VAYNOR

A Study of the Welsh Countryside

By

Dr Elwyn Bowen
M.B.E., M.A., M.Ed., Ph.D.

Illustrations by

Dewi Bowen A.T.D., N.D.D.

Published by Foxgate Ltd 1992

ISBN 0 9513706 1 8 – Casebound
ISBN 0 9513706 2 6 – Paperback

Typeset in ITC Galliard

Printed and bound in Wales by Stephens & George Ltd
Merthyr Industrial Estate, Dowlais, Merthyr Tydfil, Mid Glamorgan CF48 2TD
Telephone: 0685 388888

To my family, past and present.

Where we live when we are growing up moulds our lives. We carry it with us wherever we go.

It shapes us, deflects us, half blinds us. Where our roots are first put down, the place, the people, the air we breathe determines our growth. We may react against it. We may have to leave home to free ourselves and see clearly, but we cannot tear ourselves away from our roots. From them we draw strength, vitality, the symbols of our imagination and the images of our art.

Anon.

A WEDDING AT ST GWYNNO'S CHURCH VAYNOR c1875

Believing that evil spirits would be kept at bay at weddings by loud detonations, farmers fired their shot guns, into the air when the wedding service was in progress. A much older custom in local weddings was to light a bonfire in the churchyard, which was fed by each well-wisher a branch on top of the fire.

(Reference page 373.)

FOREWORD

by Professor Glanmor Williams C.B.E., F.B.A., M.A., D.Litt., F.S.A., F.R.Hist S.

Chairman Ancient Monuments Board for Wales

The church and parish of Vaynor have had a unique place in my affections ever since my childhood. On all the dozens of occasions that I came to Vaynor in days gone by it always seemed to me to be the very epitome of rural peace and tranquillity; a place which never appeared to change and where time passed very gently. That may, no doubt, once have been true; but nowadays not even such an idyllic spot as Vaynor can escape the inexorable march of events or fail to feel their force. Within the twentieth century the parish has changed faster and more dramatically than for hundreds of years beforehand. All the more reason, therefore, why it needed an historian to chronicle its ancient and recent past with care, understanding and affection before it disappears for ever.

How fortunate it has been that Elwyn Bowen undertook that task! If Vaynor is one of my favourite places, Elwyn Bowen is one of my favourite people. I vividly remember him coming to me many years ago and rather diffidently showing me the fruits of a lifetime of the most diligent inquiries into Vaynor's past. Not just the history that could be gleaned from manuscripts, maps, newspapers, and the printed record, but better still that history that could only be brought to light as a result of regularly tramping the highways and byways of the parish and endlessly observing with keen and questioning eyes all the material traces that the past had left: in churches and chapels, farms and houses, fields and hedges, streams and rivers, sticks and stones – everywhere and anywhere. Nor had he neglected to unlock that rich treasury of recollection and reminiscence, Welsh and English, stored in the marvellously retentive memories of older inhabitants. His thesis was literally a labour of love, and it was awarded a richly deserved MA degree. I am delighted that he has now decided to publish his findings in this printed history of the parish he loves so deeply, so that thousands of interested readers will be able to profit from the choice harvest he has garnered as the result of his long, patient and discerning researches. We shall all derive rare enjoyment and enlightenment from the delights he spreads before us.

Glanmor Williams

PREFACE

In this book I have attempted to describe some aspects of the history of the parish of Vaynor from the early seventeenth century down to the present day. I have also tried to indicate some of the social, religious, educational and cultural changes of the period. This research formed the core of an M.A. Thesis presented to the University of Wales in 1981. It has since been modified but inevitably, this is still an academic study.

For those readers unfamiliar with the study area perhaps I should give some relevant details. The parish of Vaynor is situated south of the Brecon Beacons and immediately north of Merthyr Tydfil, the town of Tydfil the Martyr and once the iron metropolis of the world. The parish reflects in its history, culture and settlement patterns, those polarities of upland agriculture and urban industry. The Tâf Fawr and Tâf Fechan rivers mark the parish boundaries as they flow through a rural landscape to converge below Cefn Coed-y-Cymer, an industrial dormitory village, which developed in the wake of Merthyr's iron and coal industries. Pre-historic artifacts, Roman roads and nearby Norman castles confirm the presence here in earlier times, of other cultures.

Over the centuries peasants and farmers have wrestled here, at Vaynor in unrelentless toil and hardship, to obtain a meagre living from an upland area with an unyielding soil, a climate of high rainfall and a brief growing period. Travellers such as Daniel Defoe and Malkin and local poets, mystics and scholars have written graphically of the awe-somely beautiful Tâf Fawr and Tâf Fechan valleys. With the advent of industrialisation however, in the mid-eighteenth century, the area around the hamlet of Merthyr Tydfil was within a few decades, trans-formed into the most ravaged and exploited acreage in the world. As virtually a suburb of Merthyr, Vaynor has shared in this black legend of riots and reform, of poverty and prosperity, of ravish by industrial predators and of decimation by plague and disease. No place suffered greater torment than Merthyr during the years of the industrial depres-sion between the two Great Wars.

A work such as this must rest in part on the enormous support and advice given to me by friends and advisers. I am greatly indebted to Mr Gareth Jones, Managing Director of Stephens & George, Printers, Merthyr Tydfil for sponsoring and printing this book. I am also very grateful to Mr William Bird and Mr Martin Wehko for the patience and encouragement which they have shown me. I am also profoundly grateful to my friend, Professor Glanmor Williams former Professor of History at the University College of Wales, Swansea and Chairman of the Ancient Monuments Board for Wales for kindly providing the Foreword in this book, and also for his encouragement over many years, for his professional advice and for so many innumerable acts of personal kindness, which went far beyond the call of duty.

Finally, I would wish to express my sincere gratitude to my brother Mr Dewi Bowen N.D.D., A.T.D., former Head of the Department of Art at Cyfarthfa High School, Merthyr Tydfil for the cover designs and the many excellent illustrations, and also to all the very kind people who loaned the photographs, I offer my appreciation and thanks. I trust that my bibliographies indicate my indebtedness to other historians. The place names have followed a vernacular form.

ELWYN BOWEN
June 13th 1991

CONTENTS

CHAPTER I

The Topography, etc

The Reverend J. E. Jenkins, former Rector of Vaynor writing in "Vaynor: Its History and Guide"[1] in 1897 described the location of the parish of Vaynor thus, "The parish is surrounded on the east by Llanddety, on the south by Merthyr Tydfil, on the west by Penderyn and on the north and north east by Cantref, Llanvigan, and Llanfrynach... Two noted rivers form the boundaries of Vaynor for a considerable distance, viz the Tave Vechan on the east and south side, and Tave Vawr on the west side". Another accomplished local historian, William Morgan (Pant)[2] writing a little earlier in 1893 stated, "The Parish is in the hundred of Pengelli, in the County of Brecon. It has an area of 6,957 acres, a rateable value of £6,559 and a population, according to the census of 1891 of 3,057. It comprises the hamlet of Cefn Coed-Y-Cymer including the village of that name; Dyffryn, extending from the village of Cefn Coed through the valley of Tâf Fawr, including what is known as the Vaynor, together with Pontsarn and Pontsticill, as far as the brook of Cwmcar, in the valley of Tâf Fechan".

The origin of the parish name, 'Vaynor' or 'Faenor' has evoked considerable discussion among historians and scholars. Generally place names are associated with physical features in the locality such as mountains, woods, fields, mills, rivers or brooks which contribute so much to the treasury of nomenclature. Theophilus Jones[3] the Breconshire county historian in discussing the origin of the name 'Vaynor' suggested in 1809 that "our 'maenawr', which according to the idiom of the language and the orthography of the country, is changed into 'Faenor' or 'Vainor', was as I apprehend, the manor or demesne attached to Marlais Castle". He adds "in old manuscripts of different periods, the parish is called 'Y Faenor Wen', 'Faenor Winoe' and 'St Winoer' ". William Morgan totally disagreed pointing out that "if 'maen-mawr' is really the original form of the word 'Vaynor', we contend that it is much more probable that the name was given to the locality, on account of the innumerable massive stones that are to be found on the Tâf Fawr side of the Cilsanws mountain". He also suggests that it might be derived from the word 'van' or 'ban' meaning a high mountain peak or from the "light coloured limestone, rocks of which there is an abundance".

The Rev J. E. Jenkins[4] offers the explanation that "Vaynor is an Irish word, pronounced "Aynor" in that language and means 'alone', or 'solitary' ... what was Vaynor ... even until a hundred years ago ... a solitary place ... and the inhabitants, what were they but "Aynorawns" – hermits, with few exceptions, dwelling in houses half hidden by tremendous oaks". More recent explanations have been offered by Canon Silas Harris[5] a native of Pontsticill, and brother of T. H. Harris M.A. former Professor of Welsh at St David's University College, Lampeter, and Canon Jones Davies of Llywel, Trecastle. The former has written pointing out that "Among the Harley Charters in the British Museum there are three (in Latin) which deal with land transactions in Vaynor. One of these dated 1387/8 refers to the place as "the parish of Guinaw" (i.e. Gwynno)". Another drawn up at Vaynor itself (Maenor Wyno) and dated October 20th 1481 speaks expressly of the parish of St Gwynno and a similar charter of 1525 has the parish of 'Maynor Weno'. While stating that the name of the saint, Gwynno, has been associated with the name "Maeno Gwynno" for over thirteen centuries, he has offered no explanation for the parish name. Canon Jones Davies[6] however was quite sure when he stated "Actually I do not think there can be much doubt about its meaning. It refers to a division of land, not unlike the English 'manor' and 'maenol' was, I suspect the original form of the word in 'Y Faenor Wynno'."

In discussing the Welshry, Professor William Rees[7] formerly of Breconshire and a distinguished Welsh historian, has indicated that in some commotes the administrative area most in evidence was the 'Maenor'. The term also seems to have been applied to a special "tref" having bond tenants. When used in this sense the work takes the form "Maynor". Of interest here is an agreement in the Mayberry Collection dated July 15th 1861[8] which refers to a lease of land from "Anna Gwynne Holford of Buckland to William Hughes, Postmaster, Coed Y Cymer, "formerly enclosed from the waste of Penkelly Castle Manor". Professor Stephen J. Williams[9] claims that "Faenor" (Vaynor) is derived from "maenor" but then the late Sir John E.

Lloyd said "It has nothing to do with the English manor, but is connected with "maen" (stone) and probably it was first applied to the stone girt residence of the chief. It would seem therefore that many scholars have over the years, offered various explanations for the parish name without coming to any collective agreement as to its meaning.

Topographical descriptions of Vaynor abound from around 1534-42 when John Leland[10] who was Librarian and Chaplain to Henry VIII was sent on an antiquarian tour of England and Wales collecting manuscripts scattered by the dissolution of the monasteries. Writing of Vaynor he stated "Morelays Castelle standith in a good valley for corn and grass and is on the ripe of Morelais Brooke. The Castelle is in ruine and longith to the King ... The water of Taphe cummith so doun from woddy hilles, and often bringgith down such logges and trees, that the cuntery was not able to make up the bridges".

Some two centuries later between 1724 and 1726 Daniel Defoe[11] came down through the Tâf Fawr valley and mentioned rather gratefully, "We began with Brecknock ... we were saluted with Monuwchdenny Hill on our left ... and all a ridge of horrid rocks and precipices between, if we had not had trusty guides we should never have found our way". Another traveller G. W. Manby[12] proceeded in the opposite direction, in going from Merthyr to Brecon in 1802 and commented on the glacial boulders found on Cilsanws mountain facing the Tâf Fawr valley in the upper part of Cefn Coed with the following description, "After leaving Merthyr a few miles I

Upper High Street, Cefn Coed (c1930).

Cefn Coed High Street (c1910).

Lower High Street, Cefn Coed (c1950).

entered Brecknockshire; for some distance the country was thickly strewed with rude stones ... the face of this terrific mass was bedecked with wild vegetation, flowers and patches of sportive ivy ... I was soon driven by the pitiless storm to seek shelter at the Half Way (Inn?), a very humble pile indeed ... neither the good old woman nor her hand maid could speak English".

Writing about the same time, B. H. Malkin (1803)[13] refers to Tâf Fechan dingle as "deep, wild and precipitous" and to "Pontsticill, a bridge of one arch crossing the Taff Fechan river ... the scenery of the dingle, on the right, becomes wilder and less verdant". Theophilus Jones the county historian and deputy Registrar to the Archdeaconship was obviously unimpressed with Cefn Coed when he wrote in 1809 that it was "A barren and hilly tract, upon which not a twig now grows is still called Coed y Cymer (the wood near the conflux of the two waters). The village so called and raised in consequence of the neighbouring iron works at Merthyr is built upon the waste (common land) and houses are seen starting up without the slightest attention to regularity or arrangement, the convenience of each other or the preservation of health". His picture of the old Vaynor Church of 1809 is that of a poor, neglected rural church when he states, "This building having a small tower with two bells and consisting of a nave and chancel only is low and dark, the roof not ceiled, the floor of earth uneven, the seats decayed and irregular. This building having a small tower with two bells and consisting of a nave and chancel only is low and dark, the roof not ceiled, the floor of earth uneven, the seats decayed and irregular". The floor of the church was uneven because it was the custom at that time to bury the more affluent parishioners within the church building while the poorer members of the community were buried in the churchyard.

The account by Samuel Lewis in 1849[14] provides interesting information regarding population, agriculture and local industries within the confines of the parish. As he writes, "Vainor has 2,286 inhabitants ... it comprises 6,600 acres of which 4,000 are common or waste land; the remainder produces very good crops of grain and excellent pasturage for sheep and cattle ... Limestone is found in various parts and the procuring of it affords employment to a portion of its inhabitants; the people are chiefly engaged in agriculture and in the iron works at Merthyr ... Some lead ore has been occasionally discovered above Coed-Y-Cummer near the turnpike road ... Two woollen manufactories have been carried on for some years".

Mr Tegwyn Harris has justifiably claimed that "The parish of Vaynor has been particularly fortunate in the number and quality of its local historians because it was the favourite and most picturesque beauty spot near Merthyr Tydfil, "the greatest mining place in Britain which may be called with much propriety the capital of iron and coal". In addition the transactions of the Cefn Coed and Vaynor Local History Society have covered a range of topics some of which include 'The Prehistory of Vaynor', 'The Roman Period', 'Old Characters', 'Cultural Changes in the Tâf Fawr and Tâf Fechan Valleys', 'The Cefn Coed Schools', Vaynor Gleanings', 'Life In 19th Century Cefn Coed', 'Flora', and 'A Brief Topographical Sketch of The Parish of Vaynor". The N.U.T History of Merthyr Tydfil written by Merthyr Teachers in 1932 has frequent references to the parish of Vaynor. The chapter on the pre-history of this area includes an excellent account of the prehistory of Vaynor with many photographs by J. R. Evans a former Cyfarthfa Grammar School teacher with strong connections with the Hen Dŷ Cwrdd Chapel through his marriage to the daughter of William Harris formerly of Penderyn and a descendant of the Gwilym Harri family of poets and weavers.

Of the local historians Charles Wilkins[15], the Merthyr Postmaster provides an imaginative account of Vaynor Church as it might have been on a "Sabbath morn, two or three centuries ago; and venerable and attractive looks the primitive structure, with its fringe of meadow and corn lands". Edwin Poole[16], founder of the "Brecon and Radnor Express" mentions in his Breconshire Illustrated History in 1886 that a new church had been recently built at Vaynor and that the viaduct over the Tâf Fawr had been completed at Pontycapel, Cefn Coed. The parish of Vaynor history by William Morgan (Pant) has already been referred to. This is an excellent parish history containing invaluable information and old pictures of intrinsic interest to general readers and historians alike.

William Morgan[17], writing in 1893 provided a comprehensive and detailed account of Cefn Coed. "This pretty Village" he stated with its "600 houses and population of 2,500". Of the accommodation he says, "The old houses are small, with low roofs, and are of primitive appearance". He refers to "the numerous villas which dot the side of the hill, built mainly by 'well-to-do' tradesmen" and to "Holford Street where within living memory the last bull fight was held". He further claimed that "Cefn Coed was, in its early life, a notoriously wicked place, for here lived the chief pugilists, racers and gamblers of the whole district". He however added that "the village can now boast of seven Nonconformist Chapels

View of Merthyr and the village of Cefn Coed in the foreground (c1850).

An interesting view of Cefn Coed taken from a field where Bryn Tâf now stands. This photograph was taken by Mr Robert Thompson Crawshay of Cyfarthfa c1870s. South Terrace has not yet been built and Aubrey Chapel (built 1876) is brand new. There is a field enclosed by stone walls where the present Vaynor and Penderyn Comprehensive School now stands.

and two Episcopal Churches" and that the schools were "in an exceedingly efficient condition". He gave a special compliment too to the Reading Room and Library for its "intellectual contribution" to Cefn Coed. Pontsarn had become he claimed, "the rendezvous of thousands of tourists and pleasure seekers from all parts of the Principality", standing as he said "in the foremost ranks of summer resorts in the whole of Wales". The "Garn, Pontsticyll" he has referred to as "This somewhat straggling village ... exposed to the severity of the northern blasts and the biting eastern winds."

The Rev J. E. Jenkins' history of the parish is a collection of parish folk tales and stories and was published in 1897 some four years after his advent to the living of Vaynor. He highlighted local tourism and the physical benefits of residing within the parish boundary thus, "today with its Pontsarn and Coed Cymer and its twenty one passenger trains coming and going daily, Vaynor is in the world and the world comes to Vaynor. The air is pure and the average age of death for the last ten years was thirty three whereas the average at Merthyr was only twenty six".[18] Matthew Owen a local headmaster at Cefn Coed writing in 1912 painted a dark picture of the village life "of sixty years ago" when it was "notorious for brutal pastimes". After noting the significance of the "Stocks" at Cefn Coed he ends on a happier note when he claims that "the social and moral life of the village has long been reclaimed from such sordid pastimes".[19]

In more recent times Tom Lewis (Mab y Mynydd) the Vaynor poet historian, a man of considerable native talent, who in writing the history of "Hen Dŷ Cwrdd Cefn Coed-Y-Cymmer" in 1947 provided us with not only a brilliantly written and carefully documented account of the Hen Dŷ Cwrdd but also penned a scholarly social history of the parish of Vaynor. Tom Lewis was born in 1885 at Cefn Coed, a descendant of Dafydd Lewis who came here in 1810 from Carmarthenshire and who was later a local leader in the Merthyr Riots of 1831. Mab y Mynydd received no formal education after the age of twelve when he left school to work with his father in the coal mine. Nevertheless he was endowed with a keen intellect, together with the poet's insight and a rare facility with words which enabled him to describe scenes, events and characters with the beauty, integrity and understanding of a true creative artist. His literary achievements have made him an essential part of the historical tapestry of Vaynor.

In referring to the origin of Cefn Coed he describes the large tract of woodland which once covered the slopes of Cilsanws mountain, where as

The late Alderman Tom Lewis J.P. (Mab-y-mynydd) Poet historian of Vaynor. (Photograph courtesy of Mr Morien Lewis, Llyswen, Cefn Coed.)

he states, "In its deep recesses wild life teemed, where the poacher plied his illicit craft and found its heart's desire. When however, Anthony Bacon built his furnace at Cyfarthfa in 1765 the wood was denuded of its trees in order to provide fuel to smelt the iron. In the clearings, an occasional cottage was erected and as time wore on, and Anthony Bacon's works expanded, a small picturesque village grew and was given because of its natural features, the lovely name of Cefn Coed-Y-Cymer"[20]. He sadly reflects in 1957 upon the fact that the hamlet of Ynysyfelin, Cwm Tâf and the "Picturesque, white-robed farmsteads that used to nestle in snug glens, now lie derelict at the bottom of the artificial lakes of Cwm Tâf Fawr". Later in his "Topographical Sketch of the Parish of Vaynor" (1957) he portrays the Vaynor Church with "its own spirit of antiquity and hoary old age"[21], and he adds "As you enter its modest portals under the dangling rope that rings the two tiny bells in the stairless tower above you, you instinctively remove your hat even when there is no service in progress, and quite instinctively, you tread lightly as you walk down the aisle, as if afraid of crushing a fragile flower growing there. When the hot sun pours its brilliant rays through the stained glass windows, settling in mellow radiance on the empty pews and deserted altar, you linger there..."[22].

He pointed out in 1957 that "the little hill village of Pont Sticill" was "in marked contrast with the soft, soothing environs of Pont Sarn" and also that while becoming urbanised, "the village retains some of its former sense of permanence and stability, the customs and language of other days have gone the way of the blacksmith, the wheelwright and the miller.

The First Iron Furnance, at Cyfarthfa constructed by Anthony Bacon in 1765 for the production of pig iron from local ironstine – (A reconstruction of the scene). Cyfarthfa – (Cyfarth – Barking) (Fa – Place) – Barking place.

Morlais Castle was built about 1275 by Gilbert-De-Clare, Norman Lord of Glamorgan known to the Welsh as Gilbert Goch.

Gone too, are those hard-working, God fearing old natives whose rubicand cheeks and gnarled hands marked them out as weather beaten quaryman". Of Trefechan he writes thus,[23] "The estate is set amidst delightful natural surroundings", and expresses the hope that time will allow the "cemented exterior of the houses to sink its identity into the green of the mountains and nearby fields". He reflects that "Before corn had to give way to concrete, the productive pastures to pylons, the site occupied by Trefechan was one of the prettiest spots in Vaynor". He paints a rather sad canvas of Cefn Coed at this time when he says "Cefn Coed is becoming a suburb of Merthyr Tydfil with that bustling town's way of life ... Today, however the rumble of traffic in the streets deafens the ear and dulls the

Charcoal burners working at the confluence of the rivers Tâf Fawr and Tâf Fechan which gives Cefn Coed-y-Cymer its lovely name, which means "the woody ridge near or by the confluence of waters".

senses, and a horse-drawn vehicle is remorselessly becoming a thing of the past. Rare, too, on the lips of the inhabitants are the rich, lilting cadences of the Welsh tongue ... its death-knell has also been sounded in the places of worship, where large Welsh congregations no longer hold sway"[24]. Poetically however he claims that, "there are still to be found there some old natives who are untouched by the revolutionary changes that Time has wrought in its wake. On fine Summer days, they may be seen sitting on their accustomed seats on Twyn Gwladys (the hillock near the Black Patch), like swallows on a telegraph wire, half hidden by banks of cool, green bracken. Enjoying their pipes ... and watching with dimming eyes the new world and the cars go by ...".[25]

Old maps are an important source of topographical information and for this reason a number covering the last four hundred years have been examined. These include the Saxton Map (1578): Speed (1610); Kitchen (1754); Emmanuel Bowen (1760); The Ordnance Survey Map (1814); Ordnance Survey (1832); Ordnance Survey (1891). The Saxton map shown overleaf refers to "Tâf Flu" which is the Tâf Fawr; to "Tafuachan flu" which is Tâf Fechan; "Capel Nantye" which is Capel Nantddu (St Mary's Church, Nantddu) and of interest is the fact that "Morlafhe Caft" which is Morlais Castle is shown on the wrong side of the Tâf Fechan river. Speed has likewise placed the Morlais Castle on the northern side of the Tâf Fechan river and also refers to "Tave Vaure Flud" (Tâf Fawr), "Tave Vachan Flud" (Tâf Fechan); "Capel Natye" (Capel Nantddu, St Mary's Church); "Capel Tavechan" (Capel Tâf Fechan); and "Monuwchdenny Hill" (Brecon Beacons).

Thomas Kitchen's County map (1754) shows "Nantddy", "Capel Tâf Fechan", "Castell Merlis" (Morlais Castle) now in the correct position and farms are shown in the Tâf Fawr valley, for example, "Y Wern Vawr", "Pont ar Dâf", "Gronvan" (Grawen); and "Tu yn y Graig". In the Tâf Fechan valley there are references to "Stickel" and "Pontstickel" (Pontsticill), at Cefn Coed (which is not shown) one notes "Pont Capel" (Pontycapel). The 1814 Ordnance Survey shows the turnpike road running along the Tâf Fawr valley. By this time of course there was considerable traffic in the form of carrier vans, carts and stagecoaches running between Brecon and Swansea on this road. The map shows the "Blaen Tâf" Turnpike gate set at a most strategic spot on the Brecon Beacons where the road divides for Hirwaun and Merthyr some seven miles north of Cefn Coed. Another turnpike gate shown is the "Darren Gate" situated about two miles north of Cefn Coed and controlling access to the numerous

TWO EARLY MAPS OF VAYNOR

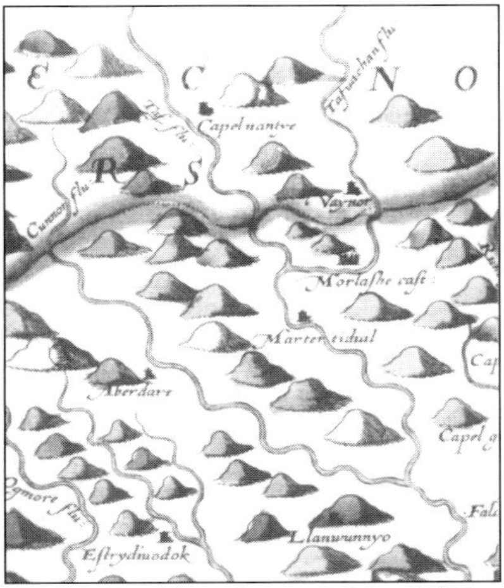

Vaynor parish on Saxton's Map 1578.

Vaynor parish on Speed's map 1610.

kilns located at the side of Cwm Tâf road. Though the parish registers refer to the "Cefn Coed Gate" it is not shown on this map possibly because it was a "chain gate". The map however does indicate an expanding Cefn Coed with enclosures of the common land and fields that have crept up the hillsides well above the limit of economical production. These enclosures of land were accelerated by the effects of the Napoleonic wars which were not over until 1815.

Much more detail is provided by the 1832 Ordnance Survey where one notes the names of the farms in both valleys. Farmhouse names such as Troedyrhiw, Abernant, Penpound, Penpont, Pontardâf, Abercar and Hendre disappeared with the building of Llwyn-On reservoir between 1914 and 1927. Similarly farm houses such as Llwynyreos and Blaendyffryn shown on this map have been demolished for expansion of the Vaynor Quarry located between Cefn Coed and Pontsarn. The 1890 Ordnance survey map indicates quite dramatic social changes within the parish of Vaynor. The route of the Brecon and Merthyr and North Eastern railway along the Tâf Fechan valley is shown with viaducts at Pontsarn and Pontycapel. The Roman road is quite clearly defined on this map, crossing at Pwllglas (the Blue Pool) Pontsarn and proceeding then behind Penrhiwglais farm and then towards Dôlygaer and Brecon. The church is incor-

Cwm Tâf and Cefn Coed in the parish of Vaynor O.S. Map 1890

rectly ascribed to St Gwendoline instead of to St Gwynno, a mistake which was perpetuated until 1939 even in official records. Pontsticill is now shown having a railway station, Post Office, school, corn-mill, two inns – the Pontsticill inn and the Butchers' Arms. Likewise a number of inns are shown at Cwm Tâf namely the Red Lion, the Farmers' Arms and the Tredegar Arms. The parish pound is located near Nantddu cottage and the stone, recently found by the author has the inscription "Nant Ddu pound. Brecknock Lordship". The Jews' cemetery is shown attached to Garn Gwilym Goch farm (later known as Tirbach, fifty metres north of the Cefn Hotel). The trackway from the Fedw farm, Cwm Tâf over Cilsanws to Berthlwyd farm, Vaynor and thence to Vaynor Church is shown. This was formerly used for conveying the dead from Cwm Tâf to Vaynor and continued eastwards past Ynysyfelin hamlet, to Cwm Cadlan and Penderyn.

The topographical picture which has been drawn of the parish of Vaynor from the antiquarian tours, maps and local histories describe a "V" shaped area situated between the Tâf Fawr and Tâf Fechan rivers. Tongues of good agricultural land are found along the river valleys with sheep walks and some "coedcae" above. The cottages of the Crawshay dynasty still remain at Cefn Coed with the Heads of the Valleys road acting as a demarcation line between the old and new housing located on the upper slopes of Cefn Cilsanws. Only the Cefn Coed and Pontsarn viaducts and railway track remain of the 1866 Brecon/Merthyr railway. New estates at Pontsticill have changed the rural aspect of the village while the closure of the school, shop and two Nonconformist Chapels have likewise denuded the local cultural landscape. Trefechan has had additional small private estates added to it in recent times while at Cefn Coed many of the loved and familiar landmarks such as the Morning Sun Inn and John Lewis's Primrose Hill cottage now belong "to the snows of yesterday".

The earliest reference to Cefn Coed at the National Library of Wales, Aberystwyth is to be found in correspondence in 1799 between Thynne Gwynne of Talybont and his Attorney-at-law concerning a meeting of the Leet Court at Cefn Coed. The name 'Cefn Coed-y-Cymer' is found spelt quite differently in old documents. The accounts of the Parish Vestry meetings of Vaynor for the later decades of the eighteenth century refer to "Coedycymmer" and to "Coad y Cymmer". The name means "the woody ridge near or by the confluence of the waters" and refers to the joining of the Tâf Fawr and Tâf Fechan rivers near Godre'r Coed which in turn means 'The bottom of a wood or forest". The name Pontsticill means the bridge of the stile, while Pontsarn is derived, claimed Tom Lewis, from

By courtesy of Mr and Mrs Morgan Jones.

An old view of Cefn Coed (c1910) showing the General Stores owned by Mr. W. R. Hughes, father of Mr Edgar Hughes, former Surveyor of the Vaynor and Penderyn R.D.C.), Mrs Davies' Clothier's Shop, Mr Phillip Pembridge's Shop (now a video shop) and on the right the shop owned by Mr Barnett, shoe maker and later occupied by the late Councillor Eddie Harris.

"Pont" which is Welsh for bridge and "Sarn" which in "ancient days meant a path made by laying down flat stones to cross over a bog or quagmire". He further adds, "The full name of this pretty pastoral retreat is "Pont y Sarn Hir" the "bridge of the long road". "the picturesque hamlet of Ynysyfelin refers to "the river-meadow of the mill" i.e. the Pwllcoch mill.

A full and fairly recent topographical description of the parish of Vaynor is to be found in the Vaynor and Penderyn District Council Official Guide written in the immediate post Second World War period of the 1940s and states:

> "The district is within easy reach of the main population centres of South Wales, both by road and rail ... The nearby town of Merthyr Tydfil is connected by a frequent service to the village of Cefn Coed and Pontsticill, the new village of Trefechan and the village of Pontsarn ... The largest village in the parish is Cefn Coed with a population of 3,000 ... which is extremely fortunate in having the amenities of a town as large as Merthyr (pop: 60,000) within a

This well known shop known locally as "Siop Marie Price" was kept by Mrs Price and her highly respected husband Councillor Joseph Price J.P. who was at one time Chairman of the Penderyn Petty Sessions Bench of Magistrates and founder Governor of the Vaynor and Penderyn Secondary School opened in 1932.

two penny bus ride. The village has excellent public services, for apart from buses there is a railway station giving access to Newport, Cardiff and Swansea ... It is well served too as regards educational facilities, the Vaynor and Penderyn Secondary School supplying the needs of the children throughout the rural district. Shopping facilities in Cefn Coed make the inhabitants quite independent of their large neighbour in this respect.

Farming employs many of the people in and around Cefn Coed, although a considerable number work at a recently established factory (Teddingtons Aircraft Controls, Gwynne's Field, Cefn) which produces various kinds of instruments and equipment for aircraft.

In its topographical setting the village is peculiarly fortunate ... a free translation of its full name 'Cefn Coed-y-Cymer' is usually given as 'the wooded ridge near the confluence.' On its eastern side the village is bounded by the Tâf Fechan whilst on the western side is the Tâf Fawr and just below the village of Cefn the two rivers join to form the Taff which finds its outlet to the sea at Cardiff.

Councillor Isaac Morris Chairman of Vaynor and Penderyn Rural District Council laying the foundation stone at the Teddington's Aircraft Controls factory at the Gwynne's Field on April 26th 1946.

Also present were Alderman Tudor Watkins M.P., Mr Ieuan Rees, and Mr Martin Hurst (Manager). By courtesy of Mr L. Morris, grandson of Coun Isaac Morris

The natural beauty of the valleys has been enhanced by the construction of three Cardiff City reservoirs in the Taf Fawr valley and of the Tâf Fechan Water Board reservoirs in the Tâf Fechan valley... both rivers have been bridged by viaducts carrying the railway from Merthyr Tydfil to Brecon and Abergavenny ... Pontsticill, translated means the "Bridge of the Stiles" ... Needless to say ... the stiles have long since disappeared ... The chief occupations of the people of the village, who number about 300 are connected with the Tâf Fechan reservoir, with farming, and with quarrying ... The hamlet of Pontsarn ("Bridge of the Long road") lies between Cefn Coed and Pontsticill is situated Vaynor Parish Church and churchyard containing the burial place of the former iron master, Robert Thompson Crawshay, over whose remains lies a huge slab of stone weighing some ten tons carrying the brief inscription "God forgive me."

REFERENCES

1. REV J. E. JENKINS. *Vaynor. Its History and Guide* (1897). p.5.
2. W. MORGAN (Pant). *The Illustrated Vaynor Handbook* (1893) p.3.
3. THEOPHILUS JONES. *History of Breconshire* (1809) p.p.472-6.
4. J. E. JENKINS. *op.cit* p.1-3
5. CANON SILAS HARRIS writing in the *'Brecon and Radnor Express* 6/8/59 and *Merthyr Express* 10/10/57.
6. REV JONES DAVIES. An article in *Brecon and Radnor Express* August 11th 1966.
7. PROFESSOR WILLIAM REES. *South Wales and the March* (1924). 1284-1418.
8. *Mayberry Collection*. National Library Aberystwyth. M.D.5741.
9. STEPHEN J. WILLIAMS. Some Breconshire Place Names. *Bycheiniog*. 1965. p155.
10. JOHN LELAND. *Itinerary in Wales* 1836-39. Quoted by Tegwyn Harris in the Vaynor Transactions 1959.
11. DANIEL DEFOE. *Tour through the whole of Britain 1724-26*. Quoted by Tegwyn Harris op.cit.
12. G. W. MANBY. *An Historic and Picturesque Guide from Clifton through the Counties of Monmouth. Glamorgan and Brecknock 1802*. Quoted by Harris op.cit.
13. B. H. MALKIN. *The Scenery, Antiquities and Biography of South Wales 1803*. Quoted by Harris op.cit.
14. SAMUEL LEWIS. *A Topographical Dictionary of Wales 1849*. Quoted by Harris op.cit.
15. CHARLES WILKINS. *History of Merthyr Tydfil (1869)*. P.88.
16. EDWIN POOLE. *Illustrated History and Biography of Breconshire 1886*. Quoted by Harris op.cit.
17. WILLIAM MORGAN. *op.cit.p.4-8.*.
18. REV J. E. JENKINS. *op.cit.p.5.*
19. MATHEW OWEN. *Story of Breconshire 1911*. pp 98-102.
20. TOM LEWIS (Mab-Y-Mynydd). *Hen Dŷ Cwrdd Cefn Coed-y-Cymer (1947)*. pp.22.
21. TOM LEWIS. *Topographical Sketch of the Parish of Vaynor*. P.6.
22. *I bid* p.7.
23. *I bid* p.9.
24. *I bid* p.9-10.
25. *I bid*. P.11.

CHAPTER II

Social And Cultural Changes

INTRODUCTION – THE RURAL SOCIETY

Prior to the industrial revolution and the growth of population at Cefn Coed, Vaynor Parish was essentially a sparsely populated rural society. This rural society persisted in Cwm Tâf, Pontsarn and Pontsticill until the middle of the nineteenth century, when the valley floors of the Tâf Fawr and Tâf Fechan began to be flooded for the building of reservoirs. One can date traumatic change in this rural society from this period of reservoir building.

This rural society had remained virtually unchanged in many respects for centuries; its members understood what their society was all about and their roles within that society. Theophilus Jones has described this type of rural society thus, "people long seated in the same country and have had little intercourse with strangers commonly retain the same national character, manners and customs through a long succession of ages, they become proud of their antiquity. The sequestered peasant who rarely quits the vicinity of his mountains, who speaks no other language than his mother tongue, still adheres with infinite attachment to old habits and customs of his ancestors – on all occasions he adapts their sentiments and dwells with fond delight upon the traditions of old times".[1]

Within this society there was adequate role-differentiation and assignment. The family farm was the basic institution and almost all the population was concerned with the way in which farm work and duties were organised and allocated between men and women, and between the various male and female servants that constituted a farm's labour force. An essential feature of the organisation of farm work was its division of labour among the sexes. The men were responsible for the cultivation and labouring work of the farm while the women were largely confined to the house and farmyard. The success of the farm depended largely on the efficiency of the master and mistress, who were respectively the heads of each major division of labour. The prestige work of the farm belonged to the men, and this was concerned primarily with the cultivation of the land.

Much of Vaynor was isolated and life was extremely hard in a climatically unkind environment. An essential element for living fully in this virtually monoglot Welsh society was to be able to speak the language. As Theophilus Jones has written, "In general, the inhabitants of Breconshire retain an enthusiastic veneration for their ancient language ... uneducated in the refinements of that new philosophy which ostentatiously affects an universal citizenship, the Welshman thinks no country equal to his own, and even in the midst of poverty is happy to acknowledge as his proudest boast that he was born an ancient Briton".[2] Unfortunately the number of Welsh speakers has fallen and today (1980) there is not one Welsh speaker in the Cwm Tâf valley farms apart from Mr Morgan John, Ffrwd Farm, and among the farming community of Tâf Fechan only Mr David Williams, Coedhir Farm, Dôlygaer and Mr David Meredith, Berthlwyd Farm speak the language. This recent decline in the Welsh language in the Parish of Vaynor is shown by the fact that whereas 1087 local residents could speak English and Welsh in 1951, this figure has fallen to 440 by 1971, a fall of 58%.

Although this rural society in Vaynor was scattered, it did afford opportunities for shared experiences through the Church, later the chapels and within farming life by the 'mutual aid' practised during periods of intense seasonal labour such as haymaking or shearing. In addition, practically every farmer in Cwm Tâf, for example, was related by ties of kinship and marriage, this was the traditional "extended" family, now replaced by the modern "nuclear" family. The coming together of the people of the valley had both a manifest and latent function – the manifest function of appearing at a shearing was to help, likewise the presence of a farmer at a funeral demonstrated possibly his kinship relationship or his respect for the dead; but the latent function was to demonstrate the family or tribal strength. Non-appearance at these functions without a reasonable excuse would have invoked severe sanctions from the family and neighbours. This usually took the form of non-support in times of intense seasonal labour.

Though often-times remote from one another in upland farms, these isolated farmers and their families together with their servants lived in a structured world or society, with established values, mores and sanctions which made for stability and a sense of security. Moreover, many of the families were of the extended family type with the parents living on one farm and the married children living round about, often-times on neighbouring farms. This was clearly advantageous both to the parents and children in terms of shared machinery, mutual aid and support in times of illness or difficulties.

This rural society had over the years established a shared and articulated set of goals. While it is clear that members of this society had individual and personal goals, they also had a comprehensive vision of shared goals such as the need for co-operative activities in times of shearing and haymaking. Furthermore, there was the added realisation that unless these acts of co-operation did take place the economic life of the countryside would collapse. Sprott's own definition of society is both interesting and revealing in the present context of the articulation of social goals. He states, "A society consists of a collection of individuals whose patterned interaction takes place more frequently amongst themselves than with members of other collections, who share a belief that they are co-members of the society, who also share beliefs about the structure of the society, the different activities that have to be carried out for the benefit of at least some, if not all members of the collection, who also share beliefs about the standards of appropriate behaviour, and who interact in terms of these beliefs".[4] Having established its goals over centuries, this rural society in Vaynor also prescribed the means for the attainment of these goals through role-differentiation and role assignment. The means adopted and employed represented the way in which this society was governed, controlled and organised, and sanctioned ethically and socially.

When one asks for a definition of 'culture', one is faced with all the problems associated with a word which has popular, literary and historical as well as more scientific connotations. This discourse has so far been largely sociological, and E. B. Taylor has provided one of the best definitions of culture from this point of view. Culture he said is "that complex whole which includes knowledge, belief, art, morals, law, custom and any capabilities and habits acquired by man as a member of society".[5] One is thinking, therefore, of this old rural society of Vaynor as having a particular culture, i.e. a rural culture and as something which was built up by generations of people existing in the past and who transmitted a culture to future generations by the socialisation of their children and through a corpus of ideas, knowledge, and certain patterns of living and behaviour broadly described as "a Welsh way of life".

AGRICULTURAL LIFE IN VAYNOR FROM 1750

For many centuries man has tilled the soil and cared for his domesticated animals and the study of any region which has had a history of human settlement indicates that the cultural landscape has many elements other than those associated with the present day life of the inhabitants. The changes from the middle of the eighteenth century far exceed in magnitude anything that has previously occurred. On a national scale the population doubled itself between 1696 and 1811 and in nearby Merthyr Tydfil, which is contiguous to the parish of Vaynor the population rose from 7,705 in 1801 to 46,378 by 1851. This explosion of population created an inevitable demand for more farm products in ever increasing quantities, and conservative ideas and rigidity of farm practices were swept aside by the needs of this increasing population.

By 1831 at least 9,000 of the local Merthyr population were employed by four great iron companies and around 4,000 families of workers slaved for four capitalist families with little regard for their hours of labour, squalor, accidents or mortality rates. Merthyr's Court of Requests created in 1809 as a tribunal for the recovery of small debts embraced Vaynor as one of its parishes which also came under the jurisdiction of Merthyr's Stipendiary magistrate. The new parliamentary borough of Merthyr which was created by the 1832 Reform Act included the growing industrial village of Cefn Coed as did the Poor Law Union of 1836. By 1831, in Merthyr and Vaynor, which in practice meant Cefn Coed, 96 per cent and 82 per cent respectively of all families worked at non-agricultural jobs. At Vaynor 50 per cent of the adult males were hard workers at the forges and furnaces of Merthyr, concentrated at Cefn Coed as a dormitory suburb to the north of the town. Vaynor was now witnessing a transition to an industrial society within its borders and along its southern flanks. The demand for limestone, charcoal, food supplies and water following the nineteenth century cholera outbreaks at Merthyr Tydfil and Cardiff crucially changed the economic, social, cultural and agricultural life of the parish of Vaynor.

In Breconshire, the early founders of the Brecknock Agricultural Society formed in 1755, realised that a new situation in agricultural matters was about to develop and they had the needed spirit of enthusiasm, enterprise and energy to hasten it along. They ventured forth in several directions – social, industrial and agricultural. Some of these ventures failed, while others such as highway improvement succeeded and initiated subse-

Immigrants to Merthyr C1830

Immigrants into the Welsh valleys in the nineteenth century were Welsh and non-Welsh. Some walked or came on gambos, while later others arrived by train. They came to the nursery of the industrial revolution, a social and political storm centre and a crucible of suffering and change.

Castle Pit, Troedyrhiw. 1860-1935.

Blaenglais farm, the home of Howell Rhys (1718-1802).

quent large scale action by the state. In the purely agricultural sphere the early emphasis on a more productive system of crop husbandry created a foundation for a completely new form of cattle husbandry. By the early years of the nineteenth century many of the projects encouraged by monetary premiums (awards) had come to fruition. The evolution of the Brecon Agricultural Show in the 1820s was a gradual one but behind it was the realisation that the agricultural economy of the county was best linked to livestock. The Agricultural Show in its present form naturally reflects a farming economy very different from what it was two hundred years ago.

The cultural landscape of the parish of Vaynor has changed considerably during the last century. Agriculture in the parish has declined as a result of reservoir building and afforestation mainly, and also due to the technological, economic and social changes of this century, particularly since the end of the Second World War. A gradual change in the economy has taken place, the mixed largely self sufficient economy of the nineteenth century has disappeared. Because of the change of emphasis and the introduction of new cultivating and harvesting machinery, the paid labour force on Welsh farms has rapidly declined – only two farm servants for example, remain on Vaynor farms today. In the agrarian changes that have taken place, rural industry has declined spectacularly and the local craftsmen of Vaynor have now virtually disappeared.

The yearly round of life on a Vaynor farm has been described by the poet Howell Rhys (1718-1802) of Blaenglais Farm, Vaynor in his poem "The Farmer's Song" where he refers to growing corn for bread, paying rent, hiring labour, ploughing, harrowing, hedging, carrying lime and coal, manuring, threshing, feeding stock and taking corn to be ground at the local corn mill. The thresher he pays "one in twenty" while "for every fifteen I take home the miller keeps a pound". In addition "the parson takes his tithing" and "then on May Day my workmen will all expect their pay as well the landlord on St Michael's Day". The Vaynor Terrier, an agreement between the Parson and the freeholders of Vaynor dated 19th June 1689, states that the following tithes were to be paid annually to the Parson:- "Every owner of sheep to pay the tenth fleece of wool ... a lamb out of every ten ... calves in like manner ... corn the tenth sheaf thereof ... colts a penny a male and half penny a female ... the tenth of cheese, pigs, geese, kids, hemps, honey and garden fruits".[7]

THE ECONOMY

In common with other areas of the highland zone in Wales the uplands of Breconshire were for centuries inaccessible and sparsely populated, with their predominantly pastoral population scattered among farmsteads and cottages. Today, there are a dozen scattered farms in the parish of Vaynor compared with fifty five in 1893. This dramatic decline in the number of farms in the parish testifies to the changes made by reservoir building, housing afforestation and limestone quarrying during the last centuries. In the late eighteenth and nineteenth centuries a considerable number of small holdings were established by squatters (tai unnos) on the fringes of the surviving common.

A comparison between the 1840 Tithe Survey Map and the present situation indicates clearly the considerable change which has taken place in the rural landscape. It is of interest to examine a particular area of the parish and to evaluate the changes between 1840 and 1980. If one selects the area surrounding the Glais Brook, Vaynor, one notes that in 1840 there were thirteen farm units, now there are only two. One notes too, in

1840 the presence of William Crawshay of Cyfarthfa Iron Works. In Vaynor, he owned Godre'r-dyffryn, Llwynyrhyddod, Dreinos, Llwynyreos, Lan Ucha, Tir Jenkin Soch and Tŷnewydd, in total an area of 278 acres. By comparison with the 1980 Farm Owner/Occupier Boundaries Map one notes that the whole area of farmland owned by Mr Crawshay is now (1980) owned either by Powell Duffryn (Vaynor Quarries) or the Merthyr Council. The enclosure of new land had virtually ended by 1840. There has been some recession since for example, Cwm-moel Cottage in the Glais Valley was occupied in 1840 but is now derelict.

The most significant changes over the last 140 years have been in land use. In 1840 almost 25 per cent of the total land use was devoted to arable farming. This was confirmed by Morgan (Pant) writing in 1893 when he stated that a hundred years previously there was a quantity of corn grown here and enough to keep four corn mills on the Tâf Fechan alone fully employed.

It is apparent from the Tithe Map and Tithe apportionments that each farm in 1840 combined arable meadow and pasture as key features in their land use. Clearly the emphasis in 1840 was on self-sufficiency, probably due to the remoteness of the area and lack of communications. Even then, in 1840 the Industrial Revolution was affecting the land use. Farm prices in South Wales from 1843 for butter, pigs and sheep were increasingly influenced by the state of the iron industry at Merthyr. In addition, the development of communications ushered in a new era of easy access to an expanding market due to the population explosion on the southern boundaries of Vaynor at Dowlais and Merthyr. Vaynor's population correspondingly grew as the following figures show:- 1871 – 2792; 1881 – 2851; 1891 – 3057; 1901 – 3420 and 1911 – 3857 residents of Vaynor.

In the succeeding years the Agricultural emphasis changed to accommodate the demands of the coal mining communities for milk, butter, meat and cheese. With this demand for food supplies one notes a bias towards milch cows in Vaynor. By 1893 Morgan was stating "There is not much corn grown by the Parish at the present time". The only cereal grown in the 1890s was oats and rotational grasses occupying as much as the total arable acreage of a farm.

The fields used for growing arable crops in 1840 were generally small – often below five acres in size. The average over ten farms was just three acres, but pasture, however, was the exact opposite, usually being large fields, for example, Godre'r-duffryn had one field of fifteen acres and Dreinos one field of twenty six acres. The pasture also tended to be the highest land and each farm had hill grazing rights. Only one field in the area of the Glais Brook has been ploughed up since 1977; this is not really surprising because the land has been classified as Grade 5 by the Ministry of Agriculture, which means that it is land of very restricted potential.

The climate is heavily against agriculture. This area receives over 1524 mm (60 inches) of rain annually and has relatively few hours of sunlight for arable farming. The spring is very late (April-May) and the onset of winter very early (November). This results in a very short growing season and very little time for harvesting and drying grass.

The seasonality of agricultural activity was reflected in the social life of the agricultural community. Leisure and ready money marked out May and October-November as holiday periods. Farm workers were given time off from work in May and November to attend the hiring fairs at Brecon. Social events held in summer, such as preaching meetings, singing festivals, Sunday School tea parties, etc were fitted into the slack periods as far as possible. The yearly round of agricultural work still preserves something of the old Celtic division of the year into two halves – May to October and November to April.

It is extremely difficult to present an accurate historical account of agriculture in Vaynor during the first half of the nineteenth century because of the almost total absence of records. We are extremely fortunate, however, that the Breconshire Country historian, Theophilus Jones has devoted a detailed chapter of his county history (1809) to agriculture. While his account is devoted to Breconshire in the main, he does refer specifically to the agriculture of this area. One is also aware of the fact that the upper reaches of Vaynor Parish are only six or seven miles from the main stream of agricultural life in the County, at Brecon, with its Brecknock Agricultural Society founded in 1755 exerting an immensely beneficial effect upon the agricultural, economic and social life of the County, which included the parish of Vaynor. Furthermore, Vaynor's principal landowners, such as Sir Charles Morgan and later Lord Tredegar's family, the Gwynne's of Buckland, Morgan Bolgoed and Rogers Pontardâf, were very closely associated with the Brecknock Society and would no doubt have encouraged their tenants and bailiffs to note "the encouragement of agriculture and manufactures"[8]. They were undoubtedly prompted by this active Society, which from 1755 offered premiums (awards) for example, for the improvement of roads, afforestation and crop husbandry which included the growing of turnips, potatoes, swedes, and mangolds. Premiums were also offered for the development of agricultural machinery, land reclamation, drainage, for the use of new fertilisers and there were livestock premiums for horses, sheep and cattle. In retrospect, the period 1755 to 1817 was one of pioneering on a scale of considerable magnitude, often unsuccessful in some respects but nevertheless successful especially with their crop and machinery policies.

In referring generally to the southern and eastern parts of the county, which as stated, includes Vaynor, Theophilus Jones (1809) writes of the poor drainage resulting in wet, boggy commons, "upon which something like hay is mown at the latter end of the summer". He adds that "it is so short as to be carried home in a sheet or thrown into a basket placed upon a sledge".[9] This is particularly interesting since the late Mr Tom Jones formerly of Danydarren Farm refers to the same practice at Cwm Tâf occurring a hundred years later, which he referred to in a tape recording made by the Department of Rural Life, at the Welsh Folk Museum, St Fagans in 1955. Theophilus Jones accurately points out that the farms of this district "are generally small and the general terms of leases are from seven and fourteen, to twenty one years current". He also informs us that the charge for land here was "From six to seven shillings per acre, and the poorest grounds from three shillings to four"[10].

He also states that the "local inhabitants do not raise a sufficiency of corn for their own consumption". This is difficult to understand since there were at least seven corn mills in the Tâf Fawr and Tâf Fechan valleys at the beginning of the nineteenth century. Morgan (Pant) writing in 1893 stated, "It appears that there is not much corn grown in the parish at the present time ... that there was a quantity of corn grown here, a hundred or a hundred and fifty years ago, is testified by the fact that there were no less than four grinding mills in the Tâf Fechan valley along at that time". These were the Pontsticill, Cwm Farm, Glais and Gurnos Mills.[11] David Davies, the Penderyn Parish historian, writing in 1905 stated, "Hen Felinau y plwyf oeddynt, Melin-y-Pwll-Coch a Melin Pont-y-Capel yn Nghwmtâf".[12] (They were old Parish mills, Melin-y-Pwll-Coch and Pont-y-Capel mills [were both] in the Tâf Fawr valley.) In addition the mill at the Millers' Arms, Cwm Tâf might have been working, so that Vaynor was well supplied in having seven corn mills around the beginning of the last century. Surely, therefore, considerable corn must have been grown here.

Although not an agriculturalist himself, Jones suggests that "there is no doubt, that if the land were well manured and limed, tillage would become as profitable in the vales here (i.e. Vaynor) as in other parts of the country: the farmers, however, at present depend principally; if not entirely, upon the sale of their butter, cheese, cattle and sheep". However, in a later report, on the Parish of Vaynor, he repeated himself in stating that compared with other parts of the country, "the agriculture of this neighbourhood is not so favourable ... though it is certainly in an improving state".

One gleans some further information regarding crop rotation in Vaynor where he states "About five or six years ago their general practice was to plant potatoes, after which to lay on lime and sow wheat for several years successively and as long as the ground would produce it; others, after potatoes sowed white oats, then manured for barley, and then oats and grass seed on the third year".[13] The influence of the Breconshire Agricultural Society upon agriculture in Vaynor would seem to be confirmed by his statement that, "Wheat, rye, barley, oats, vetches, turnips and potatoes are the common arable crops of the South and South Eastern (this must include Vaynor) parts of the County, and they are cultivated with tolerable success".

Theophilus Jones informs us too that carts and waggons were being used in the valleys but that the sledge was the only mode of transport in the upland regions. As stated in the section on "Transport in Vaynor", he refers to "the usual teams in tillage, are four or five horses, otherwise six oxen, or four oxen and a horse ... that curse to labouring oxen, the heavy yoke is still in common use and they are worked in pairs".[14] He was very critical of the plough in general use in Breconshire, which presumably would have been used in Vaynor. He describes it thus, "The county plough is a heavy, clumsy and inefficient implement, but long custom has prejudiced our husbandmen in its favour. Within the last few years, however, the short Rotterham has been introduced".[15] Whether this plough was used in Vaynor is unknown but Jones hoped that in view of "the reduction of expense, and the lessening of labour, that our farmers, I trust, will shortly see them, and we may hope in a few years to find it in universal practice".

Sowing was generally performed in broad-cast and the harvest commenced in August and ended about the middle of October, Jones claimed that the reaping hook was "the favourable instrument of the country; though of late years the scythe and cradle will cut at least three acres a day. Reapers are paid from one shilling to eighteen pence per acre with meat and drink from two to three shillings when they find their own provisions".[16]

Referring to the livestock he pointed out that the cattle and horses were generally small but that both had been considerably improved in recent years by crosses from other counties. With regard to cattle, cattle premiums had been started by the Breconshire Agricultural Society in 1796 and with heavier hay crops and the growing of winter fodder more cattle were kept. From Hereford in 1815 came the early maturing Hereford cattle, deemed by Jones "the first breed in the island, their frame is altogether athletic; for the purposes of travelling, the form of many of them as beasts of draught is nearly complete". Since these cattle passed through Vaynor as they passed from Brecon to Merthyr to be slaughtered and en route for the English markets with Welsh drovers, Vaynor farmers undoubtedly soon knew of this new and favourable breed of cattle, and were probably not unmindful of their excellent qualities as early maturing animals and also for their ability as beasts of draught.

Horses were the first type of livestock to be awarded premiums by the Breconshire Agricultural Society about 1780. By 1810 the favoured breed was indicated by the premium "for the best Suffolk Punch Stallion". This was broadened by 1818 to the best stallion for agricultural purposes. By this time the use of a travelling stallion was widely adopted as the best means of improving stock. This emphasis on farm horses remained until 1864 when there was a class for Welsh ponies, and by 1873 there were twenty-one horse classes.[17] Involved as they were in the activities of the Brecon Agricultural Society and the Breconshire Agricultural Show, it is very likely that Lord Tredegar and the Gwynne's of Buckland kept their tenants in Vaynor alive to the virtues of the Suffolk Punch over the ox as a draught animal, as Jones himself wrote, "It is a satisfaction to observe, that our farming teams have been greatly improved by these encouragements".[18]

The fact that Theophilus Jones refers to the smaller species of sheep found living in the Breconshire hills than across the English border is borne out by a later testimony given by Mr Tom Jones of Danydarren (Wrlod-ddu) when he spoke of the truly old Welsh breed of sheep of Vaynor as being small – ("Defaid bach penwyn roedd yr hen frîd cyn y Cheviots – y real Welsh").[14] Again, undoubtedly the proximity of Vaynor Parish to Brecon with its influential Society was a most fortunate circumstance for Vaynor Farmers in that it was within the 'zone of influence' in terms of agricultural experimentation and news. Vaynor farmers walked and rode to Brecon to buy and sell stock, so that they were very differently placed in terms of agricultural knowledge than say the farmers of Llanwrtyd Wells or Abergwesyn over thirty miles away from Brecon. Furthermore, Lord Tredegar and Rogers Pontardâf would have seen to it that they had the best available stock and the services of the best pedigree stallions, bulls and rams on their own farms in Vaynor. The Vaynor farmers were aware, too, of the premiums offered by the Breconshire Agricultural Society for the best ram (1796), the best Merino ram (1810) and for long and close wool sheep. The introduction by the Society of Cheviots, Rye-lands and Shropshire Downs undoubtedly improved the quality of stock in the County[20] – and in Vaynor, Mr Tom Jones in his tape-recording of 1955 referred to this fact when he said, "Mae'n wyth deg i gan mlynydd ers pan ddaeth y Cheviots, cyn hynny roedd y defaid yn fach" (It is 80-100 years since the Cheviots came here, before that the sheep were small).

There is ample evidence in Vaynor today, in the form of old lime-kilns that lime has been extensively used as a fertiliser in Vaynor over the years.

By courtesy of Mrs Monica Evans formerly of Coedowen Farm.

A sheep sale at Coedowen Farm, Cwm Tâf (c1977).

Theophilus Jones indicates how it was used in the eighteenth century. He states that it was usually laid on in the proportion of thirty barrels to the statute acre, each barrel containing three bushels or thirty gallons. With regard to general fertilising he includes with lime, yard muck, "scourings of headlands", coal ashes, fern and straw. He was severely critical of their management of their muck yards, as he stated "most inconsiderately do they suffer those valuable juices to run in waste along the roads to the annoyance of the travellers".[21]

At the beginning of the nineteenth century, we are informed "that the common price of mowing hay was from two shillings, to ten shillings and sixpence per statute acre, with a limited quantity of ale or cyder; in some places a gallon to the acre. Most of the farmers, however, pay by the day, viz a shilling and find the mower both meat and drink – female haymakers receive from sixpence to nine pence a day and usually stipulate for an allowance of drink".[22] The influence of industrial development in Glamorgan and Monmouthshire is reflected in the shortage of agricultural labour in Breconshire, as Jones states, "the wages of farming servants have increased very greatly within the last ten years, mining, collieries, limekilns, iron works, canals and railroads, whereby the labourer is enabled to earn his half crown or three shillings a day, have thrown the husbandman very far into the background; and it is often with difficulty that he can find a sufficient number of hands to cut and house his crops".[23]

REFERENCES

1. THEOPHILUS JONES. History of Brecknock (1908) p.135.
2. Ibid .135.
3. Office of Population, Census and Surveys. Fordham Hants (1980).
4. The School Council. The Social Implications of Social and Economic Change. H.M.S.O. (1968) p.22.
5. K. MANHEIM. Diagnosis of our time. Routledge (1943) p.72.
6. GILLIAN PALE. Cultural Changes in the Tâf Fechan Valley Breconshire (1858) p.2-3.
7. REV J. E. JENKINS. Vaynor: Its History and Guide (1897) p.18-19.
8. THEOPHILUS JONES op.cit., p.149.
9. Ibid p.153.
10. Ibid p.153.
11. W. MORGAN (Pant). The Illustrated Vaynor (1893) p.26.
12. DAVID DAVIES. Hanes Plwyf Penderyn (1905) p.19.
13. THEOPHILUS JONES op.cit., p.476.
14. Ibid p.154.
15. Ibid p.154.
16. Ibid p.155.
17. HENRY EDMUNDS. 'History of the Brecknockshire Agricultural Society', 1755-1953. Brycheiniog. Volume 3 (1957). p.103-5.
18. THEOPHILUS JONES op.cit., p.157.
19. Tape recording made by MR TOM JONES, Danydarren Farm, Cwm Tâf in 1955 for the Department of Rural Life at the Welsh Folk Museum, St Fagans.
20. HENRY EDMUND op.cit., p.108.
21. THEOPHILUS JONES op.cit., p.158.
22. Ibid p.161.
23. Ibid p.161.

AGRICULTURAL SELF-SUFFICIENCY

The two hundred years whose history on the production side has already been outlined was a period of gradual transition from an economy essentially concerned with producing the requirements of the community to one depending upon the sale of a limited range of products and the purchase of consumption goods produced elsewhere. Until recently rural communities were largely self-sufficient and rarely was it necessary for the countryman to leave his locality for the necessities of life. Most rural dwellers lived and died in intimate co-existence realising all their ambitions within their own communities to which they were bound by ties of kinship and neighbourliness in a social and economic entity.[1] All the food needed by the community was grown locally and from their animals they had meat, skins, wool and milk from which they made butter and cheese. To augment the food supplies, they might have bought, wheat, sugar, salt and spices. From the gardens, fields and orchards they had vegetables, root crops, cereals and fruit. Crucially important to farmers and cottagers were pigs which not only provided a supply of meat which was salted but also a supply of lard. The size and condition of the pig was a source of great personal pride to the owner and pig killing day was an important day. A pig killer from the immediate locality was usually employed to kill and cut up the meat. The pig meat was invariably shared with a group of friends and in this way it provided a meat supply at a time, when, people in the nineteenth century could rarely afford to purchase meat.

Ironwork of all kinds from nails to ploughs were made by the smith – Thomas Lewis formerly of the Crown Inn and later of the Morning Sun Inn, Cefn for example made hatchets, horse shoes, gates and repaired the stage coaches and shod the horses on the Brecon-Merthyr stage coach route in the early nineteenth century. Daniel Evans at the Pwllcoch Mill made blankets and there were seven corn mills for milling on the Tâf Fawr and the Tâf Fechan rivers. Carts and waggons were made by the wheelwright, while the carpenter made the furniture, the coffins and implements. Many other articles were made at home on the hearth on winter nights – the men made handles for implements and nets while the women were busy knitting and sewing. Reference has been made to Mr Tom Jones of Danydarren making his own baskets, "legs" for scythes and flails. Today none of these things are made in the Parish because there are no traditional craftsmen left. Creativity has degenerated to mending and patching and most of the crafts of the hearth have disappeared.

Until the end of the nineteenth century farming depended upon a wide range of hand tools worked by a large labour force, for example, according to the 1851 Census, Danygraig Farm (173 acres) Cwm Tâf had three house servants, a servant man and two 'farm labourers' in addition to the master and mistress. It is clear that because of the changeable weather conditions of upland Breconshire, the farmers of Vaynor could not safely garner the harvest successfully year after year without outside help. This mutual assistance in farm work was the central theme of neighbourhood feelings. Each farm saw itself as the focus of a small group of six or seven farms.[2] Assistance was given freely and through friendliness and co-operation the countryman overcame the isolation imposed upon him by his environment.[3] By welcoming his neighbours to his home, by visiting them and helping them in the performance of certain kinds of farm work he maintained a form of society which did not require a central meeting place in a village or town.

Refusal to accept assistance implied unfriendly independence, for to assist a neighbour imposed upon him an obligation to reciprocate in time of need. In a farming community made up of isolated farmsteads a good neighbour was invaluable in so many spheres, ranging from expertise in form filling, attending sick animals or in personal illness. Death could cause serious problems and in Vaynor when a death occurred in Cwm Tâf it required the services of many neighbours to carry the body of the deceased to Vaynor Church four miles distant over Cilsanws mountain.

Co-operation in farm work included the lending and borrowing of horses, implements or workmen depending upon the particular task. The work groups were generally kinsmen and neighbours. In Vaynor the work groups were drawn from the separate valleys except on occasion, when friends or farmers sharing the same hill for grazing purposes were invited members. The size of the work group naturally varied with the task whether it be harvesting, shearing, pig-killing or sheep dipping. There was then a seasonable labour need.

No one received payment on these occasions except those who could not be repaid with services. What was given and received varied with need, thus a small farmer might receive for his labour corn for his poultry, or the services of a bull for his cows, or a boar for his sow. In Vaynor only one farm in five possessed a bull. In Cwm Tâf, this was usually at the largest farms such as the Neuadd or Danygraig. Mr David Richards formerly of the Wern, Cwm Tâf informed me that Gellia Farm and Penyrheol Cwm Tâf each kept a Hereford bull for three years alternatively. Local farmers

By courtesy of Merioneth County Record Office, and the Welsh Folk Museum, St. Fagans

Horse power and the new mowing machine.

had the service of the bull for their cows free of charge. Since the income of most farms in Vaynor depended very largely on the sale of store cattle, milk butter and cheese, the bull was an essential farm animal. In the nineteenth century the Welsh Blacks and later the Herefords calved in the spring months thus ensuring a high milk yield in the Summer.

Cows were taken to the bulls usually in June or July and there was therefore a constant traffic of cows from one farm to another. Without this co-operation between farms the economic basis of farming would have broken down. If there was no man on the farmyard, the maid released the bull for which she was given a penny and as was explained to me by a number of farmers, this was not a payment but a custom. No cash payment was made in either Cwm Tâf Fawr or Tâf Fechan except when cows were taken to the Shorthorn bull at the Gurnos Farm, Merthyr when a charge of a pound was made probably because there was little possibility of repayment through labour services or the loan of equipment. In the same way only one farm in eight to ten kept a boar but since bacon pigs were so important in the economy, boars were a necessity. For the efficient running of a pastoral economy co-operation was critical. With sheep farming every farmer bought in new rams annually.

The co-operative nature of local farming was most clearly seen in the hayfields, for not only did neighbouring farmers help one another in harvesting this vital crop but their wives and maids, together with cottagers and their families were also expected to help. Cereals and hay were cut with a scythe before the introduction of implements such as mowing machines, reapers and binders. In those days, it was one day's work for one man to cut one acre of standing corn. In addition to the outdoor staff, the farmer's wife and the wives of neighbouring farmers were involved in the preparation of food. Only maid servants and the wives of cottagers were expected to do the more lowly job of raking hay in the fields.

Local custom determined which of his neighbours a farmer co-operated with, and when a farm changed hands the newcomer usually accepted the same partners as his predecessor. The system was however complicated by the fact that the obligation had a different range for different tasks. The borrowing and lending of horses or implements was normally limited to the closest neighbours, this applied to harvest time and shearing.

Shearing day was a very important event in the agricultural and social life of the parish. Shearing day was usually held on the same day for each individual farm from year to year and brought together relatives from the neighbouring valleys. Shearing day was essentially a "farmer's day". Labourers were not considered good shearers and if they had been it would have been considered an insult to send one to assist a neighbour or kinsman. In the event of the farmer not being able to attend it was necessary for him to be represented by a son if he were of age.

I have been informed that the status and prestige of farmers in Vaynor was reflected in the positions taken up on the shearing bench. At the turn of this century, the shearing day did not commence in the Cwm Tâf Fawr valley until Mr Jenkins, Crawen Farm took up his position at the end of the bench reserved for the most respected shearer. This respect, I understand, was engendered in others by the fact that Mr Jenkins was a staunch Sabbatarian and "a good man". His "goodness" was exemplified in his behaviour to his servants – he fed them well and they ate at the same table and in the same kitchen as his family. This was not always the case in Welsh farmsteads. On the shearing day farmers and servants sat at the same table and there were no social distinctions whatsoever.

The economic status of the farmer was reflected in the quality of the shearing feast. Hospitality and generosity were pre-eminent among the traditional values and were determinants of local status.[4] Some farmers and farmers' wives commanded respect which was out of proportion to their wealth, through kindness and readiness to help the needy. On the occasion of a shearing, a lamb was killed and the traditional dinner and tea prepared the day before. Some difference of status was reflected on the shearing day, at meal times when the more lowly ladies were in the kitchen and the most prestigious persons attended to the men at the dining table which was large enough to sit a dozen men.

The harvest was so important that the supply of labour could not be left to chance. It was provided through an exchange of labour with other farmers or as payment in kind to cottagers in the form of milk, cheese, butter, sacks of swedes, corn for the poultry or being allowed, to plant potatoes in the farmers' fields. Mr Richardson living at the Cross Roads, Vaynor recently informed me that for the last forty years he had helped at haymaking at Pengellifawr and Llwynyrodyn farms, Vaynor. In exchange he was permitted to grow a few rows of potatoes, received a load of manure free

By courtesy of the Welsh Folk Museum, St Fagans.

A nineteenth century pig killing day.

and a sack of swedes annually. In the case of the farmer, while the cottager supplied the seed potatoes, the farmer undertook the preparation of the ground, weeding and sowing the growing crop and supplying the manure. The cottager was expected to work a commensurate number of days for his rows of potatoes. This custom of work debt was in vogue in Vaynor until recently, vestiges of it have remained up to today where farmers give loads of manure in return for labour at the hay harvest.

Farmers and cottagers only very rarely had fresh meat except when they killed a pig and shared small portions among neighbours and friends. Salt bacon was the basic item of possibly two or three meals every day. The potato harvest coincided with the pig killing season in October so that a young porker could then be reared on the new supply of potatoes. Each pig was an object of family interest and its development was a matter of concern because it involved quite a considerable financial investment. Pig killing was literally and metaphorically a "big day" starting at five in the morning when a fire was lit under the cauldron to provide boiling water. It involved the services of a neighbour to catch and tie the pig to the bench and the services of a slaughterer. From the different parts of the carcase several meat foods were prepared, namely faggots, chitterlings, brawn, lard and scratchlings. Lard mixed with soot was used as a form of water-proofing for boots; while the thin transparent membrane over the lard was used for cuts and the pig's bladder was used as a football by the local boys.

In addition to their value in the farming community, these co-operative activities were important social events. The preparation of elaborate meals etc., was a token of hospitality. When the evening feast was over and shearing tools put away, they gathered round the hearth and gossiped, reminisced, speculated about market prices and when all time honoured topics had been fully reviewed and discussed they returned to their lonely farmsteads.

In terms of self-sufficiency, they processed their farm products, and every rural neighbourhood had its craftsmen responsible for producing tools and equipment for the farm. Essentials such as gates or ploughs could be produced locally by wheelwrights, carpenters and blacksmiths. All the furniture of the home could be made by specialised local cabinet makers and carpenters; all the utensils of the dairy, horse harness, wearing apparel, boots, clogs, indeed everything the countryman required, could be produced locally.

The period 1900 to 1939 however, saw a distinct widening of the horizons of the Welsh farmer and a new emphasis on production for the market. Perhaps the most significant single event of the period was the establishment of the Milk Marketing Board in 1933.[5] Almost immediately the production of butter and store cattle declined, sheep and pigs declined in numbers and the production of milk became the basis of the economy. The self sufficient economy of the nineteenth century gave place to a specialised dairying economy by 1935. This change of emphasis completely altered the pattern of work on Welsh farms. Whereas even in the first decade of this century most medium sized mixed farms kept two or three male labourers, who spent a great deal of time cultivating and harvesting the arable crops, by 1935, the farm labourer was a rarity in Vaynor. Because of this change of emphasis and the introduction of new cultivating and harvesting machinery, the paid labour force on Welsh farms declined rapidly.

A feature which characterised the period above all else was mechanisation. Mechanisation not only contributed to depopulation but also affected rural social life in all its aspects. In the early decades of the century the horse drawn mowing machine quickly replaced the scythe on the larger farms for harvesting corn and hay. The large gangs of farmers and cottagers required for the harvesting could largely be dispensed with now for all this work could be completed very quickly by the farmer himself with little assistance. The purchase of mowing machines, binders and tedders meant an appreciable capital outlay which few farmers could afford. The problem was overcome by a co-operative effort, where groups of farmers pooled their resources to buy the new machines.

Since 1939 the agricultural economy of Vaynor and of Wales has been completely transformed and the technological, economic and social changes, brought into being since 1945 have completely changed the life and outlook of the Welsh farmer. Among the most significant social chances which arose as a result of technological improvements was the almost complete disruption of the neighbourhood group with its traditional intimacy of association and co-operative organisation.[6] One finds in Vaynor today that each farm is an economic unit, virtually totally independent of its neighbours. Only two farms in the Parish of Vaynor, i.e. Berthlwyd, Vaynor and Coedowen, Cwm Tâf employ labour on a full time basis.

In the agrarian changes that have taken place, rural industry has declined dramatically. Local craftsmen – all those enumerated in the occupational list of the Parish registers have disappeared and rural industries such as clog making etc, have ceased to exist. As a result of these changes, the countryside has lost something more than economic units producing essential goods, for in the social history of the countryside the significance of the craft workshop, whether it be the blacksmith's shop or the cobbler's shop as a focus for a rural community cannot be overestimated.

REFERENCES
1. J. GERAINT JENKINS, Life and Tradition in Rural Wales (1976) p.18.
2. DAVID JENKINS, The Agricultural Community in South West Wales (1971) p.48.
3. ALWYN REES, Life in a Welsh Countryside (1951) p.92.
4. ALWYN REES, ibid., p.95
5. J. GERAINT JENKINS, op. cit., p.25.
6. J. GERAINT JENKINS, op. cit., p.28.

THE ROLE OF FARM WORKERS IN VAYNOR

The division of labour on the farm was into male and female labour coming under the master and mistress respectively. The agricultural labour force grew rapidly between 1801 and 1851 – outside Glamorgan and Monmouthshire by 64 per cent. It fell however from mid-century, between 1851-1911, the overall decrease of male agricultural workers fell by 45 per cent and the recorded fall in the female labour force over the same period was 94.9 per cent.[1]

This decline was due partly to migration to the industrial areas of England and Wales especially to areas of industrial growth in South Wales, Migration was being felt by the 1870s in the growing scarcity of farm labour. The decline of labour was also caused by such important factors as the fall in grain prices from the mid 1870s which accelerated the switch to permanent pasture at the expense of arable farming, the introduction of agricultural machinery, the amalgamation of farms and bye-takes and to the general conditions of employment.

The maids were not generally employed as domestic servants. The greater part of the maid's time was not occupied in the farm house but on the farmyard. On the other hand maids did not work in the fields except during the harvests. According to the Third Report of the Committee on the Employment of Children etc, in Agriculture 1870: "in the ordinary routine of farm work, the women servants tend cattle, clean out the stables, load dung carts, plant and dig potatoes, hoe, take up, top and tail turnips, and in the Spring, drive the harrow, but they are never trusted with horses and carts".

By the end of the century the 1893 Commission Report stated "that maids were employed in housekeeping, preparation of food, gardening, feeding of pigs and poultry, dairy work, including milking, the feeding of milch cows, sheep milking, helping with harrowing and threshing and occasional help at harvest time".[2] There was a great scarcity of female servants for agricultural work throughout Wales and among the reasons for

The old Grawen Farmhouse, Cwm Tâf. Described by Theophilus Jones, Breconshire County Historian in 1809 as a "house of the gentry".

this state of affairs were the long hours which were comparatively harder than for male labourers. They were the first up and the last to retire and continually under the vigilant eye of the mistress throughout the day. Town life had a greater fascination for them than for men. Many daughters of agricultural labourers took up dressmaking and domestic work in urban areas of England and Wales".

As recently as 1940 the conditions of employment for Mrs Mary Richards[3] housemaid at Grawen Farm, Cwm Tâf were as follows: She commenced work here at the age of 14 years at a wage of 5s.0d. (£0.25) per week of seven days. Her hours of duty were from 7 a.m. to 9 p.m. in Winter and from 7 a.m. to 11 p.m. in Summer. She was responsible for the poultry, milking, housework, cleaning out the cattle and had to work in the fields at harvest time. She and the two men servants ate at the same table as the "Missus" but was never offered a second helping. Her breakfast was a duck egg ("because they could not sell them"), dinner every day was fat bacon, eggs and potatoes. Tea was bread and jam or bread and cheese without butter; one cake for Sunday tea and for supper anything left over from dinner and cold milk. Leisure time was confined to going to chapel and Sunday School and occasionally to Brecon Fair. As a special treat, she was permitted to visit a neighbouring farm with her master and mistress on Christmas night. After working at this farm for seven years, her wages were increased to £1.0s.0d. (£1.00) a week and when she left she was given a wedding present of £2.0s.0d. (£2.00).

In 1851, Census Returns[4] for Vaynor show that every farm in the parish had "house servants" coming from the neighbouring parishes, from around Brecon and some from as far as Carmarthen. Very many were over fifty years of age suggesting that perhaps they had been employed by the same family over two or three decades. The youngest noted in the returns was "Margaret Prosser, aged 10. House Servant at Nantgwineu Farm, Cwm Tâf". It is noticeable that most of the farm workers come from the Brecon area and were probably hired at Brecon Fair.

A farm servant (gwas fferm) was quite different from a farm labourer (gweithiwr). Farm servants were always unmarried men who were engaged to work with horses and who lived in at the farm, while farm labourers were usually married men who lived in their own homes away from the farmstead, and were employed in general labouring such as hedging and ditching. The farm servant became a farm labourer upon marriage and henceforth he accepted a different contract. When farm servants became old their duties were relaxed and when unable to do more arduous duties became cowmen. This was considered to be the least prestigious work on the farm because it was often considered degrading for a man to milk.

Farm servants and farm labourers often worked from about 6-7 a.m. to 9 or 10 p.m. while married labourers worked from about 5.30 a.m. or 6.30 a.m. to 8.30 p.m. Wages were curtailed by natural adjustment, employees were normally in short supply as were wages, and were highest around the industrial and mineral centres. A farm servant in Vaynor could therefore command a comparatively better wage than his colleague at Builth. The average day for married labourers was 10½ hours to 11½ hours during the summer exclusive of meal times while in the winter months he worked from dawn to dusk. Sunday work was confined to winter time and involved only the indoor servants looking after the animals. The longest hours were worked as already stated by the maid servants.

There were no fixed holidays but generally most servants were granted three or four days holiday a year to attend weddings, funerals, eisteddfodau, or a cymanfa. One or more days of the year were usually set aside for hiring fairs such as those held annually at Brecon in May and November.

These hiring fairs have declined in importance from the last decades of the nineteenth century because of labour scarcity. When the hiring was completed in the morning, the rest of the day was given to pleasure and even after hiring had ceased as a function of the fair, the fairs continued as major social occasions.

A wide diversity in wage rates existed between various regions. Local factors were significantly responsible for this lack of uniformity especially the distance from competing industries, such as the iron industry at Merthyr Tydfil. Often times the agricultural wage earners were so attached by sentiment, tradition and habit to the practice in a particular area that they were only vaguely aware of the quite distinct roles on the farm for example, if there were too few sons for the work of cultivation it was farm servants, (single men living in) who were employed to supplement them and not farm labourers. Sons and servants (not labourers) were equivalent in the way that the farm staff was organised as a production unit but obviously different in terms of status.

Danygraig Farm, Cwm Tâf had three male and three female employees in 1851. The oldest employee was "William Watkins aged 63, farm labourer" and he was probably the chief servant in charge of stables and horses. It should be noted that there was more than one kind of labourer. They were engaged by the year, but unlike servants they were paid by the week and did not work on Sundays. In addition, there were casual labourers employed and paid by the week or the day. They were often very highly skilled men who undertook hedging contracts for example, but in the hierarchy of farm workers they were the lowest.

Against the background presented so far, the prestige of different farm occupations can easily be understood. The chief servant did the highest work, namely working with horses under the supervision of the master. Next came the second and third servant etc. Lastly came the hired casual labourer. Maids were engaged by the year and lived in at each farm sleeping in the house. On fairly large farms such as Danygraig there were as stated, three maids. the senior maid helped the mistress with the butter making and in preparing the food while the second and third maids were employed on the farm yard and in harvesting.

The wages of labourers, i.e. farm workers, varied with the level of wages and working conditions in neighbouring industrial districts. Proximity to the iron works at Merthyr and Monmouthshire was advancing the price of rural labour in the South Eastern areas of Wales, such as Vaynor, where the outdoor labourer on his own food earned from 8s.0d. (£0.40) to

10s.0d. (£0.50) a week in winter and from 9s.0d. (£0.45) to 12s.0d. (£0.60) in the summer. The drastic fall in farm prices after the war of 1914-1919 led to a reduction in cash earnings.

Two indices i.e. diet and accommodation may be applied for measuring the standard of living of labourers. Before the middle of the nineteenth century labourers virtually existed on oaten or barley bread, potatoes and milk. Fresh meat was a luxury and usually came from poaching game or fish. The diet was almost totally deficient of green vegetables and fruit. The aspect of the labourers' condition which came in for most criticism was his accommodation. The worse possible conditions prevailed on the farm premises among the indoor servants where the conditions actually deteriorated in the late nineteenth century. Male servants preferred sleeping in outbuildings since it afforded greater freedom but they hardly ever got away from badly lit, badly ventilated insanitary conditions. The parish records of Vaynor relevant to illegitimacy bear testimony to the lack of strict division in the sleeping accommodation of servants.

The section on illegitimacy in the Chapter relating to the Parish Records indicates an average illegitimacy rate of 12.8 per cent in Cwm Tâf for the first half of the nineteenth century. Some girls had a few illegitimate children and some farmers were apparently guilty of fathering some illegitimate children for their servant girls. Since so many of these young servant girls were often totally illiterate and a considerable distance from their parents, lack of parental supervision has also been suggested as a possible reason for this very high rate of illegitimacy.

Farm servants ate their meals sometimes alone in the back kitchen and occasionally in the same kitchen and at the same table as the family. Occasionally too, they shared the hearth, after supper. This concession was increasingly withdrawn towards the end of the nineteenth century when relationships between employer and employee became in some cases, tenuous. The general lack of supervision of farm servants was blamed for inducing moral laxity in rural areas. The indoor male servants were in the main free to roam the countryside at night in pursuit of farm maids, who were allowed to admit them. The custom prevailed in this area of 'sitting up' all night courting in the farmhouse kitchen while "bundling" or courting in bed was less common in Vaynor. In some places indoor servants often insisted upon permission to practise this custom when engaging themselves for farm service. This custom declined in Wales under the strong influence of Nonconformity.

There was acute dissatisfaction with the quality of housing for married labourers in the early nineteenth century. Walter Davies writing at this time described the majority of the mud walled and thatched cottages in South Wales as "huts". There was some improvement by 1840 when walls were now being made of stone and mortar with roofs of slate but they were still badly lit and poorly ventilated. The general conditions of the agricultural wage earner until about the middle of the nineteenth century, were harsh and impoverished in the extreme. The hours of work were strenuously long, wages low, accommodation poor and the diet meagre and undernourishing. The worst conditions were those experienced by married labourers who were uncertain of employment and existed oftentimes, through the winter only by relief from the Parish. Many made the journey to the iron works to ward off the threat of the workhouse. This drain of rural labour to the iron works sometimes improved the lot of the remaining labourers by creating a local labour shortage.

There was an improvement from 1850 and one of the significant factors in the change was the development of the railways. Compulsory education arrived in 1870 and henceforth young children could not slave in the fields. Due to higher wages the wife did not have to go out to work but it really depended on the number of children. The diet improved and the influence of nonconformity exerted some influence on the labourers' drinking. The individual acquired some personal respect as the result of gaining a vote in 1884 and by changes in local government in 1888. The improved conditions of the agricultural wage earner in Wales after 1850 was accompanied by the growth of independence.

The 1851 Census Returns indicate that in 1851 there were 68 farm servants on the 35 holdings referred to in the Census of that year for the Parish of Vaynor. In the two valleys of the Tâf Fawr and Tâf Fechan however there were over a hundred holdings so that one can estimate up to two hundred servants here in 1851. In the two valleys today (1980) there are two full time farm labourers. This is partly due to the reduction in farms resulting from reservoir building in the latter half of the last century and in the early decades of this century, together with other factors, such as the change of emphasis from arable farming to milk production and most importantly to mechanisation which made farm servants less essential to the smooth running of the economy. As a result then of the technological, economic and social changes of this century and since 1945 in particular,[6] the farm servant has now virtually disappeared from Vaynor.

REFERENCES
1. The Royal Commission on Labour. The Agricultural Labourer Volume II (1893), p.9.
2. The Royal Commission, ibid., p.11
3. The recording made by MARY RICHARDS, Pant Cefn Y Ffordd, Penderyn, formerly a house mad at Grawen Farm, Cwmtaf in 1950.
4. 1851 Census Returns for the Parish of Vaynor.
5. WALTER DAVIES, General View of the Agriculture and Domestic Economy of South Wales, Volume III (1815), p. 136.
6. J. GERAINT JENKINS, Life and Tradition in Rural Wales (1976), p.28.

THE EFFECTS OF RESERVOIR BUILDING ON VAYNOR AT CWM TÂF FAWR

As a result of cholera outbreaks in South Wales and following Parliamentary legislation the Cardiff Waterworks Company was granted permission in 1884 to impound water in the Tâf Fawr valley. The Cantref reservoir was completed in 1892 resulting in the demolition of four farms, namely Glancrew, Crewisaf, Abercrew and Blaentâf. The Beacons reservoir was later constructed and opened in 1897. The greatest changes to the cultural landscape however occurred with the construction of the Llwyn-On reservoir completed in 1926.

The hamlet of Ynysyfelin, Cwm Tâf (c.1910).

An accurate picture of the area prior to the building of the three reservoirs is difficult to obtain. The Tithe Map and approprionments indicate that in 1840 the Cwm Tâf portion of Vaynor Parish had 75 per cent under grass, 14 per cent was arable and the rest was bracken covered, woodland or waste. Each farm had an area of land near the river called a 'cracwydd'. The enclosed farmland bounded by the Llysieuog to the north and the Tâf Fawr to the west amounted to 1,607 acres made up of twenty two holdings, of which:- 9 were less than 10 acres, 12 were between 10 and 200 acres and 1 over 200. Each farm would have had between 10 and 20 cows and up to about 600 sheep with grazing rights on the mountain. This was a largely self-sufficient community with its rural craftsmen, cottagers and farmers working in co-operation especially at times of high seasonal activity such as at the shearing or haymaking. Thus as Gillian Bale has concluded, "Thus before 1892 the cultural landscape was one of close adaption to environment, buildings of local stone, farming economy adapted strictly to soil conditions and good growth of grass; the only

By courtesy of J. Williams, Trefechan, Cefn Coed.

This railway engine, the 'Abernant' was used in the construction of the Llwyn-On and Cantref filters until around 1926. The "navvies" line, which was the railway line which ran from Cefn Coed to Cwm Tâf was connected up to the main line at Cefn Station. Abernant was one of six locomotives used full time in the construction of the works. After delivering the workmen the train would return with two railway coaches of children en route for the Cefn Coed Schools.

A group of men working at the quarry under the Ffrwd farm (c1926).

industry being based completely on local material".[3]

In Cwm Tâf there were two small settlements. Ynysyfelin was located on the right bank of the river near the bridge across the Taf. Here there was a small cluster of four or five holdings, the Red Lion Inn, nearby the Farmers' Arms, and the Pwllcoch woollen mill which for centuries had been listed as the "Pwllcoch mill in the Great Forest of Brecon". In addition there was Capel Bethel, a Baptist chapel built in 1799. About a mile to the north of Ynysyfelin was Nantddu situated at the confluence of the Nantddu brook and the Tâf Fawr. Here grouped around St Mary's Church were according to the Parish Registers a number of pubs including the Tredegar Arms next to the church, an animal pound, a vicarage and the shooting lodge owned by Lord Tredegar. With but two exceptions all the holdings and buildings belonged to either Lord Tredegar, Lord Merthyr, Vaughan Rheola or Rogers Pontardâf. The only signs of local industries were the lime kilns situated on Cwm Tâf road and the fulling mill referred to above at Ynysyfelin. Stone for the kilns was obtained from the slopes of the Darren Fawr and from 'Cwar Moses' opened by a local minister around 1848.

During the period of reservoir building hundreds of 'navvies' came to work and live in Cwm Tâf. Their presence here is recorded in the 'navvies line' which runs from near Cefn Coed to Cwmtaf and was used for conveying men and limestones from the quarry under the Ffrwd farm to Cwm Tâf. In 1926, forty two men were employed at this quarry, twenty eight were stonemasons and the remainder worked on cranes, the steam navvy, compressors and locomotives. The navvies resident at Cwm Tâf lived in what were called "the huts", about thirty to every hut and supervised by the ganger's wife and two maids. The huts were suitably divided into eating, cooking and sleeping areas. Smaller huts called the "bathroom" and the "boiler house" provided facilities for bathing and drying clothes. The spiritual welfare of the navvies was catered for by the missioner, Mr Gasson, assisted by Mr Harry Hicken, lay preacher and ambulance man. A sixteen page pamphlet called the "Navvies letter" kept them informed of employment opportunities in other parts of the country. Names of men listed as "navvies" in the Nantddu Church registers refer to "Charles Smallman, John Hope, Benjamin Almond", and surnames such as "Hart, Trickett and Thompson" have survived in this locality until recently. Their favourite hostelry was the Morning Sun, Inn, Cefn Coed kept by the Lewis family for over a century. Here they mixed with iron miners, colliers and iron workers and listened to the ballads written and played by Joe Mainwaring, a platelayer and small holder.

Illustration by DEWI BOWEN

A nineteenth century navvy arriving in Merthyr. They were easily recognised because their clothes were distinctive. They wore moleskin trousers, double-canvas shirts, velveteen square-tailed coats, hobnail boots, gaudy handkerchiefs and white felt hats with the brims turned up.

The greatest changes which have occurred are in the agricultural economy of the Cwm Tâf valley. Writing in 1957 Gillian Bale stated that "The farm and acreage amounts to 3,570.5 acres of which rough grazing constitutes 81.0 per cent, permanent pasture 10.9 per cent and hay 4 per cent with arable land only taking up 0.8 per cent of the total farmland. Within the area taken over by the Cardiff Corporation, 30 of the original 31 farms have now been vacated and as a result Coedowen farm has grown from 45 acres in 1840 to a total now (1980) of 600 acres. This traumatic change in the agricultural life of Tâf Fawr is due to reservoir building and also to the

Building the dam at Llwyn-On reservoir, Cwm Tâf (c1925-26).

establishment of the Coed Tâf Fawr in 1946 when the Forestry Commission purchased 2,342 acres of land in the upper Tâf Fawr. The establishment of Coed Tâf Fawr has greatly affected the number of livestock grazing in the fields. By 1957 the number of sheep had fallen from 20,000 in 1946 to around 9,000 by this time. This decline in sheep population is directly attributable to the reduction of pasture available to them and because the rough pasture has been taken over, there is less winter protection for the flocks and for economic reasons the sheep farmers have cut back on their stock numbers. Furthermore, there are increased losses from pests such as foxes due to the increased cover afforded by the dense woodlands. Coedowen now has 4,700 hardy Cross Cheviots and 60 Welsh mountain ponies (1980); The Grawen has 600 Cross Cheviot; Pentwyn Isaf has 600 Cross Cheviot sheep; Danygraig has 900 Welsh Mountain sheep; the Ffrwd has 850 Welsh Mountain crossed with Cheviot while Penmoelallt has 100. Bale recorded in 1957 that "Herefords and Cross Herefords are the chief breeds maintained, but the two farms which have dairy cattle only keep Friesians and cross Friesians. There are ninety nine beef cattle and fifty six dairy cows on these farms". She further adds, "Thus of the seven farms:- 2 keep dairy cattle, 3 keep store cattle only and 2 keep both kinds".[4]

The presence of limestone has continued in the post-reservoir construction period to promote the local lime burning industry with two kilns on the west facing slope of the Darren Fawr adjacent to the main Brecon to Merthyr road. These kilns now both closed turned out quite different types of lime products. The Danygraig kiln established in 1948 was a Price family concern, they had previously had a long association with the old round kiln lower down the valley opposite Danydarren farm and just north of the Jews' cemetery. The Danygraig kiln produced burnt lime which was later crushed to make 'kibbled lime' for lime spreading on fields. The other quarry owned by Calcium Products and Fertilisers Ltd, was working from 1939, when a large two bay kiln was built near the old round kiln dating from the early nineteenth century. Until it closed in 1972 this kiln employed about ten men and produced roughly 8,000 tons of burnt lime annually for agriculture, factories and collieries. They also produced about 7,000 tons of crushed limestone used as a fertiliser in agriculture and also as a 'dust' for collieries in the National Coal Board area to reduce the danger of fire damp explosions and of pneumoconiosis.

The 'hamlet' at Llwyn-On comprises the two groups of Corporation houses and the Forestry houses together with the Community centre, the old Llwyn-On farmhouse and the new Capel Bethel built in the period 1915-26 to replace the former 1799 Capel Bethel situated near Ynysyfelin prior to the valley flooding to construct the Llwyn-On reservoir. At Nant-ddu the St Mary's Church is now not used for worship and is fast falling into decay. Most of the employees at Cwm Tâf belong to an urban culture and are alienated in this area from their sources of leisure, from shops, from schools and places of employment for their wives. In conclusion, the chief causes of social and cultural change in the Cwm Tâf valley have been the construction of the three reservoirs during the last hundred years and more recently since 1946 the establishment of Coed Tâf Fawr.

CWM TÂF FECHAN

During the mid nineteenth century there were at least four outbreaks of cholera at Merthyr and other South Wales' towns. To counteract the disease local authorities decided to establish reservoirs and in 1858, by an Act of Parliament, the Merthyr Tydfil Local Board of Health established the Pentwyn reservoir (Dôlygaer Lake). The building of this first reservoir in the Cwm Tâf Fechan required 122 acres of land and the valley land of two farms which later became derelict. The Dôlygaer Lake area became a favourite rendezvous for Sunday Schools, for summer visitors for the regattas and for those seeking pleasant walks and afternoon teas at Dôlygaer farm and Pentwyn Inn.

With the construction and completion of the Merthyr to Brecon railway thousands of people visited the Tâf Fechan valley. We note for example, that about 700 people are said to have travelled from Pant to Dôlygaer for a picnic at the reservoir in July 1863 while the station at Pant issued between 4,600 and 4,700 tickets to Dôlygaer for the Pentwyn regatta of 28th June 1866. Trains ran from Merthyr to Dôlygaer at intervals of half an hour for the regatta of 24th June 1869. On this occasion 1,600 to 2,000 passengers went by rail from Merthyr, about 1,200 from Cefn Coed-y-Cymer, a further 1,200 from Dowlais and a large number from Brecon, Newport, Cardiff and other places. With these quite astounding figures one can understand the comment made by the Rev J.

By courtesy of Merthyr Tydfil Central Library.

Cefn Coed railway station (c.1900).

E. Jenkins at this time when he stated:- "But today, with its Pontsarn and Coed Cymmer, and its twenty one passenger trains, coming and going daily, Vaynor is in the world and world comes to Vaynor".

Because of the increase of population at Merthyr Tydfil it was necessary to build reservoirs at Lower Neuadd in 1884 and the Zulu reservoir, Upper Neuadd in 1902. Here the area of grazing land taken over was 116 acres. Then in 1913 it was decided to construct a fourth reservoir to be called the Tâf Fechan reservoir located to the south of Dolygaer Lake. Because of the first World War this reservoir was not completed until 1927 and involved the submergence of the land belonging to eight farms, the vicarage, the 15th century Dôlygaer Church (Capel Tâf Fechan), Bethlehem Congregational Chapel, some cottages and small holdings. It became a valley of flooded memories. By 1926, 1157 acres of land to the north of Pontsticill had been acquired by the Tâf Fechan Water Board and in 1938 six more farms were taken over by the Tâf Fechan Compulsory Order making a total of 3,077 acres owned by the Board, with 2,567 acres being farmed in a restricted way resulting in the eventual abandonment of some more farms.

In order to evaluate the social and cultural changes which have taken place in the Cwm Tâf Fechan valley during the last century one has to try and create a picture of this area prior to reservoir building, railway construction and the acquisition of land for forestry. The Tithe Maps for the parish of vaynor and for the adjacent parishes of Llandetti, Llanfeugan and Llanfrynach which lie within the valley indicate that in 1840 there was a total of sixty eight holdings here making up a total farmland acreage of approximately 4,146 acres. The Vaynor parish portion of the Tithe Map shows that the farmland was 43.5% under pasture, 27% was meadow, 20% was arable and the remainder was woodland and non-agricultural land. The farmland of the Vaynor parish portion amounted to 1487.5 acres. The inclement weather, soil quality, high rainfall and a short growing period from May to September were the controlling factors in the agricultural life of the valley and the poem, "Can yr Hwsmon" written by the Vaynor poet, Howell Rhys of Blaenglais farm highlights the problems of the farmers at this time in obtaining money for the purchasing of seed, hiring servants, paying the tithes, and the local craftsmen. The Tithe Map also shows that the main settlement was not around the church of St Gwynno but at Pontsticill, where in 1840 there were about ten houses which by 1847 had risen to fourteen. The inhabitants were mainly quarryman, colliers and iron workers at the Dowlais Company Works.

A Blast Furnace – Dowlais c1870.

DIAGRAM SHOWING THE PROGRESSIVE DECREASE IN THE NUMBER OF FARMS FROM 1890 TO 1960 IN CWM TÂF FAWR (By G. Bale)

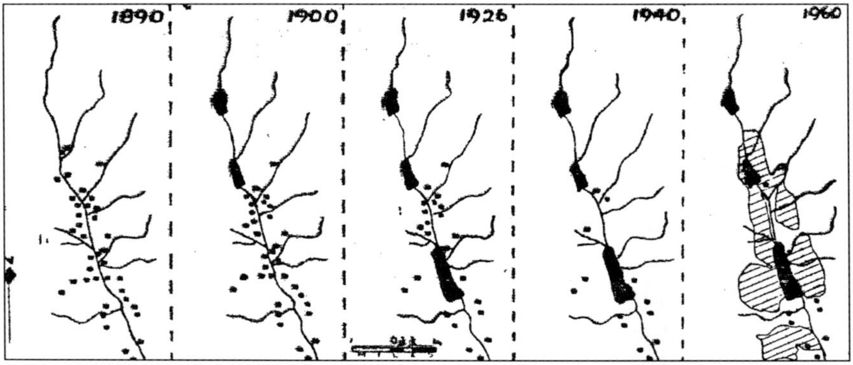

FARMHOUSES – EACH A NUCLEUS OF FARMLAND

CARDIFF CORPORATION RESERVOIRS

ACREAGE OWNED BY FORESTRY COMMISSION

DIAGRAM SHOWING THE PROGRESSIVE DECREASE IN THE NUMBER OF FARMS FROM 1840 TO 1960 IN CWM TÂF FECHAN (By G. Bale)

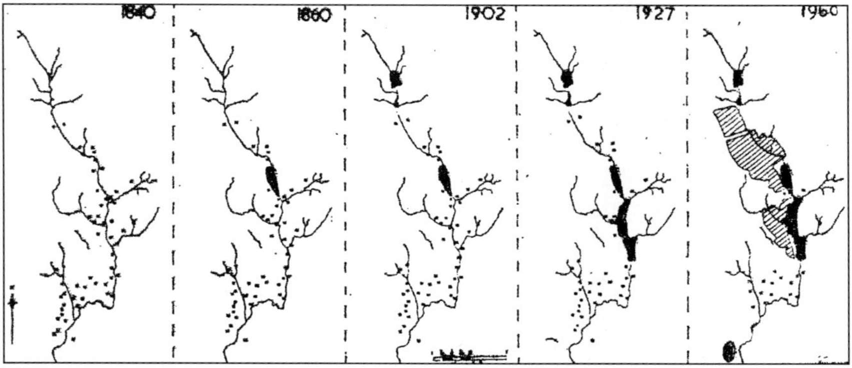

FARMHOUSES – EACH A NUCLEUS OF FARMLAND

ACREAGE LEASED BY FORESTRY COMMISSION

DEVELOPMENT OF HOUSING – TREFECHAN

TAF FECHAN WATERWORKS

As stated in the section on Education, in 1738 the Circulating School movement in Wales set up four temporary schools in Cwm Tâf Fechan at Blaenglais farm, Cwm-moel (70 pupils), Vaynor (39 pupils), Taf Fechan in Llanddeti (Dôlygaer) (54 pupils) and at Taf Vaynor (41 pupils). Later schools were established in Pontsticill and Groes. There were some rural craft workshops located at Pontsticill for blacksmiths, and weavers and there were corn mills at Gurnos, Glais, Cwm farm, Pontsticill and on the Callan brook. The 1832 Ordnance Survey map shows quarries on Morlais Hill connected with the ironworks at Merthyr by a mineral railway. The main parish road ran from Vaynor Church via Berthlwyd into the Tâf Fawr valley, crossing the Tâf Fawr at Ynysyfelin and subsequently to Penderyn. Another road led via the 'gap' to Brecon.

Pontsticill village (c1900).

The process of social change has continued with the Tâf Fechan Water Board leasing 1,137 acres of its catchment area to the Forestry Commission to establish Coed Tâf Fechan in 1947. This acquisition included the land belonging to twelve farms, all of which was to be planted. In 1947 further farmland was lost when the Vaynor and Penderyn Rural District Council purchased land around Vaynor House, between Cefn Coed and Vaynor Quarry in 1947 for the building of a new village, Trefechan. With the development of Trefechan and the expansion of the Vaynor quarry there was a further decline in the amount of agricultural land available for farming. Gillian Bale has shown that by 1958 the total number of holdings for the various parishes in the Tâf Fechan valley had fallen from sixty eight in 1840 to 18. Furthermore the total acreage of farmland was now 1,606 acres which was about one third of the 1840 acreage. In 1958 the Vaynor parish portion of the valley, the farmland was 896 acres of which 4.5 per cent was arable and 90 per cent pasture the remainder being non-agricultural land.

Commenting on stock rearing in Tâf Fechan in 1957 Gillian Bale reported that because of the restrictions imposed by the Water authority and the Forestry Commission regulations, Neuadd and Coedhir farms could only keep sheep. Below the catchment area farms such as Tyle'r-bont and Pengellifach could keep sheep and cattle. Of the fifteen farms in the lower parts of the valley at the time of her survey in 1957, six kept dairy cattle only, five kept store cattle only, one kept both and three did not keep cattle. The main breeds of dairy cattle kept were Shorthorn and Ayshire crosses with a few Friesians while Hereford and Cross Hereford were the usual breed of store cattle. She further indicated that there was a growing number of ponies reared locally. In 1980 the Cwm farm had about eighty and Berthlwyd about fifty, each having their own stallions. These ponies were sold locally, on the Continent and in America as riding ponies.

Limestone has continued to be the chief source of mineral wealth in the valley but the only quarry still in production is Vaynor Quarries Ltd and in 1957 was producing road stone, railway ballast, reducing dust for coal mines and ground limestone for agricultural purposes. It was then producing about 1,000 tons per day and had a labour force of 154 of which 70 were quarrymen. By 1980 the quarry covered 179 acres and the number of employees had fallen to 112. The population of Pontsticill has increased in recent years with the building of houses in both the private and public sectors. The school closed in 1951 and children up to school leaving age now attend the Cefn Coed schools. There are two Inns, the Red Cow and the Butchers' Arms still functioning but the village shop and the two Non-conformist chapels have closed and have been converted into private dwellings. The last train from Merthyr to Pontsticill junction was on Saturday November 11th 1961.

The social and cultural landscape of the Tâf Fechan valley has completely changed over the last century. It is no longer a self sufficient community with rural normative values. It is fast developing an urban culture with closer links with the outside world than with the Tâf Fechan valley.

REFERENCES

1. GILLIAN BALE. Cultural Changes in Cwmtaf 1840-1957. Pamphlet of the Cefn Coed and Vaynor History Society (1957) p.9.
2. Ibid p.23. (Map)
3. Ibid p.5.
4. Ibid p.18.
5. Gillian Bale Cultural Changes in the Taf Fechan valley Breconshire 1840-1958 p.9.
6. Ibid p.2-3.
7. Ibid p.16. (Map)
8. Ibid p.14.

LIFE AT DANYDARREN FARM, CWM TÂF FAWR TOLD BY MR TOM JONES (1875-1962)

Fascinating historical insights describing fully life on a Cwm Tâf farm are provided in a tape recording made by the late Mr Tom Jones of Danydarren farm who was born in 1874 and died in 1962. He spent the whole of his 88 years at Danydarren farm and was an acknowledged expert hedger, shepherd and farmer. His memories of the last quarter of the nineteenth century were colourful and vivid. He recalled the building of the 'Navvies line', the building of the three reservoirs, the demolition of the hamlet at Ynysyfelin, using the 'car llusg' in the fields, carrying home 'gwair mân' in a sheet from the Darren Fawr to feed calves, of poaching and of acting as beater for Lord Tredegar on the 'Glorious twelfth of August'. His life time covers the period of greatest social change in the valley of his birth. The tape recording is in Welsh and was made by the Department of Rural Life, Welsh Folk Museum, St Fagans in 1955.[1]

By courtesy of Mrs M. Thomas, formerly of Nant Ddu Lodge, Cwm Taf.

Mr Tom Jones of Danydarren farm, Cwm Tâf Fawr (c1960).

From the tape recording we find that his home at Danydarren was a thatched farmhouse until 1951. The date 1772 has been carved on one of the kitchen beams but the family believe it was built around 1693. It was a farm of 48 acres carrying a stock of 600 sheep, about five cows, a mare, a few pigs and some poultry. He could clearly recall the year 1880 and the whole panorama of life both on the farm and in the valley back to that time of his childhood.

He had spent much of his life shepherding on Cilsanws mountain and many of his references are to sheep. He refers to the old Welsh breed of sheep found at Vaynor during the last century and he describes them as "Defaid bach penwyn" (Little white headed sheep). He also refers to the introduction of the Cheviot breed to Vaynor during the middle of the nineteenth century. He states that his own particular breed dating from the end of the last century had been "Cross o Gardi a Cheviot oedd yma" (we had a cross Cardi and Cheviot here). He gave various reasons for keeping this breed, there was he claimed better wool with the Cheviots and too much hemp with the Cardies but the latter were hardier and better suited to the climate of the Brecon Beacons. Whereas the old breed of Welsh sheep were hardy too, they were unfortunately far too small. The Cheviots however were bigger and more compact. The cross between the Cardi and Cheviot breeds produced a hardy and compact animal ideally suited for this upland area.

Danydarren farm, Cwm Tâf (1991) (formerly called 'Yr Wrlod-ddu', meaning 'The black ditch'). The upper part was thatched until 1951 when it was raised to its present height.

He recalled buying Cardi lambs at Talybont at the end of the last century for seven and eight shillings each. They walked them home, marked them with pitch or by searing a mark on their noses with a hot iron and then tried to settle them on the hill. They inevitably tried to return home and he spent much of his time coursing them back to his own hill. When they were particularly difficult, he cut their hoofs to make walking difficult, ("Torri o dan bôn y droed a chyllell poced yn ffordd o'u setlo").

Mr Jones crossed a Cheviot ram with the Cardi ewes which were kept for three years. He kept the male Cardi lambs for a year and then sold them for twice as much the following year. When the ewes were four years old, they were fattened and sold to local dealers. About 150 breeding ewes were kept and the lambs were usually born in fields near the house, about the 12th to the 14th March, the ewes having been brought down to the coedcae in February. The word 'coedcae' is very common in Vaynor, every farm having what is called locally a "coeca".

The researches of Dr W. Linnard of the Welsh Folk Museum indicate that the word 'coed cae' is typically a word of South West Wales, especially of this region where it is used to describe a wooded area on the steep upper wooded slopes of the valleys. The coedcae were usually enclosed by a wall, fence or hedge. Sometimes the name is applied to a farm such as Coedcae-du situated on Cwm Cadlan Road near Cwm Tâf. In a survey of the lands of the Earl of Plymouth conducted by John Eyre in 1766, the largest "Coed Kae" recorded in the survey was one of 61 acres in Merthyr Tydfil parish. The form of use of each of these woodland areas is described generally as 'pasture and wood'. This confirms the recognised importance of these coedcae woodlands for regular winter grazing of livestock.

Mr Jones described methods of castration used in Vaynor involving the use of a hot searing iron, heated in a wood fire because a coal fire was too hot, or of using two pegs tied with hemp and bees wax. He also described how "Mae dyn yn sbaddu efo'i ddannedd" (A man could castrate them with his teeth). After marking and pitching and castration, the lambs were taken up to the hill on the 13th or 14th May. The sheep were taken on tack about the 15th October, when they were walked to Usk, Cardiff or Bridgend at a tack charge of between four and five shillings a head. They were taken up to the hill immediately upon their return from tacking on the 12th April. He brought in new rams every year and sold about twenty which he had reared from his best male lambs. The wethers were kept on the hill until they were four years old and then sold to dealers, one of whom was known as "Quick Johnny", or in the markets. He mentioned that they often sold sheep in the market in the yard behind the Crown Inn at Merthyr. The ram was put to the ewes when they were eighteen months to two years old and, interestingly he mentions "a phrynu maharen ar gyfer y rhai gwanaf a'n cadw lawr" (and buying a ram for the weaker ewes and keeping them down on lower ground).

By this Mr Jones meant that the ewes which were "doing badly", i.e. those that were weak and could not withstand the rigours of the Brecon Beacons in the winter months were kept down on the meadows. One of the rams was put with these. Danydarren shearing was by tradition always on the last Saturday in July – every farm had a recognised day for shearing. The shearing was done on benches in the barn and a lamb was killed for dinner.

There were a few well-known sheep complaints and he recommended certain treatments which were thought to be efficacious. They were as follows:- 'Gwaed yn y dwr' (blood in the water) – change the land; sheep with sore tongues – stop them eating dandelions; to stop the grub – (probably referring to liver fluke) tea grounds every morning or salt petre in clear water; constipation of cows or blockage – hot beer and bran, footrot – cut out the infected part and apply Stockholm Tar or clean out the foot and make them walk over burnt lime; maggots ("a bad place at Danydarren because of flies living in the fern") – clean out the wound and apply oil; and for sheep scouring – a lump of lard. Mr Jones mentioned that one could evaluate the general health of a sheep by examining the eyes. If the veins were not red then the sheep was unhealthy. He recommended putting salt-petre in the eyes of a sheep to gain this red and healthy appearance prior to taking them to market!

Sheep were marked by cutting their ears when they were lambs. He claimed to know every sheep ear-mark over a considerable distance. An additional form of marking was to use an iron and hot pitch, while the best sheep mark was to sear or burn a mark on the sheep's nose and then to rub in fat.

They kept four or five cows for their own milk supplies and for the making of butter and cheese. Calves were fed on 'gwair mân' and sold when the prices were highest. Some were kept for two years, bullocks were castrated in the Autumn, "before the hoar-frost". He does not indicate the breeds kept but further investigation has shown that he had a mixture of Jersey, Short horns and Friesians.

They kept a mare for general farm work but were not concerned with the keeping of horses because it detracted from their main interest, which was sheep farming. He described the traditional way of breaking in horses by leading for a few days, teaching the horse to turn right or left, to pull by fastening a log and then finally when the horse was considered ready to work the collar traces, backband and "langtree" were put on the horse. Particularly difficult horses were 'broken in' in boggy ground.

Having spent over seventy years on the hills as a shepherd, Mr Jones was regarded locally as an authority on sheepdogs. He claimed that Scotch dogs were unsuitable for the craggy slopes of the Darren Fawr because they had too much hair on their feet. Traditionally, the shepherds of Cwm Tâf favoured mottled dogs, or close-haired dogs and they usually worked in pairs, one for coursing and the other for collecting. He recalled buying two excellent dogs at Llangynidr for £1.0s.0d. (a trained dog today [1980] costs £250).

He recalled methods of training sheep dogs. Invariably, the golden rule was to wait until the sheep dog indicated that it was ready for training. "Readiness" was shown when the dog started rounding up the farmyard poultry. Training proper began with two sheep on the farm fold and this was developed so that the dog would recognise the meanings of particular whistles. Much of the training came incidentally by learning from an older dog. Killer dogs never attacked their own flocks but have been known to travel as far as Penderyn or Vaynor to kill, sometimes working in pairs. Recently (1968) Mr Sivill of Coedowen Farm had three hundred sheep killed by a killer dog over a period of three months, it was finally caught with the traditional wire snare.

Mr Jones referred to traditional ways of stopping a dog from excessive barking while working sheep, namely, to split the tongue or to tie a cork on the tongue. When a sheep dog rushed at the sheep it was useful to tie one fore leg up to its neck, and where a dog disobeyed, 'rhoi leriad iddo fe' (give it a good hiding) and then it would obey the whistle of command. He discussed ways of whistling and commanding. A good dog would be rounding up sheep on the yard in three months and working on his own on the hill in ten months.

Cutting and harvesting the hay usually took a fortnight with a scythe; he recalled the first machine coming to Vaynor at the end of the nineteenth century. Payment for mowing hay was at the rate of five shillings an acre, which was considered to be a day 's work. Everyone carried his own sharpening stone, or a "rip", which was an eight-inch long, two-inch square block of ash wood covered in grease and mixed with sand. He recalled that the scythes were bought from Isaac Nash, the ironmonger, but that the farmers made their own handles or "legs". It was rather interesting to hear him say that the legs were cut "when the ewes went to the ram" (October/November); that they were left to dry (to season) for six months and then shaped in the Spring. During hay-making time everyone worked in an effort to cut three or four acres between five and nine in the morning before it became too hot.

Mr Jones refers to the gambo being used for conveying the hay from the meadows to the farm yard where some was stored in the barn or made into ricks. Women helped in making food, turning the hay and in loading hay and corn. The drink was "diod fain" (small beer) and skimmed milk. He discusses at length the fact that gwair mân was cut on "Bryn Meilad (Brynmoelallt) and Cwm Meilad (Cwmmoelallt), Sychpant, Penyrheol and other places". He refers to the excellence of its food value because it contained so many herbs and for this reason was kept especially for the feeding of young calves and for pregnant cows. He mentions, understandably, the difficulty of cutting short hay like gwair mân, of turning it and of collecting it.

He states that the 'Welsh waggon', 'y carbach' or the 'car llusg' was used for carrying the gwair mân, hay and oats. He recalled seeing two or three in the hayfield at the same time in the nineteenth century and indicated that they were quite easily made on the farm, using ash or larch for the shafts. The car llusg, however, was not used for carrying manure to the fields. The manure was carried in panniers strapped to the sides of the horse. The panniers had bases fastened by a peg so that unloading was easily facilitated by merely removing the peg and the contents fell out on the ground. He mentioned that this was the traditional method of manuring and was very convenient for fertilising side land. Provided that the car llusg was loaded properly and the load tied, he claimed that it was possible to carry as much hay or corn on a car llusg as on a gambo. Its greatest virtues were that it could easily be made at home from locally grown timbers and that it was very safe especially on sideland such as that found at Cwm Tâf in general. The car llusg was also used for collecting rushes on the waun and for conveying peat to the farmhouse.

Mr Jones does not say much of arable farming, nevertheless he states that they grew barley, wheat and oats, the latter being the chief cereal crop. He mentions that wheat was brought at Pontypridd in the old days and that they had a choice of white and red wheat. Cwm Tâf farmers always used the red variety of wheat because it was hardier and more suitable for this altitude but that the white variety produced more flour. Barley was grown to feed the pigs for the winter. Wheat was sown in May and was ripe by September – we have a late Summer and early Winter in Vaynor. Everyone grew oats, they used the car llusg for conveying the crops up to the house and they stored it in the towlod, i.e. the room above the cowshed.

They threshed whenever the need arose and the milling was done at Trebanog mill, Penderyn, indicating that by the end of the nineteenth century Melin Pontycapel, the mill at the Millers' Arms and the Pwllcoch mill, Cwm Tâf were no longer operational as corn mills. Oats were traditionally bought at the March fair at Brecon and was planted in April. The rotation which he and his parents followed was oats, potatoes, swedes (or mangolds), then corn with clover. He mentions that they kept half a field for wheat and always kept the best ground for this crop, sometimes using a sickle for harvesting. Soot was spread with wheat to prevent blight.

Looking back over nearly ninety years, he said, "Gwaith caled oedd cael bywoliaeth yn yr hen amser", (It was hard work making a living in the old days). He added that there was no market for calves, stating that they could not sell them for a halfpenny a pound. As late as Christmas 1914 the Grawen Farm buried forty turkeys which they had failed to sell at three or four pence a pound at Merthyr Market. Fully-grown sheep were only worth twelve shillings each in the 1930s.

One can understand why the Cwm Tâf farmers had to be self-sufficient. Using native skill they had to make all kinds of traps ranging from the stone trap called the 'gyst' for foxes, to mole-traps and also their own tools and implements. Mr Jones mentions that he made his own car llusg, baskets for carrying potatoes and cart shafts, "legs" for all the tools, loops for carrying hay and flails for threshing made from ash, holly and hazel. The flail normally has two wooden parts attached by cord or leather, Mr Jones mentions that the flail which they made had no leather attachment but a piece of hazel, – as he states, "Dim lledr yn y ffust-roedd y rhwymyn o gollen". Whether this type of flail is peculiar to Cwm Tâf is unknown but what is known is that they made their own nutcrackers from the hazel, this I have used and they are most efficient.

Mr Jones lived a hard life and there was little time for recreational activities. Nevertheless, he provides interesting information about the sporting life of the local aristocracy – Lord Tredegar, Lord Merthyr, The Bolgoed family and the owners of the Rheola estate. At the end of the nineteenth century and in the early decades of this century, he said that the valley was teeming with bird life. Game such as grouse, pigeon, pheasants and partridges was plentiful.

Grouse were shot all over the moorland – in the Great Forest of Brecon which comes down to Cwm Tâf, above Coedowen and over to Penderyn. In his youth he was employed as a "beater at the shoots" and recalls that eighty grouse weighing between 1½ and 1¾ pounds each, were shot in one day in August 1912. On another occasion, at the turn of the century, he recalled that 300 pheasants and 40 hares were killed in another shoot. The owner of the Rheola estate, Vaughan Lee, had 900 acres of land in the Tâf Fawr Valley and kept a keeper at Penmoelallt who reared up to a thousand pheasants ready for the beginning of November. They shot around the outskirts of the estate first and then by the third week of November they shot in the "preserve". The beaters were given food and drink – in the case of Lord Tredegar at the Shooting Box. It was a time of high revelry when the local farmers who acted as beaters were given grouse sandwiches while out beating and as much beer as they could consume after their return to the Shoot-

The peregrine falcon still found nesting on the cliffs of the Darren Fawr Cwm Tâf and in the Taf Fechan valley. It has been claimed that King Henry VIII sent down to the Great Forest of Brecon for his falcons.

ing Box by night. Each tenant was given a brace of grouse or of pheasants, the surplus game was sent by train from Merthyr to different parts of the country. The keeper reared the young pheasants on a different field every year in order to keep down disease. The keeper fed the pheasants apparently after they had been freed – Mr Jones states that they came to be fed when the keeper whistled to them. The grouse however were not fed because they lived in the heather on the hills.

Farmers were not allowed to poach and were given only one warning if caught. They were forbidden to trap or shoot game but he admits that he had killed three grouse with his stick and that his dog had killed three hares in one day, one weighing ten pounds. There was also on abundance of woodcock, snipe and partridge in his youth, together with hundreds of rabbits and hares. The farmers, he said, were troubled by hares and complained so bitterly to the landowners about the damage done by them, that they were finally permitted to kill them. The partridges have gone he claimed because there is too much disturbance now. Badgers on the other hand had come recently into the valley – they were not here when he was a boy. He stated that he had not taken much interest in fishing but some locals caught up to forty pounds of trout in a night by poaching using poles and nets with which they swept the pools, or by groping with their hands. The Tâf Fawr he said was traditionally a better river for trout than the Tâf Fechan because there was less peat in the water. He concluded his tape recording by stating that eels up to two pounds were very common; and that a lot of fish were caught by the locals when the trout proceeded up the brooks to spawn in the Autumn.

REFERENCES
1. Tape recording made by Mr Tom Jones, Danydarren Farm, Cwm Tâf Fawr 1955 for the Department of Rural Life, Welsh Folk Museum, St Fagans.
2. Public Record Office, County Hall, Mid Glamorgan D/D P.I. 1-5.

Cyfarthfa Ironworks, watercolour by Penry Williams (c1825).

By courtesy of Cyfarthfa Castle Museum, Merthyr Tydfil.

THE INTER WAR YEARS

From the beginning of the nineteenth century the parish of Vaynor became closely attached to Merthyr economically, socially and politically. Cefn Coed became an industrial village, a dormitory for the miners, colliers and iron workers working for the Cyfarthfa works, while the farms provided supplies of food to the growing population located in the Merthyr area. Vaynor residents shared in the vicissitudes of industrial depression and periods of prosperity, as they did in the riots of 1831 when Dafydd Lewis of Cefn Coed was one of the local leaders.[1] They likewise participated in the nineteenth century strikes, 'lockouts' and Chartist meetings with the Cefn Unitarians playing a leading part in the cry for reform and social justice. From the time that the Crawshay dynasty took over Cyfarthfa, Vaynor became economically largely dependent upon Merthyr Tydfil.

Vaynor residents were all to frequently among the dozens of children, men and women killed or permanently maimed in the accidents caused by roof falls, gas and powder explosions in the mines and collieries or by burns, scalds and explosions in the iron works.[2] Hundreds succumbed to

THE CRAWSHAYS OF CYFARTHFA

Richard Crawshay (1739-1810); William Crawshay I (1764-1834); William Crawshay II (1788-1867); Robert Thompson Crawshay (1817-1879).

A haulier with his pit pony. The haulier has a 'peg and ball' lamp fixed to his cap. This produced a naked flame and was a contributory factor in the large number of pit explosions in South Wales.

A miner cutting coal with his mandrel.

chest complaints such as chronic bronchitis, pneumonia, silicosis, pneumoconiosis and the scourge tuberculosis. Overall the dangerous working conditions, poverty, cholera, poor housing, insanitary conditions resulted in an appalling mortality rate. Merthyr and its environs became notorious for its number of hideously deformed beggars and its crippled and blind musicians seeking a scanty and precarious living by learning to play the harp and playing on the streets and in pubs.

The second half of the nineteenth century witnessed a tremendous expansion in the South Wales steam coal industry and a downward trend in the local iron and steel industry. At the beginning of the twentieth century Merthyr was experiencing a new wave of prosperity in the pits and in 1911 for example, over nineteen thousand men were employed in local collieries and produced over three million tons of coal that year. Both the Dowlais and Cyfarthfa iron works were however struggling to survive with the latter works closing in 1910 but re-opened, in a temporary lease of life in 1915 to supply munitions during the First Great War. The war produced massive changes in the social and economic life of both urban and rural people alike.

After the apparently limitless industrial progress during the war years the country became almost paralysed from around 1922 by a collapse of its industrial, manufacturing and commercial life. South Wales suffered mass unemployment and poverty without parallel in the British Isles and the Merthyr area was one of its most serious victims. In Merthyr in 1930 for example, 3,000 men were made unemployed by the closure of the Dowlais works. In one case at Cefn Coed six members of one family lost their jobs at Dowlais including one member of the family, Emmanuel Lewis who was the Mill Manager. With a further closure at Dowlais in 1936 another 800 men joined the ever increasing dole queues.[3] Following the closure of the iron works 69.1 per cent of the men registered at Labour Exchanges at Merthyr were recorded as unemployed while the figure for Dowlais was a staggering 73.4 per cent.[4] Industrial depression was paralleled by a depression in agriculture during the thirties when it was claimed that Welsh farmers were struggling to survive on an average income of around £100 per annum. Sheep were being sold on Vaynor farms for thirteen shillings per head in 1935 (i.e. 65 pence in modern currency).

Following the First World War the 1921 Census returns indicated a sharp decline in Welsh speakers and it became clear in the aftermath of the armistice that the Chapels were no longer the social or spiritual forces that

By courtesy of his daughter Margery Lockwood.

Mr Tom Wade's Ironmonger's Shop, High Street, Cefn Coed (c1935).

they had been. The most drastic human effect of the prolonged mass unemployment was to be seen in the large emigration from South Wales. The net effect was that 430,000 Welsh people left their native country between 1921 and 1940. Merthyr displayed an equally drastic loss of its people in that a total of 16,900 left this district between 1921 and 1931 while a further 9,668 were estimated to have left by 1939.[5] This was for many families a violent emotional uprooting and for the communities, a cultural shock and inevitably a permanent loss of many of its best scholars and natural leaders.

The effect of the industrial depression on families, on young scholars in the run down schools, upon towns, villages, housing, health, shops and services, and commercial life was widespread. This was also reflected too in the continued deaths due to malnutrition and diseases such as tuberculosis. The depression was calamitous and South Wales in the thirties bore all the symptoms of a sub-standard society made manifest to the most casual observer in the hundreds of men seen standing forlorn, in thread bare clothes at street corners, or wending their way to the distant coal patches. Some villagers at Cefn Coed can still recall local men carrying up to three hundred weight of coal on their backs from above Clwydyfagwyr nearly three miles away. In 1934 I recall finding a well known local character lying dead beside his heavily laden wheel barrow near Pontycapel bridge. Respectable men were forced to raid neighbouring fields in search of potatoes or swedes for their starving families while others resorted to sheep killing and poaching.

What emerges very clearly in one's folk memory is a world which was intensely local with children fainting in school for want of food, of shoes being given out by Mr Matthew Jones the Headmaster, to disadvantaged families. Of boys with ropes over their shoulders going after school to pull their fathers and their specially designed wheelbarrows up the steep incline from Pontycapel to the village of Cefn Coed, where as stated above a sack containing two to three hundredweight of coal hewed and then carried or wheeled along three miles of uneven or unmade roads was sold for one shilling and three pence (7 pence now). One recalls also the weekly fish sales on the Twyn, the constant traffic to Mr Tom Wade's Emblem Stores to buy leather to repair shoes and the talk of pigeons and allotments. The well loved Dr Flood was nursed by my mother until he died on March 15th 1941 aged 88 years. When illness and death were frequent visitants during these years of perpetual poverty and torment our nights were all too often disturbed by those who could not afford a doctor and sought

A drawing of an unemployed man carrying coal from the coal patches at Clwydyfagwyr to Cefn Coed (c1930).

medical help, professional advice or the loan of something from the local nurse. Such was the communal feeling at this time that help was freely sought and given without thought of financial recompense.

While many gained spiritual strength from the chapels and churches and the Sunday School outings afforded days of excitement and pleasure beyond all measure, it was the local libraries, miners' clubs and welfare halls that provided intellectual stimulus, political inspiration and human comradeship for so many of the unemployed. It has been claimed that

A group at St Tudor's Church, Cefn Coed 1934. ***Back Row:*** *M. Arthur (?), Mr D. R. Davies, Mr Jones, A. N. Other, A. N. Other, Mr Price.* ***Second Row:*** *Mr Jones (Library), Mr Sam Evans, Mr Francis, Mr Bob Rogers, A. N. Other, Mr W. Thomas, Mr Owen Morris, Mr Mog Davies.* ***Front Row:*** *A. N. Other, A. N. Other, Rev John Davies (Rector), A. N. Other, Mr Jones, A. N. Other.*

Cefn Coed Allotment Association (c1937). ***Back Row:*** *Penry Morris, Bill Howells, Bill Ellis, George Batten, Fred Alban, Tom Wade.* ***Front Row:*** *A. N. Other, L. Johnson, A. N. Other, Joe Nicholls, Tom Lewis J. P., Morgan Thomas, S. Lewis.*

during the mid-thirties there were 109 Workers' or Welfare Institutes in South Wales containing 750,000 books. By contrast with the post 1945 era this was a cultured, inquiring generation of people, well read in history, philosophy and literature.

The intensity of suffering in South Wales during these years of the locust; the total dependence of these communities upon their own resources and their continued feeling of a shared heritage and destiny made them more strongly cohesive, supportive and self reliant. Self help groups were established to repair shoes at 82 High Street, Cefn Coed and at St Tudor's Hall. Allotment associations, pigeon clubs and choirs were but a few of the recreational activities set up in the valleys. Whippet and greyhound racing became very popular while the hungry boxers of this period were some of the finest ever. Thus somehow the valley people survived the long winters of mass unemployment and poverty to emerge with a strong sense of belonging to a community that had been ravaged, but proud of its sacrifices and character in the face of insuperable difficulties. They were led by men whose total commitment in politics was to alleviate the suffering of their fellows and out of this period came some of Wales' greatest leaders and scholars.

Mr 'Moss' Evans, formerly of Cefn Coed, General Secretary of the Transport and General Workers Union.

It was inevitable that boys like Arthur Mostyn Evans, better known throughout Great Britain as 'MOSS' Evans, General Secretary of the Transport and General Workers' Union and once voted by a Gallup poll as the "most powerful man in Britain", should have grown up to be a fierce Socialist. He was born into hard times in 1925, in a one-up and one down terrace house at Cefn Coed. His father, was an unemployed miner for fourteen years. His mother started work in a brickyard at the age of twelve, was widowed during the First World War, remarried and bore in all, twelve children.

At twelve he moved with his family to the Midlands where his father eventually found work in a factory and family fortunes improved. Not far away in other factories were scores of local boys including Noel Lewis, Albert Williams and Tommy Mason who died there as a result of an industrial accident.

It is almost impossible to imagine the chagrin, the humiliation, the lack of educational opportunity and the resulting intellectual wastage caused by mass unemployment. Some sought expression for their frustration and ability in the sphere of politics and the Trade Union Movement. Moss Evans has been referred to, and another who hailed from Cefn Coed who distinguished himself in this field was Lance Rogers.

After leaving school at fourteen years of age Lance found employment at Lucy Drift, Merthyr Tydfil in 1930 only to be made unemployed in 1934 with the closure of this drift mine. He became a committed socialist, took part in several hunger marches and in April 1937 left Merthyr to fight in the Spanish Civil War. By this time he was politically very active and frequently shared the political platform with such noted orators as Aneurin Bevan, MP for Ebbw Vale and later Health Minister. It was ironic in the extreme that on the eve of his departure for Spain that he was informed that he had won by written examination, the Foundress Open Scholarship to study for two years at Ruskin College, Oxford. After World War II he became a County Councillor for Breconshire, a Miners' Agent for Ogilvie Colliery and until his retirement in 1981, Miners' Agent for the Rhymney Valley. He was nominated for four different Parliamentary constituences and on the last occasion lost the nomination to Neil Kinnock by one vote.

In later years from nearby Pontycapel came Brynmor Thomas, Professor of Anatomy and Experimental Pathology in the University of St Andrews and Professor Felix Beck of Loughborough University and from High Street, Cefn Coed Professor Colin Evans now of Singapore.

Sadly, it necessitated another war to bring the depression to an end. The cenotaph at Cefn Coed, really the most honoured edifice in any locality, was unveiled by Col J. J. Jones, JP circa 1924 "In honoured memory of the brave men from Vaynor Parish who gave their lives in the Great War 1914-1918 for our freedom. Atgof rhag anghof". Forty men who died in the First Great War and seventeen in the Second Great War are recorded on the cenotaph at Cefn Coed while nine men of the first Great War and two of the second Great War from Pontsarn, Vaynor and Pontsticill are recorded at the Memorial Hall, Pontsticill.

Scene at the unveiling of the Cefn Coed War Memorial by Col Sir J. J. Jones c1924. By courtesy of Mr L. Morris, LLantrisant, grandson of Councillor Isaac Morris (Chairman of Vaynor and Penderyn R.D.C.) seen in the centre with Col Sir John J. Jones on his right. The Right Rev the Lord Bishop of Swansea and Brecon is also present with the Rev Lewis Davies, Rector of Cefn Coed.

REFERENCES

1. TOM LEWIS. Hen Dŷ Cwrdd, Cefn Coed-y-Cymer (1947) p.205.
2. KEITH STRANGE. Accidents at Work in Merthyr Tydfil c1840-1850 in Merthyr Historian Volume 3. p.54-60.
3. KENNETH O. MORGAN. Rebirth of a Nation. Wales 1880-1980 (1982) p.216.
4. Ibid p.229.
5. Ibid p.230.

CHAPTER III

Buildings

INTRODUCTION

In this study it is proposed to examine vernacular, i.e. cottage and farm-house homes, and ecclesiastical buildings which will include both churches and chapels of the Parish of Vaynor.

Essentially the traditional houses of rural Wales owe their design and layout to a complex interaction of geographical, geological, economic and rural factors. The climate, the local geology and the availability of suitable materials have their effect in determining the design and type of house found in a particular area. Basically, one finds that the countryman built his home from the materials occurring locally; very often he designed his own home, building it according to his needs and considering primarily not architectural beauty of design but the utility of the building.

Growth in some of the industries of late – eighteenth and early nine-teenth century Wales was very rapid. In this area iron and coal production expanded enormously, and industrial communities such as that at Cefn Coed came into existence in the latter half of the eighteenth century. In this area, the building of houses was as necessary as the sinking of shafts or the construction of furnaces. Key workmen had to be attracted to fill essential jobs, while accommodation was also needed for the many labour-ers.[2]

The siting of houses was dictated by industrial convenience, they had to be within walking distance of the occupants' places of work, for example, Cefn Coed men in the main worked at Cyfarthfa Iron Works or in local drifts and mines. Most houses provided little more than shelter and a means of heating and cooking, with perhaps some storage of food. The number of rooms were usually two to four with primitive sanitation, some having none, while others were provided with a privy set over a cess-pit and usually shared between several households. Overflow and seepage from the cess-pits, and water running off the waste strewn land around the works and houses, frequently polluted the wells and the streams, which were the only source of drinking and washing water.

These insanitary conditions were common throughout the area and in 1832, 1849, 1853 and 1866 Cholera joined the list of dreadful fevers recurrent here. Its arrival helped to stimulate public action to consider building reservoirs in the Parish of Vaynor for nearby towns, and for the City of Cardiff, under powers given first by local Sanitary Acts and then with the Public Health Act of 1848 by general regulations. Even so, the first Act which applied controls to all housing throughout Britain was not passed until 1835, though local regulations of some sort were in force in many places before that date. Thus, one finds that housing for the coal mining industry of South Wales, which was mostly developed after 1850, is built to much better standards than the housing constructed for the workers at the iron works.

In the Vaynor locality, most of the houses dating from the unregulated phases of the Industrial Revolution have been demolished as a result of slum clearance and re-development. Some, however, remain intact, while others are derelict and waiting for demolition. These have been drawn and plans have been made of them and will be discussed later. In the present state of decay and dereliction one catches a fleeting glimpse of close-knit communities scarred by poverty and hardship, drunkenness and the ever present pall of death from disease or accidents. Some historians have described areas like Georgetown in Merthyr Tydfil and Field Street, Cefn Coed as notoriously bad areas; but strangely enough, the older residents of Cefn Coed and the rehoused families of the Gurnos Estate, Merthyr speak with the deepest affection and love for these old areas, where in spite of poverty and hardship, the homes were usually spotlessly clean and where there was a communal warmth and feeling especially, for all those who were old or ill.

As we shall see later, many of the early industrial houses draw more on the farmhouse methods than on those used later for the cottages; they are well built, differing from the farmhouses only in a few important details.

As the Industrial Revolution progressed and the size and value of industrial businesses increased, housing costs became more significant and durability seemed less important. Economy was sought in cheaper materials, lower transport costs and reductions in the need for skilled craftsmanship. With the opening of the Glamorganshire Canal in 1794 builders in Merthyr Tydfil were able to roof houses with slates brought by ship from North Wales to Cardiff. Where there was no canal, the traditional stone slabs were still being used in 1830, even though they required heavier roof timbers and more skill in fixing.

Skilled carpentry in local hard wood was replaced by simpler construction in imported machine sawn soft wood, and components such as windows were made to standard designs in workshops, instead of being made up on the site for each house. In 1850 the tax on bricks was lifted, at the same time as the railway network was growing. Bricks were easier to lay than stones and gradually replaced them, first in the expensive parts of walls, such as quoins at the corners of a building and the jambs and heads of window and door openings, and then eventually throughout. Since the Parish of Vaynor comprises both rural and urban areas we now examine rural and urban housing within the Parish.

WELSH RURAL HOUSES

A rural cottage (17th Century).

A long house (17th Century).

Interior of long house.

EARLY COTTAGES

Reference has already been made to Theophilus Jones' description of Breconshire houses at the beginning of the nineteenth century when he stated that "the hut indeed upon the wilds of Breconshire where the door serves for the threefold purpose of an entrance, a window and a chimney is a miserable habitation".[4] The Commission on Education (1847) presented a very similar description of Breconshire cottages when they stated "the cottages to be very little, if at all, superior to the Irish huts in the country districts ... In very few cottages is there more than one room which serves the purpose of living and sleeping.[5] This would appear to be the typical and simplest type of rectangular cottage found in Wales. A seventeenth-century observer speaks of a Welsh Cottage as a "Dunghill modelled into the shape of a cottage, whose outward surface was so all to-be-negro'd with such swarthy plaster that it appeared not unlike a great blot of cow-turd. This structure straddled over about eight Ells of ground, above the surface whereof the Eves were advanc'd about two Yards, and the Chimney peep'd about a foot above the Eves; the light flowed in through the old circumference of a bottomless Peck; which being stuck in the Thatch, supply'd the place of an Orbicular Casement. The door-way was a breach in the wall toward one end which being of a dwarfish size i.e. two foot lower in stature than an ordinary man, we were forced to abridge our dimensions and to creep in. The Parlour, Hall, Kitchen, i.e. One room".[6] From the description given by Hugh Evans one notes that the one-roomed cottage persisted, in some places within living memory (Most of the workers' houses were one roomed. The chimney would be open, the fire of peat, a stone on the hearth and the floor of earth).

The next stage in the development of this type of house came probably when it was divided into two parts so that the window in its further end provided light for the bed place while the entrance provided light for the living end. The most usual method of sub-dividing the cottage was by arranging the furniture, the dresser in particular to serve as a partition between the living and sleeping ends. The Commissioners for Education (1847) in their general survey of Brecknockshire state that "a large dresser and shelves usually form the partition between the two ends: and where there are separate beds for the family a curtain or low board is (if it exist) the only division, with no regular partition".[8] Similarly Hugh Evans states, "rhoddid dresser a chwpwrdd pres ar draws yn aml i wneud siamber"[8] ("a dresser and a 'press' cupboard were often placed across to form a 'chamber' "). The single-roomed cottage divided by means of a partition became widespread throughout Wales and there are constant references to it and again in the eighteenth century Warner described a 'tenament' ... divided into two apartments in Brecknockshire. Because of the size of families it is very likely that most of these two-roomed cottages had a bed in the kitchen and in the parlour, or 'pen isaf' as it was called. This type of cottage is still to be found at Cefn Coed. A plan and drawing of this cottage will be discussed later under 'Urban Housing' and is shown in that section.

A further development in this type of cottage may be compared with the development of the lay-out of the long house, which in Vaynor so predominates over other types of rural house that it must be given pride of place.[10] A plan of this type of single-storyed cottage is shown overleaf. From a description given by Lleufer Thomas these cottages had two rooms from 10 to 12 feet square; there was generally no loft, the roof being open to sight with a dividing partition about five feet high between the rooms. The major problem confronting the families occupying these cramped cottages was that of accommodation. The various Government reports of the nineteenth and twentieth centuries all bear witness to the unsatisfactory housing conditions, especially of the sleeping accommodation. If these deficiencies were apparent to outside observers then, it is certain that they posed very severe problems for the inhabitants of these cottages. This problem of accommodation gave rise to another development in rural domestic architecture in the form of the 'Bwthyn crogloffft' or 'cock loft cottage'. The Crogloffft cottage was a single roomed cottage which had been divided by a thin partition so separating the living room from the bedroom which was ceiled at a height of around seven feet. Above it was a loft, a "dark and airless triangular space" the floor of which was the ceiling of the bedroom. This constitutes the additional accommodation, which, by this simple expedient, is doubled without any actual addition to the house itself.

This sleeping accommodation was divided into an upper and lower floor and access to the crogloffft was by means of a ladder from the living room. Evidence is lacking as to whether this type of dwelling was to be found in Vaynor cottages, but a modification of it will be discussed when farmhouses are examined and reference will also be made to two-roomed houses in the Cefn Coed area, which had access to an upper room or loft by means of a ladder.

The rural cottage with bedroom on the upper floor was introduced into Wales in the early nineteenth century, but in fact it was no more than a long loft stretching along the length of the cottage, access being obtained by means of a ladder. It was un-partitioned and light was invariably provided by a small window. The walls were about eighteen inches high and the roof sloping up to about eight or nine feet. Welsh cottages in Vaynor have belonged, possibly until the eighteenth century, to the single-room tradition for living and sleeping.

Bragdŷ cottages, Vaynor with a "cwrw bach" on the right.

The cottages at the Bragdŷ Vaynor date from 1795. The ground floor plan shows a front room which was formerly a kitchen with a stone staircase leading to a bedroom above. There is a catslide roof at the back covering a small back kitchen probably added in the last century.

Tredegarfach, now derelict but standing, was a small-holding of six or seven acres. The plan indicates the typical and traditional kitchen, a small room 9 feet by 5 feet, a dairy 5 feet by 5 feet, and a stone staircase, at the side of what was once an open hearth in a kitchen approximately 15 feet square. The built-in oven was probably absent in the Bragdŷ and Tredegarfach until the last century and, because of the absence of ovens, bakestone bread was generally used. In the early cottages, ovens were not provided nor were facilities built for their insertion. The kitchen lay-out at

Tredegarfach, although on a small scale, was exactly the same as that found in some of the larger farmhouses such as Danydarren (Wrlod Ddu to give its old name) and at the old house at Danygraig.

Danydarren Farm (Wrlod-ddu) – Cwm Tâf.

Illustrations by DEWI BOWEN

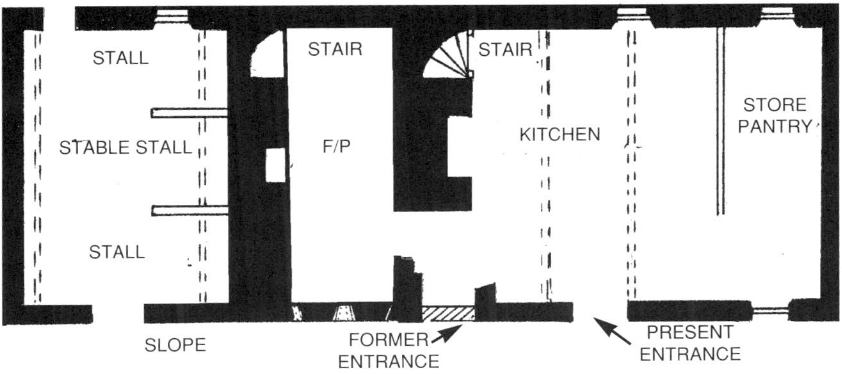

Ground Floor Plan of Danydarren Farm, Cwm Tâf.

THE LONG HOUSE

Students of vernacular architecture will no doubt search for this important type of house defined and illustrated by Peate in a notable chapter on the 'Welsh House' and named by him as the 'Long House'. Strong objections have been raised to the name, some arguing that it is an ancient type going back at least eight centuries, others that it is a product of the Industrial Revolution. By true long houses we mean all buildings which shelter both a family and their cattle and have direct access between the two parts. In Wales, it was as far as can be judged, the predominant type over large areas of the moorland plateau. As the term implies, the long house was a single, long low building; the dwelling itself is always at one end, generally called the 'upper end' (Pen uchaf) though this depends upon the situation of the house, while the other end (Pen isaf) houses the cattle. Between the two is the door leading into a passage called the 'penllawr'. The upper end was always paved while the cow house floor was always of earth.

A true long house in the parish of Vaynor is the old Danygraig farmhouse situated on the main Brecon to Merthyr Tydfil road, two miles north of Cefn Coed. This long house is of modest proportions, linking it with a lower rural class than Hepstefawr farm described by Peate at Penderyn. In the plan of Danygraig farm, shown overleaf, one notes that the kitchen adjoins the byre or 'penllawr' and is clearly seen. To the right of the kitchen is a raised floor indicating where the dairy and, possibly a small bedroom were in former days. Incisions in the beams indicate where the partition separated the kitchen from these small rooms. Between the joists nearest to the fire place and on each side of the fire place are inset rollers used with a length of material for drying corn. A detail of interest is the small original window lighting the attic at floor level and the entrance to the 'towlod' or 'taflod' for storing wool, cheese and corn or sometimes used as a bedroom for the servants.

In the simpler kind of false long house, the former existence of a way through from house to byre is perfectly clear because it has been blocked up.[12] A good example of the modified long house is Ffrwduchaf Farm, actually in the parish of Penderyn but since it is in the Cwm Tâf valley is considered part of this study. Although from the front it appears like a long range of buildings erected at various times during the nineteenth century, an examination of the rear, where the stair projection has a three light wooden window with diamond mullions, indicates that part belongs to the early seventeenth century. Then the house comprised a hall entered

Old Danygraig, Cwm Tâf.

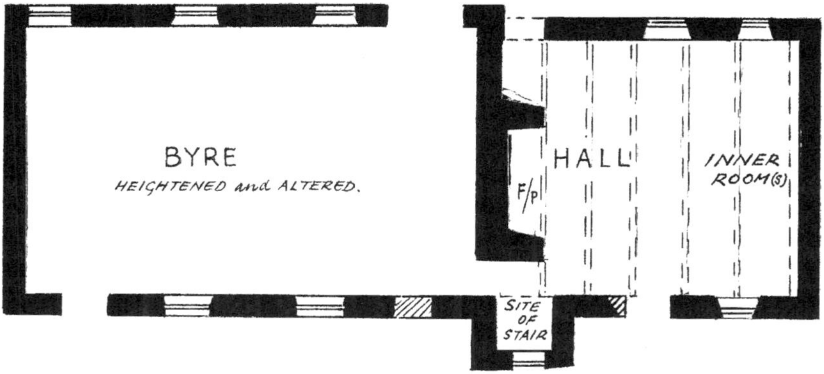

Ground Floor Plan of old Danygraig Farm, Cwm Tâf.

from a cross passage within the byre, and two small inner rooms as shown in the plan overleaf. In subsequent changes at Ffrwd Farm one notes that the focus of life has moved to an extension at the upper end which includes kitchen, scullery and dairy. The parlour has retained its old function, but the hall, which seems at one time to have been used for farm purposes, has a large arched opening, now blocked, on the northern side of the yard. It has now in effect, become an extra parlour, as the occupiers stated, “the front room”.

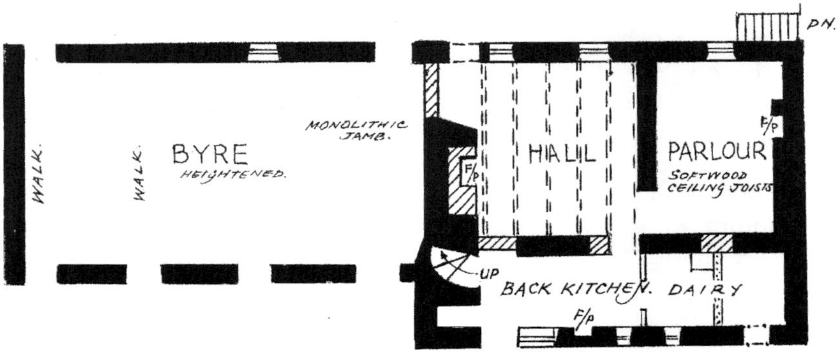

Ground Floor plan of Blaendyffryn – Vaynor.

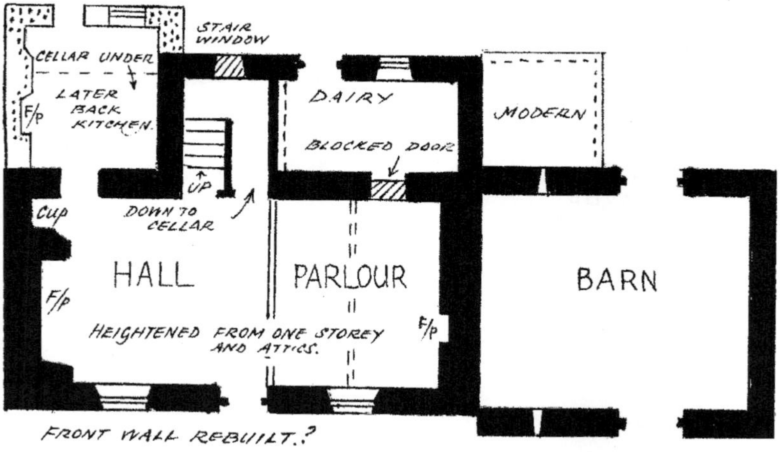

Ground Floor Plan of Brynrhŷs – Vaynor

Ffrwd Uchaf was undoubtedly the earliest and best of its type. Cwm Farm, Vaynor is similar in incorporating the side of the passage into the house to give an extra room. Here a lobby entrance has been made to avoid going straight into a room. Blaendyffryn Farm, Vaynor, now in ruins, had the same kind of development in piecemeal fashion.

HOUSES OF THE GENTRY

The Vaynor parish is lacking in houses which have a specifically gentry type of plan. Theophilus Jones the Brecknock county historian has referred to this fact thus, "Though this parish cannot boast of the splendid seats of opulence or of any families long settled here, (the Gunters of Ynis-fawr now extinct and Morgan of Carawen of later introduction only excepted)". Grawen, as its known locally has been considerably altered by the addition of a new wing comprising a kitchen, a large parlour and a smaller additional room. The original farmhouse still stands and is used as a store. The salting slab has the date 1773 inscribed on it but the house could date from the late seventeenth century. Jones has referred to it as "Carawen or Carw-waun, the buck's park".

There is then little evidence of gentry status in the parish of Vaynor and the families of Ynysfawr and Grawen would seem to have been of minor importance. The families were probably not above minor gentry or yeo-man status and were perhaps hardly more than superior peasants until late in the seventeenth century. A more general explanation for the scarcity of gentry in the parish was the sheer poverty of the region. This high barren moorland area, with its two tongues of tolerably good land in the Tâf Fawr and Tâf Fechan valleys, would not have permitted much accumula-tion of capital to buy land and erect fine houses. On architectural evi-dence, the late sixteenth and early seventeenth century was a period of rebuilding new and greatly improved housing but there was none in this parish, but the Neuadd Farm, Llanddeti in the Tâf Fechan valley was an outstanding example before it was demolished.

At a somewhat lower level, some men could afford, before the Civil War, to rebuild in this new way. Ffrwduchaf farm is one of the first long-houses to be so reconstructed, without much modification on the ground plan but greatly improved by the addition of a chimney stack and an upper floor throughout. Still, up to the middle of the seventeenth century, the vast majority of peasant farmers will have had houses less like Ffrwduchaf and more like the ill-built croft or wretched huts which represented the general peasant housing prior to the 'great rebuilding' which took place in the second half of the seventeenth century when these primitive long houses were rebuilt to the new standards.

Unfortunately, the chronology of change is imprecise. The most we can say is that many of the old houses of the Vaynor Parish, seem to have been built or rebuilt in the second half of the seventeenth century with some overlap into the early eighteenth century. By the end of that period the process of improvement and the raising of living standards which it implies would have reached all the peasantry, or small farmers, whichever one chooses to call them. Thereafter, so far as the evidence goes, these was a slackening of building activity.

In fact it was the industrial revolution in this immediate locality at Merthyr Tydfil which provided the great impetus to improvement, beginning slowly, perhaps around the 1820s, and then reaching a peak towards the middle of the nineteenth century. It is to this period, more than any other that the buildings owe their appearance. It was during this time that many old farmhouses were heightened from one storey and an attic to two storeys. With the building of the Merthyr-Cardiff Canal, blue slate was made available to replace the thatch and, in many cases, there was an increase in the number of rooms through heightening, so making more bedrooms, and by extensions which provided additional kitchens and parlours. Dairies were often added, and their proportions indicate the great demand for milk and its products and salted bacon in the industrial towns of South Wales in general, and Merthyr Tydfil and Dowlais in particular. In the latter half of the last century farmhouses such as Danygraig, the Fedw and Pengellifawr were completely rebuilt while the old farmhouses were kept as stores.

FARM BUILDINGS

BARNS

Because of its high altitude and high rainfall the Parish of Vaynor is not particularly suited for corn growing. Some corn however, had to be grown to feed humans and livestock. The barn design is a carry-over from the days, when corn was threshed with flails on the barn floor. The barns are easily recognised by their large doors, usually between nine and eleven feet high and about nine feet wide, which rise to the eaves to facilitate the unloading of corn or hay. A feature of the Parish farm barns in the structure shown is referring to Coedhir barn Dôlygaer. An explanation given to

Feature at Coedhir Farm, Dôlygaer to extend the width of barn for the unloading of corn and hay during inclement weather.

me by Mr Trevor Owen of the Welsh Folk Museum, St Fagans was that this feature facilitated the covering and unloading of two loads of corn or hay during inclement weather. In some cases this awning was supported by stone pillars on each side and in other cases by stone or oak supports as seen at Coedhir farm Dôlygaer.

The great doors open on to the middle section, the paved floor (y llawr) with occasionally lower doors opposite. Most of the local barns are two-bay and the floors are raised two or three inches, above the middle paved floor and cobbled. Threshing with flails on the barn floors of this parish was practised sporadically until the 1920s. The oldest barn examined was that of the Grawen, Cwm Tâf which still retained the pegged stone tiles on the roof (1980). Unfortunately, the stone tiled roof of the Grawen Farm was replaced by corrugated sheeting in the mid 1980s. At most of the farms visited the barn was separate from the farmhouse.

COW HOUSES

The cow houses visited in Vaynor housed very few cows due to restrictions imposed by the water authorities or for other reasons, such as the keeping of store cattle rather than dairy cattle. In the main, the cow houses were long buildings with one or two rows of stalls facing a range. In most cases the passage for the cows had an exit on the other side, while the range invariably had a trap door leading to the loft (taflod) for storing hay. Attached to the cow houses were calf pens without stalls. A most interesting feature was found at Coedhir farm, where the cow stalls were separated by slabs of stone.

An interesting feature of Coedowen farm, Cwm Tâf is the awning running along the length of the cow shed stables and barn and is a characteristic of farms in the Cwm Tâf and Tâf Fechan valleys. In an area of high rainfall this feature was invaluable since it facilitated the carrying of hay from the barn to the cattle and horses under cover. All the cow houses examined were of nineteenth century construction. They were slated, whitewashed and well-built.

Canopy supported by oak or stone wall supports. The base stones are large untrimmed boulders with 3-4 inch spaces between them. Coedowen Farm, Cwm Tâf.

STABLES

Every effort seems to have been made to have the stable as near the house as possible, probably because the horses were considered to be the most valuable creatures on the holding. The general substitution of working horses for oxen on ordinary farms in the Parish of Vaynor dates from around the late eighteenth and early nineteenth centuries. Horses brought the traps and waggons to Merthyr, and cart sheds are still to be seen on some farms. While horses have been replaced by tractors they are still retained at Danygraig and Coedowen farms for the shepherding on the Brecon Beacons, while at Cwm Farm and Berthlwyd farm the shire horse has been replaced in the stable by Welsh cob and Welsh mountain pony mares and stallions kept for breeding purposes only.

BUILDING CONSTRUCTION

Evidence of cruck construction of houses shows that this method was at one time wide spread through the country. Unfortunately none of these buildings still exist in this Parish and indeed the only clue that we have of their existence in the area is the possibility that 'Taicwpla' in Penderyn, might refer to houses of cruck construction. Cruck constructed buildings consist of pairs of curved timbers set up in inverted V form, the timbers crossing at the apex of the triangle thus formed, so forming a fork in which the ridge piece is fitted. The rafters and purlins are placed on the crucks which therefore support the whole weight of the roof. The walls were of secondary importance.

Reference has already been made to the very poor houses in rural Breconshire in the eighteenth century. Prior to the use of stone, there would seem to be a natural development from daub and wattle to the use of turf or clods on the one hand and mud prepared in various ways. These were the normal materials used in many parts of Wales until recent times and in houses constructed of these materials, the older technique of wattle and daub persisted in the interior partitioning. The earliest use of stone in folk building appears to have been to form a foundation on which rested the sill of the wooden framework of the wall and such stones were used without having been dressed – and were often river stones or stones from boulder clay.

Dry walling is met with throughout Wales in old buildings and it has been found that clay mortar was used for folk building into the nineteenth century. It is likely that in this area a lime and clay mortar was used for filling in the spaces in the walls of houses. Dry walls are an essential feature of the Vaynor Parish landscape and clearly indicate how skilfully the walls were built, using long stones for binding the walls and also as gate posts. Some of the walls measured at Pengellifawr were between four and five feet thick at the base and six feet high. The largest boulders were the base stones and the size of stones used in the construction of these walls tended to get smaller as the walls rose from the ground. There are miles of stone walls in the Parish of Vaynor, the stone having been obtained by field clearance or from the small quarries to be seen on the farms and hills of the parish. The stone was conveyed probably by the car llusg in the late eighteenth and early nineteenth centuries, during the Napoleonic Wars, to build these boundary walls.

"Native Earth" was more commonly used throughout Wales for floor than it was even for walls "the floor" states J. Evans in 1798, "of a cottage was the native soil, rendered very hard and uneven from long and unequal pressure". The author recalls, as stated elsewhere, cottages in Cefn Coed with earthen floors up to 1935 and had flag stones in his own home until about 1936.

Roof coverings in Wales have consisted until recently of two classes of materials; thatch and stone. Thatch, in the sense of vegetable matter, in Wales has consisted of many materials, turf, fern, heather, heath, rushes or reeds, and straw.[15] The author recalls straw thatch on Danydarren Farm, Cwm Tâf until 1951. Jenkins has referred to Dafydd Sakry "a poet, a worker in straw, a maker of beehives and a thatcher",[16] and the Parish Vestry records refers to "Do for attend the thatch of the Church 2s.0d" (£0.10p). The use of fissile stone for roofing has been known in Wales from at least 'Roman times"[18] and examples of stone roofing are still to be found in the Parish, for example, on the barn at Grawen Farm, Cwm Tâf.

In the past, the cottages and farmhouses of Wales have provided evidence of almost every stage in the development of the chimney ranging from the simple hole in the roof, the wattle and daub louvre to the stone or brick chimney. With regard to doors, the door hurdle was in existence in Wales in 1888, Evans describing (in 1798) a cottage writes, "door there is none, but this deficiency is supplied by a hurdle formed of a few wattlings and rushes, which in bad weather is raised perpendicular to stop the gap".[19] Another feature often met with down to the second half of the nineteenth century was the harr-hung door. An examination of old prints and photographs of farms in this locality show the windows to be small.

Apparently few were made to open, a fact which explains why windows were broken in some places when an inhabitant died, so that his spirit might escape to heaven.[20]

The fireplace and chimney not only varied in their siting within the house but also in their construction. During the sixteenth century a drastic change took place in the location of the fireplaces. Formerly an open fireplace in the middle of the floor, it was now placed against one of the walls. The placing of the fire against a wall, instead of in the middle of a room, posed a special problem. Thus, from this period, cast iron fire-backs are known[21] and continued to be made until the nineteenth century as a means of protecting the stone wall at the back of the open fire on the floor. More common in houses of a low social order was to build the fire back stone against the wall, as a form of buttress or reredos, and against which the fire would be placed. The top of this is known as the 'pentan', it served to hold the kettle, and so forth. The hearth itself could be a single slab, even the living rock, but it could equally well be a section of pitched stone defined by a stone kerb. There is evidence from Breconshire to suggest that it was this type of hearth that was found in houses erected as late as 1850.[22] The author has recently found an iron gravestone used as an iron fire-back at Danygraig farm, Cwm Tâf.

The built stone fireback proved so useful to rest things on that it developed outwards on both sides of the fire, to become the familiar hob or pentan. With the introduction of coal as a common fuel, something was needed which would hold the fire together, and allow for some ventilation underneath. One way of securing this ventilation and enabling the ashes to be easily disposed of, was by having a hole covered by a grating, underneath the fire. In this warm hole under the fire such things as weak chickens were laid to strengthen and this is one explanation of the proverb 'A chick nurtured in Hell will insist on remaining in Hell'.

The early grates, introduced with the use of coal, were simply a grating, a criss-cross of iron bars, raised a little on short legs, and provided with sides to prevent the coal from falling out. Typologically, the stage has now been reached where the fire burnt in a grate elevated above the floor, and with stone hobs on either side. The range will not be discussed in detail here but it should be mentioned that it was a product of the industrialised areas, particularly Coalbrookdale and, in Wales, it was in the industrialised areas that it gained the greatest foothold in the South Wales mining valleys. In the valleys it seems to have developed from a fire burning in a grate to what was termed on 'oven and sham'. This was a central grate, with to one side of it a cast-iron baking oven, the other side was bricked up, but the bricks were hidden by a moulded cast iron plate called the "sham". The author recalls practically every house in Cefn Coed having an 'oven and sham'[24] until the Second World War. These were replaced in the valleys by an oven and boiler, and ultimately by a one-piece range such as the 'Yorkist' or 'Chattan Special'. The whole process of the introduction of the range meant new work for the housewife, for the hearth had to be washed, coloured, sanded, the fender scoured, the range black leaded and the attendant brasswork polished. It provided great decorative scope which was often carried to excess.

With regard to one of the most important features of the hearth, namely the bread oven, it seems that up to about 1600 the common baking utensil used all over Wales was the metal pot-oven, used either with a metal cover, or more probably inverted over a bakestone. Cast iron had probably only reached Wales shortly before this date, so perhaps we should postulate some kind of earthenware predecessor to the pot oven.[25] Around 1600, wall ovens, either built-in examples of stone or brick, or portable clay ones from North Devon began to be used in Glamorgan and Gwent. Evidence of wall ovens have been found in the cottage at Cwm-moel and the small holding at Tredegarfach, Pontsticill.

INDUSTRIAL HOUSING

The examination and measurement of both rural and industrial housing in this area indicates very clearly a close relationship between the earliest industrial houses with the rural dwellings[26] which have already been described. Undoubtedly during the first phase of the Industrial Revolution the decisions about plan shapes and constructional methods were left to local builders and craftsmen, who followed the traditional practices of rural Wales and eventually the district. The industrial nature of such houses is shown mainly by the way they were grouped around the works and usually arranged in rows. With the great increase in population in this district one finds that houses were compacted together so that every conceivable space and corner could be utilised. One finds in Cefn Coed therefore still standing, a single-storey dwelling, until very recently two-roomed houses and cottages, following traditional plans. We now look at the different house or cottage plans of Cefn Coed and district.

SINGLE STOREY DWELLINGS

83 High Street, Cefn Coed. A single storey dwelling (late 18th century).

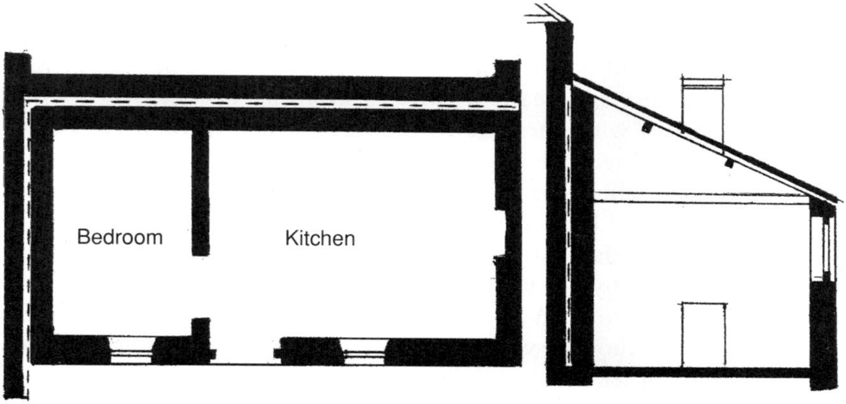

Ground Floor Plan of 83 High Street, Cefn Coed.

It is very likely that there were single-storeyed, one-roomed dwellings at Cefn Coed similar to those found in Vaynor and throughout Wales - "the miserable huts and habitations", referred to by Theophilus Jones around the turn of the eighteenth century. It was natural, therefore, that they should have persisted after the Industrial Revolution. The example at 83 High Street, Cefn Coed is a 'lean to' or back-to-back type of dwelling which was occupied until 1936. Since then it has been used as a store.

The single storey cottage at 83 High Street, Cefn Coed.

TWO-ROOMED COTTAGES

Two examples are shown. The first was located at 46 High Street, Cefn Coed and was occupied until 1936. Its measurements indicate how very small the only living room was. The main entrance was 4ft 9ins high, the room measurements 11 feet wide and 8 feet long. The house had, a fire-place downstairs with an oven. There was a fireplace upstairs in a small undivided room. A cupboard set in the wall downstairs acted as the pantry. There are no indications of where the toilet might have been, the occupants were obviously sharing this convenience with neighbours.

46 High Street, Cefn Coed. A two-roomed cottage with ladder access to upstairs (19th century).

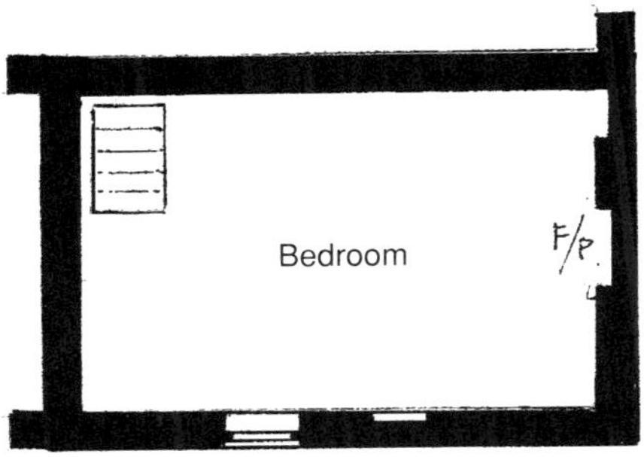

First storey.

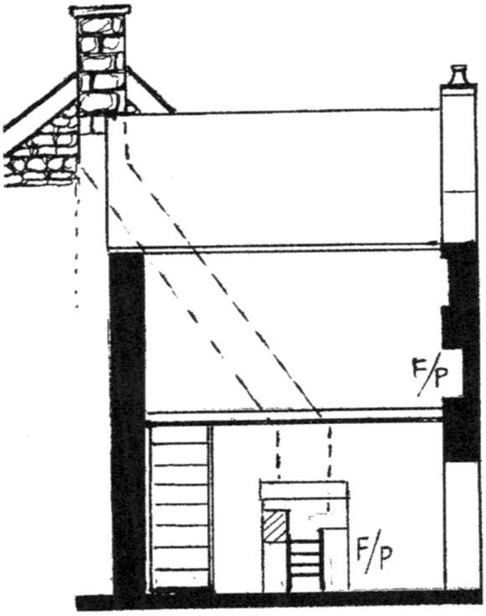

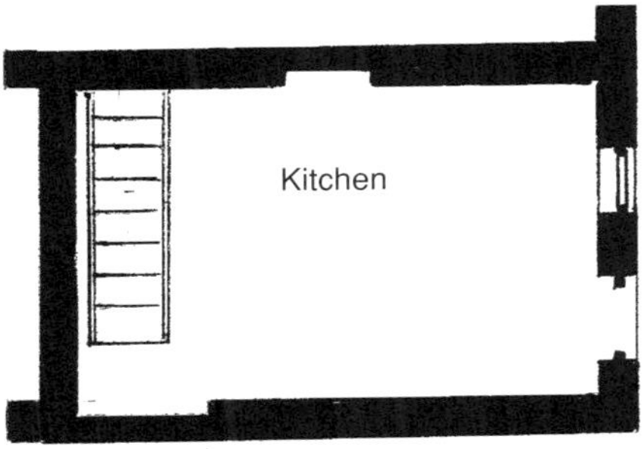

Ground floor plan of 46 High Street, Cefn.

The second example shown of a two roomed cottage is shown in the drawing of 82 High Street, Cefn Coed which was used until recently as a workshop by the author's father. The ground floor plan shows a traditional fireplace with oven, a 'cwts dan stâr' and a fairly large window opening on to the Cefn Coed High Street. The upper room was illuminated by two small windows, and furniture was taken up by means of a trap door set in the floor. The cottage was occupied by a family until the First World War and since then it has variously been used as a meeting place for the local Guides, as a distribution centre for the boots and shoes for deprived families during the period of industrial depression in this area in the 1920s and 1930s and latterly as a builder's store. In design and structure it shows an advance upon the type referred to above. Unfortunately this building was demolished in 1975.

82 High Street, Cefn Coed. A two roomed cottage (early 19th century).

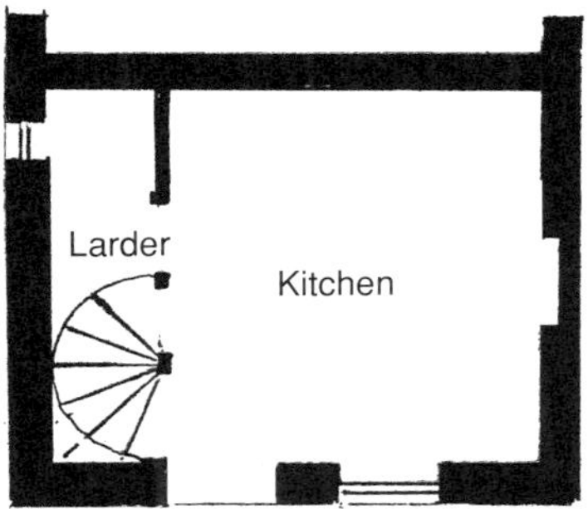

Ground floor plan of 82, High Street Cefn.

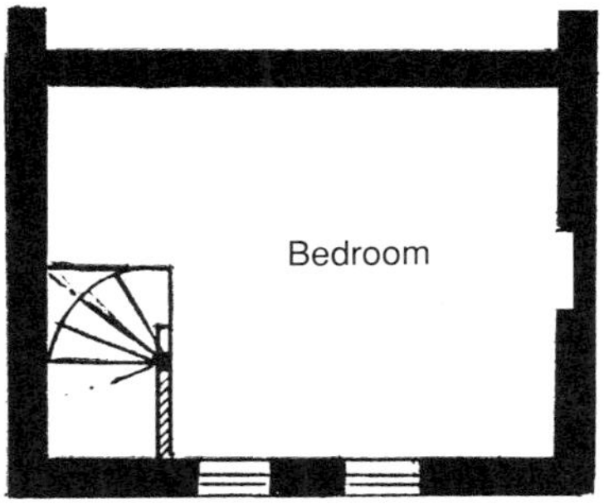

Plan of first storey.

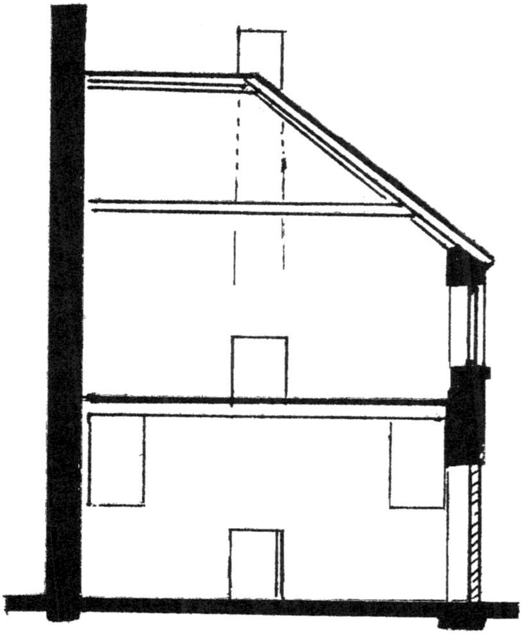

Vertical section

THREE ROOMED COTTAGES

Many of the three-roomed cottages were originally two-roomed cottages with a back kitchen added in later years. In these three roomed cottages one finds that the stone staircase is still to be found at the side of the fire place in the 'front room', giving access to the undivided bedroom on the first floor, which of necessity accommodated the whole family. Many houses of this type were to be found on Cefn Coed High Street until about 1935 (the same as Bragdŷ Cottages Vaynor).

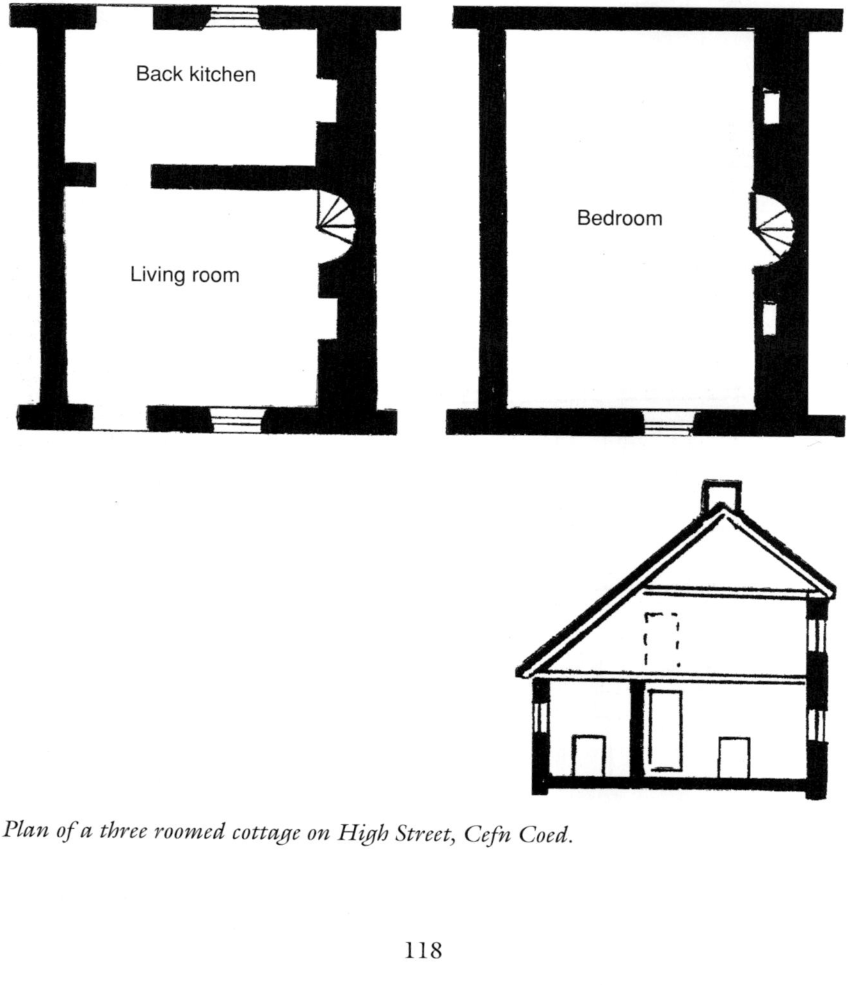

Plan of a three roomed cottage on High Street, Cefn Coed.

Another form of three-roomed cottage was found in this locality. Here one notes a rather different plan; on the ground floor there is a kitchen, a larder and a small bedroom. Access to the first storey was by means of a stone staircase at the side of the fire place to an undivided room above. Very many of these early cottages had oak roof structures like that of rural dwellings and would have been covered originally by stone slabs. A row of this type of cottage may still be seen at Gellideg, Merthyr Tydfil and at Rhydycar. Another form of three-roomed houses was to have one room on the ground floor and two small bedrooms upstairs such as those found at Pond Street, Dowlais.

FOUR ROOMED COTTAGES

Typical four roomed ironworker's cottage found at High Street, Cefn Coed and at Holford Street.

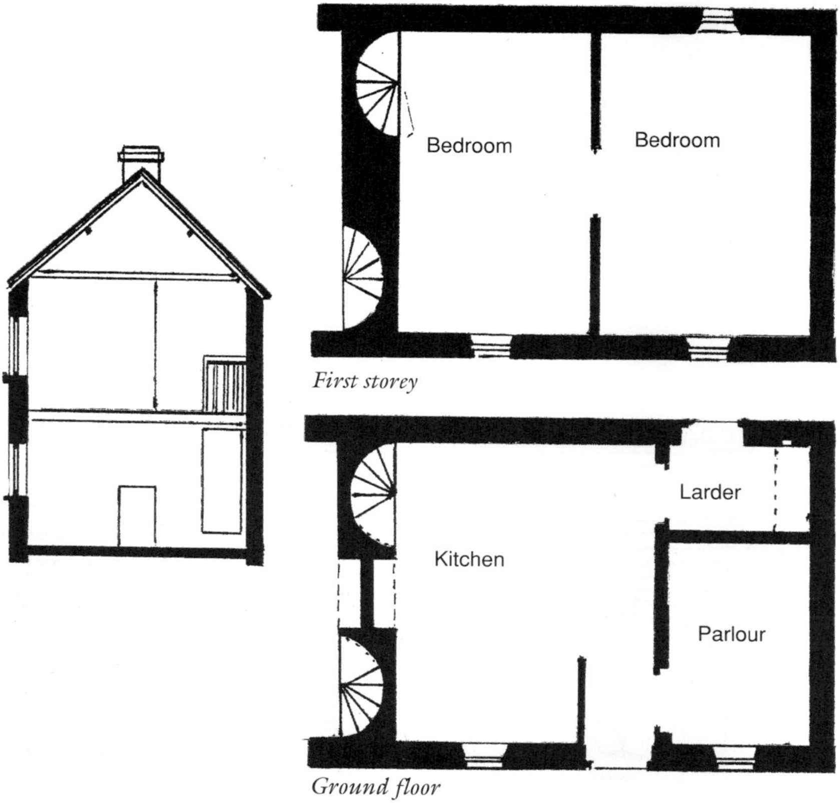

Plan of a four roomed cottage such as those found at High Street, Cefn, Holford Street and Tai-Grawen.

Most four roomed cottages have conventional plans, with two rooms on each floor and a larder. Their construction is quite traditional, too, with stone walls outside and oak beams and partition inside. It is important to note the identical plan here with that of the long house type farmhouse kitchen with dairy and bedroom, fire place and stone stair case. These four roomed cottages are still very common at Cefn Coed and Pontsticill, where they are built in rows as at Holford Street, Cefn Coed. The partition walls between the houses are four feet to five feet thick to allow for the stone stair cases which are then found on opposite sides of the chimney. Entrance was made into the kitchen from the front and the rear exit was either through the larder or through the rear wall near the larder entrance. In recent years, back kitchens have been built behind the kitchen and a further development has been the building of a bedroom with small bathroom above the kitchen addition. Some houses such as the Primrose Hill Cottage built by Mr John Lewis himself in 1902 contrasts with the three or four roomed traditional plan discussed above. This house was demolished in 1990.

The detached, stone built Primrose Hill Cottage, Cilsanws Lane, Cefn Coed built in 1902 by Mr John Lewis.

BASEMENT DWELLINGS

Another innovation tried out in the period from 1790 to 1840 was the 'dual' row, in which one range of house formed the basement of an entirely separate range above, as shown in the sectional drawing. This design was well suited to sloping sites, common enough in this industrial region where building space was extremely limited. The row was placed along the slope with the doorways of the upper houses at ground level on the uphill side and of the lower houses on the other, downhill side. Usually the lower houses had only one storey and were to be found in Cefn Coed until five years ago at Well Street, and at Lower High Street (i.e. 1975). They are still to be found in a few houses at Pontycapel Road. These single-storey houses (or flats) were of course ideal for the newly married or for the elderly. The rents were low and, although small, they fulfilled a social need. On occasion, however, they were not used for domestic accommodation and the planning of them was rather different as shown in the block of buildings situated at Lower High Street, Cefn Coed. Until after the Second World War the lower storey faced the High Street and was used as a fish and chip shop, while the upper storeys were used for domestic accommodation. Access was gained to these upper storeys by means of a flight of stone steps on the outside. This building is an excellent example of the attempt in the nineteenth century to accommodate as many as possible in the small spaces available. While the countryside was never very far away, the physical setting of valley and mountain imposed a limit on urban expansion. A section through the lower High Street, Cefn referred to above, and Well Street, would clearly illustrate how the natural slope was utilised for basement housing.

THE VALLEYSCAPE

It would seem that the older parts of Cefn Coed had been built by 1860. Further expansion was mainly in the form of infilling within the earlier housing and expansion up the side of Cilsanws mountain for the middle-class housing. Cefn Coed, like Merthyr, was largely unplanned in the sense of planning for the convenience and comfort of its inhabitants. According to Malkin, who visited the town in 1803, the "first houses that were built were only very small and simple cottages for furnace-men, forge-men, miners and such tradesmen as were necessary to construct the required buildings. These cottages were built in scattered confusion, without any

42 and 42 High Street, Cefn Coed (showing basement dwellings).

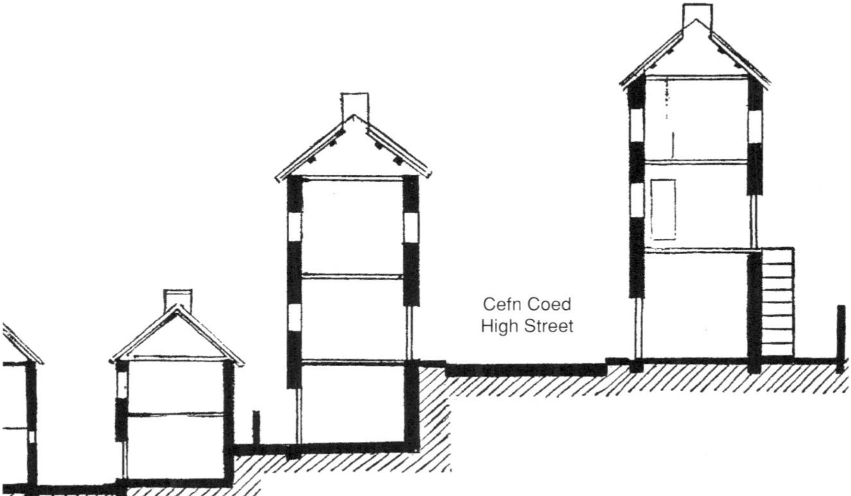

Section through Lower High Street and Well Street, Cefn Coed, showing how the natural slope was utilised for basement housing.

order or plan. As the works increased more cottages were wanted and erected in the spaces between those that had been previously built".[27]

Three years later, Malkin revisited Merthyr again and found that great improvements had already taken place and that "many new streets have been built, which are sufficiently straight and wide, and more have been laid out. The new houses are in general good, and some of the older strees have been rebuilt on an improved plan".[28] The formless and apparently haphazard lay-out of Cefn Coed, sloping down from the steep flanks of Cilsanws to the Tâf Fawr and Tâf Fechan, has given it a certain natural· charm which persists and can be appreciated even today.

Throughout the nineteenth century, the houses were built predominantly of rubble pennant sandstone with floors covered by flagstones and roofs covered by slate. The use of local stone in its rich variety of colours enabled the buildings to harmonise with the surrounding landscape to a surprising degree. This is particularly so with much of the early nineteenth century housing which, though sub-standard inside, is warm and full of character outside. Unfortunately, it is these houses built of stone, sometimes laid random but often coursed and trimmed, that were being rapidly demolished everywhere in the Valleys. These terraces were far more pleasing in appearance than the late nineteenth and early twentieth century housing, yet at the present rate of 'progress' there will be no examples left within a decade.

A popular type of early terrace house seems to have been the two-storey, single-aspect design with short roof spans, narrow window openings and wide double frontages (two rooms down and two rooms up). The reason for the short spans and wide fronts may well have been that the dwellings were built by masons rather than carpenters and it was therefore essential to keep timberwork with all its joining problems to a minimum. Certainly the stonework is usually of high quality with well cut and well laid arches over doors and windows and neat circular stairs built into the thickness of party walls. The roof span of these houses were exceptionally small and varied between four and five metres overall.

In 1875 Sanitary districts were established and with these came the general introduction of building by-laws, to continue the form of housing developments. It was the rigid application of by-law planning to the mining towns built in the latter part of the nineteenth century that was responsible for the regular grid-iron layouts which distinguished these settlements from the earlier iron towns. These by-laws ensure that each new housing estate has proper streets, rear access lane, good drainage, piped water and so on. Thus the majority of late nineteenth century housing was built as monotonous houses in serried terraces. The houses were still largely built in pennant sandstone but gradually red or yellow brick was introduced first for chimneys, then for arches to openings, and finally for quoins and complete surrounds to doors and windows.

Internal planning also underwent considerable change and double-fronted elevation gave way to single-fronted treatment. The single-aspect dwelling, with a single entrance at the front, was abandoned, house plans became more square and finally a house plan was evolved, with a narrow frontage and two entrances – one from the street and the other from the rear garden. The double access, such as South Terrace, Cefn Coed normally had a separate parlour which was usually reserved for births, deaths and marriages at the front, with a passage alongside leading to a large backroom (kitchen) and the staircase to the bedrooms. By the end of the century many of the terraces, such as Vaynor Villas, Cefn Coed and the Morning Sun houses were being built with bay windows overlooking handkerchief size front gardens but, by and large, these houses accommodated the middle class strata of society at Cefn Coed.

In terms of social stratification at Cefn Coed at the turn of this century it has been described by Morgan (Pant) (1893) thus, "Cefn Coed may be divided very properly into two parts; the more ancient part, which was principally built on the bank of the Tâf Fawr, and is now known as Cefn Isaf. These old houses are small, with low roofs, and are of very primitive appearances, affording an accommodation quite inadequate to the sanitary requirements of the present day. The more modern position of Cefn Coed forms the main street ... more modern still are the numerous villas, which dot the sides of the hill, built mostly by well to-do tradesmen".

During the last fifty years considerable changes have been made in the cultural landscape of Vaynor as a result of slum clearance, the building of council estates and private building. Bryn Tâf was built in 1936 to rehouse families from Field Street, Cefn Coed and immediately after the cessation of World War II a number of prefabricated bungalows were built at Maesygarreg, Cefn Coed on the site of the former Garregfawr farm which was the ancestral home of the family of Roy Jenkins former Member of Parliament, now a Member of the House of Lords. The new village of Trefechan likewise came into being after World War II as did the new estates at Pontsticill. The Gersanws estate now stands on what was known as the 'Conservative Hall Field" and on land formerly owned by the late Col Sir John J. Jones T.D., J.P.

The official opening of the Maesygarreg prefabricated bungalows in the late 1940s. Included in the photograph are Mr Vernon Rose (Clerk to the Vaynor and Penderyn Rural District Council), Mr Penry Morris (Chairman of the Housing Committee), Mr and Mrs Morgan (new tenants and formerly of Cross Keys Court, Cefn Coed), Mr Spencer Harris (Sanitary Inspector), Mr Edgar Hughes (Surveyor), Mr R. Boulter and Mr Ieuan Rees. (Donor Mrs Roy Lewis).

THE CHURCHES AND CHAPELS OF VAYNOR

Vaynor Churches

The Church standing at Vaynor in 1291 is supposed to have been burnt down during the Battle of Maesyfaenor in that year. A new church, rebuilt of stone in 1295, stood it is claimed, until it was replaced by a new church on the present site in 1870, only the tower now remains of this old church.

Reference has already been made in the section on the 'topography of the Parish of Vaynor' to the description given by Theophilus Jones in

1809 of a church "having a small tower with two bells and consisting of a nave and chancel ... the roof not ceiled, the floor of earth uneven, the seats decayed".

The building of churches in England and Wales progressed on distinctly national lines and the parish churches of the medieval period indicate the evolution of this style in church building. Vaynor church, i.e. the church of 1295, had its own peculiar attraction resulting from pleasing proportions and well defined outlines. The exterior is simple, bold and straight forward with it single western parapeted tower and aisleless nave and porch. The principal entrance was through a semi-circular headed door under the tower in the west facade. In later years this entrance was dispensed with and a new entrance, a south porch, was built into the south wall of the nave near the tower. One porch was planned deep and narrow so as to act as a screen against the direct blast of the wind.

The high-pitched stone tiled roof designed to throw off snow and rain, was another result of climatic conditions. The interior was on the lines of many parish churches with open timbered roofs in the nave. It is natural that in early times the material at hand should have been employed and this in itself gave local character. The sandstone of Vaynor is so hard in texture as to admit of little sculptural ornament, and this provides an added serenity to the architecture of the Vaynor Church. The fine oak trees of the Vaynor Parish undoubtedly provided the building material. This timber was specially serviceable for posts, beams and braces of the roof nave and this gave the old church an intimate and attractive interior.

During the last nineteenth century three new churches were built in the Parish, namely, St Tudor's, Cefn Coed in 1889, St John's Cefn Coed in 1874, and the new church of St Gwynno at Vaynor in 1870. St Tudor's as stated elsewhere was demolished in 1936 to make room for the gymnasium of Vaynor and Penderyn Secondary School. The present Vaynor and Cefn Coed Churches are almost identical except in size, Cefn being larger, but having a nave, chancel and tower each end, both being made of local sandstone.

Chapels

It is of interest to consider Baumgart's definition of what constitutes the artistic element in buildings, i.e. architecture as art. Briefly it is that, up to the beginning of the twentieth century at least, "A building had to have a constitutional or representative role, and has to use a richer variety of forms than a purely utilitarian structure". As to the representation role, the Non conformist chapel became transformed into an essentially Welsh vehicle of religious expression. Throughout the nineteenth century and the early part of the present century, chapel society dominated the religious, cultural and social life of the valleys which at the time were still generally Welsh speaking. In a society more concerned with rhetoric and revivals than with the visual arts, the chapel was often the most important building and the only evidence of anything approaching deliberately conceived architecture.[30]

With regard to the variety of forms, here too there can be little doubt as to the relevance of chapel architecture and in this a strictly limited structural range. The chapel builders eminently succeeded in achieving a rich diversity of designs to suit all purses and creeds. While concentrated almost entirely on the front facade, the designs display a virile imagination, part folk-art and part an adaptation of historic styles introduced from England.[31]

It is immediately apparent that without these often times very beautiful buildings many parts of the Valleys would be architecturally barren and devoid of any relief from the monotony of industrialisation.

The Royal Commission Census of 1911,[32] revealed that there were about 800 chapels in South Wales. Two factors were responsible for these high numbers. In the first place, there was the need to build chapels to serve a growing population and linked to this was the fact that the mining valleys had an unusually high proportion of worshippers, for example, in 1851 in Merthyr Tydfil 64 per cent of the population went to religious services. Enthusiasm for religion was, no doubt, partly a means of retreating from the often appalling miseries of industrial life in mid century. The second reason for the large number of chapels was the rivalry between different sects. Each chapel built its own chapel regardless of whether or not the area was already served by other places of worship. In addition, chapels were established independently by the laity, often, as in the case of Tabor Chapel Cefn Coed, as splinter groups of the mother chapel, giving rise to duplication within each denomination.

Apparently, the majority of early chapels were not designed by architects, but were generally the products of local builders as in the case of the early building of the Hen Dŷ Cwrdd in 1747 and also in the rebuilding of the Hen Dŷ Cwrdd, Cefn Coed in 1853 by ministers or members of the chapel, who gleaned their ideas from the illustrated catalogues of the period. The result is that chapels tend to have a similar character, although the window arrangements often differ and there may be local variations of window tracery etc. Of the local architects, William Gabe and his father built many of the chapels in the Merthyr Tydfil district. Unfortunately, none of Gabe's work has survived intact and it is difficult to appreciate the architectural importance of their buildings. Often times the 'chapel' was designed by the minister concerned, the Reverend Evan Harris of Merthyr for example, had been a carpenter and builder before entering the ministry and he designed a large number of Methodist Chapels in Glamorgan. His own Chapel, Capel Pontmorlais is now the Merthyr Blind Institute.

The most striking architectural aspect of the Welsh Chapel, whether designed by a local builder, minister or architect, is the consistency with which the barn like form of building had been adhered to for over a century, i.e. from the early years of the nineteenth century until well into the twentieth century. The gable-ended roof, traditional in Wales and easier to construct became the dominant feature. The design of the gable facade characterises the development of the chapel style, more than any other single feature. Here is the focus of all the artistic and architectural expression of Nonconformity and this, with one important exception is nearly always a classical rather than a Gothic expression. The exception is the English-language chapels of the latter half of the nineteenth century.

The few English chapels built in the early years of the century followed the traditional architectural design of the chapels built for the Welsh-speaking congregations. They rejected all forms of symbolism connected with the Church and were concerned essentially with the provision of rooms for preaching rather than settings for religious rituals. From the middle of the century onwards, however, the English chapels became more and more like simpler versions of Anglican churches. The design of the main facade of Welsh chapels in the area falls into definite groupings. By comparing facade design it is possible to classify them and trace the evolution of the chapel styles. As in most styles, there is the familiar rise-and-fall sequence; an ascent to a golden age and then a decline into decadence and eccentricity.[33.]

FACADES OF SOME OF THE CEFN COED CHAPELS

Hen Dŷ Cwrdd Unitarian Chapel. Built 1747 and rebuilt 1853 and 1895.

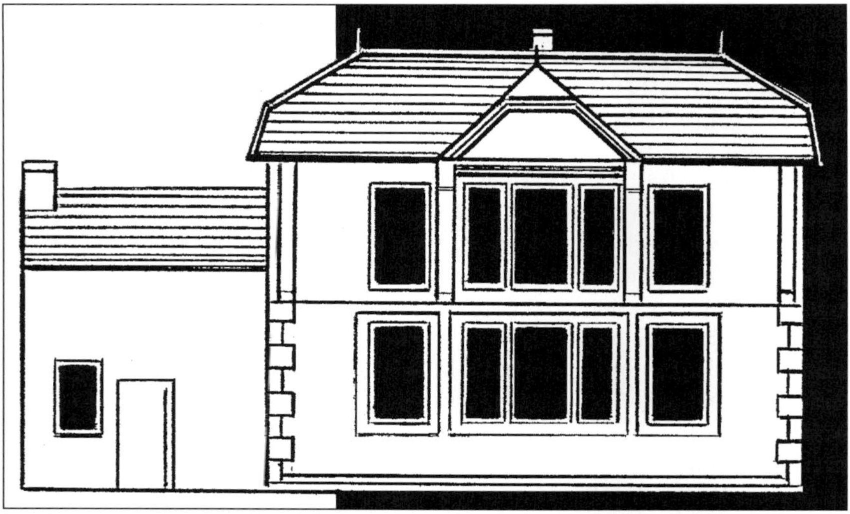

Moriah Calvinistic Methodist Chapel. Built 1807 and rebuilt 1873 (demolished 1972).

Carmel Welsh Baptist Chapel. Built 1844 and not rebuilt.

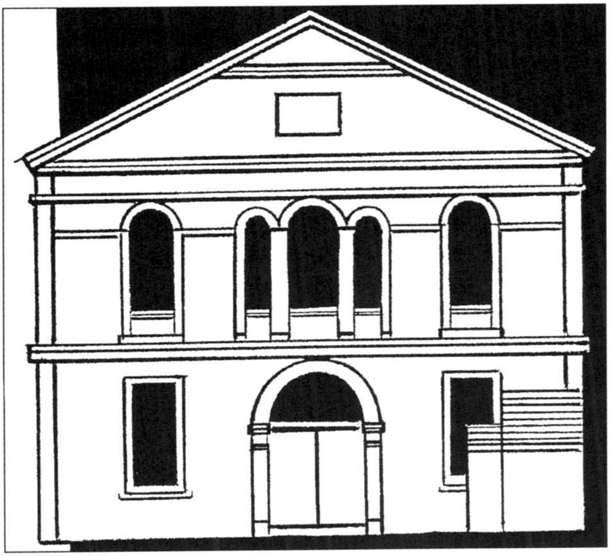

Ebenezer Welsh Independent. Built 1837 rebuilt 1861 and partially rebuilt in 1913.

Tabor Welsh Independent Chapel. Built 1845 and rebuilt 1905.

Aubrey Welsh Wesleyan Chapel built 1876. Demolished 1972.

In the earliest or primitive phase, the domestic long wall facade, which had been adopted by the eighteenth century meeting houses was continued and the traditional position of the pulpit in the centre of the long wall was retained in some cases. The chapel buildings can be divided broadly by period into the following categories. Firstly "the golden age" made up of the Early Classic period (1800-1835). The Classic (1835-1845) and the Late Classic (1855-1865) and Post-Classic (1865-1910). One cannot, however, strictly adhere to these dates as indicating particular styles, Carmel Baptist Chapel, Cefn Coed for example, has the general architectural features of the primitive phase, in that it has the pulpit in the central position of the long wall but it was actually built in 1844 which has been described as the 'Classic Period', i.e. 1835-1845. This Chapel could well have been a replica of the original chapel which is alleged to have collapsed. The following table indicates when the Vaynor Parish Chapels were built and rebuilt and their respective styles.

Chapels In The Parish Of Vaynor And Their Styles Of Architecture

Name of Chapel	Date of Original Building	Style	Date of Rebuilding	Style
Hen Dŷ Cwrdd Unitarian	1747	Primitive, pre 1800	1853 & 1895	Post Classic 1865-1910
Bethel Welsh Baptist, Cwm Tâf	1799	Primitive, pre 1800	1927	
Moriah Calvinistic Methodist	1807	Early Classic 1800-1835	1873	Post Classic 1865-1910
Bethelhem, Independent Pontsticill	1828	Early Classic 1800-1835	1924	
Ebenezer, Welsh Independent	1837	Classic, 1835-1845	1861 & 1913	Early Post Classic 1855-65
Carmel, Welsh Baptist	1844	Classic, 1835-1845	Not rebuilt	
Tabor, Welsh Independent,	1845	Classic/Late Classic	1905	Post Classic 1865-1910
Aubrey, Welsh Wesleyan	1876	Post Classic	Not rebuilt	
Seion, Welsh Baptist, Pontsticill	1901	Post Classic	Not rebuilt	

We now examine the architectural features of a sample of three of the chapels of the Parish of Vaynor as they are today (1980).

Carmel Welsh Baptist Chapel (Classic 1835-1845)

Carmel was built in 1844. The colour is a restoration of the original which was restored in 1890. The pews are original and seat 300. The plan is square, 36ft by 36 ft.

General Characteristics

The starkness of the earlier chapel forms is relieved by the introduction of mouldings around the windows, and sometimes delicate keystone emphasis. The surface is of stucco, colour having been added in the pilasters and mouldings. The sense of proportion is remarkably sure, a rather "feminine" quality is to be seen. The facade is on a flat plane, this type is frequently seen in a non-pedimented form in the first half of the nineteenth century. There has been a clear move of emphasis to the gallery floor (the upper storey), the two floors are sometimes divided by a drop moulding. Upper storey windows are not centralised, they are framed with a moulding and the sills are delicately corbelled, frames are continuous and have corbels and pilasters. The tracery springing is emphasised. Windows have little headroom in the facade. The lettering is heavy, shaded sans-serif with an alternative slab serifed form. The interior is simple, iron pillars support the gallery and the pew boxes are low in relationship to the wall.

Ebenezer Chapel, Cefn Coed
("The Decadence" Early Post Classic 1855-1865)
Built 1838, Rebuilt 1861 and 1913

General Characteristics

In some cases there is an emphasis on the corners and the style. The proportions are heavy, there is emphasis on the horizontal, the mouldings being introduced wherever possible. A most important factor is the connecting of the windows by a drip moulding. The emphasis seems more or less equally divided between the storeys. The surface treatment remains coloured stucco, but in one or two cases brick has been extensively used. Heavy tracery is used in the windows and the proportions are much heavier and coarser, the slender panels found at the sides of the windows in the earlier styles are missing. The windows have more headroom in the facade wall. The window disposition is similar to the preceding style. The lettering is a crude sans-serif.

Hen Dŷ Cwrdd Unitarian Chapel (Post Classic) Built 1857, Rebuilt 1853 and 1895

Hen Dŷ Cwrdd Unitarian Chapel, Cefn Coed is a remarkably restrained and unified design of its time (rebuilt 1895), and one is led to believe that it is an adaptation of the second chapel erected in 1853. The most interesting features are the windows which are emphatic without being overornate. On the upper floor the centre is filled with a triple group of round headed windows linked by Romanesque pilasters. The windows of the outer bays are circular with stone trefoil tracery which is repeated in the round headed windows of the ground floor.

The Interior

Chapel interiors vary considerably. In early buildings decoration was kept to a minimum but later as chapels became larger and more imposing, greater attention was given to furnishing, usually in pine wood, either highly polished or varnished, with cast-iron pillars and brass fittings. The pulpit, usually in a raised and central position on the end wall opposite to the entrance is the focus. In front of the pulpit is the 'big seat' (sêt fawr), separate and reserved for the elders and deacons, in the form of an enclosure with bench-type seats, and the communion table. Within the two-storeyed chapel the gallery is an important element in the design and invariably is supported by slim cast iron columns, often supplied by the local ironmasters at Merthyr Tydfil. Floors are generally covered by earthenware tiles while the ceilings and walls are plastered. Frequently, the wall behind the pulpit is ornamented with classical pilasters and stencilled decorations incorporating scriptural texts. The best ornamentation is found in the ceiling in the form of a ceiling rose highlighted by colourful and intricate plasterwork designs making them exceptionally attractive.

Engraved glass is to be seen, mostly in the doors of the porches. Generally, stained glass is very rare, probably the cost restricted further use. Brass is used for door handles, umbrella stands, locks, hinges and various other fitments. During the latter part of the nineteenth century, large organs became important features, either designed as an integral part of the building, or added later as funds became available. The organ position varies from the centre of the gallery, facing the preacher, to above and behind the pulpit, or on occasion below and in front of the pulpit. The serried rows of organ pipes, decorated with various designs or biblical texts often form an impressive climax to the chapel interior.

Windows

In the early chapels the windows are evenly spaced in the facade, the upper storey lit by three or four windows, the ground storey by the side windows. The lower facade windows were used to light the stairways which led to the upper storey gallery. In later style the position of the lower storey windows does not change but the upper storey windows become centralised after 1845 (the late Classic decade). Occasionally the upper storey windows are rounded. Window tracery is varied to such an extent that no definite trend can be traced. The glass used in the windows is household glass, although in some cases thick, frosted coloured glass is used. The disposition of the windows is relationship to the rest of the facade may be noted by reference to the drawings of the chapels.

Lettering

The lettering forms on the facades of the Non-conformist chapels are of great interest. They reflect the character of the period; of the builders and of the chapels. The variety of lettering is quite exclusive, many typographical forms being used and may be described as follows:

1800-1835	Bold, black serifed and unshaded type
1835-1845	Heavy, shaded, sans-serif, with alternative serifed form
1845-1855	Heavy block letters, close spacing
1855-1865	Crude sans-serif type
1865-1910	Varied forms freed from a plaque spread across the facade

Iron Work

Most of the chapels have iron railings, or iron gates. These railings and gates were made, as were the interior support pillars, by the great iron masters such as Crawshay, Guest and Hill. There is considerable variation in the design of the railings and especially in the railing terminals (Finials). Some of these finials and brackets have been examined and they illustrate this unusual aspect of chapel design and to exemplify the high degree of artistic skill of the local craftsmen.

REFERENCES

1. J. GERAINT JENKINS. Life and Tradition in Rural Wales 91976) P.117.
2. J. B. LOWE. Welsh Industrial Workers Housing 1775-1875 (1977) P.3.
3. J. B. LOWE. Op. Cit. P.4.
4. THEOPHILUS JONES. History of Brecknock (1809) P.139
5. IORWERTH PEATE. The Long House (1946) P.89.
6. W. RICHARDS. Wallography on the Britton Described P.P.17-18.
7. H. EVANS. Cwm Eithin (1931) P.63.
8. The Commissions for Education (1847) in their survey of Brecknockshire, Radnorshire and Carmarthen. P.56.
9. H. EVANS. Op. Cit., P.63.
10. J. T. SMITH. The houses of Breconshire. Part VI. Brycheiniog Volume XVI (1972) P.4.
11. I. PEATE. Op. Cit., P.93.
12. J. T. SMITH. Op. Cit., P.10.
13. THEOPHILUS JONES. Op. Cit., P.476.
14. J. EVANS. Letters ... North Wales in 1798. P.115.
15. I. PEATE. Op. Cit., P.176.
16. J. E. JENKINS. Vaynor. P.129.
17. J. E. JENKINS. Op. Cit., P.149.
18. I. PEATE. Op. Cit., P.179.
19. J. EVANS. Op. Cit., P.161.
20. I. PEATE. Op. Cit., P.186.
21. EURWEN WILLIAMS. Yr Aelwyd. Folk Life. Volume 16. (1978) P.89.
22. S. JONES and J. T. SMITH. 'The Houses of Breconshire'. Brycheiniog. IX (1963) P.60 and P1 XIV B.
23. EURWEN WILLIAMS. Op. Cit., P.92.
24. EURWEN WILLIAMS. ibid P.92.
25. EURWEN WILLIAMS. ibid P.98.
26. J. B. LAWE. Op. Cit. P.8.
27. B. H. MALKIN. The Scenery, Antiquities and Biography of South Wales (1804) P.177.
28. B. H. MALKIN. The Scenery, Antiquities and Biogrpahy of South Wales. (2nd Edition, 1708) P.276.
29. FRITZ BAUMGART. A History of Architectural Styles (1970) P.7.
30. JOHN B. HILLING. Cardiff and the Valleys. (1973) P.127.
31. JOHN B. HILLING. ibid P.127.
32. Royal Commission on Church of Encland and Various Religious Bodies in Wales, and Monmouthshire. Vol 6 (1911).
33. JOHN B. HILLING. Op. cit. P.130.

CHAPTER IV

Rural Industries And Craftsmen

INTRODUCTION

In a mountainous area such as Breconshire the population has tended to be concentrated in lowland areas. Craftsmen were usually centred in hamlets or villages and by tradition and partly through poverty, many of the upland farmers made their own equipment ranging from shepherds' crooks to their own wheel-less sledges made from timber growing on their own farms. Mr David Richards of Penderyn formerly of Gellia Farm, Cwm Tâf informed me that he could recall Mr Jones of Llysieuog Farm, Cwm Tâf using a car-llusg in the early 1930s for carrying "gwair mân" – moorland hay cut to supplement a poor harvest, down off the Llysieuog hill. Similarly, Mr David Williams of Coedhir Farm, Dôlygaer informed me that he recalled a wheel-less sledge being used in Pontsticill in 1935.

The dispersed nature of the settlement in Vaynor, especially in the upper reaches of the Tâf Fawr and Tâf Fechan required the services of itinerant craftsmen. The 1851 Census provides some clues for example, the following craftsmen were found on the farms when the census was taken: Richard Hughes, carpenter (Wrlod-ddu farm, later called Danydarren farm), David Griffiths aged 28, Shoemaker (Born in Carmarthen), Evan Watkins, Wheelwright (Nantgwineu Farm), Levi Thomas, Wheelwright (Blaenduffryn Farm). More recently, an itinerant carpenter known locally as "Llandeilo" was found seriously ill in a barn at Trebanog Farm, Penderyn. Presumably between "calls" they slept at wayside barns.

Rural craftsman have traditionally produced essentials in the form of tools and equipment to accommodate specific and local needs. For example, they considered such factors as soil, topography and local traditions. The Breconshire type of billhook used in Vaynor for laying hedges of willow, hazel and hawthorn was almost straight bladed with a short pistol-shaped handle. This was very different from the type of billhook used in Cardiganshire, or even as near as Llandeilo, which was curved and designed to keep the users' hands clear of brambles.

Vaynor is conspicuous for its stone walled boundaries which climb the steep and dangerous slopes of the Beacons. An excellent example of the adaptation of country-made equipment to local topography is provided by the use of the wheel-less sledges used, as already stated, in this area until the 1930s. The great danger in using wheeled vehicles in steep slopes is that they over-turn but it is almost impossible to over turn the wheel-less sledge and the greater the load the safer they become. They were used extensively for centuries in Vaynor for the conveyance of stone for farm house building, for harvesting, for field clearance and for the building of boundary walls. The deep ruts made by the runners may still be seen on Cilsanws mountain, Vaynor today.

Although much of Breconshire was concerned with pastoral farming, fruit cultivation and cereals were grown in other parts. In Vaynor, the main crop throughout the nineteenth century was oats which would account for the large number of corn mills. Of the 107 corn mills located by the author in Breconshire there was always at least one set of stones for animal grist, i.e. oats or barley and one set of French burrs from the Paris basin for grinding wheat.

Very many parts of Breconshire, especially along the southern fringe were within easy reach of the thickly populated industrial districts of Monmouthshire and Glamorgan and were naturally concerned with supplying the needs of these industrial populations. The woollen and leather industries in particular were in the nineteenth and early twentieth centuries largely dependent upon the nearby industrial markets. The Priory woollen mills at Brecon, up until the Second World War, were almost entirely concerned with the production of shirt and underwear flannel for the South Wales market. This was the case too, for the woollen mills of Vaynor some of which had been converted from former corn mills.

TYPES OF RURAL INDUSTRY IN VAYNOR

Rural industries may be classified into four groups namely extractive industries, processing industries, service industries and creative industries. We now look at these industries in Breconshire, firstly to extractive industries in the Parish of Vaynor:

Geological Map of South Breconshire showing the limestone rocks, i.e. Carboniferous rocks of this region

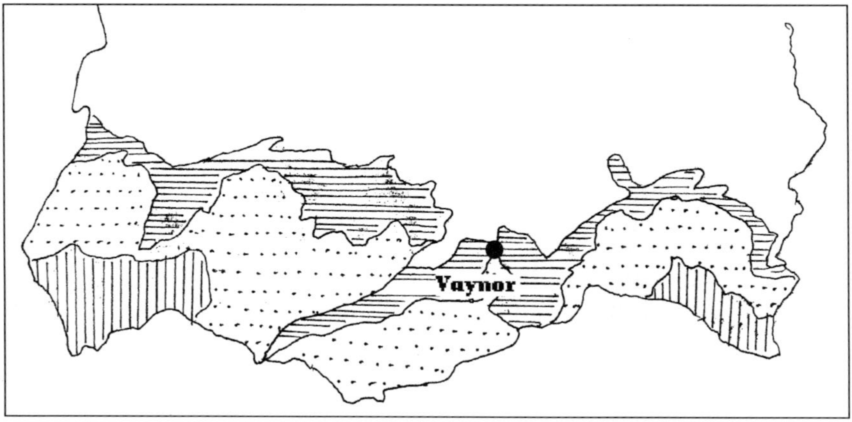

KEY

Carboniferous rocks

Lower coal series

Millstone grit

Carboniferous limestone series

EXTRACTIVE INDUSTRIES

i.e LIMESTONE QUARRYING AND LIME BURNING

The limestone industry has been important in southern Breconshire for centuries largely because of an abundance of limestone and because there has been a local demand for limestone and lime in agriculture, building and the iron industry. Quarrying in Wales appears to date from prehistoric times and there is evidence form Roman and Norman times of quarrying and lime burning. A letter in 1763 from George Jones of Carmarthen to Roderick Gwynne after the purchase of the Buckland Estate and Penkelly Manors, with which Vaynor has been associated for centuries, outlined the respective rights of the Lord and tenants thus for this locality:-

> "Ye tenants enjoyed ye Commons over ye four Parishes and dug stones upon ye wastes for repairing their walls adjoin to ye mountains without any the liest interruption til very lately"[1].

It would appear from this document therefore that tenants had the right to collect stone from the Commons probably for buildings, walls and for lime-burning. When the Great Forest was enclosed in 1815-1819 quarries were set apart for the use of the allotment holders and from what can be ascertained from old records, the commoners had enjoyed the right of obtaining both building stone and limestone previously.

The presence of limestone in the Tâf Fawr and Tâf Fechan valleys in the parish of Vaynor has been a source of income since the late eighteenth century when quarries were developed to provide limestone for the iron industry located at Merthyr Tydfil. Similarly the iron works at Hirwaun founded in 1757 had limestone from Penderyn brought down on the tramroad from 1780. The earliest references to limestone quarrying in this area are to be found in the registers of St. Gwynno's Church Vaynor, which testify to large numbers of quarrymen in Vaynor in the latter half of the eighteenth century. A later reference is to the quarry on the slopes of the Darren Fawr near Danydarren Farm opened around 1848 by an Independent Minister, the Rev W. Moses, of Cefn Coed, and the quarry was known then as "Cwar Moses".[2]

It is apparent that lime-burning in this country and in this area has spanned many centuries. Quite apart from its use as a constituent of mortar for building, lime has also been used as a fertiliser in agriculture. As early as

1523 Sir Anthony Fitzherbert referring to land improvement, wrote:-

> "Another maner of mendying of errable lande is to muck it, marle it, lyme it or dong (dung) it ... where plentie of lyme stonne with wood and secole (coal) and make lyme thereof and do it upon their landes".[3]

It is apparent that coal was being used as a fuel and it was thought at this time that it was the heat in the dung and lime which contributed to soil fertility. The beneficial effects of liming in Glamorgan was noted by Rice Merrick in 1578:-

> "Now of late years since the knowledge or use of lyming was found, there groweth more plenty of grayne".[4]

A description of early seventeenth century kilns was provided by George Owen in 1603 when he stated:-

> "The same (limestone) put into a kill (kiln) made of wall six foot high, four or five foote broad at the brimme but going narrower to the bottom. In this kill is made a fire of coles or rather colm (clay and small coal mixed) with some sticks ... then is the kill filled with small pieces of lymestone ... then the same burneth ... is suffered to cool ... carried to the land ... the next shower of rayne maketh it to molten and falle into dust".[5]

By the mid seventeenth century Walter Bligh could declare that counties formerly barren were now growing corn because of the greater use of lime. F. V. Emery has referred to Horton in Glamorgan and to Landimore where in 1639 there were "Quarries for limestone where tenants, out of mind have used to burn lime for the composing of their lands".[6]

The 1801 Report on the Great Forest of Brecon referred to the fact that horses used for hauling lime were charged at the rate of one penny per season and that all the persons living within the Lordship of Brecknock were allowed to dig and burn lime, dig tile stones as well as to cut turf without payment.

The Brecknock Agricultural Society founded in 1755 encouraged the use of fertilisers and the widespread use of lime in Breconshire drew favourable comments from Arthur Young in 1776 and Theophilus Jones writing in 1805 claimed that:-

> "Lime is an acknowledged native of the country easy of access and cheap of purchase, is the general favourite manure with the greatest part of the farmers in Breconshire and is commonly laid on in the proportion of thirty barrels to the statute acre: each barrel containing three customary bushels or thirty gallons".[7]

He further added:-

> "I am not acquainted with any country (county) in which lime is held in such high repute, nor where the manufacture of it is so common practice among farmers".

Lime became so popular and important in the science of agriculture that it was included in general terms of leases in Breconshire. As Theophilus Jones the County historian stated:-

> "The landlord upon tenant's first entry allows 20 barrels of lime (some more some less) per customary acre for the arable: the tenant engages to lay an equal quantity in this the last year of his term.".[8]

Farmers living south of the Brecon Beacons were fortunately placed with regard to the availability of low cost lime because the cost of the lime, cost of transport and the payment of tolls at the Turnpike Gates had to be set against the amount of extra crop yield by buying lime. The cost of lime in 1816 was 10s 3d (£0.51) per barrel. For agricultural purposes lime was used usually on one field on every farm annually and liming was always undertaken in the Summer because roads were often impassable in Winter. The lime was usually applied to a field prepared for Autumn wheat at the rate of about three tons of lump lime per acre. This was the accepted practice in Breconshire until the end of the nineteenth century. For building purposes this quick lime was slaked with water to produce what is called hydrated lime and ashes or sand was added to this to make a suitable building mortar.

The importance of the lime burning industry is reflected in the number and variety of kilns found in this locality. The remains of a large number of mountain kilns are to be seen on Cilsanws mountain (OS 032 110) overlooking the Glais valley. In addition, on the opposite bank of the Glais brook are the remains of a kiln with the two draw arches intact and provides some indication as to the shape and size of these mountain kilns.

They appear to be built into the sides of hills with the sides supported by earth and rubble. The top of the kiln was usually at the same level as the floor of the small quarry of outcropping stone at the rear which provided the stone. The kilns would have been approximately six metres square of dry stone and probably lined with fire-clay. If we accept the evidence of Mr Cyril Price who in the 1960s was proprietor of the Danygraig kiln and pre-World War II of the round kiln at Danydarren Quarry, he obtained the fire-clay from Heolgerrig coal levels. These mountain kilns have been referred to by Tom Lewis where he states, "Every farmer had his own small kiln at Cilsanws Mountain. The burnt lime was carried down to the lowlands in sacks bourne on the backs of sure footed ponies".[9]

The kilns at Danydarren, Danygraig and those half a mile south of Pontsticill were commercial kilns which are invariably located near major roads, railways, canals or ports. Lime burning was discontinued at Danygraig in the 1960s and at Danydarren in the early 1970s and both are now falling into decay although they were not built until the 1930s. Between these kilns there is considerable evidence of lime burning possibly dating

The Danydarren lime kiln (disused since 1972).

from the eighteenth century and below the present road near the Turnpike on Cwm Tâf road one can still see a road built through the woodland to avoid the payment of tolls at the Turnpike gate situated near the lime kilns during the nineteenth century.

The lime burning season began in May or June and farmers from outside the parish assembled at the nearest toll gate at midnight hoping to make the journey to the kilns and return before midnight on the following day to avoid a double toll at the numerous tollgates. Long strings of carts traversed the roads every night cutting in and out of parish roads to avoid turnpike tolls. These carts ruined the roads especially in wet summers. The enforced payment of tolls at the tollgates were such that on a cartload of lime which cost two or three shillings at the kiln, tolls of five shillings might have to be paid within a distance of eight miles. As Howells has stated:

> "The spark which ignited the Rebecca Riots was the multiplication of toll gates along the various Trust roads which made the vital carriage of lime in particular, unbearably expensive".[10]

With the building of the Merthyr to Brecon railway line from Pontsticill lime was now available for Breconshire farmers in larger quantities and at a cheaper rate. In 1863 lime was available at the kilns at Pontsticill for 3s 6d (£0.17) a ton;[11] at Merthyr Tydfil for 4s 8d (£0.24) a ton and at Talybont at 12s 0d (60p) a ton. Mr William Morgan, Tredegarfach, Pontsticill informed me in 1950 that he could recall in his childhood in the 1870s, mules loaded with panniers of lime leaving Pontsticill for Herefordshire, and older residents have informed me that Dafydd Lewis, son of the Morning Sun Inn, Cefn Coed worked a small quarry at the turn of this century near the rear of the Cefn Hotel and close to the stables more recently used by the England family of coster mongers. Much of this stone was used for road making at Cefn Coed and Vaynor and for lime burning in his garden kiln.

The first limestone extracted in the Tâf Fechan valley for purposes other than lime burning was probably during the 1870s when William Crawshay, who owned the land, began quarrying to provide limestone for his iron furnaces. This can be seen on the 1840 owner/occupier Tithe Map where it is clear that the Crawshays were consolidating possession of the land south west of the Glais Brook. During the period of the development of the waterworks at Pontsticill, numerous small quarries were worked in the valley. The Chief quarry was that at Abercriban owned by Mr A. W. Lewis father of the late Lord Brecon. He worked this from 1903 to 1923 to provide roadstone. In 1923 this quarry was bought by the Merthyr Corporation who made use of the stone to build the dam of their newest reservoir at Pontsticill.

Working conditions at the quarries of Vaynor have been described to me by the late 88 year old Mr John Evans of Bryn Tâf, Cefn Coed in 1980. He commenced work in 1903 at 10s 0d (£0.50) a week at Cyfarthfa Quarry (Vaynor Quarry). After a while at Gethin Colliery he returned to Vaynor Quarry in 1914 where he was paid 1s 8d(£0.08) for every two tons of rock cut and loaded. In one day he filled 29 "skips" (waggons) of rock each holding 32 hundredweight for which he was paid £1.18s.8d (£1.93). In the same week he filled 129 skips of rock each weighing 32 hundredweight, a total of 206 tons of rock for a wage of £8.12s.0d (£8.60).

Mr A. W. Lewis then re-opened the old Vaynor quarry which had been worked in Crawshay's day when silica was brought down from the top of Cilsanws Mountain by aerial ropeway. Its present extent (i.e. in 1980), is

Vaynor Quarry (c1970).

179 acres and employs 112 people made up of 32 office workers, 60 labourers, i.e. dumper drivers and machine operators and 20 haulage drivers. Twelve of the employees are female clerical workers. If permission is granted by the planning authority to Powell Duffryn for expansion, northwards to utilise the land of the last two farms in the Glais valley, namely Llwyncilsanws and Blaenglais, then quarrying is likely to continue in this area into the twenty first century. If however, permission is refused that it seems likely that all economical seams will be worked out before the year 2000 and the quarry will close.

LEAD MINING

"Lead mining in Brecknock was on a very small scale indeed until almost the middle of the sixteenth century", states W. J. Lewis in referring to Breconshire. He continues "A little ore was raised in the parish of Penderyn (adjacent to the Parish of Vaynor) and in the hills of Llanigon but they were unprofitable ventures. The same can be said of the workings noted by Rees in 1815 at Dinas Rock near Pontneathvaughan and at Coedycymmer (Vaynor). They were none of them worthy of development ... The only mine to be worked during the eighteenth century seems to have been near Llanwrtyd Wells and several tons of its ore were sold at £12.0s.0d each".[12]

There is a shallow hole on Cilsanws mountain on the Darren Fawr, overlooking Cwm Tâf Fawr approximately 1½ miles north of Cefn Coed which is known locally as the "lead mine". An abortive attempt was made in the first decade of this century by Mr Gus Rees, Tynygarn, Cefn Coed and members of the Lewis family of the Morning Sun Inn to mine lead at "the lead mine". While humourous stories relating to the "lead mine" are legion there is no information regarding the amount of lead mined there.

Clarke writing in 1848 of lead mining in this area stated "Lead ore is found above, below, and in the limestone rocks of Glamorgan, both northwards and southwards of the basin ... North of the basin there has not been much of it tried except a little near Morlais Castle and in the rocks between the two rivers, Tâf Fawr and Tâf Fechan, about a mile above Coed-y-Cymmer".[13]

PEAT CUTTING

In the cottages and farmhouses of rural Wales the hearth was the centre of family life and a fire of peat or of peat mixed with coal dust and known as "culm" was kept burning on the hearth throughout the year. Peat cutting has gone on in Vaynor for centuries in both the Tâf Fawr and Tâf Fechan valleys. The late Mr W. R. Evans, Coedowen Farm, Cwm Tâf informed me in 1976 that he had personally cut peat in Cwm Tâf until the late 1930s. His peat cutting tools have recently been found at Coedowen Farm. Near to the Coedowen Farm house I recovered a stone bakestone which had been used for baking oatcakes over a peat fire in the nineteenth century.

By courtesy of the Welsh Folk Museum St Fagans.

Cutting and drying peat in Breconshire 1938.

The late Mr Richardson, Cross Roads Bungalow, Vaynor informed me recently that most Pontsticill residents were cutting peat up until 1936-1937. It would appear that Mr W. R. Evans, a farmer, had used the correct tools for the job of cutting and paring etc., whereas Mr Richardson, a cottager, used the only available tool which was a spade. Mr Richardson informed me that "the peat was cut the width of a spade, one or two inches thick in June, July or August. It was then left on the mountain to dry for a few days, and then carried down by wheelbarrow or failing that in sacks carried on the back. Mr Evans used a car llusg at Cwm Tâf. Mr Richardson further informed me that in the 1920s he had lived at Cwm-moel Cottage which was the remotest and most northerly habitation in the Glais Valley. While there he carried on the age-old tradition of cutting peat "in the bog". The peat supply was augmented by cutting down trees and as he stated, "the peat was burnt in an ordinary grate".

CHARCOAL BURNING

Over much of Wales the woods and forests had for centuries been worked at a low level of subsistence utilisation, to satisfy the needs of a rural population, for fuel, agricultural implements and vehicles, domestic utensils, tanstuffs, furniture and constructional timber for dwellings and larger buildings such as castles and mills.[14] The woodlands were also important for grazing and pannage. In general, this widespread dependence on the native woodlands persisted until the Industrial Revolution.

One gleans from a written description given by Tom Lewis that prior to two hundred years ago a large portion of Vaynor was covered by natural woodland, he writes thus:-

> "The Hen Dŷ Cwrdd of 200 years ago was built in a clearing in wood. The wood formed part of a larger wood which stretched from the confluence of the Tâf Fawr and Tâf Fechan rivers to the higher slopes of Cilsanws Mountain. In its deep recesses wild life teemed, where the poacher plied his illicit craft ... When however, Anthony Bacon build his first furnaces at Cyfarthfa in 1765 the wood was denuded of its trees in order to provide fuel to smelt the iron.[15] In the clearings, occasional cottages were erected, squatters built their "tai-un-nos", and as Anthony Bacon's works expanded, a small picturesque village grew and was given because of its natural features the beautiful name of Cefn-Coed-Y-Cymer".

Wood and charcoal have probably been used locally and sporadically for the smelting of metal ores since pre-Roman times. After the Norman Conquest of Wales there was increasing development of mining and smelting especially of iron and lead. Charcoal burning was associated with smelting operations from the thirteenth to the fifteenth century in Eastern Monmouthshire (iron), around the rim of the South Wales coalfield (iron, lead) in North Carmarthenshire and Western Breconshire (iron, lead).[16] Charcoal continued to be used as a fuel in the iron industry in some places until well into the nineteenth century.

In the sixteenth century the iron industry was transformed by the introduction of the blast furnace and the power forge, and this resulted in an unprecedented increase in the demand for charcoal from the local catchment area, the radius of which was governed by the economics of horse or mule transport. The iron masters of Merthyr had a vital interest in maintaining their charcoal supplies and therefore wanton destruction of the raw material resources is unlikely to have taken place. However, complaints against the iron masters and their ill-effect upon the environment were doubtless sometimes justified.

Early environmentalists complained of the numerous traditional forest products and services lost such as fuel, game, pannage etc., resulting from charcoal burning. However it could be claimed that iron works prompted the development of woodlands, for example, David Davies writing in 1905 refers to the fact that great improvements had been made at Garwnant, Wern and Pentwynuchaf Farms Cwm Tâf, by planting trees. This improvement was accomplished by the industrialist Lord Merthyr, the owner.[17]

Small wood was the most convenient materials for charcoal burning and therefore when timber trees were felled, it would be a reasonable assumption that in the rapidly growing Merthyr the large timber assortments could probably be sold off for building purposes. This would ensure maximum financial return, as well as avoiding the laborious cross cutting and clearing of large timber to make charcoal billets. Undoubtedly, a large charcoal burning industry developed in the Merthyr area, based on the iron industry and involving selection and purchase negotiations, the actual felling, cording and coaling operations and then the bagging and transport of the charcoal to the works. Oak and beech formed the best charcoal but a licence in Glamorgan allowed the use of aspen, beech, birch, blackthorn, hawthorn, hazel, sallow, willow or any other trees except timber trees of oak, elm and ash. The prime hardwoods species (oak, elm and ash) were however used because a charcoal analysis at Coed Ithel furnace, a seventeenth century blast furnace at Llandogo shows oak to be the main constituent of the charcoal.[18]

The organisation of the early woods operation in Wales can be inferred from surviving iron works' accounts. Employment in woodcutting and charcoal burning fluctuated seasonally. The felling and cording work was concentrated in the Winter and especially in early Spring. Little felling was done in the Summer, when the woodcutters were probably engaged in harvest work on the farms. More men were engaged in woodcutting than in the actual charcoal burning. Wood was felled, cross cut and corded close to the stump. In general the wood was cross cut into one of two standard billet lengths, either 'long' (4 foot or 4 foot 4 inches, or 4 foot six inches) or 'short' (2 foot or 2 foot 2 inches). Cord size varied in South Wales, both between regions and in time. These widely divergent cord sizes present a serious problem in trying to assess the amount of wood or charcoal required to produce a ton of iron. In the eighteenth and nineteenth centuries, wood for charcoal was often sold, by the ton instead of by the cord, taking $2^1/_2$ tons as the weight of a statute cord of 125 cubic feet. The amounts of wood and of charcoal needed to produce a ton of iron decreased during the sixteenth and seventeenth centuries, as technical efficiency in smelting improved.

Production in the charcoal iron industry was typically intermittent, for example at Clydach, Breconshire 1704, the furnace was worked from September to January, the rest of the year being used to lay in stocks of raw material, particularly charcoal. At Merthyr where the first furnace was built in 1765, the pattern was that work at the furnace should be carried on three days a week, and the other three be devoted to woodcutting "which the men enjoyed immensely, especially as they combined it with snaring game, shooting blackcock".[19] Charcoal was produced close to where the wood was felled, because charcoal was always cheaper and easier to transport than wood. The charcoal-burners were known as 'colliers' or 'wood colliers' (colier coed) and they lived rough in the woods during the charcoal burning season.

The normal charcoal burner's hut or cabin was a structure shaped like a wigwam, constructed of poles and covered with brushwood and turves. In later years, canvas or tarpaulin was used like a tent to cover the conical framework of poles. The charcoal was made by stacking the mixed hardwood billets closely to form a regular conical or domed mound with a central vent for firing. The mound was covered with turves or earth laid on straw, furze or bracken. The cordwood and charcoal agreements often included the purchase of sufficient rods and poles to make hurdles to serve as windbreak screens. The charcoal sites were called 'hearths' (aelwyd cols) and on a steep slope a platform would be made by 'cut and fill' to form a level surface for the charcoal burning operations.

Charcoal was also made in holes or pits (holocols) dug at 5-6 yards in diameter and 6-8 feet deep. These pits and platforms can still be traced at many places in South Wales. Good examples are to be seen at Garthmaelwg. The burning or charring of the wood usually took 10-12 days. The piles first 'sweated' and then 'breathed', the piles gradually shrinking and the smoke thinning. The charcoal-burners could regulate the burning by manipulation of vent holes, and the burning heaps were protected from wind by screens of hurdles backed with straw, bracken or heather. Finally the soil cover was removed and the charcoal raked out. After cooling, the charcoal was bagged in sacks usually made up locally from canvas or sacking stitched with twine and tied with cord.

As demand grew, a class of middle-men arose to negotiate the purchase of woods and the delivery of charcoal, contracts being based on the costs of transport and the quality of the charcoal supplied. Transport was generally by trains of pack horses or pack mules, carrying sacks or panniers of charcoal for distances up to 12-15 miles, but occasionally for as far as 25 miles.[20] In Glamorgan in 1831 the standard price for a short cord was 7s 0d if within 5 miles of Pentyrch works, 6s 0d (£0.30) if 5-10 miles, and 5s 0d (£0.25) if over 10 miles. At Margam in the mid eighteenth century, indentures stipulated that horses carrying charcoal should be muzzled in such a manner that they could not browse the young growth in the woods.[21]

During the eighteenth century, the gradual use of coke from coal resulted in the decline and eventual collapse of the charcoal iron industry. However, charcoal burning persisted in Wales until about the end of the nineteenth century and gave rise to many place names throughout Wales. There are public houses called 'The Wood Colliers' and place names containing the elements 'golosg' (charcoal), 'gloddaith' (charcoal pit), 'cols' (charcoal or coal), and 'glo' (charcoal or coal). Examples are 'Cefn Golosg' (Cardiganshire), 'Golosged Du' (Carmarthenshire), 'Gloddaith' (Caernarvonshire). The word 'glo' was used for coal and for charcoal and therefore in areas were coal does not occur 'glo' can be taken to indicate charcoal as e.g. Cwmyglo. (For further information, please see author's Ph.D. (unpublished) thesis at University College of Swansea.)

PROCESSING INDUSTRIES

In this category, the craftsman is concerned with processing some raw material so that it can be used by another craftsman or used in the home. For example, the corn miller is concerned with processing grain for use in the home or by bakers, and with providing animal food from grain grown locally.

Brecknock had a number of other processing craftsmen such as maltsters and woollen manufacturers. Since all the processing crafts demanded a range of immovable equipment and often required water power, they were usually practised in small factories or mills.

CORN MILLS

In 1893 William Morgan stated "That there was a quantity of corn grown here, a hundred or a hundred fifty years ago", and this is testified by the fact that there were no less than four grinding mills at work in the Tâf Fechan valley alone, at that time. These were the Pontsticill, Cwm, Glais and the Gurnos Corn Mills. All of these have ceased working for many years. The Pontsticill mill was on or near the present filter works, the Gurnos mill is almost level with the ground, but not a trace of the other two mills can now be seen ... The Gurnos and Glais mills were employed as Yarn factories before they were allowed to fall into utter disuse".[22]

Corn mills were just as common throughout Wales as they had been in the Tâf Fawr and Tâf Fechan at Vaynor. A hundred years ago there were over 900 working constantly throughout Wales. As late as 1900 there were 45 corn mills in full production in Breconshire but by then none in Vaynor. For many centuries the corn mill was the means by which the farmers' grain, stored and threshed in his barn, could be turned into flour for bread. The first known water mills, called the Greek or Norse mill are recorded in the first century BC. Domesday Book recorded in 1086 that there were 5,624 mills in 3,000 communities south of the Trent.

With the conquest of Wales in 1282, all the mills previously owned by the Welsh princes passed into the hands of the English crown and were administered by the English sheriffs of the new counties. As before, all Crown tenants and serfs had to bring their corn to be ground at these mills and the dues charged for this became a fruitful source of Crown income. In time, however, it became more profitable for the Crown either

Breconshire corn mills of the 19th century. (From the author's unpublished PhD thesis, Swansea 1985.)

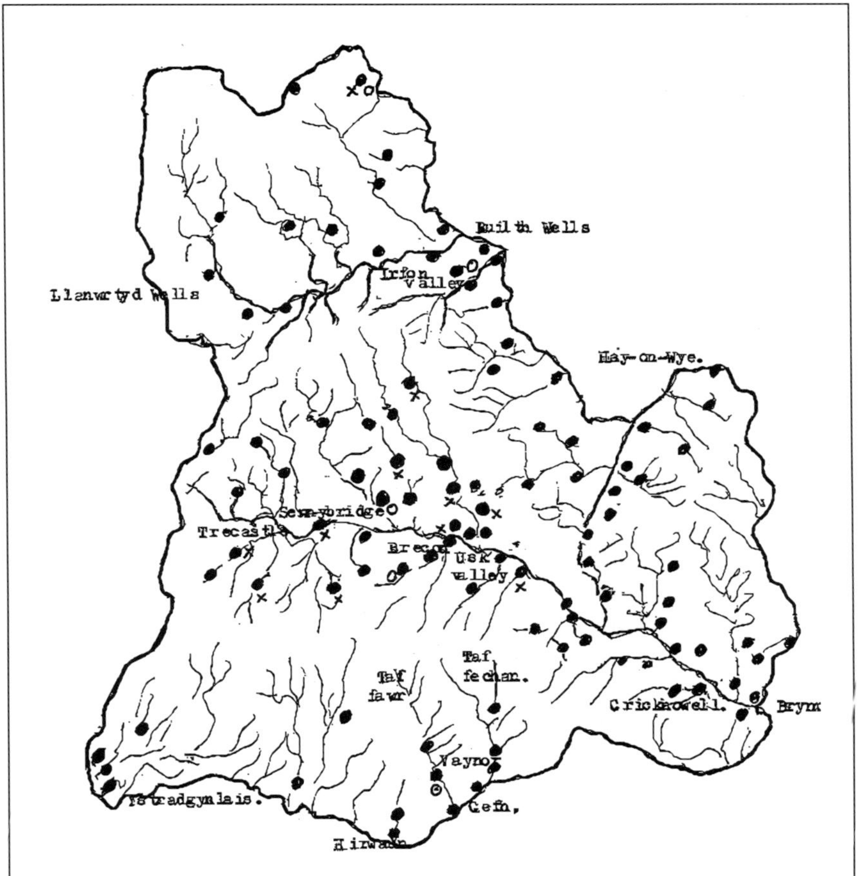

● Corn Mill

X Corn drying kiln (attached or detached)

○ Field kiln

⊙ Domestic method of drying corn as found at Danygraig in the 19th century.

Note 107 sites of corn mills were found by the author in 1984 in Breconshire which were operating in the 19th century. Note also the number of corn mills in the corn belt areas of the Usk and Llynfi river valleys.

Corn mills operating in 1926 in Breconshire. (From the author's unpublished PhD thesis, Swansea 1985.)

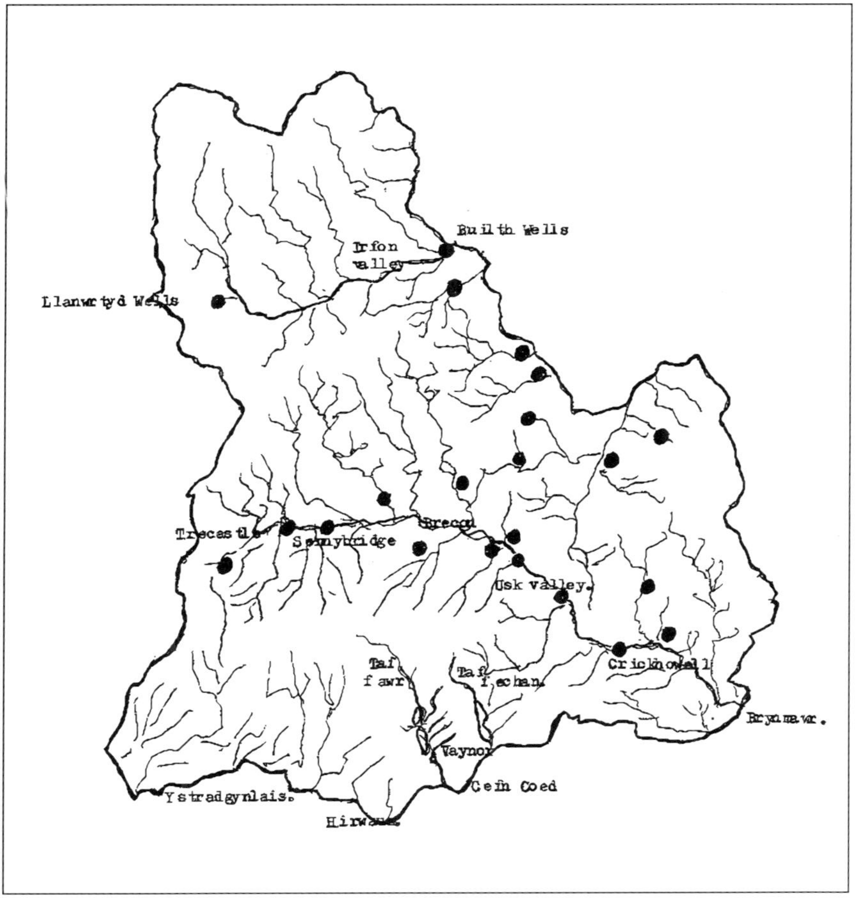

● Site of corn mill

Note. There were at least 107 corn mills operating in Breconshire in the 19th century. This had fallen to 20 as shown above by 1926, and now in 1980 there is not one working.

to lease out these mills to tenants, or grant them to favourites who, in turn, received the mill dues and since they had a monopoly, probably charged excessive rates for grinding. Lordships not under Crown control had their own arrangements: in Cantref Selyf, for instance, the tenant built the mill from the Lord's timber and kept the woodwork and roof in repair. They also made the weir and the millpond, but the Lord bought the millstones and paid for the foundations, the mill wheels and the spindles.

The Augmentation Office Parliamentary Surveys, Brecon, No. 3 contains an account of the Seven Forest Mills (Great Forest of Brecknock) among them being that of Pwllcock (Pwllcoch)[23] Mill, Ynysyfelin, Cwm Tâf. This document is particularly interesting and undoubtedly refers to the Pwllcoch mill situated in the parish of Penderyn and in Cwm Tâf Fawr near the hamlet of Ynysyfelin.

The entry fo 29th October 1651 reads as follows:-

> "Pwllcock Mill – All that Water Grist Mill with the appurtenances commonly called Pwllcock Mill situate standing and being in the Parish of Penderrin afforesaid with all Tolls Mulktures Suits Services and Customs thereunto belonging nowe in the tenure and occupacion of Mrs Games which we estimate to be worth p ann xl (£10)".

We see from this that the Pwllcoch Mill, while situated at Ynysyfelin was on the Penderyn side of the Tâf Fawr. As we note from the following statement local people using the mill had to fulfill certain conditions:-

> "There are divers ffreeholders and tenants w'thin the several parishes ... and Penniderrin aforesaid whoe doe owe divers suits services and customs to the said mills".

Failure to carry out the various annual services resulted in that one had to pay the "ffynes and Penalties they are lyable unto in default thereof". A long list is given in the survey of the local residents expected to give "suit of mill" ... "The same tennts (tenants) are to be ready upon Sumons to carry Woode Timber and Stones for the Repayrein and Re-edifieing of the said Mills at their own cost and charges upon payne of tenn shill". Furthermore we see that:-

> "The said tennts are to carrye the Mill stones to ze Respective Mills from any place wthn the Bounds of the Lordship of Brecknock at theire owne charges".

The local tenants were compelled to grind their corn at the Lord's mill,

> "Everye of the said tennts are bound to come with grist to the said Mills there to be grinded, and if any of them goe to any other Mill, to be amerced upon every default three poundes".

If they were unable to have their corn ground for some reason, they were still expected to wait three days before going to another mill. Payment for grinding corn in 1651 at Cwm Tâf was as follows:-

> "The said Tennts are to pay for grindeing theire Wheat Rye Barley and Mault the twentieth part and of their Pilt Corn the tenth pt (part) and for grinding the Pilt Corn into Meal the twentieth part".

As we see the tenants were not permitted to sell their corn,

> "the tennts may not sell any corne or graine that shall growe upon their Customarye lands to any pson (person) ... until he or they agree with the Lord or the ffarmer of the said mills".

The Lord had the right to,

> "Cutt Turfs and Wood for the Repayre of the Dams and Banks without interruption".

In addition we read thus,

> "That if any of the said tennts doe give his daughter in Marriage he is to pay to the Lord or his ffarmer ffoure shill (four shillings), and if any Mayde doe Commit ffornication to pay ffoure shillings".

The mills were apparently at the time of the survey in 1651 in a structurally poor condition, as we see,

> "That not withstanding all the said Customes Services And Priviledges belonging to the said mills that they are for the most pt (part) verye ruinous and much in decaye for want of re-edifieing and Repayracon".

The survey concludes thus,

> "This Survey was p'fected the 29th of October 1651 by us Exr p Will: Webb 1651. Jeremie Baines, John Ffiske, Joh Haddocke, Samuell Cottman".

Gillian Bale writing about 1956 states,

> "The only sign of industry in the valley was the fulling mill at Ynysyfelin. It was situated at the side of the Cadlan Brook. The fuller obtained his wool from the local farmers for whom he produced cloth in return. This mill, however, was affected by the impending construction of the reservoir and in 1891 it was closed and later demolished".[24]

It would appear then that the Ynysyfelin corn mill like the Gurnos corn mill had been converted to a woollen factory. The reasons for this was probably two-fold. Firstly there was a reduction in the production of corn (oats) because during the nineteenth century at Vaynor there was a greater concentration upon beef production for the ever-growing population to the south and simultaneously a greater demand for flannel underwear and blankets. It is very likely that corn milling at the Millers' Arms, Cwm Tâf came to an end for the same reasons which caused the conversion or adaptation of the Ynysyfelin and Gurnos Mills. The author after years of searching has recently recovered both the upper and lower millstones of the Millers' Arms Corn Mill. The Millers' Arms Inn closed in the 1920s with the building of the Llwyn-On reservoir in 1927.

The French burr mill stones from the Millers' Arms are four feet in diameter and in sections, bound by three iron bands and set in about a foot of plaster of Paris. The mill stones of the Glais corn mill, while the same in diameter, are however, solid conglomerate stones and lie on the river bank at the confluence of the Glais Brook and the Tâf Fechan river just below the Blue Pool at Pontsarn. The sectionalised French burr stones were used for grinding wheat while the solid stones were for oats. It is quite conceivable that the Normans utilised a corn mill here at the confluence of the Glais and the Tâf Fechan since it had the necessary physical features in terms of flow of water, siting etc., and was the most convenient spot for the inhabitants of Morlais Castle.

The mills during the Middle Ages and the succeeding centuries were small and simple. The millers' customers were local farmers and cottagers

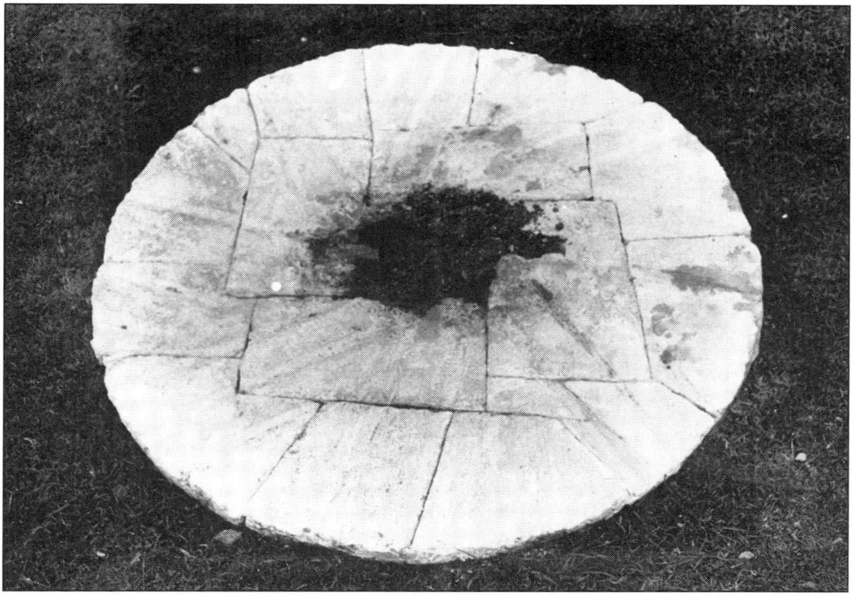

A French burr used for grinding wheat at the Millers' Arms, Cwm Tâf.

or the flour was taken to the nearest town and sold to bakers. Pack mules came from as far as Brecon in the late eighteenth and nineteenth centuries carrying flour to Merthyr, they returned carrying coal or lime.

The keeping quality of flour is poor, so that the customers would store or buy corn and have it ground in small quantities at frequent intervals. Because of the distance travelled and to avoid a second journey every sack was measured by volume, the miller then took his toll, usually one sixteenth, for payment was in kind and the rest was ground in the presence of the owner. Wheat or corn (oats, barley) can be ground only when it is dry. At the old Danygraig Farm (built about 1620-1650) Cwm Tâf, there are perforated rollers on each side of the open hearth fire place. These rollers are set between the beams of the ceiling so that a person sitting on each side of the fireplace could turn these rollers with a pole and thereby disturb the drying corn lying on a piece of canvas suspended from the rollers. (See Section on Buildings.) The author has also found a number of attached and detached corn drying kilns in Breconshire, especially in areas of high rainfall.

The author examining the conglomerate upper stone at the Glais mill, Pontsarn. This stone was used for grinding oats and barley.

Mr Williams, retired miller at the Libanus Corn Mill near Brecon, whose family had been farmers and millers for many generations, informed me that he had a small kiln where he dried damp corn; that travelling millwrights called every two years to dress the stones and that the running cost of the mill was about one shilling a year for grease for the mill wheel. He stated that there were two major problems for a miller. The first was the problem of rats which came from the rivers; this problem was overcome by storing sacks of corn six inches apart so that cats could pursue and kill the rats. The second problem was that of rat droppings in the corn – it was very important therefore that stored corn should be kept in a place at the farm safe from rats.

The miller was responsible for drying the corn in some cases but usually he was only responsible for the grinding: bolting or sifting out, the bran had to be done by the customer himself.

From various manorial documents, Professor William Rees has been able to build up a picture of a typical medieval Welsh mill. The water wheel consisted of a central oak beam, holding two sets of spokes joined by curves and strengthened by iron stays to form the wheel. Between the outer rims, a number of trough-like ladles caught the current. The axle passed through the mill building, with a single inner wheel made of wood, and banded at its other end. This wheel was cogged and turned another cogged wheel (the wallower) fitted on to the main shaft or spindle which revolved vertically on a brass bearing. The wallower turned the stone nuts which turned the upper stones.

The upper millstone was adjustable. The corn was passed from a container through the hole in the centre of the upper-stone, the flow being regulated by a hopper vibrated by means of a jack worked from below by the rind and spindle. The Gurnos mill ruins suggest that it was originally a three storey building and some distance away there are the ruins of what might have been a store or a corn drying kiln typical of those found in areas of high rainfall where oats (and barley perhaps) were an important part of the diet.

There survives a technical treatise in Welsh[25] which lists the duties of the miller as follows:

> "He is to be industrious and careful, he must dwell in the mill at all times, or nearby, where he may see its door, except when he goes to Church to hear the Mass, or when he has his master's permission to go to some other place".

He had to open the door at the second knock, he had to keep the floor of the mill level and clean at all times. He was not to allow the mill to stop when it still had corn in it, or to allow it to grind when empty, neither was he to leave the ground flour to stand in the trough; nor the sacks untied after filling them. He was also expected to tie the sacks and lift them on to the customer's pack horse. These tasks were in addition to the technical skills required of him, like judging the force of the water, preparing new cogs and spindles etc.

This type of corn mill remained common for many hundred of years, but in the eighteenth century new ideas and practices were introduced such as the underdrive spurwheel and later the introduction of cast iron as a material for wheels and shafts. Some all-wood constructed mills such as Pengelli mill, near Talybont, however survived and were used until the early decades of this century. The increased grain production brought about by the need for self-sufficiency during the Napoleonic Wars caused many new mills to be erected. Partly because of this, it is rare to find a mill older than the first half of the nineteenth century. Of the corn mills of the Tâf Fawr nothing remains of the Pontycapel Mill, home of the poet Gwilym Morgannwg and later a brewery; the Ynysyfelin Mill was demolished as was the Millers' Arms.

In the picture painted by Penry Williams of Cwmcapel c1830 one can see the Pontycapel corn mill on the site, which was later used to build Pontycapel Brewery. The mill wheel is visible and from its position one can deduce that it was either a breast flow wheel or an under flow wheel of wooden construction. The water leat running from below Pwll Tâf is still visible.

As already stated the author has recovered the stones of the Millers' Arms Corn Mill. Of interest is the fact that the Millers' Arms Corn Mill was considered by the locals to be "unreliable". This was because the river tended to freeze at this spot in winter time, due probably to the impounding of water at Cantref reservoir which greatly reduced the volume and flow of water. Cwm Tâf farmers therefore found it necessary in the late nineteenth century and first quarter of this century to travel as far as Libanus or to the Trebanog mill, Penderyn to have their corn ground. .

Of the corn mills in the Tâf Fechan valley nothing remains of the Pontsticill, Cwm or Glais mills except as already stated, one mill stone belonging to the latter. Part of the building of the Gurnos Mill remains and possibly the ruins of the nearby kiln.[26]

Melin Pontycapel, Cefn Coed-y-Cymer

Nothing remains of Pontycapel corn mill because a brewery stood on this site for about a century. The mill race and sluice gate however, may still be seen. The earliest reference found to this old mill, refers to the poet Gwilym Morgannwg living here in 1781. A painting by Penry Williams the famous Merthyr artist (c1830) shows the mill and mill wheel at this time. Dewi Davies writing in 'Hanes Plwyf Penderyn' (The history of the parish of Penderyn') states that Pontycapel mill was one of the oldest mills of the parish of Penderyn. Although in the parish of Penderyn, this mill served parishioners of Vaynor until it was demolished around the middle of the nineteenth century when the Pontycapel brewery was then built on the site.

Sites of woollen and fulling mills in Breconshire during the 18th and 19th centuries.

(From the author's unpublished PhD thesis, Swansea 1985.)

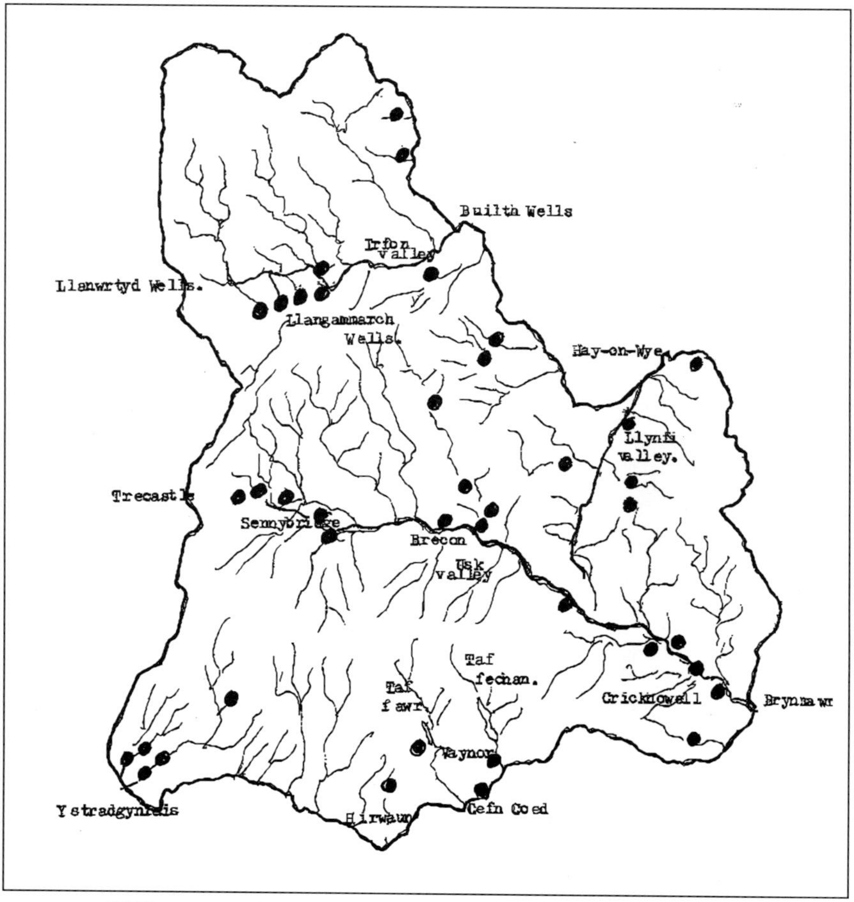

Key ● Sites of woollen and fulling mills

Note. In 1851 there were 83 employed in the woollen industry in Breconshire. By 1924 it had declined to 24, now only a few are employed at the Cambrian Woollen Factory at Llanwrtyd Wells.

THE WOOLLEN INDUSTRY

Since the earliest times Breconshire had supported large flocks of sheep and from the fourteenth century to the mid-eighteenth century domestic spinning and weaving was widely practised in all parts of the country. The area was important enough to give its name to a type of drab-coloured, rough cloth known as "brecknocks" which was exported in considerable quantities through markets at Brecon, Abergavenny and border towns. Until the last quarter of the eighteenth century, woollen manufacturing in Brecknock, as in other parts of Wales, was a domestic pursuit. The county provided all the raw material that was required and this was spun into yarn, woven into cloth and knitted into stockings. "From the latter end of the sixteenth century", says Theophilus Jones, "great fortunes were acquired in Brecon and the vicinity by the manufacture of woollen cloths".[27] During the first half of the eighteenth century, both the weaving and knitting industries were so flourishing that Brecon was described as "the richest town in Wales".

This prosperity, however, declined by the mid eighteenth century and one of the most notable efforts to revive it was carried out by the Brecknockshire Agricultural Society in 1755 when it offered premiums

> "to the person who will produce before 29th September, 1756, the best piece of cloth of drab colour, manufactured within this county, from raw wool, the growth there of measuring 21 yards long and 1 yard wide".[28]

Perhaps the most grandiose of the Brecknockshire Agricultural Society's schemes was to make the County one of the main producers in Britain, supplying weavers over a very wide area with ready spun yarn.

> "The very great quantities of wool that are sold annually of this County" states Theophilus Jones, the County Historian, "would if manufactured at home, furnish employ for all our working hands and would greatly enrich the county in general ... By offering premiums for spun yarn and establishing a monthly or quarterly market at Brecon, this would give employment to many of the idle hands that are now a burden to their neighbours".[29]

Spinning must have been very common throughout the county and the Society's concern was to expand this industry so that the demand for spun yarn in the clothing counties could be met by the spinners of Brecknock. The first yarn market was held at Brecon on the 9th June 1765,

> "but it aroused very little interest and after continuing in a lingering decline until 1780, it ceased to be held".[30]

In addition, the Society attempted to promote the cloth industry by establishing 'spinning schools' within the county with the aim 'partly to encourage children to learn the art of weaving and partly to prevent them idling and begging".[31] In 1756, they appointed the first spinning instructress paying her "half a crown a quarter for every child taught".

Further attempts were made to extend the woollen industry by actively encouraging manufacturers from other districts to migrate to Breconshire and through the efforts of Howell Harris at Trefeca between 1752 and 1773. The Trefeca experiment petered out with Harris' death in 1773, while the efforts of the Brecknockshire Society was only half heartedly supported. By the early decades of the nineteenth century the production of woollen fabrics and articles for a wider market had become unprofitable and woollen manufacturing survived in the county as only a very small scale industry.

Between 1810 and 1830, however, the rapid decline of the woollen industry in Brecknockshire was arrested as new machinery for carding and spinning was brought into the county. One cannot accurately determine when the local mills were mechanised. From what Samuel Lewis has written in 1849 it is apparent that operations were only on a small scale, as he stated

> "Two woollen manufacturers have been carried on for some years; but the number of people engaged is very inconsiderable".[32]

The industrialisation of South Wales meant an increased demand not only for knitwear and stockings, still produced under a domestic system of manufacture throughout the nineteenth century, but it also meant an increased demand for flannel, particularly shirt and underwear flannel. The mills in the south of Breconshire as at Brecon, Ystradgynlais, Crickhowell and Vaynor, took advantage of the ready market in South Wales.

From the parish records it would appear that Vaynor had a fair number of spinners and weavers during the nineteenth century. The earliest reference to a weaver is to be found in the baptismal records of the Hen Dŷ Cwrdd Chapel, Cefn Coed where it states, "Richard son of Howell Powell, weaver of Coedycymmer born 13th July 1800 was baptised by me Thomas Davies". The membership book contains the names of John Harry, Harry John Harry, Edward and William Harry, who were all weavers and descendants of Gwilym Harri, poet and weaver of Garw Dyle, Penderyn, son of Harri Harri formerly of Gellia Farm, Cwm Tâf. Gwilym Harri of Garw Dyle was the grandson of Sion Llewelyn one of the founders of the Hen Dŷ Cwrdd. The will of "Harry John Harry, Weaver of Pontsticill in the Parish of Vaynor in 1744" refers to "Thomas Shittles and weaving apparatus – £2.15s.10d and weaving apparel £2.10s.0d" and is among the Chapel Records.[33] In the Vaynor Church records there are references to Harry John, Weaver (1815), Lewis Jones, Weaver (1815), Lewis Jones, Weaver (1849), Robert Peat, Spinner (1851) and Lewis Thomas, Weaver, Factory Cefn Coed.[34] The 1851 Census refers to "William James, Master Woollen Factory", and to "John Lewis, Flannel weaver and Phillip Lewis, aged 13 apprentice at home".

Other references in the 1851 Census returns are to "Lewis Jones Hand Loom Weaver; Jenkin Harry, Woollen Weaver"; and in the same house at 100 High Street, Cefn Coed were "Dina Rees, stocking knitter, Sarah Rees (daughter), wool carder; Edward Humphreys, Flannel Spinner; and Maurice Phillips, flannel weaver".[35]

These entries are of considerable interest and clearly indicate that some were domestic weavers while others were employed at a "factory". Geraint Jenkins states that "some form of factory system had already entered the weaving industry, by the middle of the eighteenth century". Jenkins throws some further light upon this matter when he states "the process of fulling was the earliest process to become a factory one ... carding, spinning and weaving continued to be domestic pursuits long after fulling mills had been introduced".[36] There is a reference in 1832 to the "ruins of old woollen Factory on Tâf Fechan, Cefn Coed".[37] This of course refers to the old Gurnos Corn Mill adapted as a 'pandy' or fulling mill where the woven cloth was thickened. In the traditional processes cloth was first fulled with urine bought locally, then with fuller's earth and finally with soap.

The "factory" at Ynysyfelin, Cwm Tâf was a weaving factory and located on the site of the old Pwllcoch corn mill. The last weaver here was the late Mr Daniel Evans who, when the factory closed in 1891/1895 built himself a house at Cefn Coed (next door to the author), installed his loom there and operated from here until he died in the 1920s. The Ynysyfelin weaving factory known as the Pwllcoch mill was the adapted "Pwllcock" corn mill of 1651. It is, of course, quite possible that the Pwllcoch Mill at Ynysyfelin, Cwm Tâf Fawr, produced the cloth while the Gurnos mill did the fulling. In referring to Ynysyfelin the 1851 Census Returns state that the occupier was "Thomas Jones, Tailor" (not weaver) and in the neighbouring smallholding of Ynystâf lived "Gwenllian Prosser, Stocking Knitter".[38]

In conclusion, it would seem that until the end of the nineteenth century carding, spinning and weaving continued to be cottage pursuits in Vaynor as in previous centuries. The local place name and land mark called "The Pandy" points unmistakably to the importance of the fulling mill in the life of this district. The power from existing corn mills had been adapted and in this manner many fulling mills developed into small woollen factories to meet the need for blankets and flannel for the nearby South Wales market.

SERVICE INDUSTRIES

The service craftsmen was mainly concerned with the repair and renovation of farm and domestic equipment. The carpenter and joiner was concerned with building and maintenance, the saddler with saddlery and leather equipment for horses, the cobbler with the repair of boots and shoes while the blacksmith who was concerned with making shoes and household necessities is now more or less an agricultural engineer concerned with machine repairs. When the horse provided the only motive power on the farm and the equipment and machinery of agriculture remained simple, the blacksmith was a very necessary creative craftsman essential to every rural community. The account book of Robert Phillips, Penpont covering the period 1829-1850 gives an indication of the variety of work conducted by a rural blacksmith. Among the entries are the following items: Mending poll axe 3d; pot hook 1s 3d; fireback 2s 6d; gate hinges 12 pairs for 3s 0d; horse shoes 2s 6d-3s 6d a set; new swing plough £2.10s.0d and pitch fork 1s 6d.[39]

Often times there was no cash payment between farmer and blacksmith, potatoes and bushels of grain would be given in lieu of cash. The blacksmith worked in association with other craftsmen, Robert Phillips above, supplied saddlers with irons for harness, clog and boot makers with clog irons and nails. He also undertook wheel tyring, fixing irons to cart axles and shafts. The local craftsman has disappeared in Vaynor and in Wales

Sites of saddlers' shops in Breconshire during the 19th Century.

(From the author's unpublished PhD thesis, Swansea 1985.)

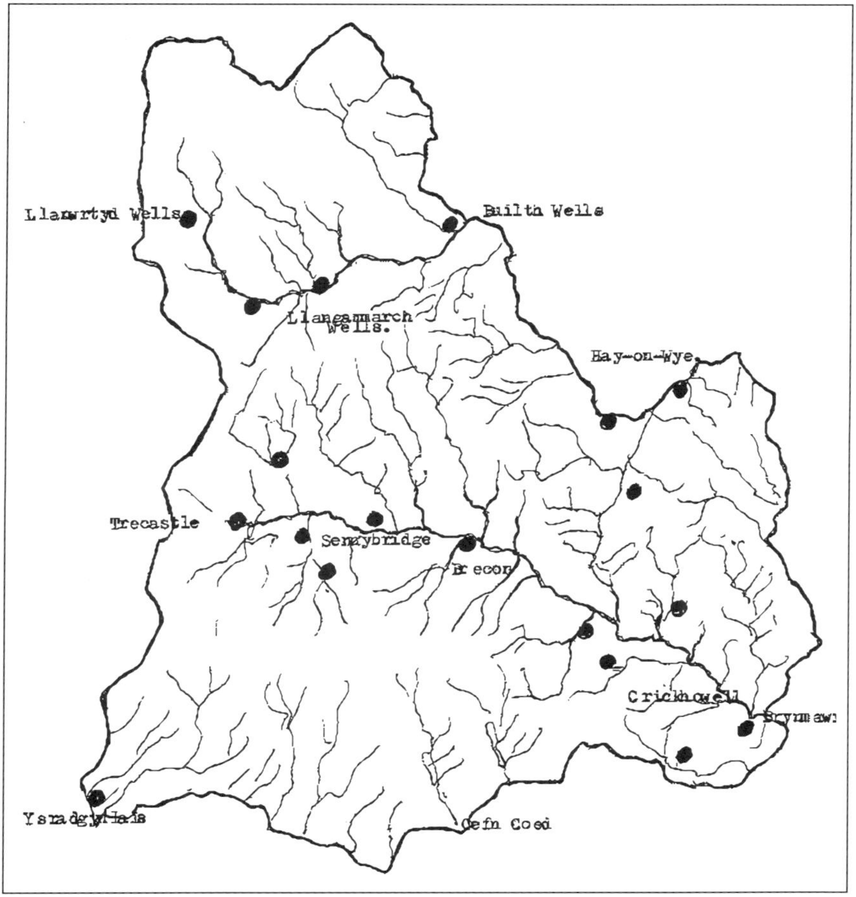

Key ● Sites of saddlers' shops

Note. In 1830 there were 6 saddlers in Brecon, 5 in Builth, 4 in Hay-on-Wye (in 1980 there were none).

generally; the only blacksmiths that have survived are those that have been able to meet the challenge of changing circumstances. The remains of smithies may be seen in practically every hamlet and village of Breconshire. A typical village smith was at the Crown Inn, Cefn Coed where Thomas Lewis was a repairer of stage coaches, parish constable, maker of hatchets, farrier and blacksmith (see back cover or page 176).

THE CREATIVE INDUSTRIES

These industries may be divided into three distinct categories. First there were industries based on local raw materials and for example, such industries as clog makers could be considered under this heading.

CLOG MAKING

The 1851 Census Returns for Vaynor refer to "William Howells, Clog Maker" from Pembroke. In the past practically every rural community in Wales had its clog maker who was fully employed in making new clogs and repairing the old. Today, with changes in fashion the clog maker is very rare. It is a trade which demands considerable knowledge not only of leather work but also of woodwork. The origin of the clog is shrouded in mystery, but clogs were worn by rich and poor during the middle ages. The clog offered great advantages over other forms of footwear in that they were inexpensive, warm and waterproof in wet mines or muddy fields.

There were two distinctly types of craftsman engaged in the trade. There was the village clogmaker such as William Howells referred to above, who in the main made clogs for a local market in Vaynor. He made clogs for individual buyers by measuring their feet and making the clogs accordingly. In the second category were the itinerant clog sole makers such as the Riggs of Northumberland who came to Vaynor annually and undertook only the cutting and rough shaping of alder blocks ready for the clogging factories of Lancashire and Yorkshire. Many of the itinerant cloggers came to Vaynor from Llandovery and during the Spring and

Summer months they wandered from grove to grove along the Tâf Fawr with, but a few simple tools, living in roughly-built huts or tents. For generations these craftsmen had utilised the alder growth of the county in order to make clog soles. For clog soles, the craftsmen needed a timber that did not easily split and was easy to shape. Alder was ideal for this purpose and after being cut in the Spring and Summer months was left to season for at least nine months before use.

The old craft of the clogger was one of the most picturesque of rural crafts. Alder trees of about 18 inches in girth were cut into logs with cross-cut saws and sorted into four sizes – "mens", "women's", "youths" and "children's". Each log was split into two with a beetle and wedge. The billets were then trimmed with a short handled axe and shaped with the clogger's stock knife to roughly the correct shape. The blocks were built into conical stacks in such a way that air could circulate freely between them to assist the drying process. The itinerant clogger did nothing more to the soles for they were sent by train to the North of England Clogging Factories.

HOME CRAFTS

While cider making and drinking in Breconshire was so widespread that a Methodist preacher in 1934 described Breconshire as a "cider besotten county".[40] Vaynor farmers were more concerned with such crafts as butter and cheese making.

Although beer making was widely practised in Welsh households such as the Bragdŷ at Vaynor, the impact of temperance leaders and a number of religious revivals from 1859 onwards greatly reduced this domestic industry. Beer was produced however on a commercial basis at two breweries in Cefn Coed. Pontycapel Brewery was built in the mid nineteenth century and supplied beer to the town of Merthyr and to the surrounding valleys until it closed in the 1920s. The 1851 Census refers to "Robert Millar, Pont-y-Capel Brewery, employing four men".

The 1851 Census mentions "John Pearce, Brewer Gwynnes Arms, Cefn Coed" but does not refer to the Meredith's Brewery (Cefn Hill Brewery) situated at Danyderi Lane about thirty yards from the Stocks at Cefn Coed. This was undoubtedly built in the latter half of the nineteenth

Pontycapel brewery, Pontycapel, Cefn Coed, owned by Thomas James Pearce until his death in 1884 when it was then inherited by his son Henry Dyke Pearce, the artist who died in 1895.

century and produced a mild sweet beer as opposed to the famous 3X strong ale of Pontycapel. Local landmarks and place names provide interesting clues. The Ordnance Survey Map 1832 refers to a hillock a half mile distant from the Pontycapel Brewery as "Bryn Cwrw", (i.e. Beer hill). The present Ysgol y Graig Junior and Infants' School is built on a field formerly known as "Brewery Field" because at the top of the drive to Ysgol y Graig on the southern side of the road leading to Well Street, was formerly the site of John Meredith's Brewery. The house on the right hand side of the entrance to Ysgol y Graig is still known as "Brewery House".

The basis of good beer is malted barley and the remains of farm malthouses are still in evidence on Breconshire farms and the names of maltsters are fairly common in the Census Returns of the nineteenth century. Malting usually took place in Winter; the barley after being steeped in water for approximately five days, then drained and spread evenly on the dry floor of the malthouse. It was then left untouched until the appearance of small roots emanated from the base of the corn. From that stage, great care had to be taken; the temperature had to be controlled and the sprouting grain had to be turned at frequent intervals with wooden shovels and rakes. The process of flooring went on for almost ten days, occasionally water was sprinkled on the grain. The green malt was then taken to the kiln, placed on the perforated tiles and gently dried by the wood fire lit in the chamber beneath. The heating arrested growth and gave the malt the characteristically 'Biscuity taste'.

To make the strong beer of Christmas, eight or nine gallons of spring water (from Bryn Cwrw?) were required for every bushel of malt, but to make the weaker brew of the hay harvest or corn harvest, the amount of water was increased to fourteen or fifteen gallons. The water was boiled and poured on the malt in the wooden brewing vessel. A bunch of gorse or wheat straw was placed over the bung holes in the base of the vessel and this acted as a filter when the liquid was drained off. The mixture was covered with an old blanket and allowed to stand in a warm place for at least three hours. More water was added, the liquid was transferred to a boiler and a half pound of hops and six pounds of brown sugar was added. After cooking overnight, two ounces of yeast were added and the beer left to ferment for two days before being casked or bottled.

The 1851 Census as already stated, refers to "John Pearce, Brewer, Gwynne's Arms, Cefn Coed". This would suggest that John Pearce was making and selling his own brand of beer as were many of the eleven "cwrw bachs" between Cefn and Libanus, a distance of twelve miles over the Beacons. Some of these no doubt came into existence at the time of reservoir building in Cwm Tâf in the late nineteenth century while others, such as the Millers' Arms, the Red Lion and the Half Way House were old wayside inns used by the stage-coaches. G. W. Manby in describing his journey along Cwm Tâf Fawr to Brecon in 1802 states "I was soon driven by the pitiless storm to seek shelter at the Half Way House, a very humble pile indeed".[42]

Blacksmiths' shops in Breconshire in the 19th century.

(From the author's unpublished PhD thesis, Swansea 1985.)

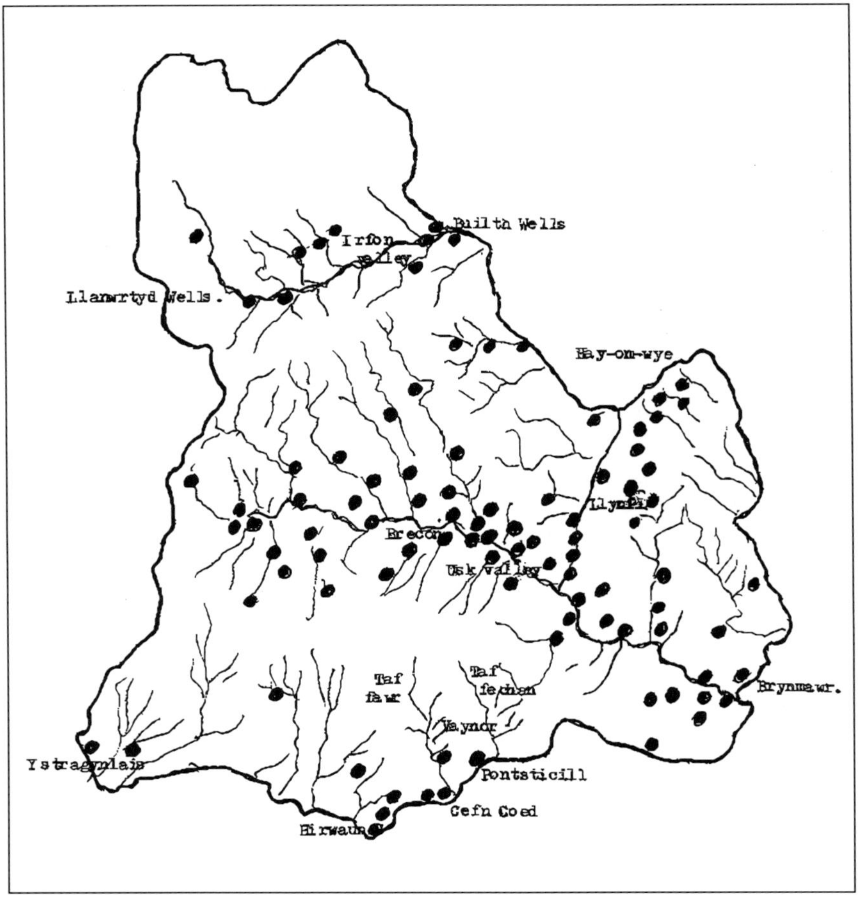

Key ● Site of a blacksmith's shop

Note. In 1851 there were 335 smiths in Breconshire. By 1980 there were only 6. Also note the number of blacksmiths' shops in the river valleys where there would have been a large number of horses engaged in farm work.

INDUSTRIES THAT CAME INTO BEING TO MEET A LOCAL DEMAND

These were the crafts necessary for every self-sufficing community. Craftsmen who met a local need were the most numerous class in Wales and because they were specifically concerned with supplying a limited market they made things well suited to the needs of local people. Craftsmen made farm implements, tools and equipment to suit local conditions, and for this reason many regional variations in tool and implement design came into being. Examples of regional variation occur in cart and wagon types and in small farm tools such as billhooks and peat cutting tools.

In the late nineteenth century, particularly during the last quarter, village blacksmiths who supplied a distinctly local market with all its metal requirements were disappearing very rapidly and their work taken over by firms such as J. E. Nott & Company, Agricultural Engineers, Brecon and large scale manufacturers in Yorkshire and the English Midlands.

The advent of mass production, television, advertising etc., has meant the demise of numerous crafts that were dependent on a local market. Craftsmen such as saddlers, coopers, turners, tanners, weavers, spinners and many others have now totally disappeared. In 1918 for example, Brecknock had the following saddlers' shops two at Brynmawr, three at Brecon, and one each at Llangamarch Wells, Hay, Crickhowell and Sennybridge.

Thomas Lewis of the Crown Inn, Cefn Coed-y-Cymer, blacksmith, hatchet maker and parish constable (c1850).

REFERENCES

1. SIR JOHN LLOYD. Historical Memoranda of Breconshire. p.153.
2. Cefn Coed and Vaynor Historical Society. November 1953. p.4.
3. SIR ANTHONY FITZHERBERT. The Boke of Surveying and Improvement (1523). In Old English Farming Books (1947) p.5.
4. ERIC KERRIDGE. The Agricultural Revolution (1967) p.249.
5. GEORGE OWEN. The First book of the description of Pembrokeshire in General (1603).
6. F. V. EMERY. West Glamorgan Farming c1580-1620 in National Library of Wales Journal (1955) p.399-400.
7. THEOPHILUS JONES. History of Brecknock (1805) p.159-160.
8. Ibid p.154.
9. TOM LEWIS. Customs and Practices. Pamphlet of the Cefn Coed and Vaynor Local History Society (1954) p.11.
10. Commission of Inquiry for South Wales. Evidence 1844. p.30.
11. V. J. PARRY, Brecon and Merthyr Railway (1970) p.6.
12. W. J. LEWIS. Lead Mining in Wales. (1967) p.252.
13. T. E. CLARKE. A Guide to Merthyr Tydfil (18) p.30.
14. W. LINNARD. The History of Forests and Forestry in Wales up to the formation of the Forest Commission (Unpublished PhD Thesis) Bangor (1979). 148-160.
15. TOM LEWIS. History of the Hen Dŷ Cwrdd (1947). p.22.
16. W. REES. Industry before the Industrial Revolution (19068) p.252-259.
17. DAVID DAVIES. Hanes Plwyf Penderyn (1905), p.19.
18. R. F. TYLECOTE. 'Blast Furnaces at Coed Ithel, Llandogo', Monmouth Antiquary (1967), Part III p.149-160.
19. C. WILKINS. The History of the iron, steel, tinplate and other trades of Wales (1903) p.50.
20. A. S. DAVIES. 'The Charcoak iron industry of Powys land'. Mont.coll., 46 (1939/40) p.31-66.
21. National Library of Wales, Penrice and Margam MS. 3666.
22. W. MORGAN (Pant). The Illustrated Vaynor History, p.26.
23. DAVID DAVIES op.cit., p.37-41.
24. GILLIAN DALE. Cultural Changes in Cwm Tâf 1840-1957. Pamphlet of the Cefn Coed and Vaynor History Society (1957) p.5.
25. N.L.W., Penarth MS. 56.
26. E. BOWEN. Some Traditional Industries of Breconshire, Chapter 3. Cornmilling. Unpublished PhD Thesis. Univ: Coll: Swansea 1985.
27. THEOPHILUS JONES, op.cit., p.144.
28. THEOPHILUS JONES, ibid p.150.
29. THEOPHILUS JONES ibid p.150.
30. W. MINCHINTON. 'Brecknock and the Industrialisation of South Wales' in Brycheiniog Volume III (1961) p.3.
31. HENRY EDMUNDS op. cit., p.74.
32. SAMUEL LEWIS, referred to in 'A Topographical Anthology of the Parish of Vaynor prior to 1900' by Tegwyn Harris in a pamphlet of the Cefn Coed and Vaynor History Society (1959) p16.
33. Chapel Records, Hen Dŷ Cwrdd Unitarian Chapel, Cefn Coed,
34. Church Rcords, St Gwynno's Church, Vaynor.
35. The 1851 Census Returns for the Parish of Vaynor.
36. J. GERAINT JENKINS, Rural Industry in Breconshire, Volume XIV (1970) p.16.
37. The Story of Merthyr Tydfil (1932) by Merthyr Teachers NUT P.147.
38. Census Returns 1851 op. cit., Vaynor.
39. J. GERAINT JENKINS, Life and Tradition in Rural Wales (1976) p.83.
40. J. GERAINT JENKINS. Rural Industry in Breconshire op.cit., p.2.
41 J. GERAINT JENKINS. Life and Tradition in Rural Wales op. cit., p.163.
42. G. W. MANBY. An Historic and Picturesque Guide from Clifton, through the Counties of Monmouth, Glamorgan and Brecknock (1802) referred to in 'A topographical Anthology" op. cit., p.9.

RURAL CRAFTSMEN

Until very recently such tasks as baking bread, making cheese, butter or beer were very much a part of the household routine of Breconshire farms. Many of the products of the farms, such as corn, wool and animal skins were taken to nearby mills for processing. The products of those mills in the form of flour, oatmeal or blankets could be used in the farm, while other products such as tweeds, cloth or leather could be used by one of many craftsmen.

Vaynor was particularly well blessed with craftsmen both rural and urban (see section on Parish records). The 1851 Census refers to a wide range of rural craftsmen, namely coopers, stonemasons, weavers, spinners, shoemakers, tailors, millers, blacksmiths and wheelwrights. The section on the Parish Registers lists the occupations in Vaynor from 1813.

Breconshire could boast dozens of rural craftsmen in the nineteenth century, nearly every parish having at least one corn mill. Vaynor was particularly fortunate in having three corn mills on the Tâf Fawr at Pontycapel, Cefn Coed, at the Pwllcoch Mill,[1] Cwm Tâf and the Millers' Arms and four in the Tâf Fechan valley at Pontsticill, Cwm, Glais and the Gurnos Mills.[2] Two of these corn mills were later used as fulling mills. Reference will be made to the historic Pwllcoch mill at Cwm Tâf later. In many cases the craftsmen who processed local farm produce were not always paid in cash, Millers for example, kept a few bushels of corn of corn for their own use, while woollen manufacturers kept a proportion of the fleeces for their own use. At the Pwllcoch mill Cwm Tâf these fleeces were converted into yarn and blankets which were undoubtedly sold in the local markets at Merthyr and Dowlais.

Other craftsmen at Merthyr were engaged in processing farm produce much of which was from Vaynor. Pigot's Directory 1830 refers to Brewers, carriers, leather sellers, saddlers and harness makers, skinners and maltsters living in Vaynor. As already stated beer was brewed at two Cefn Coed breweries, at farms and small cottages such as the Bragdŷ at Pontsarn which had a ready supply of ice-cold water in the well at the back door. Cider brewing was widely practised in the nearby parishes of Breconshire and the closure of a brewery at Sennybridge was welcomed by a contemporary writer thus:-

> "There was a here a large distillery and considerable trading was done in these damning commodities ... It is a great blessing that this trade has disappeared and we

> hope that the day is not too far distant when the business will be but history in all our towns and villages".

Craftsmen were also responsible for producing farm tools and equipment ranging from horse shoes to ploughs. David Lewis has stated, "It was not unusual in the past to see a carpenter getting up early in the morning, taking an axe on his shoulder and cutting an ash tree to make a plough before nightfall for a wage of less than three shillings ... There is no section of this Parish (Defynnog) without its blacksmith who is an expert in making iron ploughs".[4]

In the nineteenth century almost everything required in the home from furniture made by carpenters and cabinet makers, to the utensils of the kitchen and dairy could be made by coopers and blacksmiths living in Vaynor. Horse harnesses, clogs, boots, cloths, saddlery and leather goods could be produced locally and if the locality did not possess the craftsmen required then there were travelling tailors and dressmakers and millwrights who paid regular visits to the remotest parts of the parish.

While each county had its own complement of craftsmen, Vaynor was unique in the range of it craftsmen because of the fact that its largest conurbation at Cefn Coed housed men employed in the local iron works and mines. In addition too were the rural craftsmen of Cwm Tâf, Pontsarn and Pontsticill. The Burial Registers for 1897 at St Gwynno's Church Vaynor give some idea of the range of local skills:- watchmaker, mechanic, sculptor, cooper, turner, traffic arranger, joiner, cordwainer, cellarman, baker, plumber, charger, cutter.

From the beginning of the twentieth century great changes have taken place in rural Breconshire. No longer does the countryman look towards his immediate locality for the means of life. The craftsmen of Vaynor, as indeed the craftsmen of the rural districts of Wales, have lost their places as highly significant members of the rural community. The standardised products of the industrial regions, i.e. factory made hammers and hatchets, nails and even ready made horse shoes are readily available in ironmongers' shops in the market towns. With ever increasing advertising on television and better and quicker modes of transport the countryman tends to satisfy his needs in the town.

The rural craftsman is therefore less essential. Of the twenty two woollen mills in operation in Breconshire in 1900 only the British Legion sponsored Cambrian Factory at Llanwrtyd remains in production. Of the 107+ corn mills operating in the 19th century and of the thirty one corn mills operating in 1923 now there are none. The fifty three blacksmiths of 1923 are now reduced to half a dozen and of the twelve saddlers, eleven wheelwrights, tanners, brickmakers, hatters, maltsters, weavers, shoemakers, thatchers, millwrights, rural carpenters, stonemasons of Breconshire, nearly all now have disappeared and their individual expertise replaced by mass produced factory wares. This is a far cry from 1897 when the Rev J. E. Jenkins, Rector of Vaynor buried "Hannah Davydd, wife of Davydd Sakry, freeholder, poet, a worker in straw, a maker of beehives and a thatcher".[5]

REFERENCES

1. David Davies. Hanes Plwyf Penderyn (1905) p.21.
2. W. Morgan (Pant). The Illustrated Vaynor Handbook (1897) p.26.
3. D. Craionog Lewis. Hanes Plwyf Defynnog (1911) p.48.
4. D. C. Lewis Ibid p.285.
5. Rev J. E. Jenkins. Vaynor: Its History and Guide (1897) p.129.

FARM IMPLEMENTS AND TOOLS

Thomas Tusser, the sixteenth century poet and agriculturalist, wrote that the only tools required for full efficiency on the farm were a mattock, spade, pike, flail, weeding tongs and three large implements – a plough, a harrow and a cart. For centuries after Tusser's day, this was the general range of equipment, allowing for some regional variation, found on many farms. It was well into the nineteenth century before the ideas of Tull, Plenty and Ransome began to have some impact on farmers and craftsmen generally.

Primitive tools and obsolete techniques persisted well into this century.[1] For example, seeding by hand was carried out by Mr Tom Jones, Dany-darren until the 1930s. In sowing grain the seed could be carried either in a wooden or straw lip or more often in a linen bed sheet. Other farmers used a seed fiddle; the motion of the fiddle bow across the bottom of the box turned a disc which caused the seed to be thrown out on either side. Nevertheless, the late nineteenth and early twentieth centuries witnessed some improvement in agricultural implements. In threshing, the flail (see overleaf) had been replaced by hand threshers and travelling thresher box-es.

In 1970 the late Mr Morgan Rhys Jones, Garthmadryn, Penderyn informed me that his grandfather Thomas Jones, was the last person in the Parishes of Vaynor and Penderyn to plough and work with oxen in the mid nineteenth century. A plough team sometimes consisted of six, eight or even twelve oxen, yoked in pairs. The yoke consisted of a thick bar of oak or hornbeam, carved into shape. The ox was yoked to the plough team at about three years of age and remained at work for six or seven years. Although its working life was short, when it was killed its meat pro-vided food for the farming family for many months. The skin could be made into leather while the horns furnished handles and many other things. Its dung was useful as a fuel when firewood was scarce and was also mixed with clay, straw and other materials for making daub for walls of buildings.

Until the eighteenth century horses were considered noble animals and above the lowly task of ploughing. This might explain why horses were given noble names whereas cows and oxen less prestigious names. Despite the many advantages of the ox as opposed to the horse, ox teams disap-peared in the eighteenth and nineteenth centuries. Legend has it in Vaynor that oxen were shod at the Cwm Farm, Pontsticill for the whole area. This involved nailing two crescent shaped pieces of iron on each foot. Better and stronger breeds of horses, and lighter and more efficient ploughs hastened the end of the ox as a draught farm animal in Wales by 1890. Mr Tom Jones of Danydarren[2] in a tape recording made for the Welsh Folk Museum, St Fagan's in 1955, indicated that they had always kept a mare. He was born in 1874 so that one may presume that horses had been used as draught animals from that date (or possibly before) at Danydarren Farm, Cwm Tâf.

The real advance in the design of ploughs came with the patenting of Stanyforth and Foljambe's famous Rotherham plough in 1730. This plough design was based on new principles; basically it was a light wooden plough without wheels, with an iron mouldboard and coulter. Because of its lightness and design only one pair of horses or oxen was required to draw it and could be controlled by one ploughman. The design of the Rotherham swing plough spread quickly throughout Wales and was adapted by blacksmiths and ploughwrights in Breconshire to local conditions of soil and slope.

A popular plough in Breconshire was a variation of the Rotherham plough made by Josiah Evans of Pontseli, Pembrokeshire. The Pontseli plough was specifically efficient for cross ploughing.[3] Theophilus Jones writing around 1800 stated that the country plough was "a heavy, clumsy and inefficient implement". He also added that the Rotherham plough had recently been introduced to the Country.[4] The Department of Rural Life at the Welsh Folk Museum, St Fagans has provided me with a photograph of a plough used at Danyrallt Farm, Pontsticill in the nineteenth century (1850). One can read on the mouldboard 'Thomas E. Williams, Brass and'Iron Founder Brecon".[5]

Ffransis Payne points out that mouldboards of the Pontseli type were used as recently as 1935.[6] A correspondent of the Western Mail in that year stated "This type of casting, considerably improved, is still in use on scores of ploughs today and is still cast at Brecon".[7] J. E. Nott & Company in their brochure for 1900 offer "J.E. 6 or Pontselly Pattern Ploughs at £3.10s.0d".

In preparing the ground for seeding, hand tools were in the past used instead of harrows. Armed with mattocks, spades, clodding beetles men and women followed behind the plough, breaking up the soil etc. With the introduction of the Rotherham plough, these old methods of hand cultivation were suspended. By the end of the nineteenth and early twentieth centuries there was considerable variety of local types of plough but

Some farm tools and implements used in Vaynor.

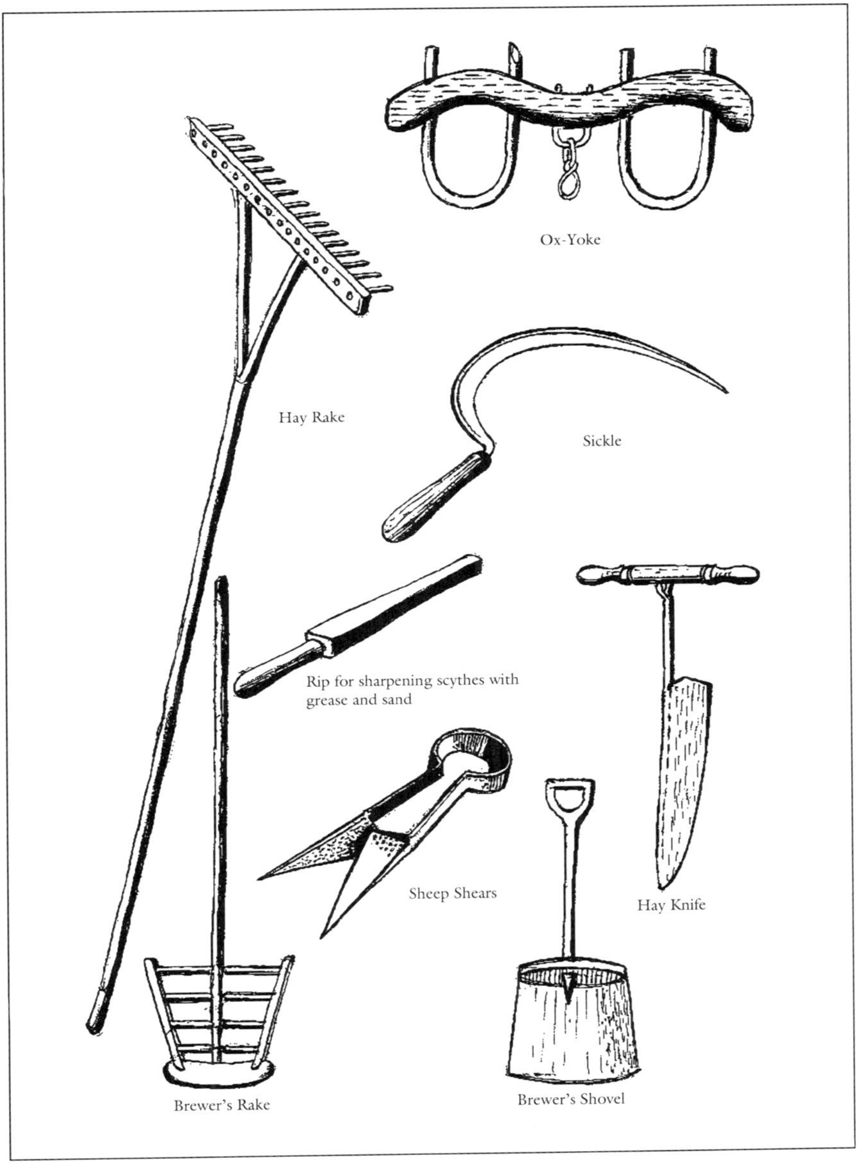

Some farm tools and implements used in Vaynor.

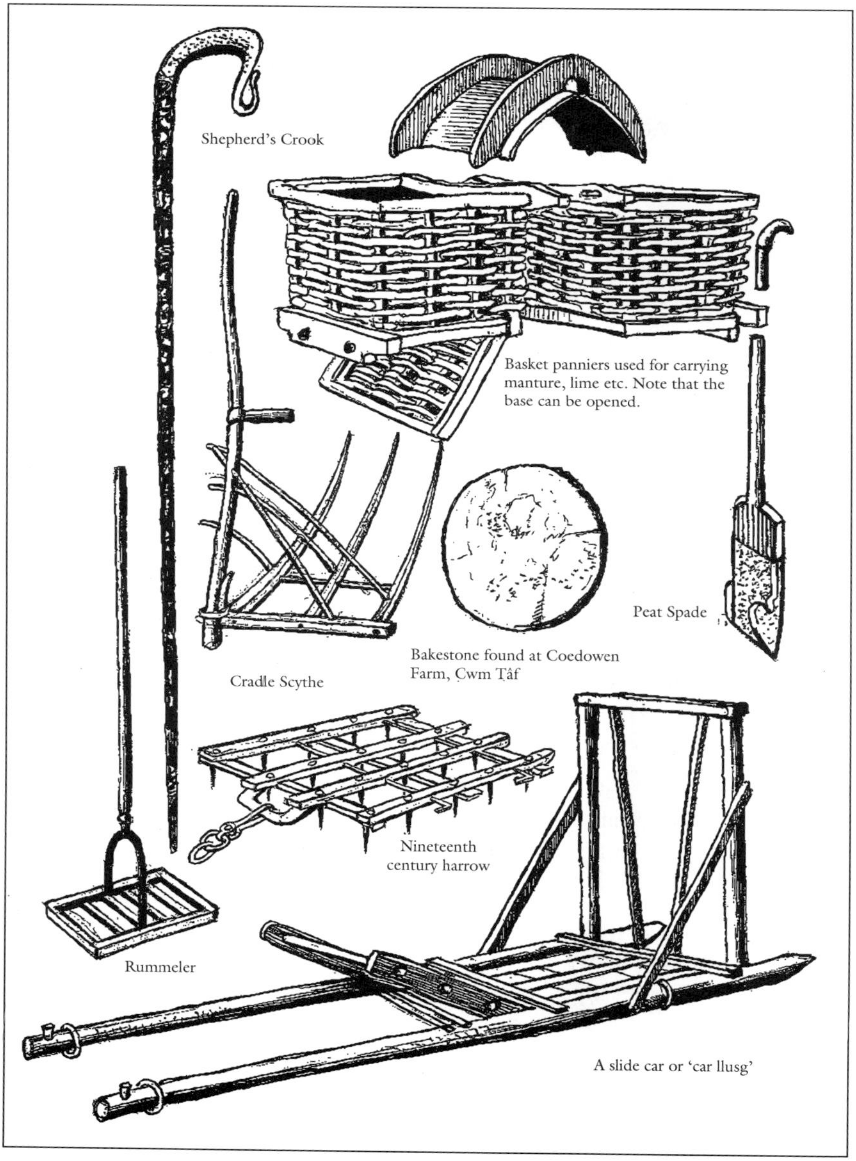

the harrow had remained virtually unchanged since the tenth century. By far the most common type of harrow consisted of a regular wooden frame, carrying around fifteen tines at intervals of eleven inches or so. Another primitive type of harrow used for harrowing grassland was the "drainglwyd". This was a wooden gate or frame to which was tied hawthorn bushes weighed down by a heavy log.

Harvesting, especially of hay, was a communal effort when men, women and children had their parts to play. In general, by the mid nineteenth century the scythe had already replaced the sickle as the implement for corn and hay harvesting. While reaping a dozen or so men worked their way in an orderly procession from one end of the field to the other. Setting the pace usually would be an experienced scyther, with the other reapers at intervals of about six feet behind the leader. Periodically, all would stop and sharpen their scythes with a rip, a wooden bar strapped to the waist which was smeared with grease sprinkled with sand kept in a horn also tied to the waist. A drawing of a rip is shown overleaf. In this fashion they proceeded until a whole field had been mown. In order to gather and hold the cut corn stalks and to facilitate putting them down in neat swaths for the binders, a wooden cradle was fixed to the scythe. For the hay harvest, a bare scythe without a cradle was always used.

Sion Llewelyn, one of the founders of the Hen Dŷ Cwrdd Unitarian Chapel at Cefn Coed was considered an expert scythesman and one day at Maesyfaenor Farm, Vaynor he completed the Herculean task of mowing unaided, a meadow three acres in extent. He was then seventy two years old and the incident is commemorated in the following verse which has been translated by Tom Lewis.

Sion Llewelyn a'r coes grwpyn
Lladd tair erw yn y dydd
Maen'n nawr yn ddeuddeg mlwyd a thrigain
Os Lladd hedwran, rhow o'n rhydd[8]

Translated it reads as follows:

Sion Llewelyn with crooked sned
In one whole day mows acres, three
Now he's seventy two, t'is said
If four he mows, then let him free

It is stated that when Sion was in his prime, he mowed at a field at Coedmeurig in Clwydyfagwyr a swath of hay a mile long without whetting his scythe and thus accomplished a feat which gained forever a name synonymous with bodily power.

Since World War I, a variety of horse drawn wheeled rakes, hay tedders and swath turners have replaced the wooden hand rakes wielded by a large labour force. Today, every stage of hay making can be done with a machine and as a result the agricultural labour force has declined. From about 1910 the string tying binder, made by McCormick Deering of America in 1878 was used for corn harvesting in most parts of Wales until the adoption of the combine harvester in the fifties and sixties of this century.

Threshing was done with and without implements but the flail was the main implement until it was displaced by the threshing machine. Threshing was usually done by the individual farmer, when he and his men servants would thresh the corn on the flag-stoned barn floor of Breconshire farms. The jointed flail with handstaff (droed ffust), beater (yel-ffust) and a joining band (cwplws) has a history going back to the late Roman period. The handstaff was generally of ash while the beater was made of a hardwood such as holly, blackthorn or ash. The joining bands were made of thongs of leather, snakeskin, willow yarn or straw rope. Flailing persisted in Vaynor until the 1920s when this old method was replaced by threshing machines.

The barns of Vaynor were equipped with two opposite doors through which a draught blew even on warm days. The threshed grain was thrown into the air with shovels so that the breeze carried the chaff away while the grain fell to the ground. After barley had been threshed, the awns or beard which was injurious to animals was removed by a hummeller.

Sheep shearing today by hand, using electric clippers and involving two or three men is far removed from the great social occasions of the past when farmers or their representatives attended from many miles' radius. The shearing contractor is becoming far more common and sheep shearing by hand which was the traditional method employed disappeared from Vaynor in the 1960s.

No vehicle shows the adaptation of design to local topography more than the sled and the simplest of all sleds is the slide car or car llusg. The car llusg consists of two stout side timbers about twelve feet long, joined together by a number of cross bars which carry the load. The side pieces project in front to form a pair of shafts, which are attached to the horse high upon the collar. The vehicle is dragged along the ground at a tilt and for this reason it is necessary to fit a wooden framework at the back to support the load. The dragging ends of the slide car are protected by wooden shoes some eighteen inches long and these can quite easily be replaced. Walter Davies, described the hay harvest as a vast communal affair, where it was 'not uncommon to see half a dozen slide cars carrying from the same field'. Mr Tom Jones refers to the fact that he could recall two or three on the hay field at the same time at the end of the nineteenth century.[9]

The sled, is very different from the slide car in that the whole body of the vehicle is dragged along the ground. Unlike the slide car the sled was in the past not limited to a mountainous terrain. Again, there were regional differences, the harvesting sled used for carrying hay and fern from upland fields consisted of two side pieces about seven feet long joined together by eight or more cross pieces. The tumbril sled consisted of a simple box on runners and was used mainly for carrying manure and lime to the fields. The vehicle in use in Vaynor until the Second World War was the slide car or car llusg and the last person to own one was Mr William Morgan, Tredegarfach, Pontsticill.

REFERENCES

1. J. GERAINT JENKINS. Life and Tradition in Rural Wales (1976), p.32.
2. Tape Recording made of MR TOM JONES (1874-1962), Danydarren Farm, Cwm Tâf in 1955 by Department of Rural Life, St Fagan's Folk Museum, Cardiff.
3. J. GERAINT JENKINS, op.cit. p.35.
4. THEOPHILUS JONES. History of Brecknock (1809), p.154.
5. THOMAS H. WILLIAMS. Brass and Iron Founder. Brecon. Acc. No. 31.51/1, Slater's Directory (1850), p.11.
6. FFRANSIS PAYNE. Yr Aradr Cymreig referred to by J. GERAINT JENKINS, op6 cit., p.35.
7. J. GERAINT JENKINS, ibid, p.35.
8. TOM LEWIS. Hen Dŷ Cwrdd, Cefn Coed Y Cymer, p.132.
9. MR TOM JONES's tape recording, op. cit.

CHAPTER V

Roads, Bridges And Transport In Vaynor

INTRODUCTION

In this age of speed and mass travel, when continents are no more than a few hours' flying time from one another, it is surprising to know that until very recently, sledges were used in Vaynor for carrying peat and 'gwair mân'. These crude home-made vehicles survived until the farms were demolished for reservoir building or until they were replaced by modern transport following World War II. These crude home-made vehicles survived because the long experience of generations of hill farmers in Vaynor had proved that these simple devices were the best suited to local needs. Until 1936, cottagers at Pontsticill were carrying peat from the mountain with broad-wheeled wheelbarrows while at Cwm Tâf, Mr W. R. Evans was using a car llusg. In the collieries and levels horse drawn trams were used for conveying coal and in the drawing on the next page, we see a typical scene at the Winch Fawr level owned by Mr Tom Lewis (Twm-y-Glo) of Cefn Coed.

The type of vehicle used depended upon the commodity to be carried and the physical conditions over which it had to be conveyed. One finds, therefore, in the eighteenth and early nineteenth centuries that the pack horse and pack mule were in considerable use within the parish for carrying lime and manure to the fields, corn to the miller and wool to the local weaver. Pack mules were also used for carrying flour to Merthyr and Dowlais from Brecon and were only replaced by wheeled vehicles with the improvement of roads by the Turnpike Trusts and the building of bridges. Heavy wagons conveying farm produce from West Wales and Mid Wales

A typical scene at the Winch Fawr coal level, Cwlydyfagwyr, owned by Mr Thomas Lewis (Twm-y-Glo) c1930.

to Merthyr Tydfil and Dowlais were part of the daily scene at Cefn Coed and the brightly-coloured stage coaches became a familiar sight until superseded by the Brecon Newport and Merthyr Railway in August 1867.

EARLY ROADS

The earliest roads in Vaynor were probably along the ridgeways. There are considerably Neolithic remains on the hilltops and moorland areas of the Parish of Vaynor but practically none in the valleys of Cwm Tâf or Tâf Fechan. This would suggest that movement was as far as possible not in the valleys which were invariably thickly wooded and to a large extend impenetrable but, as stated, on the ridgeways.

ROMAN ROADS

Undoubtedly some of the roads of the Parish of Vaynor date back to the Roman invasion. William Morgan (Pant)[1] has suggested that "this Roman road ran from Gelligaer through Twyn-y-Waun and Pen-y-Garn ddu to Pant-cad-Ivor, and instead of going straight to the Tâf Fechan Valley through Pontsticill, as at present, it made a detour, and cross the Tâf Fechan river below Pontsarn, and then followed the Glais brook and passed behind Penrhiwglais farm in the direction of the Church". He continues, "There are no traces of the road now to be seen on the west of the river from Pontsarn to the Church, but about a hundred yards from the Church there is a portion of the old road clearly discernible. It is located on rising ground, between the rectory and the river. It is pitched with stone, in the manner of Romans made their roads, and is, perhaps the best-preserved specimen of their road making in this district.

Brinley Richards,[2] writing about 1957 and discussing the possible route of the Roman road from Penydarren, Merthyr Tydfil to the Roman fort at 'Y Gaer', Brecon states, "It is difficult to conjecture the course of the road or the roads, but one road is believed to have passed close to the western fringe of Cyfarthfa Castle grounds, whence it continues to the west, passing Gurnos Farm and crossing the Tâf Fechan at Pontsarn. From the Glais brook the road travelled past Vaynor Church (100 yards from which part of the road can be seen) towards Pontsticill. The road bifurcates immediately to the south of Pentwyn reservoir at a point called Dol-y-Gaer (meadow of the camp), and is now submerged. The right fork climbed over the Bryniau Gleision and descended into the Glyncollwn Valley; the left can be traced followed the Tâf Fechan in a north-westerly direction and crossing the Beacons to the east of Pen-y-Fan the highest point".

Some believe that the Roman road may have passed to the west of Pen-y-Fan and continued along the old road from the Storey Arms to Brecon. It is not impossible, however, that an old Roman road may have passed up the Tâf Fawr valley. Canon Jones Davies[3] in considering this possibility has referred to the fact that no less than four Latin inscribed monuments have been found in the Tâf Fawr valley and states "it could not but be that there was another route here in sub-Roman if not in Roman times". Furthermore, an old Roman urn was found by the late Mr Harry Thomas "while hoeing potatoes, June 1859 in front of Abercar farmhouse, Cwm Tâf Vawr".[4]

J. E. Jenkins has a note to the effect that Ptolemy, a second-century writer referred to the Tâf Fawr at Rhatostathubius.[5] More recently, it has been pointed out that the stones near the Fedw Farm, Cwm Tâf may possibly be milestones, and situated as they are on an old track from Llwyn-On, via Cwm-moel to Glais brook, they suggest the existence of an old Roman road connecting the Sarn Helen at Ystradfellte to the Sarn Hir in Vaynor.

The following lines were composed by some unknown bard while crossing over the boggy ground from the Tâf Fawr Valley to Vaynor:

"Mi aethum i'r cwtterau,
A'r dwr yn chwilio'r tyllau;
A neidiais ar fy ngheffyl brych,
Er cadw'n sych fy sanau".[6]

Translated this reads as follows:

"I went into the gutters,
With the water searching out the holes,
And I jumped on my speckled horse,
In order to keep my stockings dry".

Morgan (Pant) has the final word; "there is not a shadow of doubt that the first road connecting Cardiff with Brecon ran through the Tâf Fechan Valley".[7]

TURNPIKE ROADS

The earliest maps of Breconshire by Saxton 1578 and John Speed 1610 do not mark roads, probably there were none worthy of the name. Each has dotted lines indicating travelling tracks, one of which traverses the parish and continues to Ystradfellte. This track could be along the Roman road connecting the Sarn Helen and the Sarn Hir. After crossing the Parish of Vaynor, one route turns northward for Brecon along the Tâf Fawr Valley. It is strange that Speed had not shown a track along the Tâf Fechan which was thought to have been the way of communication between Cardiff and Brecon. Morgan (Pant) mentions that three hundred years ago, judges travelling from Cardiff to Brecon travelled along the Tâf Fechan route and refers to a judge breaking his leg near Tyle'r-bont Farm, Pontsticill at this time.[8] Thomas Kitchen's County Map 1754 marks roads where Speed had shown trackways. The Brecon Road is along the Tâf Fechan – the old Sarn Hir, but the river is crossed at Pontsticill and not at Pontsarn. There is no road shown along the Tâf Fawr.

A Parliamentary Act of 1555 placed the responsibility of maintaining roads in the parish by the employment of individual male labour for six days during the year without payment. There is a summary of indictments against Vaynor parishioners for failing to repair their section of the Highway in 1804.[9] At this time in 1803 Malkin travelled along the Tâf Fechan to Brecon, he states, "the dingle on the left is deep, wild and precipitous. The rough and stony horse path (for the new turnpike road winds round the basis of the mountains to the west) is carried over the precipice. The winding down the hill to the waterside is picturesque and verdant, and brings the traveller back to Pont-y-sticyll, a bridge of one arch across the Tâf Fechan".[10]

Fortunately, we have a similar description of the Tâf Fechan road by Theophilus Jones a few years later, who writes, "From the Village of Coed-Y-Cymer adjoining the Turnpike to and at the distance of two miles from Merthyr, we proceed up along the banks of the lesser Tâf over Coed-Y-Cymer, a barren stony common".[11] The reference made here by Theophilus Jones to travelling along the "banks of the lesser Tâf" is particularly interesting because the roadway is still there and of course it is not referring to the present Vaynor Road, i.e. joining Cefn Coed to Vaynor. Theophilus Jones mentioned also, that the roads to the church were "impassable by carriages, and cannot without danger be travelled on horseback". From what has been stated we may conclude that the roads of Vaynor in the eighteenth century were in a truly primitive condition. Malkin has referred to them as "horse paths" – no doubt an appropriate description.

The Turnpike Acts of 1767 and 1787 are of particular interest to Breconshire and Vaynor. The former Act was concerned solely with Breconshire and it refers to the establishment of a Board of Trustees and calls for the sum of £310,000 to be expended in making and maintaining roads in Breconshire, which, of course, would have included the Merthyr Brecon Road in addition to the other roads in the Tâf Fechan valley. The influence of the Breconshire Agricultural Society in road building in the whole of Breconshire cannot be over-estimated since it offered financial grants to parishes to repair their roads.

The Turnpike Act of 1787 listed exemptions from toll, for example, for horses carrying lime or stones for road repair or carriages carrying dung.

This Act had very significant implications for Vaynor because of the number of lime-kilns in the parish and the trade conducted from them to other counties in Wales and even across the border to Herefordshire by pack mules.

The Turnpike Act of 1809 repealed all previous Acts and as a result there was an amalgamation of all Breconshire Trusts. The list of trustees included Theophilus Jones and Richard Crawshay. The tolls were revised and the newspapers of the time advertised the leasing of Breconshire gates for one year or occasionally a group of gates for a year. The 1814 Map shows the turnpike road and gates at Blaentâf and at the Darren Turnpike. The Turnpike gate at Cefn Coed is not shown possibly because it was a chain gate. Evidence of the ingenuity of local farmers in avoiding payment of tolls at the Darren gate may still be seen in a roadway passing around through the woodland underneath.

Following upon the inducements offered by the Breconshire Agricultural Society the roads upon which the stage coaches travelled were very much improved. Morgan (Pant) in referring to the Brecon-Merthyr Road suggests that it was built towards the end of the eighteenth century but Tom Lewis gives the date of the Cefn to Cwm Tâf Road as 1802. In his narrative of 1803, Malkin referred to it as the "new turnpike road". "It is known that Mr William Morgan of the Grawen, Cwm Tâf took a very active part in the promotion of this road," claimed Morgan (Pant). Previously, it was claimed by elderly people that a road through Cefn Coed passed up Field Street, along Pontycapel Road, up Job's Lane behind the Morning Sun Inn and out on to Cwm Tâf Road just below Danydarren Farm. Further information regarding the Brecon-Merthyr Road is provided by J. E. Jenkins where he states that "the turnpike road from Coedcymmer to Brecon was finished, as far as Story Arms in 1814. The extension of the New Turnpike Road from Story Arms to Brecon was carried out in 1830-1. It was diverted from the east side to the west side of the valley. The contractor from Story Arms to Tro Mawr was John Vaughan. From Tro Mawr to Ty Mawr Wood the contractor was John Probert, and the section from Ty Mawr Wood to Rai Rhos was made by William Watkins, who was also the Surveyor, the total cost being £8,000".[14]

A map attached to the copy of the Turnpike Act of 1830 gives a clear picture of Breconshire Turnpike Roads for that year and it clearly shows the deviation of the Brecon-Merthyr road passing along Cwm Tâf Fawr in the Parish of Vaynor. The 1830 Act makes the first reference to stage coaches and steam carriages and also provide for the division of the Breconshire Trust into nineteen districts, each district having a surveyor and a chief surveyor over the whole County. Entries in the Parish Vestry Record (1779-1828) reveal payments made by the Parish for road repairs, and one sees for example "Mend Llwynperchell and Heol Y Cwm 3s 0d (15p). Repairing Heol Las 12s 0d (60p)" and for the road surveyor "Jehosaphat Jones expenses to Hampshire, £10". J. E. Jenkins in a footnote states "Up to 1850, each hamlet had to maintain and repair its own roads. From that date they were to be common concern".[15]

J. E. Jenkins provides a detailed account of the making of "the new road" at Vaynor. He says "No Parish of its size ever spent more on its roads than Vaynor and up to 1850 it had to repair its own roads. Waun Dafydd and Llyngheran road were particularly expensive. In 1825 a great change took place, Car Bridge was built at a cost of £12.2s.6d (£12.13), Tyle'r Bont Bridge was also built and the new road from Glais Bridge to Cae Burdydd was commence that year". One notes from the account that it took seven years to make about one mile or less of road made up of sub-contracts for from nine to fifty perches at a time. The contract for the new road from Glais Bridge to Cae Burdydd (i.e. up to the house now called "Hy Brazil") reads as follows: "The first contract being that of Samuel Davies and William Williams for 35.15s.0d (£35.75). The next contract was 50 perches for £3.2s.6d (£3.13). Then Elias Jones made 36 perches at 4s 6d (£0.23) per perch. Evan Jones removed 157 cartloads of earth for £2.12s.4d (£2.62) and made 296 yards for £12.5s.8d (£12.28) and another length for £1 with 9 more perches at 5s 3d (£0.26) per perch". Then came "Morgan Williams to open 33 perches for £1.18s.10d (£1.94)" and Thomas Maysey succeeded in making a "cart passage" for 5s 0d (£0.25). Later there was a fall below Aberglais, and W. Meredith had to clear it, and make a wall "to stop the down the stones on the new road", and was only paid 5s 0d (£0.25). Later came other falls and "quicks and riddles" had to be planted and for all these, £20.18s.0d (£20.90) had to be paid. The work lasted seven years, and the road had hardly been finished when the funeral of Jehosaphat Jones, its surveyor, came over it on Monday August 13th 1832".[16]

It was not until the year 1835 with the passing of the Highway Act that the parishes were free from the compulsory labour system which had existed for about 300 years. From 1835 too, each parish was allowed to levy a road rate instead. The Commission of Inquiry found that very few Breconshire Toll Gates were destroyed during the Rebecca Riots. Craionog Lewis tells of an attack on the Blaentâf gate (Clwyd Turpig y Mynydd) at the junction of the Penderyn road with the Merthyr road near the Storey Arms in the neighbouring parish to Vaynor. At this time the toll-keeper received between 2s 6d (£0.13) and 6s 0d (£0.30) a week. It cost £25 a mile annually to maintain the main roads.

The surface of the roads consisted of broken stones and local farmers or carters tendered for the hauling of stone. Payment for one cubic yard was about 8 pence and for breaking the stone into suitable sizes workmen got between 8 pence and a shilling a cubic yard. The Trust provided its workmen with wheelbarrows, scrapers and rakes while the sledge-hammers for breaking stones were provided by the workmen. The general complaint was the number of gates, on average three gates to every thirty miles, while on minor roads the average was one in seven or eight miles. Some interesting evidence was given by John Jenkins and Morgan Lewis to the Commissioners of Inquiry. The large warehouses of Messrs George North, Brecon supplied farm produce to South Wales and the petition by Jenkins and Lewis included the following list of tolls:-[17]

"From Brecon to Merthyr and back – 5 horses

Llanfaes Gate out of Brecon	2s 6d	(£0.12)
Hill Gate (9 miles out) Story Arms or also known as Blaen Tâf Gate	2s 6d	
Darren Gate (14½ miles out) in the Parish of Vaynor	2s 6d	
Chain Gate, Glam. (16½ miles out) near Cefn Coed Bridge sometimes called Cefn Gate	3s 9d	(£0.23)
If load for Dowlais (17½ miles out)	3s 9d	
Parratt Gate (1 mile from Brecon)	2s 6d	
	17s 6d	(£0.88)"

In an Act passed in 1844 following the Inquiry, two important changes were instituted. These were, the consolidation of all Trusts in the county and the beginning of Government control where finance was concerned. After the paying of all debts by means of Government loans, County Roads Boards were to be set up and the administration of a County's turnpike roads was to be the responsibility of its Board. The Board was made up of 27 members, two members coming from each hundred in the County. The Board's rules were very strict, no excuses were accepted for absence from work however brief, no work was done on Sundays and absences were punished by loss of pay.

A century ago the local road mender, so Tom Lewis informs us, was a woman called "Betsi Cefn Ishaf", who was the last to undertake this work. "Her nailed shoes were those of a man, her overcoat was a muddy sack ... armed with the implements of her calling – a shovel, a sweeping brush, a scraper and a wheelbarrow, her main task was to make earth-gutters, fill up rain puddles, wheel away leaves in the Autumn and remove horse droppings which at that time littered every road in the parish".[18] A regular roadman in Vaynor at this time could expect to earn 11s 0d (£0.55) a week and if a regular employee, had to provide his or her own tools. A good picture of the situation is derived from the account books of the County for 1850, for example, maintaining the Brecon-Merthyr Road cost £324 and David Williams was paid 3s 6d (£0.18) for two days work at Blaentâf Gate, Cwm Tâf. Stones from fields were paid for at the rate of 2s 3d (£0.11) per road yard while 1s 1d (£0.05½) was paid for river stones per road yard.

With the passing of time, the use of the roads for the transport of goods as well as for private travelling became less and less. This was mainly because of the introduction of railways which brought quicker and more comfortable travelling. The amount of tolls dropped considerably with the taking down of more and more gates and by 1876 there were no more than 23 toll gates in Breconshire. The Darren Fawr Gate was abolished in 1885 and with the establishment of the County Council in 1888, the Turnpike system came to an end with the administration of the roads coming under the jurisdiction of the new Councils.

BRIDGES

Because of its mountainous nature and heavy rainfall, Vaynor is a parish of numerous streams and it has, as a result, an abundance of bridges. The small one arched bridge was a common feature of our countryside and it speaks well of the ingenuity and craftsmanship of past bridge builders to see their work still standing after centuries of buffeting by the swollen waters of the Tâf Fawr and Tâf Fechan in times of flood. The frequency of the word 'rhyd', meaning 'ford', in Welsh place-names tells us that bridges

A drawing of the wooden bridge over Pwll-dan-bont below the Gurnos Corn Mill which was later converted into a fulling mill. Morlais Castle stands in the background.

The old Pontardâf bridge, Cwm Tâf also known as "Pontyglec" (the bridge of gossip), it reappears in times of Summer drought.

were not as common as they later became. In this area we have 'Rhydycar' (The ford for carts) and Rhydyrychen (Ox-Ford). Some bridges such as the bridge over Pwll-dan-bont on the Tâf Fechan below the old Gurnos Corn Mills has disappeared – only the name of the pool provides a clue.

The frequency of flooding tended to make the fords impassible at certain times of the year, so another and more dependable method of crossing streams had to be found. What easier then than to construct a temporary bridge of wood, such as that described by T. E. Clark in 1848 when referring to the bridge at Pontsarn, he said, "The bridge is erected over two rocks of equal height having no more than 18 feet between ... The bridge is a wooden structure, nine feet in width, it was formerly much narrower, consisting only of a few planks".[19] Most bridges in early times were thus made, and Welsh place names testify to their existence, such as 'Pont bren' at Penderyn. Wooden bridges, too, proved undependable, either through rotting due to our wet climate or again by being destroyed by floods. The only course left, therefore, was to build bridges of stone and this presented no difficulty because of ample supplies of stone in the locality. These are exemplified in "Pont Garreg" referred to by Jenkins in Cwm Tâf; in Pontsarn and Pontsticill we have two very well known local placenames incorporating the word 'pont'. There was also a farm in Cwm Tâf called 'Penpont'.

The erection and maintenance of bridges had from early times been a drain on resources. As already stated, the early bridges, with very few exceptions, were made of wood and would have been in constant need of repair or renewal mainly due to the flooding of streams. By the seventeenth century the demands of trade made changes imperative. New and better roads and bridges became a necessity. In 1703, a General Act decreed that all bridges on the more important roads were to be transferred to the County as their responsibility, while the bridges on the lesser roads were still to be built and maintained by the parish in which they occurred. For this reason we see the following entry in the Vaynor Parish Vestry Records for around 1800: "Towards Pont y Sarn £1.10s.04d (£1.52)"[20] and "Paid towards Canedir Bridge 6s 0d" (£0.30).

As far as Vaynor was concerned, the next big change came in 1821 when, because of the great deal of confusion arising over county and parish bridges, Parliament was petitioned for a bill enabling all bridges in the County of Breconshire to be the responsibility of the County as a whole, leaving the individual parishes free of all obligation. As far as is known, this was the only Act of this kind ever passed. Events were to prove it to have been a wise move. In future no bridge was left to remain out of use owing to its ruinous condition because of lack of parish funds. The County Surveyor saw to all the bridges in the County of Brecknock after 1821 and it is after this date that one finds the names of the County Surveyor and Clerk of the Peace taking the place of the local justices on the contracts for building or repair.

The earliest reference to bridges in Vaynor is that on the Thomas Kitchin Map of 1754 which refers to "Pont Capel" at Cefn Coed and to "Pont Stickel". The bridge at "Pont Capel" was probably a wooden bridge built about 1650 with a stone bridge erected between 1775 and 1780. A Penry Williams painting at Cyfarthfa Museum, Merthyr Tydfil gives clear details of a hump-backed bridge of two arches and the width between the parapets was 13 feet. This bridge was destroyed on July 9th 1853 by a great flood and the present bridge was built in 1858. In the deluge of 1853 most of the Vaynor Parish bridges were swept away, Jenkins states: "the scene at Pontsarn was beyond description".

Cwm Capel painted by the famous Merthyr artist, Penry Williams (1800-1885) c1830.

In addition Jenkins added, "The following bridges were washed away:- Pont Llwyn, Pont Blaen, Pont Lydan. In the Tave Vawr Valley there was general inundation. Bridges were damaged, farming stock lost ... But great as these floods were, they were nothing to be compared to the terrible flood which took place on the 18th January, 1607 ... A great number of bridges disappeared".[21]

Other early references to bridges in the Parish of Vaynor include Malkin's 1803 description,[22] of a "bridge of one arch crossing the Tâf Fechan river" at Pontsticill. Theophilus Jones, writing a few years later, refers to "crossing the river Tâf at a little distance below the church, over a tremendous wooden bridge called Pont Sarn, thrown from rock to rock, of the height of about thirty or forty feet from the water".[23] Jenkins refers to "the footbridge below the Church" and adds in a footnote "This footbridge is the private property of H. Kirkhouse, Esq., J.P. who very kindly allows the public to use it".[24] The old bridge called 'Pontyglec' which was submerged under the Llwyn-On reservoir in 1927 re-appears occasionally during periods of drought. Translated, the name of the bridge means 'The Bridge of Gossip' and Tom Lewis has referred to the bridge as "the favourite rendezvous in the valley for news of courtings and jiltings, of wedding and illnesses, of deaths and removals".

The Cefn Bridge was built between 1775 and 1781; Ayre's map of 1776 shows this as a natural crossing point. Malkin's map, included in his book on South Wales in 1814 records Cefn Bridge, as a "New Bridge". Conversely, it was described as "old" in a document dated 1825. By the end of the century it had apparently fallen into a state of disrepair, because in 1893 Morgan (Pant) wrote "A movement is now on foot to procure the improvement of Cefn Bridge. It has been felt for years that the present one is both inconvenient and dangerous, and strong representations have been made to the County Councils of Breconshire and Glamorganshire, upon this matter".

The old Cefn Bridge (c1908).

Details regarding Cefn and Pontsarn viaducts are provided by W. Morgan (Pant).[25] Writing of the Cefn Viaduct he says, "The railway crosses the Tâf Fawr river at Cefn Coed, by a very noble stone viaduct. It was completed in the year 1866 and built by Messrs Savin and Ward from designs by A. Sutherland, Esq. It is a graceful and majestic structure ... one of the finest viaducts in South Wales. It has fifteen arches of 40 foot each, making a total length of 725 feet in all. Its height is 115 feet, and it cost £25,000. Within the space of a mile and a half the railway passes over the Tâf Fechan river by a shorter and lower bridge, called The Pontsarn Viaduct. This is a straight bridge, with seven arches. The length is 456 feet, and the height is 92 feet". More recently the Heads of the Valleys road was completed in 1964. This necessitated the demolition of some houses at Cefn Coed and the construction of two new bridges, one over the Tâf Fechan river and the other over the Tâf Fawr river.

The scaffolding for Cefn Coed viaduct completed 1866.

The Cefn Coed viaduct Pontycapel built by Savin and Ward 1866.

Building the Heads of the Valleys Bridge over the Tâf Fawr 1964.

The construction of the new bridge over the Tâf Fechan river. August 1963.

The railway bridge over Cefn High Street was demolished on July 6th 1970.

TRANSPORT IN VAYNOR

Because of the hilly nature of the Parish of Vaynor, methods of transport on the farm, and from farm, to market at Brecon, Dowlais or Merthyr remained very undeveloped until modern methods of road making became general throughout Wales.

THE SLEDGE

On the farm no vehicle shows greater adaptation of design to local topography than the sledge and the simplest of all sleds is the slide car or car llusg. It was, of course, used generally during the hay and peat harvests and was also used in Vaynor for conveying fern for animal bedding and stones either for farm buildings, boundary walls or to the mountain limekilns. The slide car was constructed of two poles which in part form the shafts and behind are braced together with cross-timbers to form a hurdle. From each corner of the frame uprights are firmly fixed; these, when necessary, are replaced by cratches. The ends or "heels" which are drawn along the ground, were frequently shod with iron. I am informed that the car llusg was used in the Cwm Tâf valley by Mr W. R. Evans of Coedowen Farm in the 1930s, for conveying peat down from the Llysieuog hill and that Mr Tom Jones, also of Cwm Tâf used this vehicle at the same time for carrying 'gwair mân' or moorland hay, down to his farm Llysieuog Uchaf.

In the Tâf Fechan valley, Mr David Williams of Coedhir Farm, Dolygaer, aged 83 years recalls Mr William Morgan, Tredegarfach, Pontsticill (opposite the Baptist Church) using the vehicle on his smallholding as late as 1936. This vehicle had many advantages, it could be easily and cheaply made by the upland farmer himself and it was very safe for working on the steep slopes on some of Vaynor's fields. Jenkins refers to this conveyance in 1897 and to a "wind bicycle", whatever that might have been. As he states "There were no roads in the parish of greater width than four feet (they are still to be seen, and even up to seventy years ago, a kind of wind bicycle and car llusg were the only conveyances known".

OX CARTS

THERE IS evidence to show that oxen were used for ploughing in the parish of Vaynor in the first half of the last century. The teams of the squires of Y Grawen and Penyradwy consisted of eight oxen pulling abreast and exhorted to work by young maidens singing Welsh ditties or traditional songs. The final call assumed a variety of forms, the most popular being 'Ma Hir' and 'Hw Mlaen'. One of the ox songs said:

> "Mu fuo i lawar blwyddyn
> Yn canu gyta'r ychin
> Bara haidd a chosyn cnep
> Dim tishan lap, na phwtin,
> Ma hw, Ma hw".

Translated it reads as follows:

> "For many years
> I sang with the oxen
> Barley bread and lump of cheese
> No cake, no pudding
> Ma hw, Ma hw".[26]

There is no evidence to show that ox-carts as such were used in Vaynor. The ox-cart had a "long narrow body on low wheels with a beam on which two oxen were yoked".[27] Gwallter Mechain throws some light upon methods of personal conveyance, "Irish cars" (Ceir Gwyddelig) he states, "are common in Breconshire".[28] Again, one is unable to say that although they were common in Breconshire, that they were also used in Vaynor, the most one can say is that they might have been used.

HEARSES, CARTS AND GAMBOS

It is very difficult to establish when drawn carts were used in Vaynor for the first time. Nevertheless, we have some references which provide some indication as to when they arrived here. Tom Lewis, in a footnote, states "William Tomos Sion of Dreinos, Vaynor was reputed to be one of the first in the Parish of Vaynor to use a horse-drawn cart. Before the advent of the cart, manure was conveyed to the fields in panniers (cewyll) strapped to the backs of horses. The cart, of course, had no wheels. It was known as a 'car llusg', and was pulled along the ground like a sleigh".[29] This information is interesting because there is no reference to the "Irish car". The Thomas family of Dreinos farm were a family of innovators, obviously, because the wife Ann Thomas was the first to drink tea in the parish of Vaynor. She died in October 1782, so could one assume that her husband was using a horse drawn vehicle about this time?

Later, in 1815 Gwallter Mechain wrote that "single horse carts gain ground but slowly",[30] when referring to South Wales in general. One can accept this view as far as Vaynor is concerned because of a report by J. E. Jenkins referring to the early part of the eighteenth century where he says "Up to 1832, there was no road by which a carriage or even a cart, of the rudest construction, could be brought as far as Vaynor Church from the direction of Coedycymmer. The steep Roman road, which can be plainly seen today, from the bridge to Penrhiwglais was even harder to climb than the old road above Rhiw-yr-ychain". Jenkins goes on to say that all funerals from Coedycymmer and "Merthyr Village" involved carrying the dead "by sturdy friends and neighbours shoulder high – the tallest bearers behind – climbing the "rhiw" with frequent changes".

Then for the first time around 1832 referring to a young man who had died of unrequited love at Merthyr he says, "His body was brought from Merthyr to Coedycymmer, and from Coedycymmer over the hill at Kilsanws – all the way from Blaendyffryn and Blaenglais, over Heol Las and Maesvaynor Road to the Church. The funeral was a memorable one. It was a sight to see, a hearse on the mountain. All the men who formed the funeral procession wore white gloves and white silk bands around their hats. this was the first, but not the last funeral that came over Kilsanws Hill in a hearse".[31] In an interesting footnote, he adds "John Richards, father of the late Mr Llewellin Richards, was the first to use a decent cart in Gelli Hamlet, Vaynor. The cart was taken up to Tylellwyd over the bed of the river".[32]

And then he is referring to 1814 when "we are told that market traps were introduced":

> "Wel, dyma gyfnewidiad
> Mae'n awr mewn llawn arferiad,
> Pob gwr o Griw i Danygraig
> Myn'd gyda'i wraig i'r farchnad".[23]

Translated this means:

> "Well here's a change. It is now the custom for
> husbands, from Crew to Danygraig Farm, to go
> with their wives to market".

He adds "the old road was too rough for spring traps". If one can relate the introduction of wheeled vehicles to the building of Turnpike Roads in the locality one should then note the fact that the Turnpike Road from Cefn Bridge to Cwm Tâf, which would include Cefn High Street was built about 1802.

Much material was carried on the backs and shoulders of men and on the heads of women. A towel was twisted into the form of a rope and coiled into a pad called a "trochan", and with this as a protection and as a cushion for her head, the woman carried a pail of milk or a bucket of garden produce over considerable distances. Several people owned donkeys which were used chiefly for the transport of grain, of garden produce and of sandstone which was crushed and thrown on the floors of the cottages. They were either harnessed to small carts or slung with panniers. Carts, it would appear, were used from the early nineteenth century in Vaynor for the conveyance of the heavier materials such as stone for road making, while gambos were used for the transport of hay, corn, fern, pigs, sheep and calves. Owing to the steep gradients which characterised the Parish of Vaynor, Clydesdale and Shire Horses were the principal draught animals although cobs were at times seen harnessed to the lighter carts. The pony and trap was also a fashionable mode of transport both in the town and country.

The horses which were the pride of the village of Cefn Coed were the Shire horses which belonged to the brewery owners, and the hackneys which were owned by the professional men. The brewery horses were paired in bays or browns and when they set off on their journeys to Merthyr Tydfil or the neighbouring valleys in their brightly decorated harnesses, they presented a beautiful sight. The carriage used by the profes-

Miss May Jones of the Rising Sun Stores, Cefn Coed with her pony and trap c1900.

Donor Mr Morgan Jones, Cefn

Mr Mathias Thomas, costermonger, Cefn Coed with his "Merthyr Cart". (c1976).

sional men of the nineteenth century in this area was the square fronted Brougham and the horse best suited to his vehicle was either the Norfolk or the Yorkshire trotter. The horse, the coachman, dressed in a livery of blue and in a black cockaded hat, and the carriage formed an artistic combination.

An outing on a horse-bus arriving at the Storey Arms at the head of Glyn Tarell. (c1910).

Brakes and wagonettes drawn by pairs of coach horses of various kinds were the chief means of passenger transport within the valley itself, but they were also used on day long trips in summer when picnics were a diversion. These vehicles, when in use, were left open during the summer but a hood of sail cloth was used as a covering during the rest of the year. They plied each day between the village of Cefn Coed and the neighbouring town and a tail-boy rode on the back steps to open the door and to take the fares. Much local news and gossip was retailed in these brakes and wagonettes during these journeys. Hawkers and fishmongers used a light sideless cart known as the flat. The market wholesalers and commission agents used a larger cart of the same design and to it was fixed a front board. This was commonly known as the Merthyr Cart.[34] Mr Thomas Francis of 82 High Street, Cefn Coed had a Hackney Carriage licence in 1903 for a "4 Wheel brake".

A party of Pontycapel friends leaving for the seaside in Mr Gough's charbanc (c1930).

By courtesy of Mr George Thomas, Pontycapel Road, Cefn Coed

Two very well known and respected businessmen were Councillor Will Morgan the local milk man and Mr Mathias Thomas, costermonger. Councillor Morgan competed annually in the pre-Second World War Fete and Galas at Cyfarthfa Park and it was always a delight to see his horse Robin, a magnificent cob with mane plaited, striding confidently down through Cefn Coed with Councillor Morgan suitably attired in white coat and black bowler, on their way to win yet again the coveted first prize in the show ring at Cyfarthfa. Both Mr Thomas and Councillor Morgan served this community with courtesy, honesty and integrity.

Councillor Will Morgan outside his home at Tai Grawen with his prize winning cob, Robin, prior to leaving to compete at the Fete and Gala held annually at Cyfarthfa Park (c1937).

By courtesy of Mr Trefor Morgan, Vaynor Villas, Cefn Coed

THE CARDI CARTS

Throughout the last century from about 1835, processions of Carts could be seen travelling along the Cwm Tâf Road because the Brecon to Merthyr Turnpike Road had been completed by 1831. With the improved deviation from the Storey Arms to the western side of the valley the gradient from Libanus had been greatly reduced, and now facilitated the movement of horse-drawn laden vehicles over greater distances with considerable less effort than previously. The carts laden with farm produce were known as 'Cardi Carts', the name 'Cardi' being an abbreviation for 'Cardiganshire', from whence very many of them came. In Autumn or early winter they would be seen wending their way towards the industrial town of Merthyr Tydfil and to Dowlais. The produce generally carried in the Cardi carts was fresh pigmeat, butter, eggs and cheese. The Cardi cart was a light vehicle with open sides except for a low upright rail each side. It was probably used during harvest time on the farm, but was always spotlessly clean when used for carrying produce. More often than not, the cart was painted a light red colour and was drawn by a typical Cardi horse, a good walker and one that did not tire too easily. The driver was usually the farmer himself though occasionally a hired carrier would be in charge.

It was a common sight to see ten or twelve of these carts in a string moving along the road from Llandovery through Defynnog, past Forest Lodge towards Merthyr. They had regular stopping places on the journey and it was a common sight too, to see a string of unhorsed carts either laden or empty outside a wayside Inn where the drivers had stopped for the night. It was the custom to leave home on Monday morning and to return by either Friday or Saturday. Sunday would be spent quietly at home.

There was considerable risk attached to the return journey to West Wales through Cefn Coed and along the Cwm Tâf valley on a Saturday night when the driver would be carrying a sum of money after selling his produce. Two carts, fully laden, would carry goods worth about £70, which was a large sum of money in those days. Thomas Thomas was hanged on April 10th 1845 at Brecon for the murder of David Lewis, murdered at Defynnog while returning from the market at Merthyr. His execution was witnessed by 15,000 persons. Very often the drivers acted as unofficial postmen. Much of the increasing populations of Cefn Coed and Merthyr had moved from the rural parts of West Wales. What better way was there at that time for sending letters to the family at home?

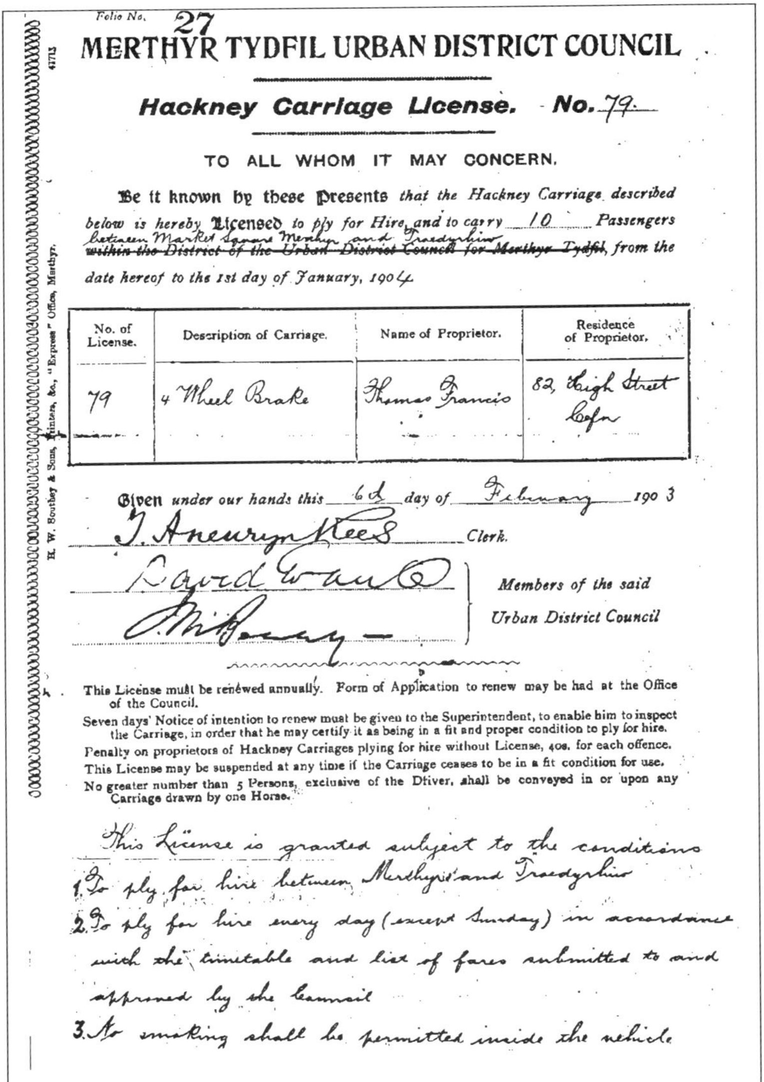

Folio No. 27

MERTHYR TYDFIL URBAN DISTRICT COUNCIL

Hackney Carriage License. No. 79.

TO ALL WHOM IT MAY CONCERN.

Be it known by these Presents *that the Hackney Carriage described below is hereby* Licensed *to ply for Hire, and to carry* 10 *Passengers* between Market Square Merthyr and Troedyrhiw ~~*within the District of the Urban District Council for Merthyr Tydfil*~~, *from the date hereof to the 1st day of January, 1904.*

No. of License.	Description of Carriage.	Name of Proprietor.	Residence of Proprietor.
79	4 Wheel Brake	Thomas Francis	82, High Street Cefn

Given *under our hands this* 6th *day of* February 1903

T. Aneurin Rees *Clerk.*

[illegible]

[illegible]

Members of the said Urban District Council

This License must be renewed annually. Form of Application to renew may be had at the Office of the Council.

Seven days' Notice of intention to renew must be given to the Superintendent, to enable him to inspect the Carriage, in order that he may certify it as being in a fit and proper condition to ply for hire.

Penalty on proprietors of Hackney Carriages plying for hire without License, 40s. for each offence.

This License may be suspended at any time if the Carriage ceases to be in a fit condition for use.

No greater number than 5 Persons, exclusive of the Driver, shall be conveyed in or upon any Carriage drawn by one Horse.

This License is granted subject to the conditions

1. To ply for hire between Merthyr and Troedyrhiw
2. To ply for hire every day (except Sunday) in accordance with the timetable and list of fares submitted to and approved by the Council
3. No smoking shall be permitted inside the vehicle

H. W. Southey & Sons, Printers, &c., "Express" Office, Merthyr.

Mr Thomas Francis of 82 High Street, Cefn Coed was "Licensed to ply for Hire and to carry 10 passengers between Market Square, Merthyr and Troedyrhiw".

PACK MULES AND WAGGONS

Prior to the making of the Turnpike Road from Merthyr to Brecon in 1831, this road was no more than an uneven track, deep in mud in winter but dusty and pot-holed in summer. The most common way of transporting goods to and from this locality was by horse or mule, a slow and arduous task. Mill-owners often used pack-mules to convey the grain from the farms and the flour to wherever it was required. The produce was carried in baskets or panniers strapped on each side of the mule. A string of mules with their panniers was a very common sight in Vaynor some two hundred years ago, wending their way to the coal and iron towns not so far distant. On the return journey the panniers would be laden with coal or lime. Jenkins states "that not a few Vaynor farmers paid their rents from profits made by carrying coal from Merthyr to Brecon, Knighton and Hereford and they had some noted mules"

"Dick, a Jack a Bwryn,
A Bal o Nantygwreiddyn,
Aeth a llawer swrne o lo
Ar hyd y fro i Gynton".[35]

Translated it reads as follows:

"Dick and Jack and Bwryn,
And Bal of Nantygweithyn,
Carried many a bag of coal
Along this vale to Knighton".

With the construction of the Turnpike Road from Merthyr to Brecon in 1831, and with the improved surface, large carts and waggons, could now be used and the carrying of flour became an important trade. Much earlier however, during a severe snowstorm in 1816 three waggons loaded with flour were trapped in deep down in the upper reaches of the Tâf Fawr valley for seven days, at a time, when "wages were low in Merthyr that year. There had been a kind of local riot and hard times were experienced. Many of the shops were without flour for several days".[36] Reference has already been made to the complaint made by the four carriers from Brecon in 1840, about the high cost of transport owing to the high tollgate charges on the numerous gates between Brecon and Merthyr, two of which, the Darren Gate and the Cefn Gate were within the Parish of Vaynor. The list of the "Carriers" to and from Merthyr is as follows:[37]

"From the Crown Inn, High Street, Merthyr:

Cardigan, Monday – returns the Friday following, William Thomas.

Cardigan, Tuesday – returns the Friday week following, David Jones.

Haverfordwest, Monday – returns the Thursday week following, Evan Jones.

Haverfordwest, Monday – returns the Friday week following, John Ormond.

Llanelly, Kidwelly, Llansaint, every Monday fortnight, Mary Hunton.

Llandeilo, passing from Llandovery, every Monday morning, and returns on Friday, in the summer – every fortnight in the winter, Jones Jones.

From Llandovery:

Every Tuesday, returning the same evening, six butter carriers. In the winter season, every Thursday about 30 carriages with pigs and numerous articles for the market.

From the Plymouth Arms, Bridge Street, Merthyr:

Carmarthen, every Monday – returns every Friday evening, David Jones.

Carmarthen, every Thursday morning, and returns following Wednesday, John Jones.

Newcastle Emlyn every Thursday fortnight – David Jones and Thomas Williams.

Swansea, every day, except Sundays, a van, at 8 in the morning, John Jenkins.

From the Iron Bridge, Bridge Street, Merthyr:

Carmarthen, every Monday – returns every Friday evening, Thomas Evans.

Carmarthen, every Thursday morning – returns the following Wednesday, John Jones.

Llandovery, every Tuesday, Thomas Jones and John Griffiths.

Llandovery, every Friday, David Saunders, John Lewis, David Davis and David Morgan."

Most of the carriers travelled through Cefn Coed and Cwm Tâf Fawr on route for West Wales. One can now understand why there were fourteen wayside inns and "Cwrw-bachs" between the Morning Sum Inn at Cefn Coed and the Glan Rhyd at Libanus and numerous blacksmiths at Cefn Coed, Nantgwineu Farm Cwm Tâf, Nantddu, Cwm Tâf, and Libanus.

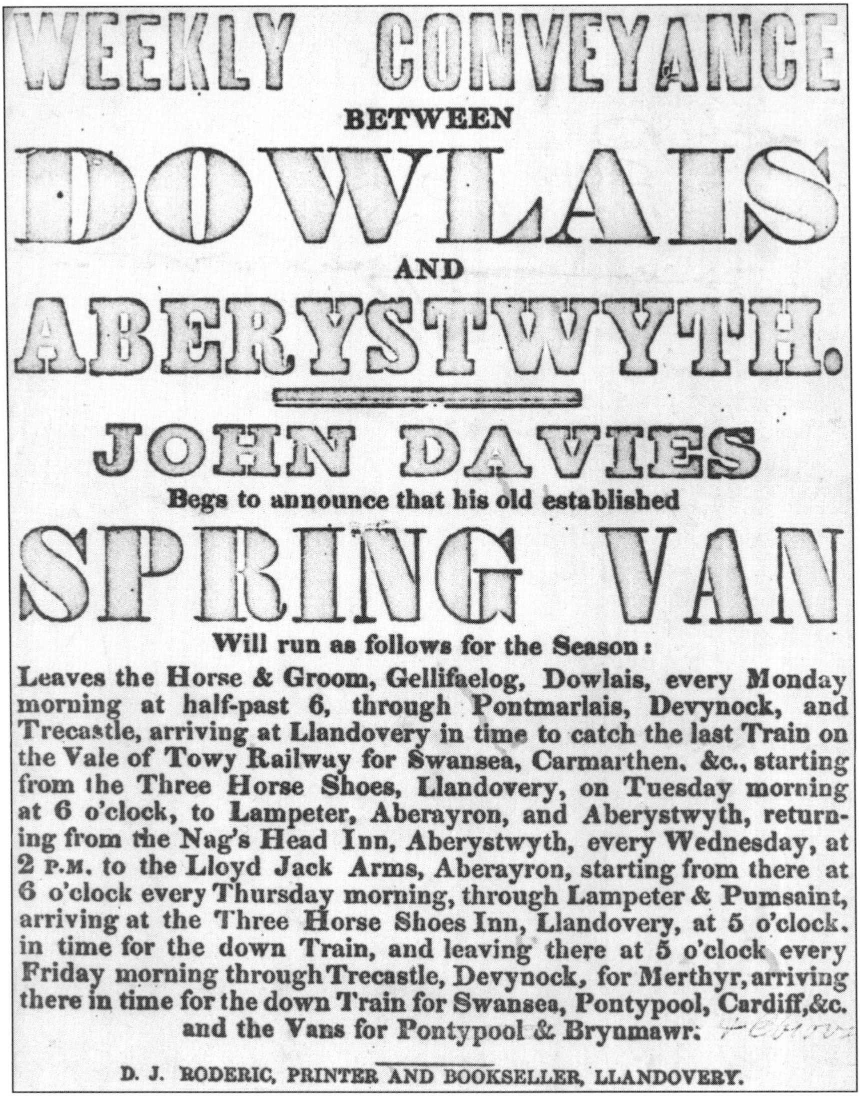

WEEKLY CONVEYANCE
BETWEEN
DOWLAIS
AND
ABERYSTWYTH.

JOHN DAVIES
Begs to announce that his old established
SPRING VAN
Will run as follows for the Season:

Leaves the Horse & Groom, Gellifaelog, Dowlais, every Monday morning at half-past 6, through Pontmarlais, Devynock, and Trecastle, arriving at Llandovery in time to catch the last Train on the Vale of Towy Railway for Swansea, Carmarthen, &c., starting from the Three Horse Shoes, Llandovery, on Tuesday morning at 6 o'clock, to Lampeter, Aberayron, and Aberystwyth, returning from the Nag's Head Inn, Aberystwyth, every Wednesday, at 2 P.M. to the Lloyd Jack Arms, Aberayron, starting from there at 6 o'clock every Thursday morning, through Lampeter & Pumsaint, arriving at the Three Horse Shoes Inn, Llandovery, at 5 o'clock, in time for the down Train, and leaving there at 5 o'clock every Friday morning through Trecastle, Devynock, for Merthyr, arriving there in time for the down Train for Swansea, Pontypool, Cardiff, &c. and the Vans for Pontypool & Brynmawr.

D. J. RODERIC, PRINTER AND BOOKSELLER, LLANDOVERY.

Public poster c1850 advertising a 'Spring van' which offered a weekly conveyance to Aberystwyth and also connected with the trains to Swansea, Pontypool and Cardiff. This van passed through Cefn Coed regularly.

By courtesy of the National Library, Aberystwyth

STAGE COACHES

As the Turnpike Trust built and improved roads in Vaynor, so the brightly decorated stage coaches became a very familiar sight as they lurched through Vaynor Parish, stopping for passengers at the Cross Keys, Cefn Coed and for the shoeing of a horse or some repair to the stagecoach by Thomas Lewis of the Crown, Cefn, village innkeeper, blacksmith, parish constable and great grandfather of the author. The high winds, ice-covered roads, floods and particularly the steep inclines at Lord Tredegar's Shooting Box, Cwm Tâf, and Crew Pitch made this a hazardous journey only for the bravest hearts in the winter-time. Stage coaches had been part of the social scene around Merthyr since about 1804 when a local advertisement stated "The populous and thriving town of Merthyr Tydfil now enjoys a post to and from Cardiff five days in each week".

Inexpensive travel between Merthyr, Vaynor and Hereford was promised, with the New Telegraph post coach called "The Cambrian" which left the Kings Arms, Merthyr every Tuesday and Saturday mornings at six o'clock during the winter season through Brecon and arriving at Hereford the same evening. There was great rivalry between the stage coach companies. In May 1827 the public was informed that a new coach, the 'General Picton,', would commence running between the Castle Inn, Merthyr and Swansea on Tuesday, Thursday and Saturday and Sunday. Bradley and Glover, however, their rivals had already sponsored the 'Imperial' in April of the same year to run from Swansea to Merthyr and then to Brecon (via Cefn Coed).[38] It left Swansea at 7.45 a.m. and arrived at Brecon at 5 p.m. It left the Castle Inn, Brecon on the return journey at 7 a.m. on Wednesday, Friday and Saturday mornings arriving at Merthyr at 10 a.m. and Swansea about 4 p.m. For 1827, the time table for the Swansea-Brecon route reads as follows:

> Swansea to Brecon, Tuesday, Thursday and Saturday. Swansea 8 a.m., Neath 9 a.m., Merthyr 1.30 p.m. (Cefn Coed at 2 p.m.), Brecon at 5 p.m. Brecon to Swansea. Wednesday, Friday and Sunday. Brecon 8 a.m., Cefn Coed 10 a.m., Neath 3.50 p.m., Swansea 5.38 p.m.

The owners of the General Picton announced suspension of service from 24th November 1827 probably because of the hazards on the Brecon Beacons during the Winter. Purchase Price and Townshend, owners of the 'Imperial', announced, however, that their carriage with a handsome head covering would continue to run from Swansea to Merthyr to

The Imperial stagecoach running between Brecon and Swansea passing the Story Arms c1830. It was Anthony Mervin Story, who later adopted his wife's family name – Maskelyne who gave his name to the "Storey" Arms. He was a man of learning, a Master of Arts, a Fellow of the Royal Society, a Justice of the Peace and Deputy Lieutenant of Breconshire. He married Margaret, the only child of Dr Nevil Maskelyne (1731-1811), the Astronomer Royal between 1770 and 1810 and the originator of the Nautical Almanac, sponsor of Captain Cooke etc, and whose sister was married to Robert Clive of India. Anthony Mervin Story Maskelyne purchased land in Breconshire and a house on the river Usk with "the aforestation of his Welsh mountain". I have not been able to trace the date of this purchase but in 1875, Story Maskelyne leased Forest Lodge Farm, Pentrenaboth, Cyfarthfa and the Gyrn, in all some 2,335 acres with hill rights to the Great Forest of Brecon to the late W. S. Miller a well known Breconshire farmer.

Brecon during the winter, twice a week on Tuesdays and Thursdays, and returning from Brecon and Merthyr on Wednesdays and Fridays starting at 8 a.m. The 'Accommodation' began running in June from Neath to Merthyr to Hereford and within seven weeks it had competition from a coach with the sturdy title of 'Ancient Briton' leaving Swansea at 5 a.m. and reaching Hereford via Merthyr, Cefn Coed and Brecon at 8 p.m. the same day.

One sees therefore that there was very considerable traffic through Cefn Coed and Cwm Tâf Fawr, throughout the nineteenth century of pack mules, "Cardi carts", carriers and stage-coaches and accidents frequently occurred. A lad of four was killed locally in 1836 while bundling a hoop across the road. The local newspaper was at pains to point out that "no blame is attached to the coachman who is a very careful driver".[39] Similarly John Prosser, aged 90 from Ruabon, North Wales was killed on the Cwm Tâf Road by the Brecon-Merthyr Stagecoach in 1837 and was buried at Capel Nantddu, Cwm Tâf. He was described as a "stranger" in the burial register but has a very good stone memorial over his grave. Was this one wonders, paid for by the Stagecoach Company?

In 1851 a public notice indicated that conveyance from Merthyr to Brecon by stagecoach cost £1.0s.6d (£1.02).[40] The death knell of the stagecoaches came with the development of railways during the 1840s and with the construction of the Tâff Vale Railway in 1841, the stagecoaches with their colour and glamour began to disappear from the local scene. It would appear that for a brief period around 1848 that trains and stage-coaches worked in conjunction. This is to be seen in the following account of stagecoaches at this time from Merthyr Tydfil which reads:

> "Coaches. From the Castle Inn to London – The Royal Mail through Abergavenny. Brecon. A coach to and from in the summer months daily, after the arrival of the morning trains from Cardiff, and a coach every Saturday, same time through the year".[41]

Pontsarn Railway station (c1912).

The last train on the Abergavenny-Merthyr line Sunday 5th January 1958.

THE BRECON, NEWPORT AND MERTHYR RAILWAY

This was one of the most important railway lines in South Wales since it offered the most direct route to Mid-Wales. The Brecon and Merthyr line opened from Pant to Talybont and Brecon in March-April 1863. The branch from Pontsticill towards Merthyr was brought into service as for as Cefn Coed-y-Cymer on 1st August 1867. The first through passenger train from Brecon into Merthyr itself (Vale of Neath Station) ran on 1st August 1868 and on 23rd June 1869 the branch from Pant to Dowlais came into full operation. The Rev Jenkins greeted this latest form of transport in Vaynor thus, "today, with its Pontsarn and Coed Cymmer and its twenty one passenger trains coming and going daily, Vaynor is in the world and the world comes to Vaynor".[42]

How right he was – on the first Sunday (4th August 1867) of the branch service from Pontsticill and again on the following Thursday, with early closing in the Merthyr-Dowlais area, the station at Cefn was "besieged" with intending visitors to Pentwyn reservoir. During the first month after opening of the branch from Pontsticill to 'Cefn Coed Y Cymmer'. 9,000 tickets were issued mainly to Dôlygaer. Trains ran from Merthyr to Dôlygaer at intervals of half an hour for the regatta of 24th June 1869. On this occasion there were 1,200 passengers from Cefn Coed alone for the fishing, the steamer, the boating, rustic sports such as quoits, pole-leaping and foot races and "Moreover the services had been engaged of the celebrated Harpist, Mr W. Frost". The average attendance for a regatta was 6,000-10,000 visitors in 1867.[43] With the dramatic fall in passenger and freight traffic after Word War II, the Abergavenny-Merthyr line was finally closed on Sunday January 5th 1958, and the last train from Merthyr to Pontsticill ran on Saturday 11th November 1961.

The last train from Merthyr to Pontsticill junction Saturday 11th November 1961.

TRAM CARS

The Merthyr Tydfil Light Railway was constructed in 1899 and was opened on Good Friday, 6th April 1901. It was run by the Merthyr Electric Traction and Lighting Co Ltd and operated 16 Narrow Gauge Electric Tramcars. There were three lines: No. 1 from Cefn Bridge to the Bush Inn, Dowlais; No. 2 from Pontmorlais Circus to Graham Street, Merthyr Tydfil and No. 3 which was a small line connecting lines No. 1 and No. 2. Originally Tramcar Railway Line No. 1 started at a point about twenty metres east of Cefn bridge but was later extended to the terminus in Cefn Coed at the Morning Sun Inn. First there were single decked vehicles then later double-decked trams were added to the service. The trams ran from 5.15 a.m. to 10.15 p.m. and the fare in 1901 was two pence from Cefn Bridge to Merthyr. The service served the Borough from 1901 until August 1939.

The first tram car over Cefn Bridge (c1910).

The tram car at the Morning Sun Inn Terminus c1937. Mr Emlyn Watkins and his cousin Mr Tom Jones are on the left of the picture.

By courtesy of Merthyr Central Library, Merthyr Tydfil

The last tram leaving the Morning Sun Inn, Cefn Coed, August 23rd 1939. (Mrs Marie Morris licensee of the Morning Sun is standing in the back row.

Re-laying tramlines at Cefn Coed, 1914.

By courtesy of Merthyr Tydfil Central Library

After 38 years of service during which time an estimated 85 million passengers had been carried and over eight million car miles travelled the Merthyr Electric Tramcars ceased to run at midnight August 23rd 1939. The author was among dozens aboard the last tram from Cefn Coed to Merthyr on that night, while thousands of local residents lined the streets and souvenir hunters stripped the trams of lamps and destination boards. From August 1939 the Merthyr Municipal Omnibus Department operated the bus service from Merthyr Tydfil to Cefn Coed at alternative times to Mr D. J. Davies who ran a private bus service.

Since the end of World War II tractors have replaced horses on local farms, horse drawn vehicles used for conveying coal, beer, refuse, milk, vegetables and fruit have been replaced by the lorry and van; people are conveyed by buses, private cars or taxis. There were a host of delightful local characters associated with particular trades and occupations. I refer of course to Mr Will Morgan (the milk), Mr Hancock (refuse), Mr Tom Francis and Mr John Francis, Mr Morgan (Vaynor Villas), Mr Joe Mainwaring, Mathias Thomas, Danny Morris and the England family of Joe, Fred and Alfie who were coster mongers. Mr Robert Lewis, far better known to Cefnites as 'Bob the Chauffeur' was for many years chauffeur to Col Sir John Jones, Fronheulog and later ran a taxi service as did his brother-in-law Mr Gwilym James.Both Mr Lewis and Mr James took inordinate pride in their gleaming Rolls Royce cars.

Mr Robert Lewis, chauffeur to Col J. J. Jones TD, JP of Fron Heulog, Cefn Coed.

By courtesy of Mrs Beryl Lewis, Cefn Coed

Mr Gwilym James and Mr Robert Lewis (Bob the chauffeur) with their Rolls Royce taxis at a wedding at St John's Church, Cefn Coed c1955.

By courtesy of Mrs Mona James and Mrs Beryl Lewis, Cefn Coed

REFERENCES

1. W. MORGAN (Pant), The Illustrated Vaynor Hardbook (1893) p.32.
2. B. P. RICHARDS, The Roman Period. Pamphlet of the Cefn Coed and Vaynor Local History Society. P.4.
3. CANON REV JONES DAVIES, Presidential Address Report from Arch: Camb: CXIVV, 1975, p4-5.
4. J. E. JENKINS, Vaynor: Its History and Guide, (1893), p.35.
5. J. E. JENKINS, op. cit., p.5.
6. W. MORGAN, op. cit., p.126.
7. W. MORGAN, op. cit., p.32.
8. W. MORGAN, op. cit., p.30.
9. Vaynor, Summary of indictment against parishioners for failing to repair their section of the Highway. C. 1804 (Sessions S1/2/1/223).
10. B. H. MALKIN, 'The Scenery, Antiquities and Biography of South Wales' (1803).
11. THEOPHILUS JONES, 'History of Brecknockshire' (1809), p.475.
12. W. MORGAN (Pant), op. cit. p.124.
13. TOM LEWIS, 'Notable dates in the History of the Parish of Vaynor' Cefn Coed and Vaynor Local History Society (1958) p.2.
14. J. E. JENKINS, op. cit., p.35.
15. J. E. JENKINS, op. cit., p.156.
16. J. E. JENKINS, op. cit., p.156.
17. DEWI DAVIES, 'Breconshire Historian' (1977), p.16.
18. TOM LEWIS, 'Old Characters' Part 1 (Cefn Coed and Vaynor Local History Society) (2958) p.11.
19. T. E. CLARK, A Guide to Merthyr Tydfil, p.39.
20. J. E. JENKINS, op. cit., pp. 148-154.
21. J. E. JENKINS, op. cit., p.108.
22. H. B. MALKIN referred by W. MORGAN (Pant), op. cit., p.33.
23. THEOPHILUS JONES, op. cit., pp.472-476.
24. J. E. JENKINS, op. cit., p.74.
25. W. MORGAN (Pant), op. cit., p.23.
26. GERAINT JENKINS, Life and tradition in Rural Wales, p.33.
27. General Survey of the Agriculture of Cardiganshire, p.12.
28. WALTER DAVIES, op. cit., p.208.
29. TOM LEWIS, Hen Dy Cwrdd, Cefn Coed Y Cymmer (1947) p.194.
30. WALTER DAVIES, op. cit. p.208.
31. J. E. JENKINS, op. cit., p.118.
32. J. E. JENKINS, op. cit., p.116.
33. J. E. JENKINS, op. cit., p.125.
34. W. J. WILLIAMS, 'Life in 19th Century Cefn Coed' (Cefn Coed and Vaynor Local history Society) 1958, p.21.
35. J. E. JENKINS, op. cit., p.126.
36. J. E. JENKINS, op. cit.,p.128.
37. T. E. CLARKE, op. cit., p.78.
38. HERBERT WILLIAMS, Stagecoaches in Wales (1977), p.44.
39. Merthyr Guardian, 1836.
40. DEWI DAVIES, op. cit., p.77.
41. T. E. CLARKE, op. cit., p.77.
42. W. MORGAN (Pant), op. cit., p.5.
43. V. J. PARRY, Brecon and Merthyr Railway (1970) p.55.

CHAPTER VI

Religion

INTRODUCTION

The migration of people into the industrialised areas of the borders of Breconshire and Glamorgan and Monmouthshire helped to determine the patterns of religious adherence and practice and also produced communities of people radically different from the valleys of Breconshire or the upland areas. These overlays of new people were richer; uninhibited by the constraints of a traditional society but oftentimes adapting painfully and violently to the cultural norms of the populous new urban towns, such as Merthyr Tydfil or dormitory villages such as Cefn Coed.

When we examine the religious background of Breconshire we find that this county evinced no great enthusiasm for either side during the Civil War. The King spent the night of August 5th 1645 with Col Herbert Price at Brecon Priory but by November the Breconshire gentry signed a declaration affirming that they believed Parliament to be the "Supreme Court of Judicature"[1] and to be legally engaged in a defensive war. There was growing evidence in Breconshire of the reformation of religion already initiated in other parts of the kingdom. Among those ejected by the Committee for Scandalous Ministers and the Committee of Plundered ministers were two local men, Josias Morgan of Vaynor and Thomas Rowell of Cantref.[2] Under the Act for the Better Propagation and Preaching of the Gospel in Wales the Rev Andrew Watkins, Vicar of Penderyn was ejected while Reginald Morgan was settled in Vaynor.[3] With the restoration of the King however in 1660 Reginald Morgan had to yield Vaynor to Owen Griffiths. In his 1665 returns Bishop Lucy named five schools in the county and Owen Griffiths was among those licensed to teach in their respective parishes.

With the Declaration of Indulgence 1671/7 dissenters were to be given complete freedom subject to the proviso that they should license their places of worship. When Archbishop Gilbert Sheldon ordered a census to be taken of nonconformists he found 4,245 in Wales, 681 in Breconshire and 110 in Vaynor. Among the elders of Henry Maurice's church at Llanigon was a former Parliamentary captain named David Williams. In 1669 he was a teacher of conventicles at Merthyr Tydfil that ranged "in numbers of their hearers from 300 to 600".[5] Wilkins has stated that Maurice was the first minister of Cwmyglo Chapel near Heolgerrig, Merthyr where he served from 1672 until his death in 1682. Throughout the sixties the Brecon Consistory Court kept a sharp look-out for nonconformist activities and the presentations at Bishop Lucy's Triennial Visitation at St Mary's, Brecon on the 24th October 1665 revealed 32 offenders for "Nonconformity" and 65 for "not attending church". Three of the former were from Vaynor and when 302 were presented for ex-communication at St Mary's, Brecon on 27th October 1668, 13 were from Vaynor. On July 14th 1685 among those who had to appear at the Sessions were Samuel Edwards, Yeomen, Penderyn and Maud Howells and Elena Morgan of Merthyr Tydfil.[7] At the Quarter Sessions held in January 1686 the following persons from Vaynor were presented for "not coming to the Church for three Sundays past", namely "Thomas John Watkins and Gwenllian his wife, Richard Roberts and Gwenllian his wife, Richard ap John and Matilda his wife, David Richard, Margaretta Rees and Margaretta Meredith".8 The Act of Toleration of 1689 allowed dissenters freedom to worship on condition that their meeting places were licensed. Among those granted a licence locally were Gladis John of Vaynor, the house of Thomas Howell of Vaynor and the house of "Noyadd Y Nantddu Cantref, Cwm-Taf".[9]

Tom Lewis in 'Hen Dŷ Cwrdd Cefn Coed Y Cymmer' traces the development of Nonconformity in the parish of Vaynor from Commonwealth times.[10] He refers to Tomos Llewelyn who around 1540 translated Tyndale's English translation of the New Testament into Welsh. He was licensed to preach in Elizabeth's times and formed religious societies in north Glamorgan. Tom Lewis refers to the early meetings of dissenters first at Blaencanaid Farm from the early 1600s and later at Cwmyglo in 1640 prior to moving to a clearing in the wood at Cefn Coed where Sion Llewelyn and others built the Hen Dŷ Cwrdd Chapel in 1747. He mentions the various Acts of Parliament enacted against the early dissenters such as the Corporation Act of 1661 which in effect prevented any Nonconformists taking part in local government. Later in 1662 with the passing of the Act of Uniformity which compelled all clergy to use the revised Prayer Book, two thousand clergy refused to obey and were ejected from their livings. From 1664 the Conventicle Act forbade more than five persons to assemble for worship except to the requirements of the Anglican Church. With the passing of the Five Mile Act in 1665 no Nonconformist was allowed to teach, preach or settle within five miles of any town or parish in which he had previously had a Church living. In 1689 the Toleration Act was passed and the dissenters were now granted religious freedom, however this Act only applied to those who subscribed to the Trinitarian faith.

The early congregations met in private houses, farms and public houses and in the space of fifty years seven chapels were built in the parish of Vaynor – two at the same time at Carmel (1844) and Tabor (1845). The extant chapel registers indicate substantial congregations with the Sunday School fulfilling an extremely important function in teaching young people to read prior to the establishment of day schools. In 1848 we find that Tabor, Carmel and Ebenezer Sunday Schools had 498 scholars and 86 teachers between them and this popularity continued. Fifty years later we still find that these combined chapels had 520 scholars and 81 teachers,[11] while the Anglican Church at Cefn Coed had at this time 160 scholars and 23 teachers attending its Sunday School.

In addition to the morning and evening services at the Nonconformist Chapels and Sunday Schools,[12] there were week-night meetings which often included such activities as Band of Hope, Bible Study, Singing School, drama or literary meetings. The Communion was held monthly and conducted by the minister who was also responsible for pastoral care, baptisms, burials and weddings. From the ranks of the deacons the officers of the church such as Treasurer or Secretary were chosen. In looking back over two centuries of Nonconformity in Vaynor it is very difficult to fully appreciate the immense contribution made by the Chapels of Vaynor towards consolidating Welsh culture, in stimulating a love of religious oratory, music, and of fostering Education and what is called "the Welsh way of life". Most importantly too Nonconformity gave the language a new status by making it the language of religion. Now with only Bethel Chapel, Cwm Tâf, Hen Dŷ Cwrdd, Carmel and the Pentecostal Chapel the continuation of Nonconformity here, as in other parts of Wales is uncertain and conditional upon a fresh glimpse "of the land beyond the clouds of time".

REFERENCES
1. From R. T. TUDOR JONES. "Religion in Post Restoration Breconshire 1660-1688". Brycheiniog, VIII (1962), p.11.
2. V. HERBERT and J. C. MORRICE. Wales in the seventeenth century (Bangor 1918) p.297.
3. Relgions Developments in Wales, 1645-1662 (London, 1923).
4. C. WILKINS. The History of Merthyr Tydfil (1867) p.90.
5. Llandaff 1669 Returns in G. LYON TURNER. Original Records.I.46. He is there called CAPTAIN HARRY WM THOMAS.
6. C. WILKINS op. cit., p.173.
7. Quarter Sessions Order Book 1685-1713 F.3-5.
8. Quarter Sessions Order Book Volume I. 1686-1713 f.10.
9. Quarter Sessions Order Book Volume I. 1685-1713.
10. TOM LEWIS. Hen-Dŷ-Cwrdd, Cefn Coed Y Cymmer (1947) p.16.
11. T. E. CLARKE. A Guide to Merthyr Tydfil. (1848) p.64.
12. A. REES. Life in the Welsh Countryside. (1951) p.120.

VAYNOR CHURCHES

(St Gwynno's, Vaynor; St John's, Cefn Coed & St Tudor's, Cefn Coed)

For many centuries, the chief centre of communal interest in every parish has been the Parish Church, which for this parish is St Gwynno's at Vaynor. Theophilus Jones, the Breconshire historian suggested that the original church here was built in 844, while the late Tom Lewis[2] appears to agree with Rev J. E. Jenkins[3] who claimed that St Gwynno's Church was built in 874 and was consecrated by Llunwerth the thirtieth Bishop of St David's and dedicated to St Gwendoline. Before proceeding with the

Vaynor Old Church (as it was in its last stages in 1865).

history of the Church, perhaps one should consider the controversy associate with the dedication.

Commenting on this the Rev Jones-Davies stated, "There is no doubt at all about the patron saint of Vaynor. The Church belongs to Gwynno and it is he and no one else who deserves the credit for being the first to make the name of Christ known in this locality. Gwendoline as a false alternative goes back over two hundred years and can be traced to Ecton who made such a hash of Welsh place names in his famous Thesaurus. Ecton himself would not have made much damage but when he was copied by Browne Willis in his 'Parochiale Anglicanum' in 1733, there were all sorts of possibilities of dire consequences for the patron saint of Vaynor".[4]

Theophilus Jones writing in 1880, found that dedication to Gwendoline strange since he claimed that there was no such saint. He guessed that it might be "Gwenfrewy" (Wenefred) but it would appear that since Willis was a more famous hagiologist than Theophilus Jones, his view carried the greater weight. As a result, the Ordnance Survey Map of 1891 gave the name of "St Gwendoline" to Vaynor Church, and more recently the Official Handbook of the Church in Wales (1939) also gave the dedication of Vaynor Church to St Gwendoline. As Canon Silas Harris, who received his early education at the "Pensteps Academy" of the Hen Dŷ Cwrdd Chapel has pointed out, the draft of consecration for the new church of Vaynor built in 1870, which is among the documents of the Diocese of St David's deposited at the National Library, Aberystwyth has "Gwynno" written over the cancelled name Gwendoline. Thus the ancient dedication was safeguarded and the new church continued securely under the patronage of Gwynno.[5]

Among the Harley Charters in the British Museum dated 1387/8 there is a reference to this place as "the parish of Guinaw" (i.e. Gwynno). Another drawn up at Vaynor (maenor Wyno) and dated October 20th 1481 speaks of the parish of "St Gwynno" (parochial Santi Gwynoci) and a similar charter of 1523 has "the parish of Maynor Weyno".

While it is very difficult to be certain in these matters, the fact that Gwynno has survived for centuries on the lips of the Vaynor people themselves does strongly suggest that Gwynno is the patron saint of Vaynor. It is also the form of the name that occurs in the earliest surviving documents, i.e. of 1387/8. Furthermore, it appears as if he is the same person as the patron saint of Llanwonno or Llanwynno in Glamorgan and also one of the three saints of Llantrisant in the same county.

St Gwynno's Church, Vaynor as it appeared in 1856.

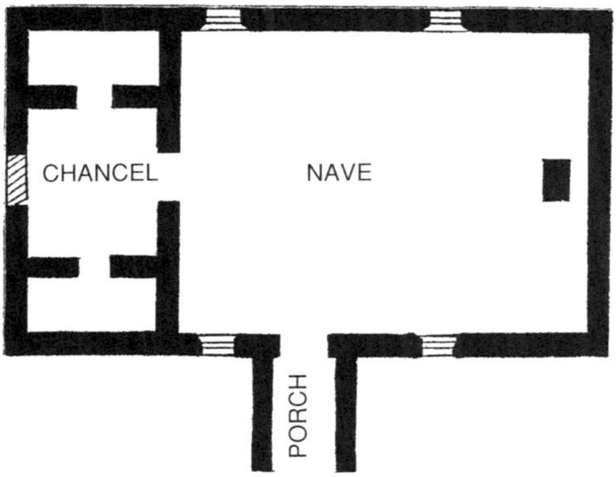

Plan of Vaynor Church

Tower of the old Vaynor Church.

The medieval espiscopal registers of the Diocese of St David's (of which Vaynor formed a part) provide the same witness over and over again. In 1401 and 1402 the Church of Vaynor is referred to as "ecclesia parochialis de Vaynor Weyno" (parish church of 'Kaenor Wynno'). Similarly, a document of the year 1488 has the heading: 'Ecclesia de Vaynor Wyno' and this form recurs thrice in this entry. In 1515 the same form (Vaynor Wino) appears twice in the same way. Not only is the parish name which embodies that of its Saint thus frequently found, but there is also express testimony to the true dedication of the church. An entry dated August 29th 1486, under the heading "Ecclesia Sancti Wynnocu alias de Vaynor" (the church of St Gwynno, otherwise Vaynor) tells us that the parish church of Vaynor is that of St Gwynno ("ecclesia parochialis Sancti Gynnoci de Vaynor').

The Rev J. E. Jenkins makes the claim that the first church was burned down in 1291 on St Thomas's Day at the Battle of Maesyfaenor. This popular history of the church is derived from a cywydd and the account of the burning of the church is found here:

> "Allor, ulw, llan rhyw elyn
> Dial Ior am Faenor fyn."[5]

So far, the author of the cywydd has eluded the searches of scholars. It is obviously important in the story of Vaynor and may well account for the supposed Battle of Maesyfaenor and the burning of Vaynor Church. The Rev Jones-Davies has referred to contemporary evidence for the burning of Penderyn Church in 1290/1 but not of Vaynor Church. He also notes "with what detail the events of that period have been recorded (Rollo, i, 70, Rat.Fin. 20. Edward I) and the strange thing is that there is no mention at all of a battle as having been fought on 21st December".

J. E. Jenkins states that a second church was built in 1295 and the tower still stands. According to Theophilus Jones the Breconshire County historian writing in 1809 this church was "low and dark, the roof not ceil'd, the floor of earth uneven, the seats decayed and irregular".[6] The ruins of this old church appear to be within an ancient circular enclosure.

A glance at the photograph taken about 1865 shows that the old church was of modest proportions. The roughly-hewn uncomfortable seats in the old church belonged to the principal farmhouses. Pews were the prerogative of the gentry or substantial farmers, while the benches were for the aged. The benches could be easily moved when required to open a grave for the clergy or the gentry. The peasantry were buried outside. The Rev J. E. Jenkins contends that the tower is a relic of the first church since it is architecturally superior to either the nave or chancel.

With the exception of one stone lying in the nave of the old church the inexorable tread of time has made the memorials laid inside the old church almost indecipherable. There is the stone to the memory of "William Watkins rector of this parish ... died April 1704 aged 43". The stone bears the coat of arms of the famous Breconshire family, the "Herberts of Penkelly" but Theophilus Jones expressed doubt as to whether the deceased rector had a legitimate claim to use it.

Interesting details of the old church membership are provided by the 1851 Religious Census which states

> "Vaynor Parish County Brecon. Diocesse of St David's
> Endowed: tithes commuted at £260, glebe 27 acres,
> Space free 42, others 72.
> Present morning 80: Afternoon school 14, evening 90.
> Average morning 100: afternoon 33, evening 130.
> Remarks. Church attendance at this time of year is never good, the farmers being more engaged than usually, their

> cattle requiring more care this time of year than any other time. Rees Williams, Rector.
> Lewis: rectory rated at £8.3s.1½d (£8.16) and in the patronage of the crown, gross income £292 arising from tithes producing £260 and glebeland £32. C and C: One service in Welsh performed by the incumbent I and C incumbent resident curate's stipend £90".[7]

In the year 1867 the old Church became so dilapidated and unsafe that the Rector and Church wardens decided to build a new church. Seven hundred pounds were quickly subscribed and arrangements had been made to build a new church when Robert Thompson Crawshay offered to build the new church provided that the subscriptions already collected would be handed over to be devoted towards building a "church at Coed-cymmer". A letter dated September 3rd 1884 written by R. T. Crawshay's son, William T. Crawshay (1847-1918) to the Rector of Vaynor confirms this. While the new church was being built, a licence to hold divine services and to administer the Sacraments at the National Schoolroom at Pontsticill was granted by Bishop Thirlwall. The cost of the new church was £1,368 and was borne by R. T. Crawshay.

On the 1st June 1870 the new church was consecrated and opened by Dr Ollivant, Lord Bishop of Llandaff, in the absence of Dr Thirlwall, Lord Bishop of St David's, who was indisposed. The morning sermon was preached by the Venerable Richard William Payne Davies, Archdeacon of Brecon (St Luke vii,5); the Rev Canon Evans, vicar of Rhymney preached in the afternoon. He preached in the open air "not far from the east side of the Tower was a thousand people before him" (from Corinthians v. 5). The evening preacher was Rev David Parry (Llywel) his text was from Colossians 1, 28. The Church wardens at this time were "Mr Richard Williams, Bryn Rhys Farm, Vaynor and Mr Evan Lewis, Coedycymmer. The choir leader was Mr David Lewis, Pant-cad-Ivor and the choir sang the anthem "Dyrchafaf Di, fy Nuw O frenin" by Eos Llechid."

"The living at Vaynor is a Rectory and the Patron was the Lord Chancellor" states Jenkins. Of 57 incumbencies in Breconshire, only 27 exceeded £50 per annum. Vaynor was one of these and it was also listed as a Rectory. Rector Jenkins has published an interesting document called the Terrier which gives details of how the Rector of Vaynor benefitted from his tithes. The original document is at the National Library, Aberys-

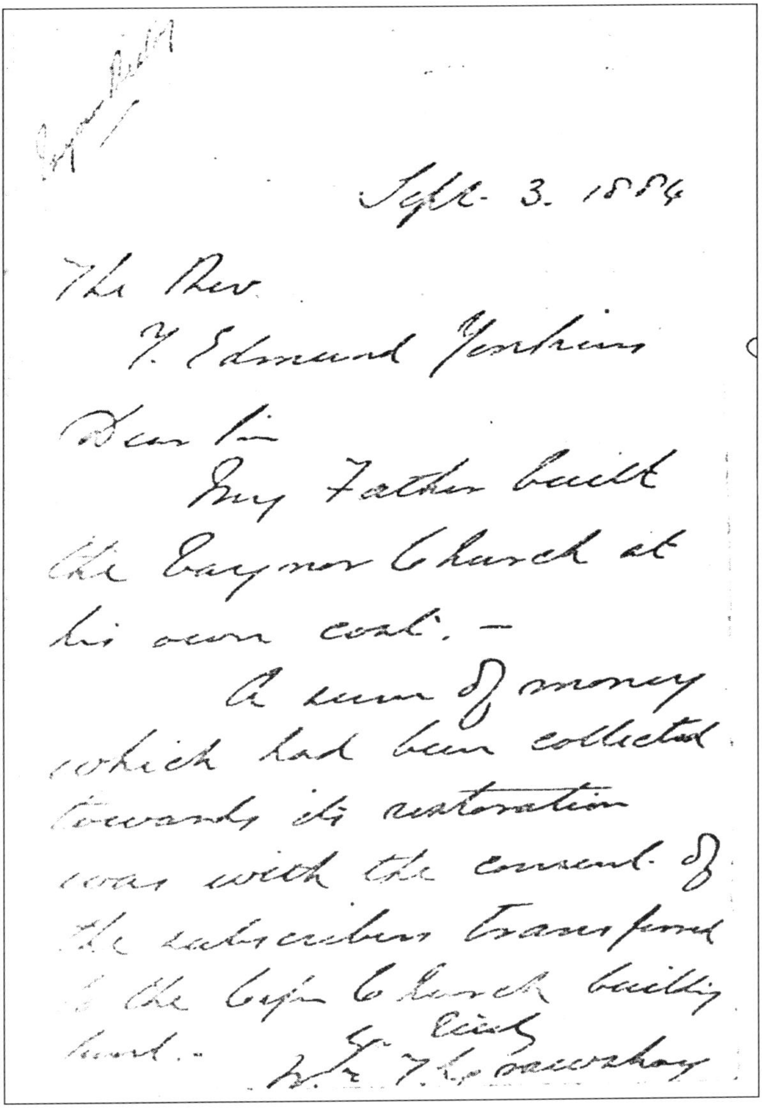

Sept. 3. 1884

The Rev.
J. Edmund Jenkins

Dear Sir

My Father built the Vaynor Church at his own cost.—

A sum of money which had been collected towards its restoration was with the consent of the subscribers transferred to the Cefn Church building fund.—

Yours truly
W. T. Crawshay

A letter from William Thompson Crawshay (1847-1918) to the Rev J. E. Jenkins of Vaynor informing him that his father, the late Mr R. T. Crawshay had built Vaynor Church "at his own cost", and that the money which had been collected for the restoration of Vaynor Church was "with the consent of the subscribers transferred to the Cefn Church building fund".

St Gwynno's Church, Vaynor, rebuilt and completed by 29th May 1869 and consecrated and opened on the 1st June 1870 by Dr Ollivant, Lord Bishop of Llandaff in the absence of Dr Thirlwall, Lord Bishop of St David's.

twyth. He mentions the fact that the old system came to an end on 1st October 1843 when the landowner and rector resolved to adopt the scheme of the Tithe Commutation Act, (6 and 7. Willi. iv. c71). The Terrier itself was a list or description of Glebe lands and tithes drawn up by the Incumbent or Churchwarden of a parish and was a local document.

Church sites are sacred and it is odd that another site was chosen for the new church which was completed on the 29th May 1869. Theophilus Jones has suggested that it was due to the nature of the old site. Whatever the reason it would seem that the parishioners were loath to leave the old site. "It is a thousand pities that it was not restored or rebuilt on the old site" said Rector Jenkins and he goes on to say "the old building, however, was held in such veneration by the people that, for some time after the roof fell in, several weddings took place in it, the last being that of our well known and generous neighbour, Mr Christmas Evans (Six Bells Brewery) and Miss Ann Jones of the Cefn Hotel by licence".[8]

The list of the Rectors of Vaynor is incomplete. Jones the Breconshire Historian mentions Howel Curties as the first rector and the date given by him is 1400. The Rev J. E. Jenkins however as a result of his researches proposed the following list of rectors:-

> "Rhys Ap Rhys 1374; Howel Curteys 1401, Thomas Ap Hywel Ap Madoc 1488; Robert Jenys 1488, Hugh Ap Rhys 1314; Josias Morgan 1609, Owen Griffiths 1660, William Watkins 1688, Howel Powell 1704, Gregory Parry 1749; Edward William 1759; Edward Thomas 1782; John Williams 1782; Morgan Walters 1814; Rees Williams 1839; J. Edmund Jenkins 1883".(p.22).

Since then the rectors have been:

> John Davies 1903; Lewis Davies 1922; Morgan Jones 1925; Chalmers Davies 1944; Gruffydd Beddoe Rees 1950; John Spencer rose 1957; Lewis Evans 1965; David Walters 1980 (also Vicar of Cefn Coed).

Theophilus Jones, Registrar of the Archdeaconry of Brecon virtually growled when referring to the absentee rectors of Vaynor. The Rectory House and glebe land was sub-let to laymen and curates were employed to serve the office at a pittance. Clerical poverty was a permanent problem at this time, about one quarter of the benefices of the established church were worth less than £50 in 1704. Returns for the diocese of St David's in 1708 revealed that half the livings were nominally valued at less than £30 and a quarter at less than £10. The most vulnerable section of the clergy were undoubtedly the curates, virtually all being ill paid and overworked. In St David's diocese it was claimed that "a poor curate must sometimes submit to serve three or four churches for £10 to £12 a year".

Testifying to the poverty of curates at this period is the home of Rev Samuel Morris, curate of Vaynor from 1790. It still stands (No. 1 Bragdy Cottages, Vaynor) having two rooms downstairs and a small stone staircase leading to a single bedroom. Outside, about ten feet up the whitewashed wall is a small elliptical stone carrying the following inscription "Habitabi lis haec domus facta erat. A.D. 1795. Sc. Pr Rev S. Morris".

The natural corollary of clerical poverty was pluralism, non residence and penury. This evoked scorn and contempt by clergymen towards their calling and laymen sometimes referred to them as "sow gelders and ale house keepers". Pluralism i.e. when a clergyman had charge of a number of livings, began in Vaynor in 1755 when Rees Thomas Powell was appointed curate in charge during the incumbency of Gregory Parry, who was rector from 1749 to 1759. This unfortunately remained the pattern of church life in Vaynor until 1839, when Rees Williams who had been the curate in sole charge since 1835, became Rector.

Jenkins lists the curates in charge of Vaynor as follows:

> Rees Thomas Powell 1755; Anthony Martin 1757; Morgan Williams 1776; Philip Charles 1783; Thomas Jones 1790; William Jones 1818 and Rees Williams 1835.[9]

"It appears" said Rector Jenkins, "that some of the old Rectors of this parish had also the charge of other livings and had curates under them, licensed to the several parishes, as the dates shown at the same time, under rules and conditions which, thanks to Providence and the spirit of the age, do not now exist".[10] the Rev Anthony Martin came to Vaynor from Penderyn but held both curacies for some time. The Rev Morgan Williams was Curate of Vaynor and Tave Vechan. "The Rev Samuel Morris was curate of Vaynor, Tave Vechan, Nantddu and Penderyn", at the same time. The Rev William Jones was also curate of "Vaynor, Tave Vechan and Nantddu" at the same time. The Rev Rees Williams came here from the curacy of Ystradfellte and held the curacies of Vaynor and Nantddu up to 1841; and "all this travelling without a nag or a bicycle!" The distances were quite considerable, from "Tave Vechan" to Vaynor was four miles, from Vaynor to Nantddu via Cefn Coed was seven miles and from Nantddu to Penderyn via Cwm Cadlan, about the same distance.

This was the unhappy state of affairs in the life of the Church in Vaynor when the Industrial Revolution started at Merthyr Tydfil. Even in localities where the church was active, its resources were inadequate and in Vaynor where the church was at a low ebb and with the population of Cefn rapidly increasing, the position was virtually disastrous. It was not surprising that Anthony Martin should inform his Bishop in 1759 about the rapid spread of Nonconformity. "Our parishioners," he said "are mostly Dissenters, they will not send their children to be catechised by the minister. But those few who belong to the church, I catechise as often as they come for that purpose".[11]

The Rev J. E. Jenkins claims that "There was a Chapel of Ease under Vaynor Church at Coedycymmer in ancient days in the field between the station and the river (not beyond the river as some say). "Tir-Y-Capel" and "Tir Pont Y Capel" are well known names of two small farms there" (page 135). This cannot be verified because "Tir Pont Y Capel" is shown on the 1842 Tithe Map of the Parish of Vaynor and "Pont Capel" is shown on Emmanuel Bowen's map of 1760. Does "Pont Capel", refer to a church here or to the Jesuit Chapel at Tai Mawr Farm? One clue is the fact that when Cefn Viaduct was being built human remains were found in the vicinity of "Tir Pont-Y-Capel". Tom Lewis (Mab-y-Mynydd) writing in 1914 stated "A Chapel-of-ease (Capel anwes) once stood near the bridge. Now there seems to be a consensus of opinion on which spot the old sanctuary stood. I have spoken to nearly all of Cefn's oldest people on the matter and some of them are certain in their own minds that it stood just underneath the forth arch of the viaduct coming from the Cefn side of the river".

Rector Jenkins provides further valuable information on the early church at Cefn Coed. As he states, "For ages after the Old Chapel of Ease above the river became a heap of ruins, the incumbents thought that Coedcymmer was near enough to the mother church of Vaynor for all religious purposes. The great "Jones of Vaynor, who came as a curate in 1818, very soon after his advent to the parish began to hold services at the Old Gate House, and afterwards at a house at Cefn Isaf, and ultimately built what was called the Old Chapel of Ease or Capel Ffeiriad (Priest's Chapel)". There is an interesting account in the Merthyr Guardian of 24th August 1833 relevant to the above which states "New Chapel at Coed-Y-Cymer. The Lord Bishop of Llandaff anxious to provide the increased accommodation required for the performance of divine service in the populous district of Coed Y Cymar which is situated three miles from the parish church, has licensed a newly erected schoolroom to be used as a Chapel of Ease to the parish of Vaynor. Tomorrow the interesting ceremony of performing, for the first time divine worship in this chapel on which occasion the Rev William Jones of Vaynor will officiate".

It is of interest to note that the Bishop of Llandaff performed this ceremony although Vaynor parish was apparently later in the diocese of St David's. One notes too that in June 1870 the Lord Bishop of Llandaff (in the absence of Dr Thirlwall, Lord Bishop of St David's who was indisposed) consecrated and opened the new church at Vaynor.

Rector Jenkins adds colourful details regarding the officers and members of the Old Chapel of Ease (Capel Ffeiriad). As he states "Rhys Jones was the first chapel clerk ... He was succeeded by Nathanial Jones, a good useful man. Other members were Thomas Williams, Shop Vach; David and Ann Davies (clochydd); Thomas John whose son died in India; John Thomas a native of Llanfynydd, a church warden and secretary of the Sunday School ... John Lewis (Goch) led the singing".12

The Religious Census[13] of 1851, Volume 1 p 181-182 gives the following information about "The Cefn Coed Cymmer Licensed Schoolroom. Licensed 1833. Erected by private subscription altogether at a total cost of £150. It had not been endowed. The Curate is supported by the Local Aid Society. The grant is £100. Space: benches 35 (total sittings 210). Present: morning 112. Afternoon school 123. Evening 202. Averages: morning 130, afternoon school 150. Evening 230. William Roberts Curate Gwernllwyn, Dowlais".

By 1867 the Old Church was showing signs of dilapidation and it was decided to form a committee to strive for the building of a new Church. As a result of their dedicated efforts a new church was built and according to the Rev J. E. Jenkins "the first service in St John's Church Cefn Coed was held in the evening of April 20th 1874 and on the following day it was formally opened by the Venerable Archdeacon of Llandaff". He adds that "St John's Church was consecrated by the Lord Bishop of St Davids on S.S. Simon and Jude's Day October 28th 1885. Towards the end of 1888, the Old Chapel of Ease (Capel Ffeiriad) was demolished, rebuilt and renamed 'St Tudor's'. St Tudor's was opened on the 27th and 28th of March 1889" and taken down in 1936 for the construction of the School gymnasium of Vaynor and Penderyn Secondary School.

St John's Church, Cefn Coed (c1945).

ST JOHN'S BELL RINGING SOCIETY, CEFN COED (c1930)

Back Row: *Mr G. W. Reed, Mr W. E. Thomas, Mr G. Ablart, Mr J. Gould.* ***Second Row:*** *Mr T. Davies, Mr E. Woosley, Mr A. E. Williams, Mr C. V. Chappell, Mr K. Gough, Mr C. W. S. Thomas.* ***Front Row:*** *Captain J. F. Thomas, Mr A. Hunt (Captain), Rev Lewis Davis, Mr I. Read (Vice Captain) Mr E. W. Read.* ***Seated:*** *Mr J. Rees (Secretary), Mr W. Chappell (Treasurer).*

More buildings meant more clergy and in 1845 the Rector of Vaynor was given an assistant curate. By 1906 there were two assistant curates receiving stipends of £120 and £110, while the gross income of the living in that year came to £246.10s.0d (£246.50) made up of £180, the value of the Annexed Tithe Rent Charge commuted at £263.10s.0d (263.50), £60 rent on the old Rectory farm and house and other lands, and £6.10s.0d (£6.50) ground rent from Derwen Cottage and Derwen Lodge. The value of the living in 1809 was £123.15s.0½d (£123.75) arising from composition for tithes, glebe and surplice fees, while in 1835 the gross value was £170, net value £88 with a glebe house unfit for residence. The old Rectory House was rebuilt in 1870.

The Rev J. E. Jenkins also mentions that "there was another Chapel of Ease, with a burial ground attached four miles higher up "in the Tave

St John's Church, Cefn Coed.

Vawr Valley at Abercar, in the same parish" (p.135). He further adds "Very interesting ruins of this chapel can be seen at present".[13] The very ancient origins of this church can be seen in the fact that no less than four Latin inscribed monuments have been found nearby in the Taf Fawr Valley, i.e. the Nant Crew monument discovered by Mr D. P. Webley in 1957, the Nantddu monument and the two discovered by Iolo Morgannwg in the Abercar beast house. In addition, two prehistoric incinerary urns were discovered at Abercar in 1859 by Mr Henry Thomas of Coedcymmer and were put on exhibition in the Cefn Coed Y Cymer Library in 1865".

It is very interesting to discover from the Rev J. E. Jenkins that there had once been an ancient chapel of ease under Faenor at Abercar Farm, Cwm Tâf. It is not however shown on any of the old maps back to Speed in 1578, neither is it mentioned in 'Parochiale Walliacanum', whereas Chapel Nantddu, a mile north of Abercar, which came under Cantref is mentioned there, as it is also mentioned by Holinshed ('Capel Nantee') in the sixteenth century.

St Mary's Church, Nantddu 1930.

By courtesy of MRS MONICA EVANS, JP of Cefn Coed, formerly of Coedowen Farm, Cwm Tâf

The altar at St Mary's Church, Nantddu c1930.

By courtesy of MRS MONICA EVANS, JP Cefn Coed

Some reference perhaps should, be made to Nantddu Church (St Mary's) Cwm Tâf Fawr and to Tâf Fechan Church in the Tâf Fechan Valley although both churches are actually just outside the parish boundaries of Vaynor. There is ample evidence to show that St Mary's Nantddu has been in existence since the earliest times but no precise information as to its foundation. The 1851 Religious Census provides the following information regarding the Church:- "Cantref Parish consisting of Cantref and Nant Ddu Chapelry. Area 20,000 acres. Population 124 males, 113 females. Nant Ddu Chapelry population 64 miles, 53 females, total 119. Endowed land £77.10s.0d (£77.50) permanent endowment £21.10s.0d (£31.50). Space others 10. Present afternoon 30. John Rogers Minster. Lewis: perpetual curacy, endowed with £1000 royal bounty. net income £60, patron rector of Cantref (600.3. 14 [22]), impropriator Rev W. Williams the incumbent. C and C: 1 service performed by the curate: Incumbent not resident. Curate has stipend of £57. Accommodation 55".

Nantddu as it appeared in 1817. The St Mary's Church appears to be behind the trees while the building seen on the roadside appears to be on the site of the Tredegar Arms Inn. A string of pack mules may be seen on the road.

By courtesy of the National Library of Wales)

With regard to Tâf Fechan Chapel of Ease, the following information was presented by the 1851 Religious Census.[14] "Endowed land £80. Space free 72. Present morning 40, David Jones Officiating Minister. Lewis sub Llanddetty; perpetual curacy endowed with £800 royal bounty and £200 parliamentary grant. C and C. One service in Welsh, performed by the incumbent. I and C: not resident".

Capel Tâf Fechan built to replace the older Church which was demolished for the making of the Pontsticill reservoir in 1927.

REFERENCES

1. THEOPHILUS JONES, History of the County of Brecknock (1809) pp. 472-477.
2. TOM LEWIS, 'Topographical Sketch of Vaynor' (Vaynor and Cefn Local History Society) (1958) p.6.
3. REV J. E. JENKINS, Vaynor: Its History and Guide (1897) p.8.
4. REV JONES DAVIES, Brecon and Radnor Express, Sept 1st 1966.
5. REV JONES DAVIES ibid August 25th 1966.
6. THEOPHILUS JONES op. cit., p.473.
7. The Religious Census of 1851. A Calendar of the Returns Relating to Wales. Volume 1 p.181.182.
8. REV J. E. JENKINS, Vaynor p.13.
9. Ibid p.25.
10. Ibid p.25.
11. REV JONES DAVIES, Brecon and Radnor Express, August 25th 1966.
12. J. E. JENKINS, op. cit p.128.
13. Religious Census of 1851, op. cit., pp. 181-182.
14. Ibid, p.181-182.

THE CHAPELS OF THE PARISH OF VAYNOR

HEN DŶ CWRDD, CEFN COED

(Built 1747, rebuilt 1853 and later in 1894)

As Tom Lewis has stated "The Hen-Dŷ-Cwrdd is an offshoot of Cwmyglo which in turn was an off-shoot of Blaencannaid".[1] Blaencannaid was, and still is, a lonely farmstead situated about a mile south of Penheolgerrig, Merthyr Tydfil. Dissenters in the seventeenth century were then persecuted and as a result, here and there is sequestered homesteads a few yeomen farmers and craftsmen held secret meetings in order to worship according to their conscience. Undeterred by threats of punishment and high fines, these defiant and courageous individuals worshipped their God. The dissenters worshipped at Blaencannaid from around 1642 and later at Cwmyglo about half a mile away.

Blaencannaid Farm, Penheolgerrig, Merthyr Tydfil, early meeting place of the dissenters.

While it is claimed that sentinels were posted on the high ground to warn the worshippers of impending danger, there is no evidence as to whether the dissenters were actually maltreated at Cwmyglo. Significantly, however, three of the fields in the vicinity are known even today as "Cae watch" (Watching field), "Maes Y Gwaed" (The Meadow of Blood) and "Cae Dial" (The field of vengence). The name of one of the sentinels has been identified as that of Edward Harri (Harri o'r Gurnos) son of the "minister" of Blaencanaid, Edward Harri who was born at Cwmyglo in 1694 and died in 1800 aged 106 years.

The Cwmyglo barn was used as a conventicle for about fifty years. In 1689 the Toleration Act was passed and at last the dissenters were now free to proclaim their faith freely. The Armenians (Unitarians), however, were still in spiritual bondage. Their freedom did not come until twenty four years later because the Toleration Act only applied to those who subscribed to the Trinitarian Creed. The dissenters of Cwmyglo relinquished the old barn and built a chapel close by.

Cwmyglo Chapel, Penheolgerrig, Merthyr Tydfil c1690.

Little is known of those who first ministered to the little flock at Cwmyglo. Vague references are made to Vavasor Powell. The first minister of Cwmyglo of whom there appears to be authentic knowledge was the Rev Henry Maurice, a Presbyterian who was the pastor of the combined Presbyterian churches of Breconshire and North Glamorgan. His pastorage lasted from 1672 until his death in 1682. He was succeeded by the Rev Roger Williams in 1698. In addition to being a minister of Cwmyglo he was also in charge of a society in Cefn Arthen in Carmarthenshire. He was assisted by the Rev James Davies of Llanwrtyd and both Calvinism and Arminianism were expounded from the same pulpit.

When the Rev Roger Williams died in 1730, he was replaced by the Rev Richard Rees of Gwernllwyn, Dowlais, a younger man of exceptional promise and fearless convictions. While the Rev James Davies was of the older school, of theologians and clung to the traditional concept of Calvinism, Richard Rees was of a more recent school of thought. Relations between the two ministers were not cordial and a serious conflict of ideals sooner or later was inevitable. This eventually came in 1747 when the Armenians who lived on the Merthyr side of the Aberdare mountain built the Hen Dŷ Cwrdd at Cefn Coed-y-Cymer. In 1749 the worshippers at Cwmyglo from Aberdare left the old sanctuary and built Hen Dy Cwrdd, Trecynon in 1749. In 1752 Cwmyglo was closed when the remainder of the congregation who were probably Presbyterians left for Ynysgau, Merthyr.

As Tom Lewis has stated "the Hen Dŷ Cwrdd of two hundred years ago was built in a clearing in a wood, denuded of its trees to provide charcoal to smelt iron at Cyfarthfa. The Nonconformist Chapels built in Wales in the seventeenth and eighteenth centuries laid no claim to any form of architectural beauty and the original Hen Dŷ Cwrdd was no exception, for its design was the architectural expression of the convictions, style and taste of the day. The old chapel probably had no fire-place, for, if tradition can be relied upon, a quantity of straw was kept in the "loft" and on wintry nights was scattered on the floor to keep the feet of the congregation warm. The timber used in the construction of the chapel was hewn in the local woods and trimmed by hatchet. The roof was probably thatched with straw or rushes and later stone-tiled because reference is made to one Rees Lodwick ("Carw Coch", Aberdare) who "roofed Hen Dŷ Cwrdd, Coed Y Cymmar in 1792".

The inside walls were treated with an annual application of lime-wash. Reference is made to this in an entry in the Chapel records of June 1842 when "17s 3d (£0.86) was spent on whitewashing the inside of the Meeting House". Apparently a gallery existed in this first chapel because it was reported to the congregation in June 1826 that "the gallery was in need of whitewash and repair" and a special coat of lime was given before the celebrations of the centenary in 1847. The duty of lime washing fell upon Sion Y Gwehydd, the caretaker whose wages were "1s 0d (£0.05) a week".

An interesting account of the centenary celebrations of July 1847 states, "On paying it a visit, we felt transported a long way into the past, and interior told of an age when wear and tear was more in the fashion than ornament and the strong substantial pews, made of oak firm as the conviction of the professors and typical in its duration of the faith professed. Among the auditors our curious eyes singled out a people characteristic and peculiar – genuine remnants of the Celtic tribes, small in stature, round bullet heads, overhanging foreheads, small sunken yet sparkling eyes and diminutive faces, whose whole expression indicated a people of superior intelligence and of a more speculative than practical cast. The chapel was numerously and respectably attended on both days, Wednesday and Thursday, and those who professed this belief reflected with pleasure upon the many changes favourable to religious freedom which have taken place within the last 100 years".[2]

The early chapel was no doubt illuminated at this time by candlelight. The candles, probably made by the chandler living in Field Street, Cefn, were stuck on to a crude wooden chandelier suspended from one of the cross beams. However, in May 1826, in keeping no doubt with contemporary fashion, a sum of 10s 6d (£0.53) was received from "Mr Wayne to have brass candlesticks in the Meeting House". In 1844 "2 snuffers" were purchased for 1s 0d (£0.05) and "two pounds of candles" which also cost 1s 0d. References are made in the chapel records to the financial support provided by the congregation for the maintenance of the original fabric. In 1825 the sum of £12.14s.0d (£12.70) was needed to repair the windows and graveyard wall. In 1826 Mathew Wayne collected £35.17s.6d (£35.88) when seats were "amended", new windows and shutters were installed, a new gate and "hinges" were provided and the "inside walls were pointed and limed". William Williams, watchmaker of Merthyr, who was one of the members of this time gave as a gift, "the shovel's head". Williams was in business at High Street, Merthyr from 1822-35.

By 1852, there was clear evidence in the structure of the old chapel of general decay, and steps were taken to arrange for the building of a new chapel on the site of the old. The contract stipulated that it should be built between the 28th February 1853 and October 1853 at a cost of £434. The architect was John Lewis, Cwm-moel, Glais Valley, Vaynor and the three Cefn Coed contractors were Watkin Meredith, Mason; Thomas Vaughan, Carpenter, and Philip Jones, Plasterer. The new chapel was opened on the 28th and 29th December 1853 and "owing to the cold weather, and the fact that the walls were not yet dry, one sermon instead of two was preached".[3] It is rather remarkable that only forty two years had elapsed before the Chapel again needed complete rebuilding in 1895 at a cost of £750.

Hen Dŷ Cwrdd Unitarian Chapel, Cefn Coed (c1930).

Schools, as we know them today, were practically non-existent. From about 1820 the Hen Dŷ Cwrdd, Cefn Coed, played the most significant part in public education in this district and this is recorded in a later chapter in 'Education in the Parish of Vaynor'. To establish the original date of the Sunday School is very difficult. It would appear from an account given by Tom Lewis that one Catherine Rees was attending a

The interior of Hen Dŷ Cwrdd Unitarian Chapel (c1980).

Sunday School in the Hen Dŷ Cwrdd in 1775, which is actually ten years before Charles o'r Bala inaugurated his famous Sunday School movement in Wales.[3] The first recorded reference in the church ledgers to a Sunday School was made in April 1838 when a "Sunday School Testament" was bought. For some reason, there is no record of a Sunday School, in 1848 but the 1851 Religious Census, while referring to morning and evening services, states "The Sunday Scholars are included in the account.[4] T. E. Clarke in referring to the Hen Dŷ Cwrdd in 1848 stated "Service at 11 and 6. No School".[5]

A concert was held in 1861, the proceeds to be used to buy new Sunday School books. The report of the concert makes interesting reading when it states among other things, that "the books were to be provided so that the children might have an opportunity of learning to read for themselves, instead of having to listen to the preacher all the time". Strangely enough ten of the books bought from the proceeds were written in English. These primers were undoubtedly purchased with a view to imparting to the children, and possibly to the adults also, an elementary knowledge of the English language.

Tom Lewis refers to the principal Sunday School teachers of the 1860s and to the instruction given to the pupils before they eventually were promoted to the "Big Bible Class". He justifiably commends the contribution made by the Sunday School training. Referring to the Unitarians of that period, he states, "Most of them were able to discuss intelligently the meaning and implications of nebulous scriptural verses, and in a theological debate there was hardly a member who could not defend the faith that was in him, in a manner that did him credit".[6] Factual evidence tends to indicate that the first Sunday School Picnic was held about 1870. The Sunday School teachers were unanimous in their opinion that, as a reward for their faithful attendance and as an incentive to continued loyalty, the children should be given a free "outing" to the country. A play entitled, "Theodore Parker", was produced in the chapel to defray the cost of the food. As Tom Lewis has so vividly recorded when he referred to the "happy throng" winding their way to Vaynor with the air rippling with "innocent merriment and reverberating with buoyant laughter. The Marshal was John Davies Y Crydd, and far behind Tomos O'r Coed coaxed an obstinate donkey to pull a heavy load up the steep incline by Clwyd Y Gelli". It was Tomos who was responsible for the conveyance of provisions to the picnic field where men "played quoits, children ran races and young ladies beguiled their time in playing "touch" or "Blind Man's Buff".

Hen Dŷ Cwrdd account books, baptismal and burial registers date from 1800 and as Tom Lewis has commented, "it is amazing to find that the chapel records were kept in English". He has referred to a memorandum found among the chapel records bearing the date 24th June 1827 which states "Names and number that partake of the Lord's Supper at the Old Meeting House, Coed Cymmer 24 June 1827". The list mentions fifty three members from the neighbouring valleys including:- "Matthew Wayne, gent and Mrs Wayne (Aberdare), Mrs Jones Maes Y Faenor, Mr Davies (Mercer Merthyr), Mrs Morgan Gurawen (Grawen, Cwm Tâf), John Williams Penrhiwglais (Faenor), Mary Watkins Ynysfawr (Cwm Tâf), Elizabeth Watkins Goitre, Merthyr, Mrs Davies Dowlais, Sarah Jones Berthlwyd Vaynor, Mary Pencoed, Penderin, Margaret William of Troedyrhiw, Anne Price, widow Aberdare".

The membership of the Hen Dŷ Cwrdd in 1837 was 36 and fifty years later in 1887 it had risen to 81. By 1900 it was 60; in 1910 it had risen to 95 and was up to 129 by 1935. The membership has fallen drastically since 1950 and the present active membership is about 20. Similarly the Sunday School membership has fallen from 159 pupils and 20 teachers in

1939 to about 10 pupils and one teacher at the present time (i.e. 1980).

The Unitarian cause attracted twice as many from the rural valleys of the Tâf Fawr and Tâf Fechan as it did from the industrial town of Merthyr Tydfil. The Chapel catered for these members who came some distance by providing a stable for the horses under the School Room. The 1851 Religious Census provides the following information about the Hen Dŷ Cwrdd membership etc:- "The Old Meeting House. Unitarian. Erected before 1800. Space 23 seats, each contains 7 persons, standing gallery will contain 200. Present morning 113. Evening 84. Average 12 months: Morning 120. Evening 100. Remarks. The Sunday Scholars are included in the account. Owen Evans, Minister".

The Baptismal register shows the number of baptisms in the period 1800-1810 to be the highest recorded. They were as follows: 1800 (24), 1801 (16), 1802 (34), 1803 (21), 1804 (34), 1805 (15), 1806 (23), 1807 (12), 1808 (13), 1809 (8), 1810 (4). Half a century later the number of baptisms was dramatically lower viz: 1850 (0), 1851 (0), 1852 (1), 1853 (0), 1854 (0), 1856 (6), 1857 (7), 1858 (0), 1959 (1), 1860 (5). During the first half of the nineteenth century most of those baptised were from the parish of Vaynor but a considerable number were from "Clwydyfagwyr, Ynysfach, Gurnos, Pantyscallog, Dowlais, Cyfarthfa, Galon Uchaf, Blaencannaid, Caedraw, Twynyrodyn, and Blaennant". Many other children were brought from as far afield as LLanddeti, Penderyn, Bedwellty, Llanelly, Rhymney, Mountain Ash, Llanwynno and Llandysul. The baptismal register for 1800 has interesting entries which throw further light upon the occupational structure of this area and upon customs that would today seem macabre. The following occupations are referred to: "Taylor, weaver, puddler, tiler, mȧson, schoolmaster, clockmaker" and to "William Price, Turnpike of this village". Mr Morien Lewis has pinpointed the position of this Turnpike Gate as between the paper shop and Castle Antiques i.e. around 20 High Street, Cefn Coed. The following entry refers apparently to an old custom "David, son of John Jones of this village, born January 24th was baptised at his mother's funeral in the meeting house February 3rd 1801 by me Thomas Davies".[8.]

The burial records for the nineteenth century are unfortunately incomplete. Again the first decade has rather high figures, for example in 1800 and 1801 there were twenty two burials for each year. The highest number of burials recorded is for the year 1838 which was 63. Many of the deceased were from without the parish, for example from Dowlais and "Gelligare", while others were from Carmarthen and Cardiganshire. The

Hen Dŷ Cwrdd graveyard was the only one at Cefn Coed during the eighteenth century. There is a reference in the chapel records to the first burial at Cefn Coed; it is dated November 2nd 1834 and states "A stone wall piece to the memory of Martha William, on the expense of the congregation 16s 0d (£0.80) and 8s 3d (£0.41). Free Gift of Robert Roberts Stone Cutter this is worth £1.4s.0d (£1.20). This was the first that was buried at Coedycymer from this money the expense paid". There is also reference to "A charity (contribution) towards erecting the stone which was received from Thomas Llewelyn Taylor, late Sergeant in His Majesty's services – 6d".

Foremost among these activities of the nineteenth century were those associated with the musical and religious life of the chapel. Much to the consternation of the local orthodox churches, musical instruments both string and wind were played in the Hen Dŷ Cwrdd in the early days of the nineteenth century. It is of interest to note that in 1860 "Thomas Beynon Blaenor Y Band of Hope" composed a "Polka" and it was known as "Beynon's Polka". In 1872 the Hen Dŷ Cwrdd adopted the Tonic Solfa system. The members were taught to read the modulator by a Miss Jones of Lampeter, a Unitarian who visited Cefn Coed for a week and devoted the evenings to teaching the members of the Chapel how to read the modulator. So blessed was the membership in musical talent that two choirs from the Chapel competed against each other in the Pontsticill Eisteddfod of 1880. A popular musical event in their chapel seventy years ago was the annual Eisteddfod. It was held on New Year's Eve, and was preceded by a tea in the school room. Iolo Morgannwg won the first prize in the first Eisteddfod held here in 1816.

The "singing School" on Sunday evenings in preparation for the Annual Gymanfa was well attended at the turn of this century. As Tom Lewis recalls "Older members can still recall walking on a week night evening through the hamlet of Clwydyfagwyr over the Aberdare mountain to attend singing rehearsals at Abernant. In 1890, the Gellionnen Unitarian Congregation travelled to Cefn Coed by horse-drawn brakes for the Annual Gymanfa". In 1900 there was formed in the Chapel an orchestra affectionately called "the string band", a chapel library and a 'Mutual Improvement Society". These activities were inaugurated by the Rev Hathren Davies and Mr J. R. Evans (formerly a schoolmaster of Cyfarthfa Castle School).

During its long history the Hen Dŷ Cwrdd has been the spiritual home of many outstanding characters such as Mathew Wayne, who in 1806 was the Manager of Richard Crawshay's iron-smelting furnace at Cyfarthfa; the Rev Owen Evans, the Rev John Hathren Davies; Sion Harri, Evan Lewis, Benjamin Saunders, the brilliant inventor; Tom Lewis, poet and scholar, but the most notable undoubtedly was Sion Llewellyn, who took the leading part in the founding of the Unitarian cause at Cefn Coed in 1747.

Sion, by trade, was a blacksmith and was born at Cwmcapel, Cefn Coed on the 30th November 1693. He had no opportunity of obtaining a thorough schooling and he informs us in his apologetic "Preface" that he knew no English. Whatever knowledge this remarkable old poet acquired was by dint of hard toil within the four walls of his rustic cottage, Ty'r Ffynnon, with its thatched roof and earthen floor. In spite of his total lack of educational opportunity, Sion Llewelyn, published a collection of his poetry in a book of 60 pages that called for four impressions, copies of this collected works are available at the National Library, Aberystwyth, The Free Library, Swansea and at the Cardiff Public Library.

Reference has been made to Sion Llewellyn the poet by Tom Lewis on 'Poets and Musicians of Vaynor'. His poetry, largely rhymed catalogues of details and events, nevertheless serves a useful purpose in that it adds to our knowledge of the bard's life and beliefs. One reads through the poetry of Sion the history of his retrograde youth, of his conversion, of his joining the Christian fold, of the divisions at Cwmyglo and the exodus to Cefn Coed in 1747. The headstone which used to mark his resting place may still be seen nailed to the chapel wall on the eastern side. It has the following verse:-

> Fe roddwyd Shon Llewellyn
> A'i wraig mewn Daiar erwyn
> I orwedd dan y garreg hon
> A saith o'u hwyrion rhynddyn.

Translated , this verse states that underneath the headstone, lies Sion Llewellyn, his wife and seven of their grandchildren.[9]

A memorial stone of unusual interest was erected to the memory of Ann Thomas, Dreinos, Vaynor who died on the 24th October 1782. In spite of her limited income, Ann Thomas, nevertheless somehow frequently procured a small quantity of tea, although it cost at that time 18s 0d (£0.90) per pound. When she died, a stone was erected on her grave on which was carved a representation of two cups and a sugar basin upside down. Do the upside down utensils suggest a "Finis" to Ann's overt tea drinking?

In the graveyard too, lies Dafydd Lewis, great-great-grandfather of the present writer. He took an active part in the Merthyr Riots of June 1831, when he led the Cefn Contingent on "Y Ddarren Fawr" and intercepted the Highland Regiment on the Cwm Tâf Road. Dafydd Lewis was one of the sixty badly wounded outside the Castle Hotel and returned to Cefn Coed with a musket ball lodged in his shoulder. An interesting tale is told by my uncle, Tom Lewis, of the encounter the following day which took place at Dafydd Lewis' house between the doctor from the Highland Regiment and the rioters.[10]

Hen Dŷ Cwrdd Unitarian Chapel Cefn Coed (c1930).

A few paces away from the resting place of the noted Unitarian divine and educationist, the Rev Owen Evans, lie Robert and Lucy Thomas, Waunwyllt. The Thomases were renowned in local annals for their spirit of commercial adventure in the steam coal trade in the 19th century. Robert Thomas opened a coal level in Waunwyllt, Abercannaid in 1828. When he died, his widow Lucy Thomas took over the mine and developed her mining interests to such an extent that she became known as the "mother of the Welsh Steam Coal trade". She attended the Hen Dŷ Cwrdd in her young days with her mother, who was a member there. She was buried here in 1847 and in looking down upon the tomb one notes signs of neglect and inattention. How true the old Welsh adage, "Tir angof yw'r bedd".

The names of Ministers and dates of their incumbences are recorded on a breas plate in the pulpit: Richard Rees 1747-1749, Phillip Charles 1749-1790; Thomas Davies 1790-1832, Daniel Davies 1832-1837; Owen Evans 1837-1865; Isaac Thomas Williams 1867-1873; John Hathren Davies 1877-1910; John Carrara Davies 1910-1918; Thomas Eric Davies 1918-1925; Thomas Lewis Jones 1931-1935; John Marles Thomas 1936-1951. The above tablet was unveiled by the late John Henry James, Vaynor, about 1904. John Henry James was a member of the well known James family, Solicitors, Merthyr, who sixty years ago were the leading Unitarians in that town.

REFERENCES

1. TOM LEWIS, The History of the Hen Dy Cwrdd, Cefn Coed Y Cymer (1947), p.11.
2. Cardiff and Merthyr Guardian, July 3rd, 1847.
3. TOM LEWIS, The History of the Hen Dŷ Cwrdd referring to Ymofynydd of 1853, p.61.
4. The Religious Census of 1881, A Calendar of the Returns Relating to Wales Vol. 1. pp. 181-182.
5. T. E. CLARKE, A Guide to Merthyr Tydfil (1848), p.73.
6. TOM LEWIS, op. cit., p.65.
7. MORIEN LEWIS, St John's Church, Cefn Coed Y Cymmer (1984) p.14.
8. Hen Dy Cwrdd, Cefn Coed, Chapel Records.
9. TOM LEWIS, op. cit., p.133.
10. Ibid p.205.

BETHEL BAPTIST CHAPEL, YNYSYFELIN, CWM TÂF FAWR
(Built 1799, rebuilt 1927)

Bethel Baptist Chapel was the oldest Nonconformist Chapel in the Parish of Penderyn having been built in 1799. With the construction of the Llwyn-On reservoir in 1927 the old shrine was demolished and a new Bethel was constructed on the present site in 1927. It is now in the parish of Vaynor and located on the side of the Brecon/Merthyr Road on land adjacent to the old Hendre Farm at Llwyn-On, Cwm Tâf.

The congregation of Bethel Chapel commenced with David Davies, Edward Evans, David Jones and Ben Richards four members of Seion Baptist Chapel, Merthyr Tydfil, meeting regularly at Penpont Farmhouse, Cwm Tâf in 1793, and later at a dwelling house at Ynysyfelin, Cwm Taf. Two of these early members, David Owen Davies and Edward Evans, became assistant preachers. Soon their numbers increased and the house was licenced for the purpose of holding religions meetings. It is apparent

Bethel Baptist Chapel, Cwm Tâf, built 1799. Demolished during the building of Llwyn-On reservoir.

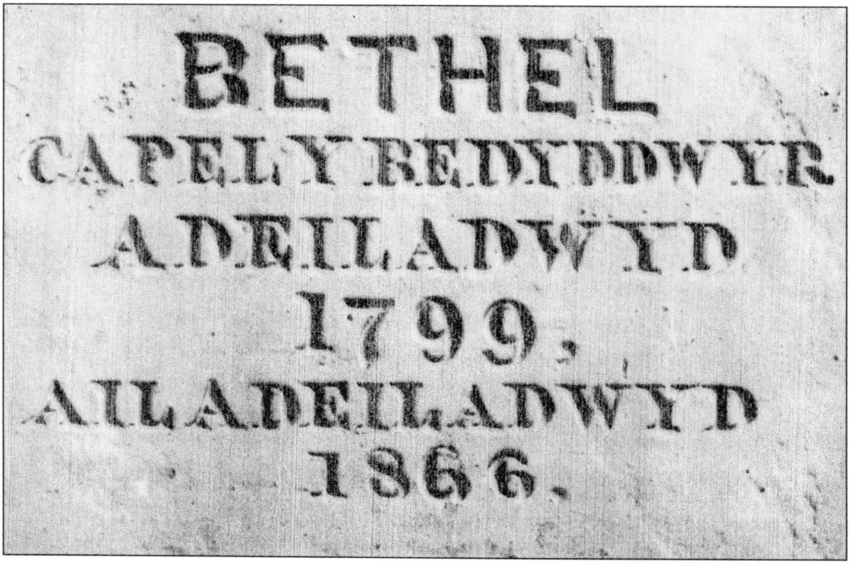

Stone wall plaque situated over the porch entrance of the original Bethel Chapel.

that a number of Seion (Merthyr) Members resided at Cwm Tâf Fawr since twelve were given letters of release or transfer from Seion to join the growing congregation at Cwm Tâf on the 25th January 1798 where Mr D. O. Davies, one of the founders of the congregation, who was a small-holder residing at Ynystâf, was ordained as their minister.

The cause prospered and eventually they built a Chapel in 1799 which they called Bethel. They also acquired land for a burial ground and by 1804 were sufficiently well established to become the venue for the Gymanfa of the three Counties of Montgomery, Radnor and Breconshire. The preachers on the first day were the Rev M. Evans and the Rev David Saunders of Merthyr and on the following day, the 6th June 1804 the preachers at 9 a.m. were the Rev John Lewis and D. Richards. In the afternoon of the Rev Titus Lewis preached and in the evening the Rev Timothy Thomas. It was decided here that the Gymanfa would be held in 1805 at Maesyberllan Breconshire, when the main preacher would be the famous Rev Christmas Evans. The statement of the Union for 1804 states:

"Beddyddiwyd (Baptised)234; Adferwyd (Restored) 124;
Cyfanswm (Total) 358 Bufarw (Died) 39; Diarddelwyd
(Expelled) 37; Cyfanswm (Total) 76
Gwlir oddwrth y ffigyrau fod y cynnydd yn = 282
(The figures indicate that the total is)
Arwyddwyd gan Mr James Lewis, Ysgynfennydd
(Allan O Hen Raglen 1804)"[1]

Three young men became ministers from Bethel, namely, David Davies, son of the minister; Richard Howell of Wernlas Farm, Cwm Cadlan, Penderyn, and Jenking Thomas of Cwm Cadlan. Richard Howell became minister of the Baptist Chapel at Pontprenllwyd, Penderyn while Jenkin Thomas became minister of the English Baptist Chapel at Cheltenham. In 1878 a branch of Bethel Chapel was established at Pontprenllwyd, Penderyn by those members who lived in the valleys of the Hepste, Cadlan and Pontpren hamlet. They congregated to worship at a humble dwelling house in Penderyn. The stalwarts of this early congregation were David and Richard Davies, sons of the Rev David Davies the Minister at Ynysyfelin; Hugh Jenkins, Penpont Farm, Cwm Tâf and Edward Lewis, Troedyrhiw Farm, Cwm Tâf. For communion the members at Penderyn joined those at Bethel and similarly for baptisms of Penderyn members when baptisms took place in the pool under Pontyglec, Cwm Tâf.

In 1838 the Rev D. O. Davies ordained his son, David Davies, as his assistant minister at Bethel.[3] Rev David Jones, Carmarthen indicates that in 1839 the membership at Bethel had reached 60, while the numbers at Pontprenllwyd, Penderyn had now reached 50. Baptists were obviously strong in both localities where neither the Methodists nor Independents had yet established their causes. After labouring for over sixty years as the Minster of Bethel, Ynysyfelin, the Rev David Owen Davies died in 1853 in his 88th year. He was followed in office by his son, the Rev David Davies who remained as minister until his death in 1869. It is worthy of note that father and son served as ministers for a period of seventy years between them. Legend has it that they did not receive any salary during this period depending entirely upon the meagre income of their small holdings at Ynystâf and Abernant.

The Rev David Davies' successor was the Rev John Hughes of Cefn Coed who only stayed for a brief period. He in turn, was followed in 1875 by the Rev T. Salathiel, Minister also of Carmel Baptist Church, Cefn

Bethel Baptist Chapel, Cwm Tâf, built to replace the original 1799 Chapel demolished in the building of LLwyn-On reservoir (1914-27).

Coed, who remained until his death in 1901. During his pastorship Bethel enjoyed an era of having a strongly supported little chapel with a rich round of social activities. Among them was included a very fine choir conducted by Mr Septimius Jenkins of Penpont. Mr David Davies recalls a literary evening at Bethel Chapel at the turn of the century. One of the items that evening was what he has called "Y Ddadl Rhannu'r Deisen" (A debate about sharing a cake) between two girls and one of the members, Dafydd Lewis. Hugh Penpont was so moved by the unfair sharing of the cake by Dafydd Lewis that he broke forth into the following triad.

> "Mae'r merched bach a'r deisen
> Ar dori 'nawr i lefan –
> Wrth weled Dafydd more anheg
> Yn stwffio ceg ei hunan".[4]

Translated it would read as follows:

> The little girl with the cake broke down crying.
> When seeing Dafydd so unfair
> In stuffing his own mouth.

It was around 1900 that the officials of Bethel Chapel were given the first warning that the Cwm Tâf Valley around Llwyn-On Farm was to be flooded and was to become a third reservoir in the valley for the Cardiff Corporation. David Davies writing in 1905 states "Mae'r achos yn wan iawn" (translated – "The cause is very weak"). By this time the pillars of the Church had passed to a greater peace than the glens of sylvan beauty in Cwm Taf Fawr. He was of course referring to the Rev David Davies, Septimius Jenkins, Penpont and Herbert Davies of the Hendre. News of the impending reservoir construction was an added blow to the officials of the Church, Mr Thomas Williams, Coedowen, David Lewis, Nantgwineu (Secretary) and Evan Morgan, Penyrheol (Treasurer).

The flooding of the valley to make the Llwyn-On reservoir, with the consequent disappearance of the hamlet of Ynysyfelin, Bethel Chapel, the Red Lion Inn, the Farmers' Arms, the Millers' Arms and so many snug white washed farms and cottages annihilated forever the old Welsh rural culture associated with Cwm Tâf Fawr. The families of Troedyrhiw, Penpound, Penpont, Pontardâf, and a host of others inevitably loaded their gambos, sang their last harvest hymns, and probably stopped for a moment, for a last tearful glimpse of the Autumn sun rising over the Darren Fawr and then departed towards a new life in Sennybridge, Ystradfellte or Brecon.

The old church of St Mary's, Nantddu has closed its doors for the last time, but miraculously Bethel Chapel built in 1927 by the Cardiff Corporation is still open. Services are held on Sunday afternoons supported by the old families of the Ffrwd, Danygraig and Gellia, Wern and a few others. There are no extant documents relating to the nineteenth century life of the Chapel. The 1851 Religious Census[5] refers to it in the following terms "Parish of Penderyn. Bethel Chapel. Baptist. Erected before 1800. Building not used exclusively as a place of worship. Space. Free 48. Others 72. Standing 40. Present morning 40. Afternoon 26. Scholars evening 54. David Davies, Abernant".

REFERENCES

1. DAVID DAVIES, Hanes Plwyf Penderyn (1905), p.98.
2. David Davies, Penderyn, p.98.
3. REV DAVID JONES, Hanes Y Bedyddwyr, 1839
4. DAVID DAVIES, Penderyn, p.90
5. The Religious Cenus of 1851. A Calendar of the Returns Relating to Wales, Volume 1, pp. 181-182.

MORIAH. WELSH CALVINISTIC METHODIST CHAPEL
(Built in 1807)

To trace the history of Moriah Chapel, Cefn Coed one has first to trace briefly the development of Calvinistic Methodism at Pontmorlais Chapel, Merthyr. The first meetings of the Calvinistic Methodists were held at the home of John Davies of Twynyrodyn, Merthyr Tydfil. As the town increased in population, the meeting place was exchanged for a house on the site of the present Morlais Castle public house. Here the members increased in number and were in a position to build a little chapel. Accordingly, a site was selected, the lease was drawn up in 1796 and the building commenced. Alongside the chapel was a smaller building intended on the ground floor to have a stable for the itinerant minister's horse and the upper storey for the caretaker. Such was the first chapel belonging to the Calvinistic Methodists at Pontmorlais, the trustees included the Rev David Jones, Rector of Llangan. The old members of Pontmorlais were zealous workers, and every Sunday several would visit the neighbouring districts and hold a Sunday School. Schools were held at various times at Aberfan, Troedyrhiw and Vaynor.

Moriah Welsh Calvinistic Methodist Chapel , Cefn Coed built in 1807.

Among the migrants to Cefn Coed at the close of the 18th century was one Rowland Pugh who came from North Wales. He soon became conspicuous because of his drunkenness and lawlessness. However, he was converted and became equally conspicuous for his virtues. He became first a member of Pontmorlais Chapel and then a deacon. At length, he started the Methodist Society in his own house at Cefn-Isaf, Cefn Coed and continued it there until the cause grew so strong that a chapel was urgently required. He is chiefly to be remembered for the great moral power he exerted and wielded so efficiently in the Cefn Coed area. Undoubtedly, it was from these very humble beginnings in a cottage at Cefn-Isaf that Moriah Chapel was built in 1807.

Local legend has it that miners and iron workers living at Caepantywyll were finding it inconvenient to walk to worship at Cefn Coed, but helped and inspired by founder members like Hannah Davies of Cefn, they built Bethlehem Chapel at Caepantywyll in 1841. "In the Cardiff Central Library there is a scrap of paper" reports Tom Lewis[2] "upon which is written a note which translated reads as follows'I do not believe that it would be wise for you to have the Meeting House, Coed Y Cymer every alternative Sunday, but Mr Davies and the congregation should have it as hitherto. Mr Williams of Hendredenny is of the same opinion as myself in the matter according to the testimony of Siencyn Tomos Sion to me' ".

It is unfortunate that there is nothing to indicate to whom this communication was addressed. It is obvious that the Old Meeting House i.e. Hen Dŷ Cwrdd was loaned to some congregation or other for the purpose of worship. Was it loaned to the Calvinistic Methodists of Cefn Coed until Moriah Chapel was built two years later in 1807? Only one record book relating to Moriah Chapel in the nineteenth century has been found and as a result one has but a vague picture historically of its early life. The earliest documentary information is that provided by the 1851 Religious Census which states "Cae Capel, Cefn Coed Y Cymer, Calvinistic Methodists. Erected A.D. 1807. Space Free 110, others 215. Standing 232. Present morning Sunday Schools, afternoon 152 and 106 scholars, evening 140 and 110 scholars. John Llewelyn Grocer, Cefn Coed Y Cymmer".

"T. E. Clarke provided a little more information in 1848 when he stated "Welsh Calvinistic Methodist Chapel. Built in 1807 and rebuilt in 1830. Service at 2 and 6. The School has 150 scholars and 28 teachers. There is a room also belonging to the Chapel at Clwydyfagwr, about one mile from Coed Y Cymmer, on the side of the Aberdare Hill, which will hold about 150 persons. A school is held every Sunday and is supplied with teachers from Coed y cymmer".[3] It is worthy of note that the room referred to was a two storeyed thatched cottage called "Yr Hen Dabernacle" at Llwynygwcw, Clwydyfagwyr. About 1823, miners were coming to services here straight from the pits. The horse named "Star" which carried the preacher became quite famous locally and was named "Star of the Cause".

After a period at 'Yr Hen Dabernacle" in Clwydyfagwyr the worshippers moved into two little cottages nearby and eventually constructed a school room which was later used by the Merthyr School Board as a school. The 1851 Religious Census, in referring to this early church, stated "Carmel, Clwyd-Y-Fagwr, Calvinistic Methodist. Erected August 1840. Space 80. Standing 20. Present morning 10 and 70 scholars. Evening 12 and 60 scholars, average (12 months) morning 10 and 70 scholars. Remarks. The Sunday School is held in the Chapel in the afternoon. John Price, Elder, Clwydyfagwr".

The Calvinistic Methodist Chapel was erected at Clwydyfagwyr in 1907. Over the years this shrine was the focus of religious and social life in the hamlet. Old residents still fondly recall the Christmas Day Eisteddfodau and the weekly meetings and tea parties. It is a memory of ordinary folk who did their duty and walked humbly before their God,

A brief analysis of the membership of Moriah Chapel, Cefn Coed shows an increase from 1888 to the Revival of 1905 with a membership for that year of 176. This membership was not sustained and from this period one notes an annual decrease. By 1910 the membership had fallen to 113 and by the end of the Second World War to 93, i.e. 35 males and 58 females. By 1939 the membership was down to 61. This trend continued until the chapel closed in 1972 with a membership of 22.

Throughout the period 1888 to 1972, men made up approximately 40 per cent of the total congregation. The number attending Sunday School in the late nineteenth century was regular and substantial. The Band of Hope attracted one third of the numbers of the Sunday School.

In conclusion, one is mindful of the very significant part played by the sons and daughters of this old Chapel, children of coal miners and iron workers, who attained eminence in the fields of Education, Science and music, and who through the sacrifices of their parents contributed so much to the religious, educational and social life of Vaynor and of Wales. Among these must be included Councillor Joseph Price JP and his nieces Miss Magdalen Morgan M. A. Principal of Wrexham Training College and her sister Mrs Elizabeth Thomas BA, the wife of Dr William Thomas, Chief Inspector of Schools in Wales.

REFERENCES
1. TOM LEWIS, The History of the Hen Dy Cwrdd, Cefn Coed Y Cymer (1947), p.23.
2. The Religious Census of 1851. A Calendar of the Returns Relating to Wales Vol. 1 pp. 181-182.
3. T. E. CLARKE, A Guide to Merthyr Tydfil (1848), p.75.

BETHLEHEM INDEPENDENT CHAPEL, PONTSTICILL
(Built in 1828)

IN OCTOBER 1968 the trustees of the New Chapel sold it to the present occupier who converted it into a bungalow. All the external architectural features remain, however, and it is easily recognisable as a former place of worship. This chapel was built in 1924 by the Merthyr Corporation as compensation for the demolition of the old Bethlehem Chapel built in 1838 which now lies under the grey shroud of water at the Pontsticill reservoir. A copy of the deed was made in 1968 by one of the trustees, Mr David Williams, Coedhir Farm, Dolygaer. He is now in his 83rd year and has spent his whole life in this picturesque and lonely area among the foothills of the Brecon Beacons. I am indebted to him for the only historical information in documentary form relevant to the history of this old Independent Chapel.

The historical milestones recorded in the deeds commence with the 10th October 1828 when it would appear that Mr Philip Watkins leased land "to the Rev Thos Evans and others" probably this lease included land for the original Chapel and possibly for the graveyard too. On 3rd December 1915, an agreement was drawn up between the trustees of Bethlehem Chapel and the Mayor and Alderman of the Borough of Merthyr Tydfil. This obviously refers to the conveyance of the old Chapel to the Merthyr Corporation prior to the building of the Pontsticill Reservoir.

Then, on the 31st December 1923 one notes the Conveyance of the New Bethlehem Chapel from the Tâf Fechan Water Supply Board to the Trustees of Bethlehem Chapel. . The last milestone was the sale by the trustees of the New Bethlehem Chapel to the present owner. The 1851 census reported on Bethlehem Chapel in the following manner: "Bethlehem. Vaynor. Independents, erected 1828. Space free 12, others 48; standing 200. Present: afternoon 50, evening 25 scholars. John Thomas. Bethlehem Dowlais".

Bethlehem Independent Chapel, Pontsticill – Built 1828 demolished during the building of Pontsticill reservoir (1913-1927).

A thorough search had failed to find a Bethlehem Chapel in Dowlais but the minister's name has been found in association with the following chapel in the 1857 Census report:-

> Pantscallog Independents. A dwelling house preaching commenced here in 1844. Space. All free. Standing 100. Present morning 30, afternoon, 50 scholars, evening 25 scholars. John Thomas, Minister Bethlehem, Dowlais".

Most of the Chapels of the Parish of Vaynor would seem to have their roots in a Mother Church in Merthyr Tydfil. This connection between Bethlehem and a Merthyr Church however has not been fully established. It was built, for example, 16 years before the Independent Church at Pantscallog with which it is linked in 1851. It is possible therefore that Bethlehem has been founded from the north i.e. from the Talybont area which was not very far distant from the early Puritan settlements around Hay-on-Wye, rather than from the south?

Bethlehem Independent Chapel, Pontsticill built 1828 and demolished for the building of the Pontsticill reservoir in 1927.

The new Bethlehem Independent Chapel, Pontsticill built 1924 but now converted to a private residence.

REFERENCES
1. The Religious Census of 1851. A Calendar of the Returns Relating to Wales.Volume 1, pp. 181-182.

EBENEZER WELSH INDEPENDENT CHAPEL, CEFN COED
(Built in 1838 Rebuilt in 1861)

Fortunately, the history of this chapel 1838-1938 has been preserved in a Welsh account written by an unknown author. It is to this writer that I am indebted for most of the general information concerning this Church. The statistical information relating to Church membership has been found in the debris in the Chapel which since its closure in 1970 has been used for storing builders' materials.

Ebenezer Welsh Independent Chapel, Cefn Coed (built 1838, rebuilt 1861).

Before the beginning of the Congregational cause at Cefn Coed there were a number of persons from Cefn Coed who were loyal and industrious members of Bethesda Chapel, Merthyr, under its minister the Rev Methusalem Jones. Among these faithful members from Cefn Coed were Jededia Jones, Thomas Williams, Morgan Morgans and Henry Thomas. They were good readers and singers and were capable of furthering the cause. They usually walked to the Troedyrhiw Chapel on Sunday morning, returning to Cefn Coed by lunch time and then back to Bethesda by two o'clock for the Sunday School.

Towards the end of 1836 they started holding meetings at Cefn Coed and rented two rooms in Cefn Isaf, Cefn Coed belonging to the "Hen Dafarn Bach". In 1837 Mr Evan Williams, who had been born at Moelfre, Anglesey and had emigrated to America, returned to Merthyr Tydfil and "kept a school" in

Ebenezer Welsh Independent Chapel, Cefn Coed (built 1838, rebuilt 1861).

Bethesda Chapel. He preached frequently at Bethesda and to the branch at Cefn Coed. Eventually it was decided that it would be advantageous to form a church at Cefn Coed with Mr Evan Williams as the minister. There were about 35 members including women and children. A plot of land was bought from Lady Gwyn Holford and in 1838 Ebenezer Chapel was completed at a cost of £400. Following a dispute within the Chapel Mr Williams left after one year and he was followed by the Rev W. Moses of Libanus, Breconshire. But again a misunderstanding arose when it was felt that the minister did not sufficiently support Chartist activities in the locality or among his members. As a result, he indicated that he intended to relinquish his duties as Minister and his letter of explanation is shown in the account referred to above.

In February 1842, Richard Evans and Walter Williams, two assistant preachers at Adulum Chapel, Tredegar, accepted the joint pastorship of Ebenezer Chapel, Cefn Coed. Invitations extended to Breconshire and Glamorgan ministers to attend the induction were refused because of their association i.e. of Richard Evans and Walter Williams, with Adulum Chapel which was a "split" from the mother church of Saron, Tredegar. The Church was, however, determined to continue independently and the

"Ministers" were ordained at Ebenezer in 1842.

The Church remained outside the "Cyfundeb" (Congregational Union) for some years and the Ministers were not invited to preach at any other chapels. Many of the members did not agree with the general situation and left with the Rev Moses to found a new chapel, Tabor, in Cefn Coed in 1845. After the Church at Ebenezer had been out of the Congregational Union for five years a reconciliation was effected between the two bodies. Following a public meeting at Ebenezer, the two men Richard Evans and Walter Williams were accepted by the Church Authorities and the Congregational Union as ordained ministers. They laboured successfully together until Walter Williams died in August 1849 and Richard Evans in April 1850. Both lie in the Ebenezer graveyard, and it is a testimony to their dedication that the debt of the first Chapel was cleared during their joint partnership.

Ebenezer was without a minister until May 1852, when Mr David Jones, a student at Carmarthen College, was ordained minister. The did not prosper during his sojourn at Cefn Coed. He left after a few years and returned to Carmarthen, where he died. In 1860 a call was given to the Rev Griffith Roberts of Llansawel, Briton Ferry, near Castellnedd. He accepted and was inducted in November of that year. He was a preacher of exceptional ability, but unfortunately his character left something to be desired. He remained at Ebenezer until February 1864, when he left and joined the Baptists. He was baptized in the river at Cefn Isaf when a large crowd gathered to witness the event. The Chapel, rebuilt in 1861 at a cost of £700, was again without a minister until an invitation was given o the Rev David Abel Jones, Minister of Pentre-estyll, near Swansea. He accepted the call and was inducted in January 1868. He laboured conscientiously at Ebenezer until 1878, when he left for Llangennech.

The Chapel, remained without a minister until a "call" was given to Mr David Rhagfyr Jones of Coleg Bala, a native of Dolgellau who came there in April 1881. He proved a talented preacher and poet, and his Bible class and Temperance Society were highly successful. He left in April 1887 for Nantgaredig and Pontargothi. He was followed in 1890 by Mr David Rees, a student at the Memorial College, Brecon. He was a very industrious and successful minister until 1896 when, owing to ill-health, he was compelled to retire.

In 1898 Mr Evan Walter Thomas of Carmarthen College was inducted as minister of Ebenezer. "He was a talented preacher and laboured successfully there with the Bible Class and the Band of Hope. He was a great help to the leader of the singing. He also started a violin class and a number played in the Chapel services."

During 1904-1905 revival over a hundred new members joined Ebenezer. Unfortunately, a large number gave up membership in a very short time. Mr Thomas stayed until 1908 when he left to take charge of an English Chapel at Tonypandy. The Rev J. T. Llewellyn Williams commenced his ministry in October 1909. He was a very good minister but left in 1910 for Bethania, Abercynon. The Chapel was again without a minister until 1915 when a call was extended to Mr J. Seymour Rees of the Memorial College, Brecon, a native of Aberaeron. He stayed until December 1922 when he left for Hermon Chapel, Treorchy. In 1913 the trustees accepted the tender of Mr Richard Lloyd, Cefn Coed for the rebuilding of part of the Chapel at a cost of £700.

The unknown author of this brief history of Ebenezer, concludes his account thus: "The Chapel today, 1938, is without a minister and many of the members having had to leave because of the industrial depression. Nevertheless a small faithful band continues". Apart from the above history of the Chapel all other documentary information is sparse. What information I have obtained regarding Sunday School membership and burials in the 19th century and of reports of the Chapel from 1932 up to the closure in 1972 have been found among the scattered Bibles, Hymn books etc which now lie in the debris in this once beautiful chapel now used as builders' store. The Sunday School members during the period 1845 to 1880 show the following membership:- 1845 – 146 pupils, 27 teachers; 1850 – 119 pupils, 25 teachers; 1860 – 153 pupils, 27 teachers; 1870 – 130 pupils, 26 teachers and 1880 – 86 pupils and 17 teachers.

The figures given for Church membership in the Religious Census of 1851 tend in some cases to be exaggerated so the figure quoted for Sunday School membership of 190 scholars is possibly inflated compared with the above figures. The Report of the 1851 Census on Ebenezer, Cefn Coed Y Cymmer is as follows:[1] "Erected 1838. Space. The whole Chapel is free except the 41 pews. Present: morning 195, evening 336 and 190 scholars. Remarks: The Chapell inside measures 30 feet by 29 feet etc. The gallary is all seated and will hold 153 persons. Henry Thomas, Manager. Cooper".[1]

T. E. Clarke in 1848 provides the following information regarding this Chapel:-

"Ebenezer Chapel – built in 1838. Welsh Independents. Ministers, Rev W. Williams and Rev R. Evans. Service at 11 and 6. The School has 130 scholars and 27 teachers".[2] In the rubbish within the Chapel in August 1980 I found a burial register containing the names of persons buried there, place of abode at death, date of death, age and remarks relating to the state of the graveyard. It would appear that this register was compiled following a public notice in May 5th 1929 requesting owners of graves to maintain them and also to submit their claims of ownership.[3]

The information in the burial register provides a fund of statistical information relating to dates of death recorded on the gravestones and also to the age of death of the deceased during the nineteenth century . It indicates quite clearly that there was a very high percentage of child deaths and as a result a low average life expectancy in Cefn Coed at this time. It was the exception for either sex to achieve the age of 70 years. One rather baffling fact emerging from the burial register however is that there are recorded burials here before the Chapel was built in 1838, for example, that of "Thomas son of John and Margaret Morgan died September 28th 1834" and far more difficult to comprehend is that of "Mary daughter of Joseph Thomas of the Parish of Eglwysian died December 1805". Does it recall a death rather than a burial? One notes that the deceased were often from outside the Vaynor Parish from such places as "Cwm Glo (Merthyr), Twynrodyn (Merthyr), Ynysfach (Merthyr), Dowlais, Cyfarthfa, Bargoed ("Gynt o'r lle hwn" – formerly of this place), Caepantywyll (Merthyr), Aberdare, Cardigan, and Heol-gerrig". In the main however, the place of death is recorded as "Of this parish" – "O'r lle hwn" or "Gynt o'r lle hwn" – formerly of this place". These burials of people from outside the parish was not entirely due to a scarcity of graveyards or to the encouragement given by Dr Dyke the Merthyr Tydfil Medical Officer of Health "to bury out of Merthyr" but also perhaps to the deep laid nostalgic affection in the Welshman's nature for the "country churchyard" or for that sacred spot where one spent those enchanting days of childhood and where one's loved ancestors lie in some sheltered glen.

Information regarding Chapel membership at Ebenezer between 1932 and 1963 has been found in the Annual Report pamphlets lying in the debris on the Chapel floor. During 1932 the members numbered 90; in 1935 – 84; in 1940 – 75; in 1945 – 80; in 1950 – 82; in 1955 – 65; in 1960 – 53. The membership of the chapel rapidly declined after this period and the members were unable to maintain the fabric of the building. Services at the Chapel were discontinued in the early 1970s and were held in the Vestry in Holford Street which is also the venue for the Sisterhood which meets weekly. Among its illustrious sons was Mr W. J. Williams MA who became Director of Education for Cardiff and whose family had been regular and faithful worshippers at Ebenzer over many years. The last minister here was Mr C. O. Devonald who was here from 1951 until 1956.

REFERENCES
1. The Religious Census of 1851. A Calendar of the Returns Relating to Wales.Volume 1, pp. 181-182.
2. T. E. CLARKE. A Guide to Merthyr Tydfil (1894). p.73.
3. Tarian Y Gweithiwr, May 5th 1929.

CARMEL BAPTIST CHAPEL, CEFN COED Y CYMER
(Built in 1844)

It would appear that most of the local congregations have their early roots and inspiration from Ynysgau, Merthyr Tydfil. In 1780, Walter Davies of Gwern Llwyn Isaf had his house licensed for holding meetings. He was assisted in his endeavours by some members of the Hengoed Chapel. The Sacrament was regularly administered in this humble dwelling every three months and the little congregation became a branch of Hengoed.

Eventually, the house became too small to contain the growing congregation, and in July 1788, the first Baptist Chapel at Merthyr, Zion (Seion) was begun and completed in seven months. Unfortunately, a dispute arose over the question of the sanctity of the Sabbath and the vexed question of working on Sundays at the local iron-works. Many members complained that Sunday labour was necessary in order to survive. This sentiment was strongly opposed and finally the newly-appointed first Minister of Zion, the Rev William Price, left with a large proportion of his congregation. Because the doors of Zion were locked to him and his followers on the day appointed for his ordination, the ordination service was performed in the burial ground attached to Zion Chapel.

During the unexpected absence of the Rev Edwards, minister of Zion in 1880, the pulpit was occupied by a young member of the congregation named Rees Jones. He apparently preached with consummate skill and power and hence forth became conspicuous for his ability and zeal. In 1804 he was appointed the resident minister of Zion Chapel. He conduct-

Carmel Baptist Chapel, Cefn Coed (Built 1844).

ed a missionary campaign in this area which was supported by his followers. By 1838 there was a branch of Zion Chapel in Cefn Coed holding Sunday Services, Sunday School and weeknight meetings in a school room.

Eventually, because of growing numbers, Carmel Chapel was built in 1844 and by 1855 had fifty members and a Sunday School of 45. Edward Morris was ordained as the first minister in 1856 and from this date there was a rapid expansion of numbers. By 1863 there were 99 members and a Sunday School of 116. The 1851 Religious Census provides the following information. "Carmel. Particular Baptist. Space, free galleries, others 32 in number let Quarterly . Standing 20. Present: 142 and 40 scholars; evening 173 and 153 scholars. Average morning 148 and 40 scholars; evening 150 and 142 scholars. John Morgan. Deacon".

The Rev Edward Morris terminated his ministry here in 1870 and was followed by John Griffiths, who was inducted in 1871 and remained until 1874, when the membership of both the Church and Sunday School just topped the 100 mark. He was succeeded in 1875 by Mr T. Salathiel from Bala, whose ministry at Carmel continued until 1889 with the Chapel membership remaining about the same. T. E. Clarke[2] does not give any information other than that for Sunday School membership and times of services when he states in 1848: "Carmel Chapel built in 1844. Welsh Baptist. Minister – Rev W. R. Davies. Services at 11 and 6. The School has 95 scholars and 12 teachers".

The Rev W. B. Griffiths was inducted minister at Carmel in 1890. He stayed, until 1897 leaving then for Tabor, Llantrisant. The church membership now stood at 123 with a flourishing Sunday School of 170. There was no resident Minister at Carmel during the period 1898-9 but in 1900 the Rev J. H. Davies moved here from Tabernacle, Coedpoeth and during the following years, the Church enjoyed its most prosperous period in terms of members which were as follows: 1900 – 145; 1901 – 166; 1902 – 165; 1903 – 167; 1904 – 183; 1905 – 269; 1906 – 203; 1907 – 180; 1909 – 1591 1910 – 134. The gains made during the 1904-5 revival were not sustained and by the time that the Rev J. H. Davies left for Killay in 1910 the numbers were fewer than a decade previously when he arrived at Carmel. This will be discussed in greater detail later.

Following the departure of the Rev Davies, Carmel was without a minister until 1916, when the Rev H. W. Hopkins was inducted. He continued as minister until his death in 1927, when the Chapel had a membership of 73 and a Sunday School of 75. The Secretary of the Chapel from 1915 was Mr E. W. Morgan, followed in 1926 by Mr David Meredith. he in turn was followed by Mr M. H. Jones, BA, during the 1930s. Membership by 1934 was down to 63. By 1947 membership was down to 43. and a decade later down to 26. The Secretary in 1947 was Miss Hettie Morris, BA, and the Chapel had now been without a resident minister since 1927. However, on July 8th 1954 the Rev J. Rees was inducted Minister, and remained until 1958.

Popular local legend has it that the first chapel was built by members carrying stones from the river. This building cracked and a new Chapel was constructed. The architect for this new building was Mr Pickerel. A description of this Chapel with photographs is given in the section on "Local Buildings". The building is unique, as on entering one does not face the pulpit.

The burial register dates from 1840 and provides information as to the place of residence of the deceased and age. It reveals the following incidence of child mortality, which represented 42% of all burials in 1850 but had declined to 17½% by 1900 and was down to 12% by 1930.

The average age of burial of both males and females at Carmel was 24 years in 1850, 44.2 years in 1900 which rose still further to 62.2 years by 1950. By comparison it was 17½ years in Merthyr Tydfil in 1850 and 25½ years by 1870. This limited investigation revealed a high mortality rate for women, probably of expectant mothers as also found by Dr Dyke, Medical Officer of Health at Merthyr Tydfil at this time.

How is the high mortality to be accounted for? It was mainly due to local and self created conditions, the very poor construction of houses, inadequate food and water supply, the absence of drainage, defective ventilation , the accumulation of filth, high risks at work and the extensive and fatal prevalence of disease.

The overall figures from 1840 to 1950 show a gradual improvement in terms of average age of death. During the nineteenth century women fared rather worse than men while there is a reversal for the twentieth century. An important consideration is the fact that Carmel burials would probably include rural residents while those of Merthyr would be almost entirely an urban population subject to for example, more deaths due to accidents. As in the case of the other graveyards in the parish, burials were mainly from within Cefn Coed but nevertheless a considerable number would seem to have come "home" to be buried from Blaenau Gwent, Pontypridd and Mountain Ash in addition to those from Merthyr Tydfil. This was hardly concurring with the statement made by Dr Dyke, Medical Officer of Health, to his Merthyr Guardians in 1865 that "It is satisfactory to know that the practice of interring the dead at a distance from the abode of the living is gaining ground ... it is admitted to be unhealthy to inter the dead among the residence of the living".[4]

Of interest is the variation of payment for graves ranging from "heb dalu dim" for half the burials in 1866 to £1.1s.0d. It had been noted that "heb dalu dim" (without payment) is written after the name of "Rees Williams, Torrwr beddau (grave digger); John James, deacon; and William Lewis, deacon". It would seem that officers of the chapel were given free graves for services rendered over the years and not as I originally concluded that "heb ei dalu" (without payment) signified extreme poverty and inability to pay for the grave.

One cleans more information regarding the social status of the Carmel members from references made to the occupation of the deceased such as "groser, cowman, roular, haulier, founder" and where, as in 1877 when the names and occupations of Trustees are given: "farmer, miner, labourer, puddler, mason, weigher, minister, rougher, roller, Brewer, fitter, finer and gentleman". Addresses such as "pen-level, Cwm-capel and tai cwar" have regrettably disappeared from the physical landscape to be replaced by such ridiculous place names as "Lupin Close and Rowan Rise"!

Whereas the Unitarian faith attracted most of the yeomen farmers of the Tâf Fawr Valley, the Baptist faith at Cefn Coed only had one adherent of farming stock from the locality in 1877, namely a trustee, Rice Thomas Abercar Farm, Cwm Tâf. His membership would seem to owe more to the result of a dispute at Bethel Baptist Chapel, Ynysyfelin, Cwm Tâf which was only a few hundred years from his home at Abercar, rather than religious attraction to Carmel, Chapel, Cefn Coed.

Recruitment of members to Carmel Chapel seemed to be linked territorially with the lower parts of Cefn Coed such as Field Street, Chapel Street and "Cefn Isha". The only trustees living outside this lower area of Cefn Coed were "Isaac Evans, near Old Chapel, Coedcymmer" and "Richard John Jones near the Church Coedycymmer, Gentleman". It is of interest to note that in the Parish records very few men are described as "gentleman". The general connotation of the term locally meant a person of private means, or a professional man, a man of the middle class who in practical terms did not have to do the more menial jobs about his home. In the vernacular of the locality he did not have "to soil his hands". An examination of the Carmel Chapel membership indicates a membership in 1896 of 121, of 145 in 1900, of 269 in the year of the Religious Revival in 1905 which fell the following year to 203. From this date there is a decrease to 98 in 1920, to 49 in 1940, to 25 by 1970 and to under 10 by 1980.

The old records of Carmel Chapel found by the author in August 1980 in an old cupboard in the Vestry throw interesting light on the life of the chapel in the nineteenth century. The account book for 1887 for example, refers to "Am lanhau y capel am Mis Mawrth 10/-" (for cleaning the chapel in March ten shillings). Of interest we see "I'r Gweinidog £4.0s.0d" (for the Minister four pounds), this would suggest that his stipend was about fifty pounds per annum. The coal bill in 1887 was "Am ddwy draft o lo 4s 7d (for two loads of coal four shilling and seven pence). Other bills indicate that water and gas had been laid on – "Bill y dwr 5/-" (the water bill five shillings i.e. 25 pence in modern coinage) while "Bill y Gass, £1.10s.4p" (the gas bill was £1.52). Accommodation for a visiting minster was relatively cheap as we note "Am lety Isaac Thomas (Persia) 2/-" (Lodging for Isaac Thomas (Persia) was two shillings i.e. 10p in modern coinage). "Am Canwyllau 4 pence" (for candles four pence), "Am Botel Dwr 1/-" (For a water bottle one shilling i.e. 10p) and "I'r tlodion 10/-" (for the poor ten shillings).

From the entries in the account books it would appear that the chapel had periods of financial difficulties and it was necessary to borrow money. An entry in 1884 for example refers to "Cafwyd Benthig gan John Williams £50 (a loan from John Williams of fifty pounds), and later, and of great interest because of the division between chapel and public house this entry "Talwyd i Glwb Y Gwynnes am log £2.10s. 7½p" (interest of £2.53 paid to the Gwynnes Arms Club"). There are references too, to "Am Ystol at yr Harmonium 2/6" (For the harmonium stool two shillings and six pence); "Am yr Harmonium £9" (for the harmonium nine pounds). To raise Chapel funds we note "Concert Isaac Lewis £3.17s.0 (Concert Isaac Lewis £3.85).

A popular way of raising money whether it was for a burial of a poor person or to help chapel finances was by having a "Tea party" followed by a concert. The first reference to a tea party in the chapel records is in 1882 where it states "Rev Salathiel oddiwrth Tea party £18.14s.5½p (from the Rev Salathiel, Tea Party £18.72) and later "Am gylleth Fara 12s 6d" (for a bread knife 63p).

In 1882 a payment of 7s 6d (£0.38) was made "Am Yr Hall" (for the Hall). Presumably this would have been for a letting of the Cefn Drill Hall for a Concert. In 1889 the Treasurer records the receipt of £5 "Oddiwrth Y Concert" (from the Concert).

It would appear from the Accounts that the money raised at the Annual Tea Party held at Carmel at Easter, possibly as a counter attraction to the notorious Cefn Fair, was utilised in 1907 to finance the tea party held at the Church Tavern, Vaynor in July of the same year. The financial account indicates that payment was made to one member for boiling water or was it a method of helping some widow whose inherent independence forbade her to receive charity? The account for 1907 is as follows: April 1st 1908:-p "Am groceries I Blod Owen £1.17s.0d" (£1.85) (for groceries from Blod Owen). "I J. D. Hughes 16s 0d" (to J. D. Hughes 80p). "Am llaeth i J. Meredith" (for milk to J. Meredith). "Am Ffwrno'r Bara Is 6d" (for baking bread 8p). "Tea Parti Church Tavern, am y tren 7s 6d" (for the train for the tea party at the Church Tavern 38p).

A full account of the Carmel Sunday School trips from 1907 to 1943 is given in the section on 'Leisure and recreational activities in Vaynor.

REFERENCES
1. The Religious Census of 1851. A Calendar of the Returns Relating to Wales.Volume 1, pp. 181-182.
2. T. E. CLARKE. A Guide to Merthyr Tydfil (1894). p.73.
3. DR DYKES Reports (1848) Merthyr Library.
4. DR DYKES Reports (1865) Merthyr Library.

TABOR WELSH INDEPENDENT CHAPEL
(Built in 1845 rebuilt in 1905)

Tabor Chapel has its beginnings prior to 1845 in Ebenezer Congregational Chapel. As a result of a dispute within the Chapel, the Rev W. Moses left with a number of the congregation and eventually built Tabor Welsh Independent Chapel in 1845.

In referring to Tabor Chapel, the Religious Census at 1851[1] states thus: "Tabor, Coed Y Cymer. Independents. Erected in 1845. Space free 84. others 110, standing 40. Present, morning 70 and 20 scholars, afternoon school, evening 100 and 30 scholars. William Moses. Minister Tydfil's Well".

Further information from a slightly earlier source is provided by T. E. Clarke[2] where he states "Tabor Chapel. Built in 1845. Welsh Independents. Minister, The Rev W. Moses. Service at 11 and 6. The school has 120 scholars and 18 teachers".

A sheet of paper found recently in a cupboard at Tabor Chapel, dated March 26th 1899, refers to a Church Meeting held for the purpose of rebuilding the Chapel. They were obviously successful in their endeavours because the present Chapel was rebuilt in 1905. The vestry was used then for many years as an annexe for the Cefn Coed Boys' School. Another document dated 1906 gives a list of persons to whom money was owed for the rebuilding of the Chapel. The highest amount loaned was £150 by Mrs Ann Davies, two sums of £100 and the rest amounting to £1,020 was made up of loans of £20 to £50.

The Nineteenth Century Burial Register[3] reveals 264 recorded burials, 41 per cent were from Cefn Coed, 49 per cent were from Merthyr and 15 per cent were from outside the local parishes of Vaynor and Merthyr. The average age of death of Cefn residents for the nineteenth century buried at Tabor was 33.1 years and that of Merthyr deceased 32.7 years. Again were these burials from Merthyr the result of exiles returning to their native village for burial or was it due to the paucity of graveyards in Merthyr and

Old Tabor (1845)
(Tabor Welsh Independent Chapel built 1845 and rebuilt 1904.)

Drawing by DEWI BOWEN

the encouragement given by Dr Dyke to bury the dead out of Merthyr?

The Burial Rates for the nineteenth century Tabor Churchyard were as follows: Re-opening grave 5s 0d. Removing headstone 1s 0d, caretaker, 6d, and Ministers fees 3s 6d.

Information relevant to the Sunday School attendance at Tabor for 1929 shows 7 teachers and 38 scholars; for 1935, 6 teachers and 58 scholars; and in 1959, 2 teachers and 30 pupils.

These figures show a Sunday School with stable numbers pre-war up to 1939. Attendance at a Sunday School offered distinct advantages to children dwelling in a poverty ridden area suffering in the throes of industrial depression between the two Great Wars. One notes an entry in the Sunday School attendance book that the "Tabor Outing Fund" for 1931 had 84 subscribers. It is of considerable interest here to note the fact that while

Tabor Welsh Independent Chapel as it is today.

the village community was divided by religious denominations, on the occasion of the annual outing, these divisions were removed and one finds in the list Methodists, Baptists and Unitarians going on the "Tabor outing".

One recalls those long gaunt winters of the depression when Chapel activities afforded some light. One fondly recalls those animated scenes of beaming faces, best suits and highly strung mothers awaiting the arrival of one of Mr Snow's buses on the morning of 'the trip'. Then again Tom Lewis has provided us with a vivid description on the occasion of the Christmas party at Hen Dŷ Cwrdd when he refers to "the bustle and mirth of excited scholars, the evident consternation of the "lady helpers" coaxing the iron boilers on the broad black hobs to a simmering murmur, the green walls streaming with condensation and the air vaporous and misty from the steam, and the spiralling smoke issuing from the ancient briars held in white scarred hands".

Other recreational activities at Tabor included the weeknight meetings of Cwrdd Gweddi, Band of Hope, Concerts, Lectures and Eisteddfodau. The financial accounts of the Eisteddfodau held in 1947 and 1948 reveal that the district was divided geographically between the fifteen ticket sellers and that about 300 attended the Eisteddfodau.

For nearly a century and a quarter the message at Tabor was delivered in Welsh. As the old people one by one passed to their rest a fragment of the language and culture passed into the grave with them. The congregation dwindled and the doors were finally closed in the early 1970s. This beautiful building which was held in solemn veneration by the old faithfuls is now used twice a week as a venue for a Judo club! (i.e. 1980).

REFERENCES
1. The Religious Census of 1851. A Calendar of the Returns Relating to Wales.Volume 1, pp. 181-182.
2. T. E. CLARKE. A Guide to Merthyr Tydfil (1894). p.73.
3. Tabor Burial Register, Cefn Coed

AUBREY (WELSH) WESLEYAN CHAPEL, CEFN COED
(Built in 1876)

AFTER closure in the 1950s the Thomas Aubrey Memorial Chapel, (the Welsh Wesleyan Chapel) served as the Chapel for Vaynor and Penderyn Grammar School for some twenty years. In 1977 it was found to be structurally unsound and demolished. Aubrey Chapel had ceased to be used for public worship with the death of the last members of the old faithful families – Mr and Mrs James Lloyd, of 81 High Street, Cefn Coed; grocers, Mrs Jones, Pontycapel Road the musical stalwart and drama producer, Mr Billy Morris and a few others.

Far more is known and recorded of Thomas Aubrey than of the Wesleyan Chapel.[1] Thomas Aubrey, born 1801, was the son of Thomas and Ann Aubrey of Cefn coed. His father was employed at Cyfarthfa and was a faithful member of the Wesleyan Chapel at Merthyr Tydfil.

When Thomas Aubrey was seven years of age his family moved to Nantyglo. After a riotous youth when he became renowned as a mountain fighter and drunkard he was converted. At the Wesleyan Synod held at Llanidloes in 1827, Aubrey passed the Ministerial examinations without

Aubrey (Welsh) Wesleyan Chapel, Cefn Coed build 1876, demolished 1977.

difficulty. From this time Aubrey's fame as a preacher increased steadily until he attained the highest offices in his denomination. This good man died at Rhyl, November 15th 1867 in his 60th year.

No records in the form of Sunday School registers or financial reports have been preserved except the foundation stone of the Chapel upon which is written "September 16th 1875", found by the author in the debris during demolition. For information relating to the life of the Chapel one has to rely upon memory and upon the reminiscences of old inhabitants.

In the first decades of this century Aubrey Chapel had a congregation of about fifty six members. It had three Sunday Services and a Sunday School supported by a large number of children. One of the Sunday services was at five o'clock and was held especially for those Wesleyans who had belonged to the English Wesleyan Chapel at Well Street, Cefn Coed, prior to its closure about 1910.

There is no record of a resident minister at Cefn Coed. The minister was shared with the Treharris and Quakers Yard Churches but was present for a monthly Communion Service at each church. The weeknight meetings included Prayer Meetings and Band of Hope. The best remembered recreational activity associated with this Chapel were the light operas produced by Mr Billy Morris whose family among others were pillars of this Chapel.

The membership fell during the period between the two Wars when this was an area of severe industrial depression and many young people sought employment in England and many of the old stalwarts passed on. The Chapel, supported by a few families, remained open until after the Second World War and then closed. In the 1950s it was bought by the Breconshire Education Committee and used, as already stated, as a school Chapel.

REFERENCES

1. MATTHEW OWEN, Breconshire, 1912 pp. 103-108.

SEION BAPTIST CHAPEL, PONTSTICILL
(Built in 1901

Pontsticill is situated approximately three miles from Cefn Coed and a similar distance from Dowlais. Sociologically, Pontsticill has closer ties with Dowlais than with Merthyr, probably because of the railway, the works, and, more importantly, Dowlais Market. Similarly, one will find a close relationship between Seion Chapel and the mother Church, Moriah at Dowlais.

As has been stated in the history of Carmel Chapel, Cefn coed, and elsewhere although Vavasor Powell had been associated with early nonconformity in the Merthyr area the Baptists were limited to meeting in private houses until the end of the eighteenth century, when Seion Chapel, Merthyr was built in 1791 and Ebenezer in 1792.

The Baptist cause was initiated locally through the zeal of one John Jenkins who came to Dowlais in 1804 and settled in the lovely smallholding known as Blaen Morlais.[1] John Jenkins, or Sion Siencyn as he was known, supplemented his income by working as an iron-ore worker for the Dowlais Iron Company.

Seion Baptist Chapel Pontsticill (Built 1901).

The early Baptist as Dowlais met at the cottage of Harri Thomas; and Sion Siencyn has described how, on occasion, he was too late in coming from work to go home and wash prior to the evening meeting. He would then wash his hands and face, refresh himself with a cup of tea and then, standing on a stool, preach to his congregation. During his evangelical campaign in Dowlais 28 new members were baptised. They were members of Ebenezer, Merthyr and when a division arose there in 1807 a group left under the leadership of William Price and formed a congregation in Dowlais in two houses which they called Bethel Chapel. This venture was however, unsuccessful and the Chapel was later used as a meeting house for the Independents and Methodists.

The Mother Church of the Baptist faith in Dowlais was Caersalem. The cause commenced here in 1819 when 144 members of Seion and Ebenezer were released from membership. The first Chapel was built in 1820 and incorporated in 1829. With a rapidly increasing population at Dowlais and an expanding congregation in the flourishing chapel at Caersalem, it was decided to build two other chapels. Hebron was opened in 1843 and Elim in 1852. Later the English Baptist Chapel, Beulah was opened in 1856 and Moriah in 1856.

Before founding Seion Chapel at Pontsticill, the Baptists met and held prayer meetings in the village. One of the meeting places was the home of Edward Williams at the old Pontsticill mill. There were about 25 members of Moriah Chapel, Dowlais, living at Pontsticill and in order to hold regular prayer meetings it was decided to open a school house there which was opened in January 1878. The first deacons were James Parry and David Lewis and they were joined later by Edward Williams the miller, Thomas Davies, Thomas Jones Llyngeran and David Watkins.

Seion was incorporated as a Church in 1901 and the Rev Richard Morris was the minister from 1901 until 1916. During his pastorship Moriah contributed £250 to Seion Chapel and supported it in every way possible.

There is little documentary evidence regarding the membership, Sunday School or of social activities of Seion Chapel, Pontsticill for the early decades of this century. The earliest record is that of the Treasurer from January 1st 1935 up to the closure of the Chapel in 1979. The Treasurer's account indicates an average weekly collection in 1935 of about 4s 0d (20P) and £2.7s.7½d (£2.28) for the harvest collection. The visiting Minister's fee was 7s 6d and there was a balance in hand of £59. In 1960 the financial account states as follows: "In hand to commence year £103.5s.9d (£103.28). Income for 1960 £82.3s.0½.d (£82.15). Total £185.8s.9½d (£116.51)". The general income, one notes has been supplemented by concerts for example, an entry for February 14th 1937 reads "Proceeds of Concert £5.9s.0d (£5.45)" and later on 12th August 1937 "Received from Moriah Dowlais for repairs £5.0s.0d (£5.00)". Ironically, the financial affairs of the Chapel when it closed showed a balance of £302.62p which was very many times more than it had been throughout its history form 1901.

The first Sunday School register found dates from January 1961 and shows a regular membership of 14. There was a Sunday School Bank at this time with a membership of 35. There is no record of a Sunday School after 1969 when the overall membership is shown as 10.

The Chapel closed in 1979 when the membership had been reduced from 19 in 1957 to 8. One of the last members was Mr Ben Wathan, aged 92, who had been the organist at Seion for 55 years. He died in 1980.

W. Morgan writing in 1893 testifies to the influence of the Baptist Chapel at Pontsticill thus "This chapel was erected by the friends worshipping at Moriah Church, Dowlais, and, as the clouds are scattered by the rays of the rising sun, so the rowdyism of Pontsticill gradually faded away before the genial influence of the Christian religion".[2]

REFERENCES
1. PROFESSOR GLANMOR WILLIAMS, Hanes Moriah, Dowlais. 1856-1953 (1956).
2. WILLIAM MORGAN (Pant). The Illustrated Vaynor Handbook (1893) p.31.

THE PENTECOSTAL CHURCH, CEFN COED
(1942)

From the evidence available it would appear that the Pentecostal Church, Cefn Coed was established here in 1942 in a building which was bought in 1946. The early meetings had previously been held at Georgetown, Merthyr Tydfil.

Pastor Horace Jones continued here from its establishment in the early 1940s until his death at Whitsun 1980. He was followed in October 1982 by Pastor Glanmor Rees Thomas a native of Carmarthenshire who had spent the last 44 years at Doncaster. The former Church was rebuilt and the new church was opened by the wife of the late Pastor Horace Jones and was assisted by the present Pastor Glanmor Thomas.

Over the years the Church has had a regular membership of about forty, and a Sunday School currently under the supervision of Miss Caroline Davies and three Sunday School teachers, with a membership of thirty scholars. In addition to the Sunday Services there is a Prayer Meeting on Tuesdays, a Bible Class on Thursdays and Youth Meetings on Wednesdays and Fridays. Currently the Elders of the Pentecostal Church, Cefn Coed are Mr Gwyn Davies, Mr Paul Beynon and Mr Sam Worrell.

In conclusion, it is virtually impossible to pay an adequate tribute to the crucial importance of the Churches and Chapels in the life of the community at Vaynor. The Church has been central to religious life here for over a thousand years while the Nonconformist Chapels have made an immense contribution to religion, music, education and provided a mode of discipline so lacking in modern times. Speaking of the Methodist Revival, Professor R. T. Jenkins stated that it was "Not a protest, not a matter of doctrine, not a matter of morality, but a spirit and power". Of its consequences for Wales he writes:

The Pentecostal Mission with Pastor Horace Jones and Elder Mr Tom Turner (c1970).

> "It took hold of a mute nation and made her articulate; it set upon her lips the rich language of the fine Tudor Bible. It took hold of a thoughtless nation and taught her seriousness ... It took hold of a nation shallow in her joy and sorrow; it shook her to the depth of her nature; it opened her eyes and sharpened her hearing".

In paying this tribute to the Churches and Capels of Vaynor one has in mind not only the institutions but those good and worthy souls who by their lives and their example made possible a richer and better world for so many. Unfortunately the Chapels, which were the most important buildings and the only evidence apart from the churches, of anything approaching deliberately conceived architecture are closing one after the other, so that now only Hen Dŷ Cwrdd, Bethel Cwm Tâf, Carmel and the Pentecostal Church remain open in the parish of Vaynor. The once intense religious passion and denominational rivalry has now cooled into a total indifference and if this trend continues the Nonconformist Chapels will soon become mere museum pieces of antiquarian interest only.

CHAPTER VII

The Parish Registers

INTRODUCTION

During the middle ages some clergymen kept records of the weddings and funerals at which they officiated, but the keeping of parish registers was not made compulsory until 1538, when Thomas Cromwell, vice-gerent of Henry VIII, required each incumbent to enter into a book, in the presence of Church wardens, the names of all who had been christened, married and buried during the previous week. Little came of this, and in 1597, more stringent regulations came into force which were confirmed by a canon of 1603. Each incumbent had to promise to keep at his church the registers in a parchment book, and copies of the entries were to be sent by the Wardens to the bishop's registry. These are now referred to as Bishop's Transcripts, which at Vaynor Church go back to 1714.

The system of registration by the clergy broke down during the Civil War and the Directory of 1645, which replaced the Book of Common Prayer, ordered that every parish should have "a fair register book of vellim" and, that births and deaths should be recorded as well as baptisms and burials. This again was found to be unsatisfactory, and in 1653, the custody of the registers was transferred to "registers", i.e. registrars, who were to be elected biennially by the parishioners. At this time civil marriages before Justices of the Peace were introduced and recorded by the lay registrar. This was generally resented and at the Restoration clerical registration was resumed. Registers were kept with greater care but they were still incomplete. During 1694-1706 and 1783-1794, for instance, when taxes were payable on registration, many births and deaths were unregistered. From this time, however, marriages were recorded more carefully, but those solemnised without banns or licence, in uncanonical hours, or elsewhere than in the parish church of bride or bridegroom, would be entered.

During the eighteenth century irregular marriages became such a scandal that Hardwicke's Marriage Act of Parliament decreed that, after 25th March 1754, all weddings not solemnised through banns or licence in some church or chapel customarily used for that purpose should be void and that separate registers for marriages should be kept "in proper books of vellim or good and durable paper", the entries to be made in a prescribed form and signed by the contracting parties and two witnesses. This resulted in a great improvement in the keeping of registers. Uniformity of baptismal and burial entries was secured by the passing of the Rose Act of 1812, which required that separate printed books, provided by the King's printers, should be used for baptisms and burials. An attempt was also made to enforce the transmission and proper custody of Bishop's Transcripts, but again, as no fees for the work involved were provided, it was without much effect. The Parochial Registers Act of 1812 provided for the safe custody of registers in "dry well-painted iron chests" and in the Vaynor Parish Vestry Accounts for 1818 one sees the following entry, "For a lock and hinges to put on the Chest of the Church, 4s.6d (23p).

In this study it is proposed to study the Parish Records of St Gwynno's Church, Vaynor and of St John's Church, built in 1874 at Cefn Coed, and also those of St Mary's Nantddu[1] which although in the Parish of Cantref, has served the Cwm Tâf valley even before Saxon referred to it as "Capel Nantye" in 1572. With the building of St John's Church in 1874 a new parish was formed at Cefn Coed, but in 1980 the Rector of Cefn Coed, the Rev David Walters MA assumed responsibility for St Gwynno's at Vaynor and St Mary's Nantddu at Cwm Tâf. The Parish Registers are to be found from 1714 at Vaynor with earlier records at the National Library, Aberystwyth; from 1877 at Cefn Coed and from 1813 at Nantddu, Cwm Tâf. We now turn to an examination of the registers.

LANGUAGE

From the first entries in the Vaynor Parish Registers all the entries are made in English. The sole use of the English language in an area which was largely Welsh speaking until the beginning of this century is difficult to understand. The ignorance of Welsh spelling is clearly demonstrated in the following place names found in the Parish Records:- "Kefen" for Cefn, "Panman (?), Garn Pontsticket (Pontsticill), Caerhaca, Suraway, Tin y Ka (Ty yn y cae) and Pont-gelli Vaylog".

PERSONAL NAMES

An important point of interest is the custom of naming a child after grand-parents, parents or a dead brother or sister. An example of this is the Christian name Emmanuel occurring since about 1855 in the name of the family of the Morning Sun Inn, Cefn Coed. This can be attributed to one Mary Manuel who married Thomas Lewis in Vaynor in 1850. She perpetuated her surname by giving the name 'Emmanuel' to three sons. As each son died in infancy, the next newly born was given the name and even today the name is still common within the family. In terms of the most popular names, J. E. Jenkins found after analysing 425 names on the Baptismal register "dated a hundred years ago", i.e. about 1800 that the most popular names then for girls were Mary, Ann, Jane, Gwenllian and Margaret in that order, while for boys it was John, William, Thomas, David and Morgan.

PLACE NAMES

By the nineteenth century farm names and names of other dwellings and other places are frequently given. Vaynor would seem to have been very popular as a burial place in the nineteenth century, or was it that urban graveyards were either few or full? One notes burials at Vaynor from 1813 from most of the farms in the Cwm Tâf valley for example, Pontardâf, Ffrwd, Grawen and Sychpant – all at least four or five miles away from Vaynor Church. Were the deceased carried all this way? Or were they brought by sledge over the old Parish Road from Cwm Tâf via the Fedw, Berthllwyd to Vaynor Churchyard? Then, again, one notes addresses of the bereaved from outside the Parish such as 'Ffynnon Tudfil, Penheoldadau'. Very many of the place names refer to farms or places that no longer exist, places such as "Abernant, Abercarr, Ponk a Furnace, Priordy, Blaenmorlais, Cwmole, Gore'r llechau, Pwllyrhiwyaid, Tyle llwyd, Ty yn y Waun, Ffynnon Rosser, Llwynmolgoch, Tyn y garn, Llwyn Yr Eos, Garn Galed, Gwaungafar, Brynshac and Franchbach". One recognises new names such as 'Danydarren' for the old 'Wrlod-ddu' (Black Ditch). This last name is of interest since one can still see the pattern of ditches which once separated the fields, 'Wrlod-ddu' was a most appropriate place name. Finally one should note that without exception every place name is Welsh.

TRADES AND PROFESSIONS

The registers indicate very clearly the great social change which has taken place in this parish during the last 250 years. Nowhere in this more clearly shown than in the description of trades and crafts in which people were occupied. Because Vaynor was a rural Parish and to a great extent self-supporting, one finds those trades associated with rural life, such as miller, weaver, etc. But since Cefn Coed was developing as an industrial dormitory for Cyfarthfa, one finds the trades associated with iron making and coal mining in the Parish registers. A list has been compiled of trades and professions as they appear in the Parish registers for each of the three Churches and these are shown as follows.

Of the first years at Vaynor, we have a gentleman (gent) who was able to sign the register and in the following years men associated with rural life and with industry. Associated with rural life in the nineteenth century we have such occupations as "carrier, taylor, yeoman, farmer, miller, weaver, groom, spinner, turner, woodkeeper, saddler cattle dealer, rural postman, castrator and game-keeper". The list for industrial trades is varied and very long, for example "metal braker, baller, rider, puddler, cinder-wheeler, furnace filler, bundler, coker, rougher-down, fitter-up, squeezer-holder, boiler-maker, sinker, melter, nailor, tin bar maker, firesmith, straightener, cleaver, ripper, charger and striker". One can pinpoint particular social changes with certain occupations, for example, the "blocklayer" with the coming of railways to Merthyr, "rail-filer", letter carrier, trained nurse (1893), navigator and waterworks labourer (1888), "sexton" in 1859 with the building of Cefn Cemetery in that year. A Police Officer is referred to in Cwm Tâf in 1891, probably to maintain law and order among the navvies working on the reservoirs, while their spiritual welfare was in the capable hands of Mr Hicken the navvy missioner.

ILLEGITIMACY

The number of premarital pregnancies in the Parish of Vaynor recorded both at St Gwynno's Vaynor and at St Mary's Nantddu shows that sexual intimacy frequently occurred during courtship. Illegitimate children are recorded as 'base', 'illeg', 'illegitimate' or as 'bastards'. Illegitimacy is recorded in the registers with a consistency which makes it seem clear that where these entries appear at all they must be taken seriously as an indication of the incidence of extra marital intimacy. The registration of children born of such unions in itself is a demonstration of the power of the clergy and of public opinion, because it must have taken some courage to offer a 'base-born" child to the priest for baptism, though some allowance must surely be made for the mother's concern for the baby's immortal soul.

It is important to note that the proportion of baptisms marked 'illegitimate' in the parish registers could well be an inaccurate indicator of moral lapse. Numbers of baptised illegitimate children may well have to be multiplied many times to guess at the number of sexual lapses which lay behind them. Evasion may have been common, of course, and it is probably wise to suspect the testimony of these records which suggest that bastardy has not occurred; for example, in Vaynor in 1821 it was recorded that there were seven illegitimacies among the thirty children recorded as baptised but for 1840 there are no illegitimate births recorded out of sixty four baptisms, yet it is difficult to suppose that morality had improved so dramatically in the course of twenty years. The illegitimacy figures for Vaynor are interesting. Between 1813 and 1850 the percentage of illegitimate births of the total was 3.2, and in the second half of the nineteenth century it was virtually the same at 3.3 per cent. The picture at St Mary's, Nantddu, Cwm Tâf however is quite different. Between 1813 and 1850 it was 12.2 per cent of the total baptisms, which is nearly four times higher than at St Gwynno's Vaynor for the same period. For the record half of the nineteenth century one finds a reverse situation in St Mary's Cwm Tâf, the percentage for the period 1851 to 1900 drops dramatically to 1.5 per cent which is now half of that at St Gwynno's. By comparison one notes that Vaynor on the whole has a lower percentage of illegitimacy than Merthyr Tydfil for the second half of the nineteenth century, which shows an average of 4.3 percent.

These facts could be regarded as evidence of greater sexual laxity in Cwm Tâf, the most rural part of Vaynor, than at Cefn Coed. More effective means of contraception, which are better known and more easily procurable in urban than rural areas, have rendered statistics of this kind largely valueless for comparing the extra marital sexual life of these communities. What is very interesting here is the fact that illegitimacy fell at Cwm Tâf from 12.8 per cent to 1.5 per cent during the second half of the nineteenth century, which coincided with two important social changes in the locality, namely the influx of workers on the reservoirs and the decline of farms and of the farming community as a consequence. The high rate of illegitimacy at Cwm Tâf is primarily associated with servant girls working on the farms. This high rate may be explained by the lack of parental supervision, because many girls had been hired at Brecon Fair and were from distant parishes. In the section on the 'Role of Farm workers in Vaynor' it was found from the 1851 Census for the Parish of Vaynor, that there were 36 servant girls working on the 35 Vaynor farms referred to in the Census. There were however, over 100 farms in the Tâf Fawr and Tâf Fechan valley, including those from the adjacent parishes, so that one can estimate over a hundred servant girls working here in 1851 on the local farms. Where the place of origin is shown in the Census Report, it is apparent that many came from Breconshire and Carmarthenshire whereas all the men were from neighbouring parishes.

It was also probably associated with inadequate sleeping accommodation. Many slept in attics for example, where the only privacy afforded to them was by a flimsy partition made of fabric. Undoubtedly, many were raped or taken advantage of by fellow-servants or by their masters. Because of in-breeding very many of the adult population were of low-intelligence. Another important factor is the low intensity of public censure because of the remoteness of the farms. Public censure in the urban areas of this locality was very severe; unfortunate girls were known to have been publicly censured in the presence of Chapel congregations. This particular form of censure had no impact whatsoever of course, if the girl did not attend Chapel or Church in Cwm Tâf.

There are very frequent references to illegitimate children born to servants on the same farm, while in some cases the same girls continue to have illegitimate children. For example, Ann .... of .... Farm, Cwm Tâf had an illegitimate child in 1836 and another in 1837. In neither case did she disclose the father's name but it is of interest that the farmer of .... Farm, Cwm Tâf is known to have fathered an illegitimate child for Mary ...., a servant girl at Maesyfaenor in 1831. Generally, if conception was not followed by marriage, compensation was paid by the parents of the man concerned. The child was then brought up by the girl's parents. From what has been seen in the Parish records, giving birth to an illegitimate child while undoubtedly a handicap, by no means debarred the woman from getting married to another partner. It is known that, on occasion, the illegitimate child was left in the porch of the farm of the supposed father. It was widely supposed, even back to the time of Giraldus Cambrensis, that the Welsh 'are not accustomed to undertaking the responsibility of marriage without previous proof of compatibility and, above all, fertility, through cohabitation and intercourse'. By noting the date of marriage and the date of the first-born child from the Baptismal Register one can calculate the number of pre-nuptial conceptions. John .... and Jane .... married at Cwm Tâf in January 1815 and their first child was baptised on September 26th which suggests that she was probably pregnant on marriage. A thorough investigation has revealed only one or two cases such as this in Cwm Tâf.

In conclusion, it would seem that illegitimacy was not widespread throughout the community at large. There is definite evidence that promiscuity does run in families. By and large, men and women lived what is termed 'respectable lives', there were exceptions such as farmer of .... Farm, Cwm Tâf who fathered at least three illegitimate children for servant girls, and who in local usage would have been termed "March y Plwyf" ("The parish stallion").

MARRIAGE

Marriage was an act of profound importance to the individuals concerned and to the social structure. It meant the creation of new economic unit as well as a life long association of persons. It gave the man full membership of the community and added a cell to village society. It is understandable, therefore, that marriage could not come about unless there was a vacant 'slot' so to speak and the aspiring couple was suitable to fill it. It might be a cottage which had fallen empty, so that a man servant and woman servant could now marry and go to live there as cottagers. It might be a small holding, or a joinery or a loom which had to be manned anew. Such circumstances ordinarily meant that young men and women in the parish had to wait until they could get married. We now turn to an examination of the Parish registers for the three Churches.

THE MARRIAGE REGISTERS

St Gwynno's Church, Vaynor

The Marriage Registers at Vaynor date back to 1755, with a gap between 1868 and 1893 due to a missing register. Records prior to 1755 dating back to 1714 are to be found in the Bishops' Transcripts at the National Library, Aberystwyth. These records show that the annual average number of marriages for the first half of the eighteenth century would appear to be 3 or 4 while for the second half 4 or 5 marriages. After 1800 there is a noticeable increase and the average number of marriages for the first half of the nineteenth century was 25 per annum and for the second half of the nineteenth century it rose to 30. The average for the first half of the twentieth century has dropped to 17 per annum and since 1950 the average is down to between 5 and 6.

An examination of the list of marriages of the three Churches in the parish shows that whereas in Vaynor in 1800 there were only five weddings, in the years between 1800 and 1837 there is a dramatic increase in marriages probably due to the effects of industrialisation and the growth of population. In the period 1837 to 1847 a period of only ten years there were 500 weddings at Vaynor. This was partly due to the compulsory registration of marriages from 1837 and also because it was considered lucky to marry in Vaynor. From 1900 there has been a decline in the number of weddings at St Gwynno's for many reasons, such as marriages at Registry Offices, Chapels and also at St John's Church, Cefn.

THE MARRIAGE REGISTER AT

St Mary's Church, Nantddu, Cwm Tâf

THE Marriage Register dates from 1813 and in that year there was one wedding, three the following year and then not another wedding for 24 years. Between 1813 and 1964 there were 53 weddings which is an average of nearly 1 wedding every three years over this period, i.e. 151 years. It is interesting to note, as already stated, that there were 500 weddings between 1837 and 1847 at Vaynor. This may be attributed to the popularity of Vaynor and also to its nearness to Cefn Coed and Merthyr Tydfil and to the growth of the local industrial population.

As one would expect, the Registers at Nantddu refer to the marriage of farmers, servants and artisans. The importance of the latter in the life of this upland area may be gleaned by the number of craftsmen referred to. One notes in 1858 that Morgan Lewis, a carpenter at Nantddu, married a widow of 45 and John Williams a miller, and the son of a miller, Humphrey Williams married in the same year. This suggests that the Millers' Arms employed a number of men. Then again, in 1860 William Watkins, a widower and son of John Watkins the wheelwright married Letitia Davies, a farm servant, while another widower, David Williams, married Harriet James, the servant girl at Coedowen whose father was James James the weaver probably at Ynysyfelin Woollen Factory. An interesting entry for 1890 reads as follows "Joseph Scragg (19) Timber man living at Crew Farm, Cwm Tâf, son of William Scragg, Figure maker, married Lucy Tricket (18) daughter of Thomas Trickett filler also living at Crew Farm". There is considerable evidence to show that many of the farms were becoming lodging houses. Abercrew was a well known lodging house. The fact that Thomas Trickett was a 'filler' suggests that he was employed at one of the Merthyr ironworks which meant that he walked about eight miles each way to work daily from Cwm Tâf to Merthyr.

The remarriage of widowers in Cwm Tâf indicates a high incidence of female mortality probably at childbirth. Research into childbirth practices at Cwm Tâf indicates that it was the custom for neighbours to help out at this time. The nearest untrained midwife would have been at Cefn Coed and the nearest doctor six to eight miles away at Merthyr Tydfil. Practically every marriage involved partners from within the valley. Over the years there must have been considerable in-breeding with its resulting detrimental effects upon the intelligence and constitution of the young. Law and order was maintained during the period of reservoir building by a resident Police Officer. An entry in the Marriage Register for 1891 refers to the marriage of one "William Colum Davies, aged 29, a Police Officer at the Police Station in Hannah Herbert's residence Nantddu". The total number of marriages for the period 1813-1850 was 6, 1851-1900 was 24 and 1901 to 1950 it was 23. Since 1951 there have been only 6 marriages there.

St Mary's Church fell into disrepair in 1980 and it is very unlikely that any marriages will take place there again.

THE MARRIAGE REGISTER AT

St John's Church, Cefn Coed

THE Marriage Registers of St John's Church, Cefn Coed date from 1883 when Dr Leigh, surgeon married Jessie Louisa Jones, daughter of William Jones, Ironworks Manager". As one would expect the range of occupations, trades and professions represent the whole spectrum of occupations one would find near a busy industrial town. One therefore finds reference to 'Engineer, Haulier, Lecturer, footballer, Solicitor, and tram-conductor', with only a few references to the rural occupations that were once common here in pre-industrial times, nevertheless one notes saddlers, carpenters and a wheelwright as late as 1930.

Whereas in Cwm Tâf until fairly recent times, marriage partners were selected from within the family, or within the valley, this was not the case at Cefn Coed. Because of the proximity of Merthyr and good communications with other districts, there is no limitation imposed by remoteness or lack of outside contacts in finding marriage partners outside the area. The total number of marriages from 1883 to 1900 was 10 and from 1900 to 1950 was 235 and from 1950 up to 1973 the total was 170.

AGE OF MARRIAGE AND OCCUPATION

An analysis of mean ages for marriage for various occupations has shown that in the nineteenth century in the Parish of Vaynor the following were the respective average ages at marriage: miners – 23.8 years, ironworkers – 22.8 years, quarrymen – 28 years, craftsmen – (masons, carpenters, painters, etc) – 29 years and farmers – 32.7 years. An explanation for these differences might be found in the fact that miners and ironworkers would have been on a full man's wage after 21 years of age and could afford to marry or at least had no incentive to delay marriage in the hope of becoming economically better off. Craftsmen, because of an extended apprenticeship, would not have been earning a full wage until after 22 years of age. Farmers were the latest getting married; this may be explained by low income, the difficulty of getting a suitable place and probably by the fact that certain circumstances might have prevented them from marrying earlier such as a widowed mother. In addition to the difficulty in getting a holding, stocking it was an added financial burden. This would explain his having to wait longer than some of the manual workers.

FATHERLESS BRIDES AND BRIDEGROOMS

Because of the extremely low life expectancy in this area, which will be discussed more fully later, an examination of the marriage registers was made in order to ascertain how many fathers of brides and bridegrooms were alive at the time of their children's weddings. The results in the following table make one fully aware of the appalling death rate for men, and it is of interest to note the improving situation with the passage of years. To take one or two examples, in 1848, there were 24 weddings at Vaynor, of the 48 fathers who might have attended these weddings, 31 were already dead, and again in 1846 there were 33 weddings and out of the 66 fathers who might have been present, 46 were already dead, i.e. 69 per cent and most of the brides and bridegrooms averaged only 21 or 22 years of age. This characteristic persisted until the turn of this century, but as late as 1901 out of 83 weddings there were 60 fathers dead. The percentage of fathers dead at the time of their children's weddings for the nineteenth and twentieth centuries is shown in the following table.

TABLE OF FATHERS OF BRIDES AND BRIDEGROOMS DEAD AT THE WEDDINGS OF THEIR CHILDREN AT ST GWYNNO'S, VAYNOR

Date	Fathers Dead	Number of Marriages	Percentage of Fathers Dead
1837-1850	362	582	31 per cent
1851-1900	654	797	41 per cent
1901-1950	188	428	21 per cent

By comparison, only 4 fathers were dead at Cwm Tâf out of 56 marriages, i.e. 3½ per cent. It is apparent that few local children in the nineteenth century knew their grandparents except at Cwm Tâf. The relatively low expectation of life combined with the relatively high age of marriage implied a relatively short duration of marriage for many and as a result upon the number of children likely to be born into a particular family.

RE-MARRIAGES

A high mortality rate resulted in a high proportion of widows and widowers in the local population. The death of a mother of a family of children or of a capable woman at the head of a farm or a craftsman's household was indeed a very serious but nevertheless common event of the eighteenth and nineteenth centuries. There are very frequent references to the deaths of comparatively young women of child-bearing age. When the father and husband died, everything upon which the family depended was put in jeopardy. The effect would vary, of course, in accordance with the point of his career when catastrophe came, with the number, age and capacity of his sons, the vigour and determination of his widow and her "attractiveness" as a possible wife for someone else. An analysis of the marriage registers shows that between 1837 and 1850,57 widows remarried and 63 widowers remarried and between 1851 and 1900, 85 widowers remarried and 65 widows did likewise. One wonders whether it was for economic expediency or was the institution of marriage popular?

These figures do not represent the total number of marriages for the period because some of the marriage registers have been lost. From these figures however it is apparent that 18 per cent or nearly one in every five weddings at Vaynor involved a widow or widower.

LITERACY IN VAYNOR

(Shown by being able to sign the marriage register)

The discovery of how great a proportion of the population could read and write at any point in time is one of the most fascinating and urgent tasks of the social historian. The challenge is not simply to find the evidence and to devise ways of making it yield reliable answers. It is also a challenge to the historical and literary imagination to recall and reconstruct, to make a present reality to ourselves at a time when, as the evidence from the information overleaf will show most men and women could only think, talk, sing, play, till the soil, tend the beasts and make ploughs, whilst only a very small minority could read or write in Vaynor. After Hardwick's Marriage Act of 1753 each bride and bridegroom was required to sign or make a distinctive mark in the marriage register, just as they had done in France for 150 years.

An examination of the Vaynor Marriage registers indicates that relatively few were able to sign their names in the Registers, fewer women than men. In 1840, for example, there were 77 weddings in which 53 men signed their names with a cross and 70 women did likewise. In 1850, 19 men out of 26 signed with a cross and 25 women, representing 99 per cent of the wives failed to sign their names. With the advent of compulsory education there was a dramatic improvement in standards and by 1900 one finds every woman out of 57 weddings able to sign her name and only three men signing with a cross. Those who married by licence were, it appears, better educated. Of the 38 weddings at Vaynor by licence during the nineteenth century, 50 per cent of the men involved and 28.9 per cent of the women were able to sign their names on the Marriage Register.

This evidence presents considerable difficulty to the interpreter, because we do not yet know what the ability to sign, often very shakily and sometimes probably by tracing or copying, really meant at these times. It seems likely on the whole that more could read, if only with difficulty than could sign their names. Many would have been taught to read in the Sunday Schools though not necessarily to write. It is even possible that some men who could write their names actually chose on occasion to make a mark instead.

BURIALS

The Burial Registers are available from 1813 at St Gwynno's Vaynor and from 1714 at the National Library, Aberystwyth. The Burial Registers for St Mary's, Nantddu are available from 1813. In the case of Vaynor one notes the very high incidence of burials from "without the parish", i.e. from "Dowlais, Merthyr, Aberdare, "Pontystorws" (i.e. Pontstorehouse, Georgetown), Gelli Gaer and Troed-y-Rhiw". A closer examination reveals that out of 3047 burials at Vaynor in the nineteenth century, 1451 or 47 per cent were from outside the parish. This tendency was encouraged by Dr Dyke, the Merthyr Medical Officer. In 1865 he reported to the Merthyr Guardian "It is satisfactory to know that the practice of interring the dead at a distance from the abode of the living is gaining ground. It is admitted to be unhealthy to inter the dead among the residence of the living".[2] This was undoubtedly the thinking behind the decision to build Cefn Cemetery for the Merthyr Parish in 1858. The Burial Registers indicate a very high mortality rate for all ages and especially for children under 5 years of age. Since so many were being buried at Cefn Coed or Vaynor, it is of interest to investigate some of the causes of this high mortality. We now examine some of the causes of death in this locality.

STARVATION

A low rate of wages co-incident with high-priced provisions necessarily led to a shortage of food. Dr Dyke reported in 1866 that 69 people died of diseases of nutrition.[3] The "starving peasantry" is a common phrase especially in popular literature. Perhaps "starving" should be taken to mean badly-fed, wretchedly clothed and housed. In this superficial survey one can only touch on the principles and open up possibilities. Starvation would not necessarily show itself in conspicuous events, perhaps perpetual undernourishment lasting for several disastrous harvests, might be its usual manifestation. The influence of climate, good and bad harvest years, mild and severe winters must be stressed as we think of these things. Where the less fortunate members of a society are at the mercy of weather and around the margin of subsistence, the tendency will surely be that the fluctuating situation will become extreme.

There are no recorded deaths due to starvation in the Parish registers but there is a very close correlation between the bad harvest years of the 1840s and a high death rate at Vaynor. Excluding the high rate due to cholera in 1849, the highest number of burials recorded in Vaynor were for the years 1840 to 1845, i.e. in 1840 there were 66 burials; 1841 – 64, 1842 – 50, 1843 – 47, 1844 – 59 and in 1845 there were 58 burials.

Referring to the industrial recession of 1875, Dr Dyke reported that "the children were very quickly affected by the diminished quantity and quality of food". As a result, however, of only one good meal daily provided by the "soup kitchens" at Cefn Coed and in the Merthyr area, he was able to report that the death rate of children in 1875 at Merthyr was less than in any previous year. He also reported in 1875 that "Famine and famine fever, this dread visitant did show itself ... relief came and the plague was stayed".[4] It would seem from the above facts that bad harvests and industrial recession were clearly important factors in determining the quality and quantity of food made available to workers and their dependents. This in turn affected the general level of health and the predisposition to disease and of course to the high mortality figures for children and adults in this area.

CLEANLINESS

Theophilus Jones writing at the beginning of the nineteenth century about domestic cleanliness, remarked of Glamorgan "the cots in the Vales of that County are externally and internally neater than in any parts of the Kingdom", but, speaking of the houses of Breconshire, and one must assume that he was speaking of Vaynor, too, he said "the hut indeed upon the wilds of Breconshire, where the door serves for the three fold purposes of an entrance, a window, and a chimney is a miserable habitation".[5] These conditions were certainly contributory factors of the many deaths in Vaynor.

SOCIAL CONDITIONS

In 1849, Dr Dyke the Merthyr Tydfil Medical Officer of Health was asked how the high mortality could be accounted for. He replied, "We believe that it is mainly referable to local and self-created conditions, and these are:- the vicious construction of houses, the inadequate supply of water, the absence of drainage, defective ventilation, the accumulation of filth, atmospheric impurity and the extensive and fatal prevalence of disease".[6] Many of the Vaynor cottages in the early eighteenth century were made of turf walls and thatched roofs. Until 1951 Danydarren farm had a thatched roof.

THE CLIMATE

Dr Dyke refers to the climate thus, "The greater humidity of your climate, the rainfull exceeding the average may and probably does act, in some seasons, especially in conjunction with other influences, as a predisposing cause in the generation and extension of sickness, – the cheapness and excellent quality of your coal go far to counteract the otherwise injurious effects of occasional dampness".[7] The rainfull in the upland areas of Vaynor varies between 76 and 90 inches of rain per annum, while the cottage roofs were made of thatch, fern and gorse, with turf walls and earthen floors. One can imagine the dampness, squalor and sickness in these hovels whose only form of heating was provided by fuels like peat or wood.

Dr Dyke reported in 1877 that 260 died "of maladies affecting the organs of breathing, nearly a fourth of the whole deaths".[8] Because of the rainfall, the nature of employment in a rural area such as Vaynor, the atrocious housing, lack of facilities for drying damp clothes, lack of fuel, remoteness from doctors, etc., one can assume that the death rate from such diseases as tuberculosis, pneumonia and bronchitis would have been relatively higher than at Merthyr Tydfil.

HOUSING AND SANITATION

Reference has already been made above to the inadequacy of rural houses in Vaynor. Referring to urban housing, such as that found at Cefn Coed or Merthyr, Dr Dyke stated "Houses built of porous sandstone, foundations of unmortared stone, floors of paving laid on the soil after the removal only of the turf, the lower floors are always damp and cold; hence arise many forms of sickness. If occupied soon after they are built a form of Typhoid Fever results ... No back doors hence no ventilation. Conveniences were rarely attached to the residences – the ash heap received the excretions which putrified in front of the house".[9] Referring to tubercular diseases, he stated, "The disposition of them is increased, if not occasioned by those causes which lower human health:- long exposure to damp and cold being one of the chief". Water arrived in the houses of Cefn Coed in 1866 and probably brought some improvement in general health.

DISEASE

Contagious diseases such as measles, scarlet fever, typhus, enteric fever, diphtheria, whooping cough and tuberculosis were rampant through Merthyr even after the introduction of vaccination, reported upon in 1867. Much of the disease was spread by overcrowding, filthy living conditions and lack of adequate ventilation superimposed upon general debility as a result of poor care, poor nutrition etc., and a general environment of rubbish and excreta near to the houses, both rural and urban. Dr Dyke has referred to "the abodes of our poor brethren covered with water, that water moreover charged with the excremitious deposits freely scattered in backyards and gardens ... The cold winds required that the doors and windows should be kept closed and thus there was no ventilation".[10] Amazingly, these housing conditions, where for example, earth floors still prevailed in the parish of Vaynor until 1935, when houses in Field Street, Cefn Coed with earthen floors were demolished. With regard to vaccination it is unlikely that Vaynor mothers living in remote upland farms would have attended the early clinics for vaccination of their babies. Sewage works were commenced in Merthyr in 1865 and completed in 1868; it did not come to Cefn Coed until the beginning of this century.

CHOLERA

It has been stated that "Cholera is the direct result of sanitary neglect – the penalty entailed by dirt, filth and impurity".[11] The names of eight victims are given for the outbreak in Vaynor in 1832, namely, a father and son – David Lewis aged 44 and his son David Lewis aged 18 years; a mother and two children – Margaret Thomas aged 30, David Thomas aged 15 and William Thomas aged 12 years. a mother and son – Ann Jones aged 46 and David Jones aged 7 years, and lastly Jane Gould, aged 13 years.

The Burial Registers indicate the following number of burials in Vaynor during the major Cholera outbreaks; in 1832 there were 47 burials with 27 burials from outside Vaynor compared with an average for the nineteenth century of 35 burials at Vaynor per annum with 16 from outside the Parish. In 1849 there was the highest number of recorded burials for any year in the nineteenth century, namely 72, of which 21 were from outside Vaynor. In 1854 there were 39 burials, twelve of which were from outside Vaynor and in 1866 there were 29 of which eleven were from outside. The 1849 figures indicate a high proportion of Vaynor people dying of cholera that year.

CHILD MORTALITY

An examination of the Burial Registers shows infant mortality to be very high. In 1820, for example, out of 38 burials, 14 were of children under five years, 8 of whom were born in Vaynor. Then in 1840, out of 62 burials in Vaynor, 35, which is more than half the total burials, were those of children under 5. Of these children under 5, 11 were from Vaynor.

Children under 5 years of age represented 42 per cent of the burials in Vaynor between 1820 and 1900 and 20 per cent of the burials were from Vaynor Parish. By comparison, in the rural area of St Mary's, Cwm Tâf, during the nineteenth century, there were 277 burials, of whom 64 were children under 5 years of age. 61 of these children were from within the parish representing 22 per cent of all the burials. 16 of the burials of under five's at Cwm Tâf included children from Cefn and other places outside the valley so that the actual number from within the valley was 48 or 17 per cent of the total burials. For the whole of the Parish of Vaynor in the nineteenth century about 20-22 per cent of all the funerals were those of children under 5 years of age. This compares very favourably with Merthyr Tydfil where, for example, the percentage of child deaths in the total deaths of 1849 was 52.6 per cent. We note here the report where Dr Dyke stated "More than half of the funerals that take place in Merthyr are those of children under 5 years of age and more than one quarter of infants under one year".[12] He continues "Of all the districts in South Wales, that of Merthyr (including Vaynor) shows much the highest rate of infant mortality" Merthyr had twice the national average of deaths at confinement, i.e. 1 in every 105 confinements against a national average of 5 per 1000, due probably to untrained midwives largely, and neglect, unsanitary conditions, malnutrition or poverty.

LIFE EXPECTANCY

The Burial Registers of Vaynor and Cwm Tâf show the frequency of early deaths to be very common in Vaynor during the nineteenth century. Dr Dyke in his annual reports to the Merthyr Guardians has given "An average age at death at Merthyr for some years of the nineteenth century. A sample of these show that in 1850 it was 17½ years; in 1866 it was 24½ years and for 1875 it was 27 years. One notes that a man living in 1875 could expect to have on average 10 years more life than one living in

1850. The Rev J. E. Jenkins of Vaynor writing in 1897 claimed that the average age at death in Vaynor was 33 years while at Merthyr at that time it was only 26 years.[13] One notes the disastrous year of 1840 when there were 62 burials at Vaynor, 35 of whom were children under 5 years and the average age of death of all burials at Vaynor for that year was 13.8 years.

Further research might indicate that it became healthier as one moved outwards from the Industrial heartland of Merthyr clustered around Cyfarthfa and Dowlais. This possibly is substantiated by the fact that during the cholera epidemic of 1849, although the population of the Upper Division of Merthyr was 23,237, which included Vaynor, and virtually the same as the Lower Division at 23,147, nearly twice as many died in the Upper Division (935 victims) as against 454 victims in the Lower Division. Dr Dyke claimed that this was largely due to the larger proportion of the labouring class in the population of Upper Merthyr. He mentions an important point with regard to the occupations in which the labouring classes of Merthyr Tydfil are engaged. "The iron works, mines and collieries must render them liable to accidents frequently resulting in death". He substantiated this by quoting the figure of 299 dying of violence (accidents) in six years.[14]

ECONOMIC FACTORS

Dr Dyke reported that the general health of people was affected by wages and the cost of good. He pointed out that for each working person employed, there were two or three dependent upon him for food, thus 45 thousand out of 54 thousand were immediately dependent upon the iron and coal trade. Poverty resulting from low wages and large families brought disease in its wake attacking most severely those whose general health was below par.[15] He also made the point that "The wages paid for work done by the majority of the persons employed, contrasted with the prices of provisions is also a measure of the healthiness or otherwise of a population".[16] Since Cefn Coed was a dormitory for Cyfarthfa, economic factors, such as wages, had a direct bearing upon life expectancy in the Parish of Vaynor as did all the factors which have been discussed. The fact that ironworkers were paid from pubs increased the incidence of alcoholism resulting in deprivation for the dependent families of wives and children.

REFERENCES
1. Parish Records, i.e. Births, Marriages and Deaths for the Parish of Vaynor.
2. The Annual Reports on the Sanitary Condition of Merthyr Tydfil 1865 made by DR DYKE, Medical Officer.
3. DR DYKE'S Annual Reports, op. cit. 1866.
4. DR DYKE'S report ibid., 1875.
5. THEOPHILUS JONES, History of Brecknock (1809), p.139.
6. DR DYKE'S Reports, op. cit., 1849.
7. DR DYKE'S Reports, ibid, 1853.
8. DR DYKE'S Reports, ibid, 1877.
9. DR DYKE'S Reports, ibid, 1869.
10. DR DYKE'S Reports, ibid, 1869.
11. DR DYKE'S Reports, ibid, 1853.
12. DR DYKE'S Reports, ibid, 1853.
13. J. E. JENKINS, Vaynor Its History and Guide (1897), p.7.
14. DR DYKE'S Reports, op. cit., 1853.
15. DR DYKE'S Reports, ibid, 1866.
16. DR DYKE'S Reports, ibid, 1866.

CHAPTER VIII

Local Government

INTRODUCTION

The Elizabethan poor-law system was laid down by Elizabeth I's ninth parliament in 1598 and re-enacted by her last parliament in 1601. With various amendments, the most significant of which was the Poor Law Amendment Act of 1834, which set the poor law on its nineteenth century footing, it remained the law of England until 1948. The National Assistance Act of that year opened with the blunt, and challenging statement, that the existing, 'poor law shall cease to have effect', and thereby brought to an end a system which had endured throughout 350 years.

The 'Act for the Releife of the Poore' of 1598 consolidated and extended laws passed earlier in Elizabeth's reign (and originating in 1536, in her father's reign) for raising local taxes (rates) and appointing in every parish "Overseers of the poor" for the purpose of "setting to work of the children of all such whose parents shall not be thought able to keep and maintain their children", together with "all such persons, married or unmarried, as, having no means to maintain them, use no ordinary and daily trade of life to get their living by; providing a convenient stock of materials 'to set the porr on work'; the necessary relief of the lame, importent, old, blind and such other being poor and not able to work; the putting out of children to be apprentices".

People evicted from the land, or without work in times of scarcity, naturally turned to begging and wandering in search of work or alms. In the sixteenth century, as in earlier periods, everyone had his 'country' to which he was bound by birth. The natural unit and centre was the parish, in which a man was born, christened and married, and in which, for the most part, he died and was buried. It was in the parish that he could look for help in times of need. If he took to wandering, it was to his parish that he was likely to be returned, especially if in need. The first check on mobility, in fact, was the parish power which kept a man literally in his place. This had long existed by a common custom and was first given statutory form by an Act of 1572, principally aimed at the removal of paupers who had flocked into towns. The later Act which finally established the 'Law of Settlement' for all parishes was passed in 1662. In 1576, an Act was passed, 'for setting the poor on work and for avoiding of idleness'. This Act also prescribed 'houses of correction' for rogues and idlers. Already 'abiding places' for the poor, the charitable 'hospitals' of earlier periods, were being provided for the impotent who for one reason or another could not earn their living, and these were made obligatory by the Act of 1598. Thus, provision was made for the three classes of the poor, for the impotent in 'abiding places', later to be known as poor houses, for the able-bodied unemployed in work houses, and for the unregenerate idlers in houses of correction.

This machinery, with modifications in 1834, was destined to stand the test of time for well over three hundred years, until 1929. Attempts had been made since 1536 to raise local funds through local officials for the relief of the local poor, at first by charity and then, from 1572, by levying local taxes. Now all this was put on a secure basis by requiring that 'overseers of the poor' should be appointed in each parish, under the general direction of the Justices of the Peace. The overseers were to provide for the poor and to tax the parishioners for this purpose. By a significant addition, which was, however, little used, the Justices, in cases where a parish was unable to raise enough money for the relief of its own poor, could levy taxes towards the use of forced labour, in effect, to penalise poverty or to deter applications for relief.

Gilbert's Act permitted the establishment of unions of parishes to set up workhouses. The spontaneous reaction to England's first serious wartime inflation was the decision of the Berkshire Justices at Speenhamland in 1795 to supplement wages from the rates on a sliding scale in accordance with the price of bread and the size of the family concerned. Whatever the long term disadvantages, the Speenhamland policy did at least prevent utter destitution and starvation in the long years of high prices before the Napoleonic wars ended and it indicated some evidence of the genuine concern for those in distress. This was followed by considerable legislation in the nineteenth century relating to poor law, health, housing and education.

We now examine the Parish Vestry Accounts for Vaynor, excerpts of which are shown in the history of Vaynor by the Rector J. E. Jenkins who has included a list of these accounts from 'the Book of the Authorities at Llanhamlech at the time by the Church wardens and Overseers'.[3] He describes the accounts as being "a hundred years old in 1897", and they therefore probably cover a period from 1797 to 1818. The excerpts selected by Rector Jenkins are of great interest and provide invaluable insights into the social and religious life of the people of Vaynor during the early part of the nineteenth century. They read as follows:-

"Do for coffin for Mary Rees, 13s" 0d; "Do for cutting grave to Mary Rees, 1s" 0d. We see that the charge for a baptism was also 1/- (one shilling), "For Mr Morris to baptise the child of Jane Rees 1/- (5p today). "Mr Morris was during this time of plurality the curate in charge of Vaynor, Tave Fechan, Nantddu and Penderyn Churches between 1790 and 1818".

This item is of great interest in that it indicates that the Vestry, was responsible for providing coffins for paupers, for digging the grave and also for "washing her body". This duty was carried out by the official Parish Body washer and in the early years he was paid one shilling for every body washed. There are frequent references to 'body washing' in the Parish Vestry Accounts for example, referring to Mary Rees deceased, "For washing her body 1/- (one shilling or 5 pence today)". Later in 1805 we find, "for cleaning ye body for Morgan Robert 5/- (25p)". It would appear that only the good and respectable were favoured thus, because the following entry records that the body of the deceased was not washed:- "To ale to the people that help us to carry old beggar that died on Coed Cymmer to Church 3s 0d" (15p); Do expenses of the burial of an old bagar that died on our parish first for coffin, £1 10s 0d (£1.50)"; "Do of trespass in the house where he died, 4s 0d (£0.20p); Do for cutting, his grave 3s 0d (£0.15p); Do for the priest 1s 0d (5p); Do for the ale to carry him to church 2s 6d (12½p)". We note the price increase in a later entry "Do to Mary Morgan for coffin to her, 15/- (75p); For washing her body 2s 6d (12½p)" but for cutting her grave 1/-. Quite a dramatic increase in prices is shown in the next entry dated about 1799, "Do to coffin to Ann Williams, £1.10s.0d (£1.50), cutting her grave and wash her body 10s 0d (50p)". One wonders why there was so much variation in the charge for coffins – did it depend on quality of timber? Or were different craftsmen involved? Or was the price pitched to suit individual circumstances? The Merthyr Vestry revealed some business acumen when they contracted with Richard Watkins on September 19th 1826 to supply them with coffins at 6s 0d (30p) each for one year.

With regard to the 'old bagar' referred to above who died at 'Coed cymmer' one notes two charges for ale for the people who carried him to church. One must assume that the first entry refers to carrying him to church at Cefn Coed and the second to Vaynor Church. A clue is provided by the Rev J. E. Jenkins as to where this very early Cefn Coed Church was sited when he states "the great Jones of Vaynor (who came in 1818) began to hold services at the Old Gate House, and afterwards at Cefn isaf". The Gate House that he refers to is probably the Turnpike House situated above the Cefn Bridge. The ale referred to was the mode of payment for carrying the body in the second instance, from Cefn Coed to Vaynor, a distance of nearly four arduous miles.

There are many entries of medical interest. The first, and one of the most fascinating, is that of "Ann Bowen and child and a man midwife to her, 21s 0d" (£1.05p). The man midwife was not trained in the usual sense but acquired expertise through practical experience. There are many references to doctors such as "Paid Powell the Doctor for cure of Peter Jones £13.12s.2½d (£13.61); to a doctor for cure the finger of Mary Martin 2s 0d (10p). To Doctor Davies for cure the leg of John Philip, £3.14s.0d" (£3.70).

Removals and settlements are very frequently referred to in the early decades of the nineteenth century, entries such as, "To moving John Jolly and family to Worcester £5.5s.8d (£5.28); Do to charge by send Jennet Abraham out of the parish 4s 0d (20p); Removing John Shir Von to Cantref, 9s 6d (48p); To journey to Brecon about Ann Morgan big with child, 7s 0d (35p); To journey for a warrant to summon her mother to come before Justice about her settlement; To my journey to Brecon with Gwennlian Morgan, 2 days, 10s 0d (50p); To order to move her to Cantref, 8s 0d (40p). To three days search for her and move her, 2s 6d (12½p); For take the wife and children of David Davies by vagrant pass to Llandovery, horses and all expenses £3.11s.0d (£3.55); To Thos Howell for move David Evan, his wife and children to the County of Carmarthen, in cart, £5.5s.0d (£5.25)". The legal wranglings involved in these cases are referred to often, for example "(1799) to Mr Theophilus Jones, (The Breconshire Historian), attorney, of cost concerning the settlement of wife and children of Williams Martin, £6.2s.6d (£6.12); Do to William Nicholas, Constable, attendance at Cowbridge Quarter Sessions, £9.0s.6d (£9.05); Do to expenses of the trial in Usk Quarter Sessions between

Vaynor and Bedwellty concerning settlement, meat and drink, hire carriages, horses, and turnpike, £20.14s.8d (£20.73); Expenses in Neath Quarter Sessions, £4.9s.6d (£4.47). Do for the trial between Vaynor and Merthyr, £3.10s.0d" (£3.50). These entries provide some interesting information regarding the re-settlement of families in their native parishes. With the influx of people into the Merthyr district during the late eighteenth and nineteenth centuries this posed a major problem for the Merthyr Vestry and the Poor Law. It has been claimed that the dying were sometimes carried into their native parishes to save the cost of a coffin which during the nineteenth century in Vaynor was about six shillings (30p).

The Vestry was apparently genuinely concerned with the poor, the undernourished and ill-clad residents of the parish. This concern is shown in the following entries between 1799 and 1828, "Do clothes to Howell Rhys 10s 0d (50p); Do to relieft in corn to Jane Zacharias, To Morgan Edward, 3 bushel and 1 peck of barley, at 7s 0d (35p) per bushel, £1.2s.9d (£1.13)". This help was of little avail as the next entry shows, "For his coffin, £1". Later we find further gifts from "the Parish" such as "To Williams Poweel a pair of shoes", and "To John Philip cloath (cloth) to make him a breeches; Do to Mary Rees, flannen (flannel) for shift, 3s 6d (17p); Mary Morgan, flannen for shift and petty coat; Paid for flannen it help shurt to Howel Thomas John, 1s 6d (7½p). For frog (presumably frock) to the child of Howel Thos John, 5s 0d (25p). To Thos David Richards, 5s 0d (25p) per week for 8 weeks, £2. To him (David Richards) load of malt, £2.19s.6d (£2.87); To Jenking John Edward, to him in time of sickness two weeks, £1.5s.10d (£1.29); To him to have bellows and other implements, £5". Also of interest were the following entries, "Do paid to the wife of Morgan Meredith for the damage to her bead (bed), of Thos Evan Jenkin, poor man, £4" and "pack saddle to Jenking John Edward 7/- (seven shillings i.e. 35p). It would appear that the Vestry considered it far more expedient to set Jenking John Edward up in his trade as a blacksmith than to support him. The next entry in 1812 might suggest that either "the Taylor" was under contract for such cases or that Howel Thomas John was "outsize" and required clothes specially made for him "to the Taylor for making frog (frock), trowser and west cost (waist coat) to Howel Thomas John, 5s 0d (25p) (1812)". The next entries for the same year illustrate the comparative cost of "shoes to Ann Din, 6s 3d (31p) against "Wooden shoes to Margaret Treharn, 1s 0d (5p)". There was quite a thriving local industry in Vaynor in clog-making and one can see from the relative cheapness that there must have been a local demand for them. The policy of helping people to earn a living rather than to depend on the parish is further exemplified in the entry "To Joan Evan Jenkin for spinning wheel, 4s 6d" (22½p).

Since the church was the focus of local government in the Parish of Vaynor one might expect entries reflecting aspects of repairs, and also perhaps of the duties of the overseers and of the Rector. In 1799, we find, "to the Priest to bury her, 1s 0d (5p)" referring here to the burial of a pauper, Mary Morgan, and later, the same burial charge for John Harry. We glean something of the physical structure of the old Church at the turn of the eighteenth century with the entry "Do for attend the thatch of the Church, 2s 0d (10p)". In this case, the thatcher was probably Dafydd Sakry who was also "a poet, a worker in straw, maker of bee hives and thatcher", because a thorough search of the parish register has not revealed the presence of any other thatchers in the parish.

The next entry refers to a custom of draping the church pulpit with black crape on the death of a communicant. There are two entries referring to this custom at the turn of the eighteenth century which state "2 yards of crape, 6s 0d (30p)", and later "To crape for Thomas John Llewellin, 9s 0d (45p)". The Rev J. E. Jenkins has added the following note to the last entry, he states "The crape was placed on the pulpit of the Church for the funeral day, and the Sunday next after the funeral, as a mark of sorrow for the departed communicant. It was not customary to use the same crape for two persons. Eglwsya, or Churching after the dead, always took place on the first Sunday after burial".[4] It is interesting to note here the intrinsic importance of maintaining, what could be described as an extravagant custom when, according to Theophilus Jones, writing at this time, about 1800, stated that the church was "low and dark, the roof not ceiled, the floor of earth uneven, the seats decayed and irregular".

The old church was heated by a fire for the Sunday and Parish Vestry meetings as we see from an entry in 1799, which records "Kindle fire in the Church, 30 times, 5/- (25p)". The entry, "To Rhys Howell to carry dust to the Church to make the floor level, 1s 6d (7½p), suggests that there had recently been a burial within the church of one of the local gentry. One would have expected here the entry "to carry dust from the church" instead of "dust to the church", because following a burial there is usually a surplus of earth. A later entry states "For make the floor of the Church level, 2/- (10p)". The Rev J. E. Jenkins has referred to the old custom of burying the "well to do" within the church. As he states, "The few pews or seats that were in the Old Church belonged to the principal farmhouses. These could easily be moved, when required to open a grave or some old family vault". The bells, made at Bristol in the sixteenth century needed repair at this time and we have the following entries relevant to their repair as follows: "For 2 horses and a man to go and take the Bells to the smith shop, and to fetch them back, 4s 0d (20p). To Rhys Howell for attending on the smith to attend the Bells, 2s 0d (10p). The Rev Jenkins , adds, "Rhys was sent, I presume, to see that the smith did not impair the sound of the bells", and later the entry "To David William, smith for mend the bell, £1.3s.6d (£1.17)". The next entry suggests that the members of the Parish Vestry were given an allowance of ale when we see, "for ale in the Vestries, 19s 0d (£0.85)". The Parish Registers for Vaynor Church are available back to 1755 because they were considered important enough to be kept safely within the church. The importance of the Parish Register is shown in 1818 when we have this entry, "For a lock and hinges to put on the Chest of the Church, 4s 6d (22½p)" i.e. containing burials, marriage and baptismal registers.

Tom Lewis states that "the duty of making census returns in the early years of the nineteenth century, was imposed upon someone who could count in English".[5] He adds, "The someone was probably Rhys Hywel Rhys", who probably made the following entries "For put down the number of people in the hamlet, 1s 6d (7½p); to my trouble by gather the number of the population, 10s 0d (50p); To fill the returns. Of assessed and property taxes throughout the parish, being 102, 12s 0d (60p)". Rhys Hywel Rhys was appointed parish Clerk and Sexton in 1800 at a salary of three guineas per annum for the clerkship only, and continued until his death in 1817. He found some difficulty in English spelling but his entries make fascinating reading for example, his references to the military, "Do to a man to go to the use of His Majesty's Navy, £3.18s.8d (£3.93); Do for my journey to Llanhamlech with list of militia, 2s 6d (12½p); Do to David Daniel, substitute in the militia for Edward Miles, 19 weeks for 4s 6d (22½p); Do to John Archbery, Captain of the Mary Ann, on pass, 2s 0d (10p); Paid towards the Melitia ye money borrow of Morgan Richards £20". His duties were varied and often times difficult. He spent "2 days in Glamorganshire to apprehend Howell Davies and put him in prison; 3 days search for Gwenlian Morgan and move her". Later "to my journey to Merthyr to stop the horse that is with Jenking John Edward to go to Pound and trespass on horse; For serve 11 notices to the women of Coed Y Cymmer and witnesses". The local Parish Vestry was responsible during the nineteenth century for the maintenance of local roads and bridges and we find evidence of this in the following entries:- "Towards Pont Y Sarn £1.10s.0d (i.e. £1.50 today); paid towards Canedir Bridge 6/- (six shillings or 30p); mend Llwynperchell and Heol Y Cwm 3/- (three shillings or 15p); Repairing Heol Las 12/- (twelve shillings or 60p)".

The Rev Jenkins claimed in 1897 that the entries in the Parish Vestry accounts indicate that "the poor were liberally, if not lavishly treated a hundred years ago".[6] He quoted the case of Rhys Hywel Rhys to provide his point, as he stated, "Christian charity, no doubt had a hand in Rhys' appointment as parish clerk, there was nothing much in him, or in his views to recommend him for the post but the church was broadminded even a hundred years ago, and would not hastily condemn an honest man. His first 'relief' amounted to 33s 0d (£1.65). In 1802, he had 5 pecks of barley, at 4s 0d (20p) per pack, and 6 packs of oatmeal at 4s 0d (20p), per peck.

He was well paid for the little jobs he did about the church, for "mend the pulpit", he was paid 8s 0d (40p). The rent of this house was also often paid by the parish. When he was bundled out of his house a cash relief of £1.12s.6d (£1.63) was then given him, "with breakfast for him and the woman 1s 3d" (11p). He was kindly treated by the parish. He had many friends ... those friends came forward and supplied all that was necessary for a decent burial". Later, a public memorial was erected to the Vaynor 'genius' who had travelled extensively in South Wales in pursuit of his duties as parish clerk. The author has recently paid for his memorial stone to be installed within St Gwynno's church, Vaynor.

The Poor Law Act of 1601, which authorised each parish to appoint Overseers of the Poor whose duty it was to provide relief for the poor, the aged, and the impotent, and secondly to produce work for the able-bodied unemployed, remained in force in principle until 1834, when some abuses which had crept into the system were removed by the Poor Law Amendment Act. By this law, adjacent parishes were allowed to group themselves into a Poor Law Union for the purpose of relieving the poor. In the year 1836 the following parishes formed the Merthyr Tydfil Poor Law Union. Merthyr Tydfil, Aberdare, Rhigos, Penderyn, Vaynor, Gelligaer, Llanwonno, Llanfabon and Ystradyfodwg.[7] The Union was altered in 1863, and the last three parishes were taken out of this union. The Poor Law Authority in the Union was the Board of Guardians, which consisted of members chosen by the electors of each of the six parishes comprising the Union. The Guardians were elected for three years and retired together.

Indoor relief was provided at the Merthyr Workhouse opened in 1853, and intended to be a home for able-bodied paupers, who had to work within its walls. It was administered by a body of officials, such as the master and matron and a staff of nurses. Another institution under the control of the Committee was the Cottage Home at Llwydcoed, which cared for poor children, and orphans. In addition there was a well-equipped hospital for the poor and those able to pay for treatment. Outdoor relief was another method of obtaining Poor Relief, which involved the awarding of an allowance in money or in kind. The money relief was distributed by the Relieving Officer at a stated time and place. Outdoor relief could take the form of a grant of food or clothing, medicine, or of money to assist the applicant to emigrate. The last Relieving Officer in Vaynor was the late Alderman Tom Lewis JP.

Since Vaynor became part of the Merthyr Union in 1836 it is of interest to examine the entries of the Merthyr Parish Vestry Record which might be considered of relevance to the Parish of Vaynor. The first of these entries relating to Vaynor is on April 20th 1800 when "it was settled to defend the Order of Appeal against the removal of Edward Rees' family in the Parish of Vaynor and that Mr Phillip Griffith be employed for the said purpose" and on September 20th 1800 "Settled to give 2s 0d a week to Mr William John Williams of Coed Y Cymmer – The Overseers are ordered to send to the House of Correction everyone that returns to the Parish after they are removed". A case of non-maintenance for an illegitimate child follows on "September 13th 1810", when "It is agreed to employ Mr Meyrick to go with the law against Mr Williams of the Parish of Vaynor for not maintaining the child sworn to him by Jane Evans".

On October 1st 1816 the power of the Cefn Unitarians increased when the Merthyr Vestry "Ordered that Mr Coffin be employed as a general overseer at a salary of one guinea a week", then at the end of October 1822 the first reference to a work house, "Resolved that the work house and Vestry Room be built" and relevant to the proposed work house we find on the 11th March 1824, the entry "Resolved that Mr Forman for the Penydarren Iron Co, Josiah Guest for the Dowlais Iron Company and William Crawshay for William Crawshay and Sons, having respectively signed an undertaking to furnish the parish with the sum of £700 each for the erection of the proposed work house". It is of interest and quite ironic to note that it was the home of Mr Coffin (a member of Hen Dŷ Cwrdd Unitarian Chapel, Cefn Coed and a radical), at the Court of Requests, Georgetown which came under attack in the Merthyr Riots of 1831.

Many of the leaders in the Riots were fellow Unitarians including Dafydd Lewis of Cefn Coed.

In the period leading up to 1834, when Vaynor formed part of the Merthyr Union, we find important entries such as in April 1824 "Resolved that a surgeon be appointed at an annual salary of £30 ... and that Mr Davies of Cyfarthfa, be asked, and he is hereby appointed for the year". Later, in November 1831, "Vestry called for the purpose of taking into consideration the expediency of employing efficient police" and on the 20th November 1831 "To take into consideration the propriety of appointing a committee as a Board of Health to take the most efficient means to prevent the introduction of spread of the dreadful disease called Cholera Morbus". The first cholera epidemic of 1832 claimed 160 victims, the second killed 1,432 people, the third killed 424 and the fourth in 1866 claimed 119 victims.

Reference has been made above to the salary of the surgeon, Mr Davies in 1824. It will be of interest to know how nurses were trained and paid nearly a hundred years later at the Merthyr Infirmary which included the Merthyr Tydfil Workhouse. When my mother, then Elizabeth Thomas of the Morning Sun Inn, Cefn Coed, applied for entry to the Merthyr Infirmary in 1914 as a probationer nurse, she first had to sit a competitive examination when three were successful out of forty applicants. She had to purchase her full uniform, her training was four years and the hours of duty were from 6 a.m. until 8.00 p.m. The weekly off duty time was one afternoon from 3 p.m. to 6 p.m. and one evening from 6 p.m. until 10 p.m. and every alternative Sunday from 10 a.m. until 1 p.m. The salary while training was five pounds per year for the first two years, seven pounds ten shillings for the third year and ten pounds for the fourth year. When a night sister in 1918 she received nine pounds ten shillings a month. The rota was three months night duty and three months days and appointments to staff nurse or sister were made by the Merthyr Board of Guardians.

The next entries to be examined were of great importance since the final execution of the proposals were to affect the physical landscape of Vaynor and with the building of reservoirs to destroy much of the cultural life of the Parish. The first proposal was that proposed by Mr Thomas Williams and seconded by Mr Thomas Stephens (the Merthyr Historian) on 8th January 1857 which stated "The Burial Board be authorised to expend any sum not exceeding £2260 for laying out the ground, building chapels, Lodge, boundary wall and other things necessary for making the

Nursing Sister Bessie Thomas (later Bowen), Merthyr Infirmary 1920 (now aged 95 in 1991).

land at Cefn fit for use as a Cemetery, and a sum of £2000 for the purchase of the same land". The second important proposal was that of the 20th November 1857 "To consider the propriety of supplying Merthyr Tydfil with water by means of a Joint Stock Company. The Merthyr Parish Vestry however strongly opposed the proposal of the Cardiff Corporation to constrict reservoirs in the Tâf Fawr Valley. On this matter we later read "Wednesday 5th March 1884. This meeting of owners and rate payers of the District of Merthyr Tydfil duly convened, hereby authorises and consents to the Merthyr Tydfil Board of Health opposing ... the application of the Cardiff Corporation made or intended to be made to Parliament in the ensuing session for an Act under the name or title of the Cardiff Corporation Act 1884".

The old Parish Vestry came to an end with the proposal by Mr Dan Thomas on November 18th 1896, when he urged that "This meeting of the Parishioners of the Parish of Merthyr Tydfil in Vestry Assembled having heard the letter dated the 12th October 1896 from the local Government Board to the Overseers of the Parish relative to the application of the Urban District Council for an order under Section 33 of the local Government Act 1894 conferring certain powers on the District Council, is of opinion that it is desirable that the powers referred to should be conferred on the Council and particularly that the District Council should have the power of assigning the duty of collecting the Poor Rate to the Assistant Overseer for the time being of the Parish, or such other person as the Council may think fit with a view to having the work of collection of local rates performed more economically. This resolution was carried with one dissentient".

William Morgan (Pant) writing in 1893 on "Local Government" provides valuable information for this period, he states "Cefn Coed has a Police Station, under the charge of Police Sergeant Hand, an able and zealour officer; and attached to it has been added, within the last two years, a commodious Police Court".[8] At this point, it is of interest to note, that the Police Station and Court House were built at a cost of £600 and that the Court held, was known, until it ceased in 1974, as the "Penderyn Petty Sessions", although held in the Parish of Vaynor. The reason for this, was that the Court was formerly held at the Long Room of the Lamb Inn, Penderyn (where Dic Penderyn was taken after his arrest on Cwm Cadlan). Later it was transferred to Cefn Coed and the appellation "Penderyn Petty Sessions", was retained. The author's ancestors, Dafydd and Evan Lewis were Parish Constables in the mid-nineteenth century and walked their prisoners from Vaynor, over Cwm Cadlan Road to the Lamb Inn Penderyn for trial. If committed to the Breconshire Goal at Brecon, they then escorted them over the Brecon Beacons either on foot or in a cart, provided by Mr Rees Gellidiafolws, Penderyn. The round trip for Dafydd Lewis, the Unitarian Innkeeper and village blacksmith at Cefn and now Parish Constable, would have been over forty miles in one day.

Tom Lewis who was Chairman of the Magistrates of the Penderyn Petty Sessions states in 1947 "The first appointed "Cwmstab" (constable) at Cefn Coed was a local ironworker, named Vaughan. He wore no uniform, but to distinguish him from other civilians he was provided with a leather strap. The Police 'Station' was his own cottage in Field Street, Cefn Coed. The present Penderyn Petty Sessions were formed in 1857. Prior to that

An impression of a man in the stocks at Cefn Coed. The actual location of the stocks was somewhere near Hen Dŷ Cwrdd, Unitarian Chapel and the nearby crossroads.

date Vaynor, Penderyn and Ystradfellte Parishes formed a part of the Ystradgynlais Petty Sessional Division".[9] The last Parish Constable appointed for the Gelli (or Pontsarn hamlet) under the old Act was Mr John Harris who was also sexton of the Parish church. "He retained his club and pair of handcuffs till his death in November, 1894", states J. E. Jenkins. 10 Petty Constables with the threat of pillory and stocks, managed to keep some order. In the early days there was a stocks located near Hen Dŷ Cwrdd Chapel and the crossroads in central Cefn. This area still carries the name, "The Stocks".

William Morgan (Pant) adds further information on Local Government, when he states "The Chairman of the Bench is Mr M. North Esq, the Stipendiary Magistrate for the District of Caerphilly Higher ... the Clerk to the Magistrates is Mr T. L. White, Solicitor, Victoria Street, Merthyr ... The Vaynor District Highway Board also holds its meetings in Cefn Coed-Y-Cymer as well as at Penderyn and Hirwaun. The Board sits monthly, and holds at present four meetings in the year at each place. Mr

T. L. White is also the Clerk to the Vaynor Highway Board. The Vaynor School Board (Mr J. H. Jones, Solicitor, Clerk) holds its monthly meetings at Cefn Coed-Y-Cymer, is included in the Parliamentary Borough of Merthyr Tydfil, but for County Council, purposes is part of the County of Brecon. For Poor Law purposes, the Parish is part of the Merthyr Union ... The meetings of the Vestry are now held at Cefn Coed, formerly the Church Tavern, Vaynor was the meeting place ... Although the village of Cefn Coed has no Board of Health, yet it is considered to be in fairly good sanitary condition ... were it otherwise, it would not be chosen by so many well-to-do people as a place of residence".[11]

William Morgan further adds, "However, it must not be forgotten that it has some auspicious sanitary defects. A complete system of drainage has not yet been provided, neither are the streets lighted with gas, and it is dependent on Merthyr for its water supply. Owing to an unfortunate litigation, the supply of water to Cefn by the Merthyr Board of Health has been temporarily withdrawn ... movement is now on foot to procure the improvement of Cefn Bridge, it has been felt for years that the present one is both inconvenient and dangerous". From 1896, with the forming of District Councils, this Parish came under the Vaynor and Penderyn Rural District Council until it was dissolved with local government re-organisation in Wales in 1974.

From its inception the Vaynor and Penderyn Rural District Council and its Officers played a crucial and significant role in the administration of Local Government in the parishes of Vaynor, Penderyn and Ystradfellte. This Rural District occupied the middle portion of the southern boundary of the County of Brecknock and covered an area of 39,271 acres, stretching from Pontneddfechan in the west to Pontsticill in the east. All three parishes topographically have much in common in having a background of picturesque farms set in magnificent scenery of lonely moorland, bracken covered hills and deep river valleys. While most of the population of Vaynor now live in Cefn Coed, Tre Fechan and Pontsticill more than three quarters of Penderyn parish residents reside either at Hirwaun or at the village of Penderyn. A large proportion of the residents of the parish of Ystradfellte reside either at Pontneddfechan (Pontneathvaughan) or at the hamlet of Ystradfellte.

VAYNOR AND PENDERYN RURAL DISTRICT COUNCIL
Members and Officers – Year 1955/56

Back Row:- V. Rose *(Deputy Clerk); W. K. Morris (Rating Officer); Glyn Morgan (Public Health Dept); Miss C. Carbin (Clerk's Dept); Mrs C. Thomas (Surveyor"s Dept); Mrs N. Thomas (Clerk's Dept); D. T. Morris (Clerk's Dept); E. J. H. Hughes (Surveyor); D. Norman Davies (Deputy Surveyor).*

Middle Row:- *R. H. Rose (Clerk); Dr James Tate (Medical Officer of Health); Councillor F. D. Jones; Councillor M. Byrne; Councillor W. J. Morgan; Councillor E. J. Richardson; Spencer P. Harris (Sanitary Inspector).*

Front Row:- *Councillor Mrs R. G. Gregory; Councillor H. T. Hamer; Councillor Havard (Vice Chairman); Councillor Ivor Davies JP (Chairman); Councillor Edward Harris; Councillor Penry Lewis.*

(By courtesy of the former Chairman, Councillor Ivor Davies)

The Roll of Honour of Chairmen and Chairladies of the former Vaynor and Penderyn Rural District Council dating for 1905 up to the dissolution of the Council due to Government Legislation, in 1974, may be seen at Cyfarthfa Museum, Merthyr Tydfil and reads as follows:-

VAYNOR AND PENDERYN RURAL DISTRICT COUNCIL
CHAIRMEN OF THE COUNCIL

1905-6	David Evans
1906-7	Joseph Price
1907-8	Rev J. Hathern Davies
1908-9	C. J. Evans
1909-10	John Rogers
1910-11	C. B. Greatorex
1911-12	D. J. Davies
1912-13	John Williams
1913-14	Roger Vaughan
1914-15	John Harris
1915-16	Morgan Thomas
1916-17	C. B. Greatorex
1918-19	David Harris
1919-20	Morgan Thomas
1920-21	Morgan Thomas
1921-22	David Harris
1922-23	J. B. Young
1923-23	J. F. Thomas
1924-25	Isaac Morris
1925-26	J. F. Thomas
1926-27	J. F. Thomas
1927-28	Isaac Morris
1928-29	David Harris
1929-30	Mrs Sarah Evans
1930-31	B. A. Williams
1931-32	William Evans
1932-33	J. B. Young
1933-34	Tudor S. Davies
1934-35	John Ivor Evans
1935-36	Morgan Thomas
1936-37	Jenkin Davies
1937-38	Isaac Morris
1938-39	David Harris
1939-40	Penry Morris
1940-41	W. G. Eckley
1941-42	Rev J. M. Jones
1942-43	Idris Silvanus
1944-46	Daniel Jenkins
1945-46	Isaac Morris
1946-47	Rev C. L. Jones
1947-48	Penry Morris
1948-49	W. G. Eckley
1949-50	T. G. Daniel
1950-51	D. C. Watkins
1951-52	Edward Harris
1952-53	F. D. Jones
1953-54	Penry Lewis
1954-55	H. C. Hamer
1955-56	C. Ivor Davies
1956-57	Morgan R. Havard
1957-8	Edward Harris
1958-59	M. Byrne
1959-60	W. J. Morgan
1960-61	F. D. Jones
1961-62	Edward Harris
1962-63	Rev C. M. Walters
1963-64	Noel C. Rogers
1964-65	A. S. Williams
1965-66	D. W. Jones
1966-67	Rev C. M. Walters
1967-68	Alfred Driver
1968-69	M. Byrne
1969-70	W. J. Morgan
1970-71	I. M. Byrne
1971-72	B. O. Jones
1972-73	John Jones
1973-74	C. Ivor Davies

Clerk of the Council F. D. James 1895-1942. Clerk of the Council Vernon Rose 1942-62. The Vaynor Community Council was formed following the 1974 reorganisation of Local Government. This Council was dissolved in May 1990 following a ballot and its responsibilities were taken over by the Merthyr Borough Council.

REFERENCES

1. MAURICE BRUCE. The Coming of the Welfare State (1961) p.32.
2. D. MARSHALL. The English Poor in the Eighteenth Century p.161.
3. REV J. E. JENKINS. Vaynor. Its History and Guide (1897) p.147.
4. Ibid p.153.
5. TOM LEWIS. "Customs and Practices". Pamphlet of the Cefn coed and Vaynor Historical Society (1958) p.8.
6. Rev J. E. Jenkins. op. cit. p.147.
7. C. WILKINS. The History of Merthyr Tydfil (1908) p.428.
8. WILLIAM MORGAN (Pant). The Illustrated Vaynor Handbook (1893) p.36.
9. TOM LEWIS, Hen Dy Cwrdd, Cefn Coed Y Cymer (1947) p.160.
10. REV J. E. JENKINS. op. cit. p.115-116.
11. WILLIAM MORGAN op. cit. p.37.

CHAPTER IX

Education

INTRODUCTION

The history of education in the parish of Vaynor has been fully researched by Mr Tegwyn Harris MA,[1] formerly Headmaster of Vaynor and Penderyn Comprehensive School, Cefn Coed and Mr J. O. Evans[2] a former schoolteacher at Cefn Coed in the transactions of the Cefn Coed and Vaynor Local History Society. Much therefore of my own research is a duplication of their work, due primarily to the fact that the same primary source material has been used.

The history of educational provision in this parish is one of great interest dating from 1650 when William Walters a schoolmaster at Merthyr Tydfil received £15 in that year and £20 the following year for teaching children "from the upper reaches of the two Taffs and from land along the Middle Usk".[3] Although the Welsh Trust (1672-1681) established 87 schools in Wales with eight in Breconshire, neither established any schools in Vaynor.[4] The Circulating Schools (1737-1761) however did with nine of their 105 Brecon schools located here at various times.[5] They were in fact more evening classes than schools where children and adults were taught the rudiments of reading over a period of three months when the class was taken by the local clergyman.

Circulating Schools were held at "Blaen Glais Farm, Vaynor in 1738 with 70 pupils, at Vaynor with 39 pupils, at Taff Fechan in Llandetti with 54 pupils and at Taff Vaynor with 41 pupils. Later in 1740 at Blaen Glais, 25 pupils; Coed Y Cymmar 46 pupils; in 1745 at Groes in Cilsanws Hamlet, 38 pupils; during 1750-51 at Garn in Vaynor, 42 pupils. Other "schools" were held at Abercar in Vaynor, Abercar in the Tâf Fawr, Pont-ar-Dâf and Ynys Fawr, Cwm Tâf".[6] Later Charity Schools in the form of the British and Foreign Schools Society (1808) and the National Society (1811) were established in Breconshire with thirty eight of the former (1,873) pupils) and five of the latter (443 pupils).[7] Vaynor National School at Pontsticill was built in 1875 at a cost of £8700 and the Nantddu National School, Cwm Tâf in 1866 at a cost of £200,[8] under a deed of that date which states, "to be used as a school for the education of children and adults or children only of the poorer classes in the parishes of Nantddu, Vaynor and Penderin".

Industrialisation created a need for an educated workforce and in this locality the first Ironmaster to promote schools was J. J. Guest of Dowlais who established a works school in 1828. The Cyfarthfa Ironworks schools came later with the Cyfarthfa Ironworks School on the Brecon road in 1848 and in 1861 the Crawshays founded the Boys' and Girls' Schools at Cefn Coed.[9] These Ironworks Schools were maintained by "stoppages" varying in amount from ½d, 1p to 2 pence in the pound. They were compulsory and were deducted from the wages of employees. The schools, owned by R. T. Crawshay the Cyfarthfa Ironmaster, were run through his manager William Jones and supported by a government grant. The children however were expected to provide their own copy books, slates, pencils and penholders and pay a penny a week as indicated in the following public notice displayed locally:-

> Cyfarthfa, June 1866
>
> On the re-opening of the schools after the Midsummer Holidays, each child will be charged "One penny per week", which must be paid in advance every Monday morning.
>
> By Order of R. T. Crawshay Esq
>
> Cyfarthfa Ironworks, June 19th 1866.[10]

Early references in the Cefn Coed Schools' log books indicate rather indifferent reports under H.M. Inspectors and these undoubtedly caused some consternation because under the Revised Code of 1862, educational grants from the government depended upon satisfactory reports. We read for example:-

> "May 1864. 'The Boys' School has not passed so good'.
> June 1865. 'The Girls' School is in about the same condition as before'.
> June 1866. 'The Boys' School has fallen off materially'.
> May 1868. 'Boys and Girls' Schools not satisfactory-half the boys failed in Arithmetic'."

The Cefn Coed ironworks school opened in 1861 now part of Vaynor and Penderyn Comprehensive School.

The "Payment by results" system which limited the curriculum to reading, writing and arithmetic continued until the Forster Act was passed in 1870 granting local School Boards the power to compel "the parents of children of such age, not less than five years, not more than thirteen years, as fixed by the bye-laws, to cause such children (unless there is some reasonable excuse) to attend School". Administration of the Cefn Coed Boys' and Girls' Schools by Cyfarthfa ended with the 1870 Education Act which now provided for a State Education. This change is reflected in a log book entry of January 1st 1875 which states "R. T. Crawshay Esq, proprietor of these Schools, having transferred the foresaid Schools to the Vaynor School Board and the buildings being sold today, the Board has possession and the Schools are now passed as the Cefn Board School".

Prior to the Ironworks schools founded at Cefn Coed there were private schools and the report of the Welsh Educational Commission of 1847, described in Wales as "The Treachery of the Blue Books" because of its attack upon the Welsh language, Welsh nonconformity and Welsh morals, has referred to two private schools in this Parish at this time. As the assistant commissioner, John Jones reported, "On February 21st I visited the above parish in which I found only two day schools, one of which, kept by Mr Owen Evans, I thought was a tolerably well conducted one. The other kept by Mr Daniel Evans appeared badly managed. There were six Sunday Schools, two connected with the Established Church, another with the Calvinistic Methodists and three with the Independents ...".[11]

The Rev Owen Evans was the Unitarian Minster at Hen-Dŷ-Cwrdd and his school was held in the schoolroom of the Hen-Dŷ-Cwrdd. A summary of the report states:- "Adventure School. Founded 1838. Good building, insufficient and bad outbuildings. Sufficient furniture and apparatus in good repair. 41 pupils on the books. Average attendance 35. Attendance for less than one year – 21. For more than one year but less than two – 7. No children under 5. Between 5 and 10 – none. Living more than 1½ miles from school – 10. No monitors. Simultaneous instruction given. No scripture or catechism taught. Instruction given in English. Only English Grammar taught. The master was 38 years of age, had had no training ... was a Dissenting Minister ... He had no other means of livelihood but the school. His salary was £70 a year which came from "school pence".

Hen Dŷ Cwrdd School Room and Caretaker's House (c1930).

The format of the report on the other "Adventure School founded in 1846" went as follows: "Bad buildings. No outbuildings. Insufficient furniture and apparatus in bad repair. One interesting comment was "41 Pupils on the books. Average attendance 52"! Under 5 years – 5. Between 5 and 10 – 23. Over 10 years – 13. No monitors and no simultaneous instruction. Scripture was taught but no catechism. Instruction was in Welsh and English but only English Grammar was taught. The master was 50 years old; had not received any training but had previously been a Baptist Minister. His only income was £30 gained from school pence".

These it would appear were the only two day schools and there is no mention of the night schools conducted by William Morris at Cross Street in 1846 or of David Thomas at the Old Meeting House. It is interesting to note that around 82 pupils attended the two day schools in the parish in 1847 but 110 of the 592 children attending Sunday Schools held in Vaynor claimed to be attending day school as well. The Commissioners reported that 320 of the 592 Sunday Schools pupils could read the Bible. The great advantage of the Sunday School to the family was that the children could learn to read without loss of earnings by attending a day school.

Mr Tegwyn Harris has compared the figures available from T. E. Clarke's 1848 'Guide to Merthyr Tydfil', with the statistics given in the 'Cronicle' and those provided by the Rev J. E. Jenkins. They are shown in the following tables:-

	1844 Y Cronicl	1847 Blue Books		1848 T. E. Clarke	
	Pupils	Pupils	Teachers	Pupils	Teachers
Vaynor Church	—	77	9	—	—
Established Church	188	—	—	—	—
Chapel of Ease, Cefn	—	64	11	160	23
Moriah	—	192	27	150	28
Capel y cae	209	—	—	—	—
Carmel	114	93	20	95	12
Ebenezer	275	133	27	130	27
Tabor	50	—	—	120	18
Bethlehem, Pontsticill	—	33	5	—	—
Totals	836	592	99	655	108

The 1847 Welsh Education Commission provided the following figures for Sunday School attendance in the parish of Vaynor and there is obviously great discrepancy. The complete 1847 Commission statistics read as follows:-

			Teachers		Usual Attendance		Also at Day	Able to Read	On the books			
									Over 15		Under 15	
Name	Cause	Date	Male	Fem	Boys	Girls	Sch	Bible	Boys	Girls	Boys	Girls
Vainor	E.C.	1846	7	2	40	30	18	25	12	15	30	20
Cefn	E.C.	1833	11	0	30	26	20	30	17	19	18	10
Cefn	C.M.	1807	19	8	95	63	34	98	67	18	45	62
Cefn	B.	1827	16	4	53	30	21	56	40	15	20	18
Ebenezer	I.	1838	22	5	42	60	13	91	25	21	47	40
Bethlehem	I.	1839	3	2	8	12	4	20	12	10	5	6
					286	221	110	320	173	98	165	156
					507				271		321	
									592			

Mr Harris provides further interesting statistical information when he indicates that the Sunday School had an attendance of 85 per cent and that 45 per cent of the total schools were adult and that 54 per cent were literate. He further indicates that 26 per cent of the local population were attending Sunday Schools in 1847 and that 29 per cent had attended Griffith Jones' schools in 1738.

An examination of this table indicates that Tabor although founded in 1844 is not mentioned. The Baptist Chapel founded in 1827 probably refers to Carmel although it was not built until 1844 while Moriah is undoubtedly the Calvinistic Methodist Chapel mentioned in the report. There is no reference to a Sunday School at Hen Dŷ Cwrdd although chapel records refer to one as early as 1775. Further information provided in the Folio edition of the Report shows that all the chapels except Moriah were maintained by subscription and no teachers were paid. All the parish Sunday Schools were supervised by a superintendent and secretary and held in the various places of worship where boys and girls were taught separately. All Sunday Schools opened and closed with prayers and lasted in Vaynor for 1½ hours, and at Pontsticill for 4 hours while all others were for 2 hours. The medium of tuition at Vaynor Church was through the English language; the Baptists employed both languages while all others taught through the medium of the Welsh language. It appears that none of the Sunday Schools taught writing or arithmetic but the Independents and Baptists taught some "other books and subjects". Without exception all schools taught children to learn the scriptures by rote and all except Bethlehem Chapel taught pupils hymns. The Sunday schools thus provided a rudimentary form of language teaching and since they were the only organised education of their day, their value cannot be over-estimated.

THE HEADTEACHERS AND TEACHERS OF THE CEFN COED SCHOOLS FROM 1861

Records are not readily available to accurately mention all those teachers who have taught in the Cefn Coed Schools since 1861. Suffice to say that very many of them were very highly respected and significant characters in the life of the Vaynor Parish Community. The very old refer to John Edwin (Davies), Emmanuel Lewis, Matthew Owen and Mrs Moss while those who attended Vaynor and Penderyn Secondary School, as it was then, speak in awe but with profound respect for the great headmaster, Mr Trevor Lovett MSc, who was the first head of the school when it was established in 1932.

The first Headmaster of the Cefn Coed Boys' School was Mr William Winterton while his wife was the first Headmistress of the Girls' School. The staff of the Boys' School in 1864 included William Davies (Pupil teacher), Lewis Williams (Pupil teacher) and the headmaster, while his wife had the assistance of one, Jane Jones. Later Headmasters of the Boys' School were:- Mr Ashworth Heys (1867), Mr John David Rees (1868), Mr Rees Price Hilliar (1882_, Mr Matthew Owen (1892), Mr Matthew Jones (1925) and Mr J. T. Williams (1938-51). A list of the Headmistresses of the Cefn Coed Girls' School reads as follows:- After Mrs Winterton, Mrs T. Heys (1867), Mrs Mary Rees (1868), Winifred R. Ransome (1872), Gaynor Edwards (1873), Elizabeth Ellen Bowen (1874), Margaret Davies (1875) and Ellen Moss who stayed from 1880 until 1917, a period of 37 years. She was followed as Headmistress by Miss Sally Thomas, who, with the reorganisation of local schools in 1932 became the first Headteacher of the new Ysgol y Graig Junior School.

Mr Trevor Lovett MSC, ARIC appointed first Headmaster of Vaynor and Penderyn Secondary School in 1932.

The Official Opening of Vaynor and Penderyn Secondary School, Cefn Coed by the Right Rev the Lord Bishop of Swansea and Brecon, October 1932.
Mr Joseph Jones JP, the Bishop of Swansea and Brecon (Dr E. L. Bevan), Rev Lewis Davies (Rector of Cefn Coed) and Professor Joseph Jones MA, BD, JP, Chairman of the Breconshire Education Authority.

The 50th Anniversary of the opening of Vaynor and Penderyn Secondary School October 1982.
Mr C. Whittingham BA (Headmaster), Owen Thomas (Head Boy), Mr Keith Davies MSc (Chief Adviser for Mid Glamorgan Education Committee), Mr Eddie Roberts MSc (Director of Education for Mid Glamorgan), Tracey Gibbs (Head Girl), Mrs Mona Shankland (Mayor of Merthyr Tydfil), Dr Elwyn Bowen MBE, MA, MEd, PhD (Guest Speaker).

Vaynor and Penderyn Secondary School opened in 1932, formerly Cefn Coed Infants' School built in 1910. (Now Vaynor and Penderyn Comprehensive School.)

CEFN COED SENIOR SCHOOL STAFF c1936

Back Row: *Mr Glyn Jones (Pupil teacher), Mr D. Stokes (Pupil teacher), Miss B. Vaughan, Mr Morien Lewis, Mr Cooper, Mr T. Lewis.*

Front Row: *Miss Buddug Wyn Jones (Mrs Morien Lewis), Miss Bessie Evans, Mr Matthew Jones MA (Headmaster), Mrs Daniels and Miss Sally James.*

Upon Miss Sally Thomas' retirement she was followed by Mr J. T. Williams who stayed as Headmaster until his retirement in 1951 when he was succeeded by Mr Dilwyn Roderick. Mr Roderick had previously been Headteacher of Penderyn County Primary School for 27 years. When Mr Roderick retired in 1968 he was succeeded by the author who stayed until he left for the Gurnos Primary School, Gurnos Estate, Merthyr Tydfil. He in turn was followed at Ysgol y Graig by Miss Mary Jones who continued as Headteacher until her retirement in the mid-eighties.

Of the Infants' School one notes that Mrs Martha Lewis served as Headteacher of the Infants' Schools at Cefn Coed from 1899 to 1935. She was followed by Mrs Mary Davies (1935 until 1967) and upon her retirement in 1967 she was succeeded by Mrs Edwards who stayed until she retired in 1980 when the Ysgol y Graig Infants and Junior Schools were combined under one headteacher. Since the Vaynor and Penderyn Secondary School (now a Comprehensive School) was established in 1932, there have been four Headmasters, Mr Trevor Lovett MSc (1932-1945), Dr Gordon Williams BSc, PhD (1945-1959), Mr Tegwyn Harris MA (1959-1973) and the present Headmaster Mr Clifford Whittingham BA (1973-).

There are frequent references in the log books of the Cefn Coed Boys' and Girls' school to Pupil Teachers during the later decades of the last century especially. The pupil teacher system was established in 1846 whereby boys and girls of thirteen years of age were apprenticed for five years and while teaching in the local schools, were themselves taught by the Headteachers after school. Headteachers instructed them for one and a half hours per day for about five pounds per year per student. Many of these young people taught classes of from 30 to 70 pupils from 9 a.m. to noon and from 1.30 p.m. to 4.30 p.m. Upon completion of their apprenticeships they then sat a competitive examination for a Queen's Scholarship and if successful pursued a two year course at a Training College to become trained teachers.

In the 1880s there are frequent references to Pupil Teacher Emmanuel Lewis of the Morning Sun Inn, Cefn Coed, who did not proceed to College to qualify as a teacher, but did in later life, become an important local business man and was Manager of the Dowlais Works. The following entries provide some information on the Pupil Teacher system in general and upon Emmanuel Lewis in particular:-

"1874. February 2nd. Pupil Teachers examination at Abermorlais School, Merthyr 10 a.m.
1875. April 28th. William Richards, Pupil Teacher terminates his fifth year apprenticeship on April 30th.
1875. May 5th. At the Managers meeting on Tuesday May 2nd it was decided to retain William Richards as Assistant Teacher until July 4th when he intends sitting for a Scholarship at Bangor.
1887. HMIs Report. Emmanuel Lewis – Arithmetic, Grammar, Geography and History. He must improve very much.
1887. April 29th. Emmanuel Lewis did not stay for lessons on Friday. On Monday he gave as explanation of his conduct that his father had ordered him to go to Dowlais respecting a colt that was dying.
1887. No lessons prepared by Emmanuel Lewis. Reason given attending Music Lessons at the Old Chapel.
1887. Emmanuel Lewis very neglectful of his lessons, too fond of playing.
1887. August 26th. Emmanuel Lewis has not got up any Euclid for today. His reason was that he was at a tea party and concert until 10 p.m. last night.
1887. September. Received complaints that E. Lewis was kicking doors and then running away."

His Headmaster was undoubtedly very relieved when he received the following information from Emmanuel Lewis:-

"1890. September 19th. Emmanuel Lewis informed me that his engagement as teacher here terminates today".

Emmanuel Lewis was buried in the Hen Dŷ Cwrdd, Cefn Coed in 1939 having been Manager of the Dowlais Iron and Steel Works from the 1920s.[13]

THE SCHOOL LOG BOOKS

The log books of the Boys' and Girls' Schools in Cefn Coed provide invaluable historical and sociological information about the school and the locality. References are made to the buildings, teaching staff, standards of attainment, health of the pupils and discipline and from these excerpts we are able to construct an accurate picture of the life of the Schools and the cultural, religious, industrial and social life of the locality during the second half of the nineteenth century and the first half of the present century. We are also able to trace the whole vista of educational provision and growth for over a century and we are privileged to read of the social and religious changes during this period. We read for example that a new Infants' School was added in 1868 and that a separate building which is the present Comprehensive School was erected in 1910. The following table illustrates the increase in pupils over the years:-[14]

Alterations brought about by the need for extra room is demonstrated in the following log books:-

> "September 1866. The great drawback to perfect order is the presence of the Infant section in the same rooms as the Senior classes."
> "February 1872. School removed to Heol Cae Library in consequence of the enlargement of the present school."
> "May 1872. Heol Cae Library was vacated and the enlarged School rooms re-entered."

This entry prompts the question, where and how large then was Heol Cae Library? The totals in the above table reflect the increase in pupils which in turn created a further expansion in buildings, as shown in the following entries-:

> "1884. HMI's Report. In recommending the Grants, allowance has been made for the lack of a class room which is now on the point of being completed. An urinal is required."

Extra classrooms were added in 1898, these proved inadequate and it was necessary to rent Tabor Vestry for the boys and Carmel Vestry for the girls in 1908. We note these changes in the following entries:-

Year	Boys	Girls	Infants	Total
1862	160	Not known		160+
1884	135	163	194	492
1903	164	166	213	543
1931	209	215	194	618

> "July 27th 1908. This morning Stds. 5, 6 and 7 have started in Tabor Vestry."

There is an entry for 14th January 1909 indicating that "The Tabor Vestry is a cold room during the wintry and sleety days we have" and that "The teachers and children are risking their health". Then three years later we note in the following entry:-

> "January 12th 1912. The children who have been for some years in Tabor Vestry have now been brought "home"."

In 1932 the whole ethos of education in Cefn Coed changed with the building of the new Ysgol y Graig Junior and Infants' School while the old 1910 Infants School became the new Vaynor and Penderyn Secondary School. The old Boys' and Girls' School became the Cefn Coed Senior School. Later in 1949 the Senior School and the Vaynor and Penderyn Secondary School amalgamated and became the Vaynor and Penderyn Bi-lateral School. In April 1981 the Ysgol y Graig Infants' and Junior Schools were amalgamated.

CEFN COED SENIOR SCHOOL FOOTBALL TEAM 1935-36.

Back Row: *John Barrie, Bryn Reed, Ronald Richardson, Mr Matthew Jones MA (Headmaster), Bobby Pointer, Gordon Roberts, Phillip Pembridge.*

Front Row: *Mr H. Cooper (Science teacher), Leo Barrie, Gordon Evans, Henry Morgan (Captain), Tom Evans, Cledwyn Saunders, Mr Morien Lewis (Geography and Games teacher).*

By courtesy of MRS OLWEN EDEARS, *Maes y Garreg, Cefn Coed*

FEES, SCHOOL SYLLABI, CURRICULA AND ATTAINMENT

Reference has already been made to the public notice put up by Mr R. T. Crawshay regarding the charge of "One penny a week" for attendance at his schools. Where parents were poor or the family large, many children were deprived of any form of education or received only a few weeks attendance at school in a year. The general method of teaching often involved employing Pupil teachers of tender age, ill equipped by lack of training and with classes of up to 70 pupils and struggling to maintain order and discipline. The position was exacerbated by rote learning of dull and uninteresting material. The discipline was invariably harsh and the general health of the pupils poor due to poverty, squalor, ignorance, large families, alcoholism and a lack of medical services. The mortality rate of children in this locality at this time was one of the highest in the country. Learning was further inhibited by additional factors such as a lack of parental interest and encouragement due to circumstances beyond their control. An additional difficulty was that the pupils were learning through the medium of English when in many cases their first language was Welsh.

The following entries refer to non-payment of school fees, they do not of course indicate the embarrassment to parents or the frustration to pupils when parents were unable to pay a penny a week for the schooling of their children. Some read as follows:-

> "1868. April. Girl taken from school because she was compelled to pay one penny arrears – the mother called me a hard woman."
> "1875. April. Several sent home in the afternoon because they had no means of paying for their schooling."

The next entry indicated that inspite of industrial recession, reduced wages and soup kitchens parents saw the advantages to be derived from an education for their children.

> "1876. December. Considering the bad times, on the whole payments are very regularly made"

But sadly we then read:-

> "1897. September Several of the older girls have left because their parents can't afford to keep them in school."
> "1855. January. Paupers' list prepared."

> "1886. March. Great difficulty in collecting School fees on account of depression in trade. Very many colliers being without work."

We then read of a very important milestone in the sphere of education:-

> "1890. December 15th. The Clerk of the School Board called and ordered the "Arrears of Fees" to be struck off the School Fees Book. "Free Education" comes into operation here on September 1st 1891. Holiday given to mark it."

Free Education rather surprisingly presented a problem for many families in that they could not afford the loss of income resulting from their children attending school.

The problem of the linguistic background of teachers and pupils referred to above is noted in the following entries:-

> "1869. September. This school in particular requires intelligent teachers, those who are brought up by intelligent parents or friends, who as a rule speak English at home. The present staff always speak Welsh at home. Nearly all the scholars speak Welsh at home, so consequently they want their reading lessons explained which the present Pupil Teachers are unable to do."
> "1870. October. Find it a difficult matter to get the children to speak grammatically, Cefn being much more Welsh than Merthyr."

The problem of trying to teach almost monoglot Welsh children is emphasised again in the following entry.

> "1872. The children so Welshy and understand so little English that there is considerable difficulty in making them discriminate the meaning of what they read."

A decade later the fact that so many children were first language Welsh was still considered an inhibiting factor in their learning when we read as follows:-

> "1883. May. Standard VII improving in Composition – this is a most difficult subject to teach, throughout the room-children speak so much Welsh at home."

When the Cefn Coed Girls' and Boys' Schools opened the curriculum was largely confined to the three R's and gradually over the years we note that there was a cautious extension into other branches of learning. It is interesting to note that Latin was taught as a specific subject in 1890 and the introduction of Welsh had to wait until 1893 and elementary science until 1898. Cookery and Woodwork were not included as subjects of the schools curriculum until as late as 1921. The curricula developments of the Cefn Coed Schools are reflected in the following entries:-

> "1872. HMI's Report. The condition of the School is not fully satisfactory either in point of instruction or discipline."

Mrs Crawshay played some part in introducing needlework to the Schools by supplying them with sewing material which the girls made into various things such as in:-

> "1865. September. Returned 12 pillow cases to the Castle."
> "1865. November. Received 2 chemises from the Castle."
> "1865. December. Returned 3 pairs of sheets to the Castle."

This support from Mrs Crawshay was undoubtedly crucial because many entries in the log books at this time indicate that the girls were unable, because of extreme poverty to supply their own materials as we see here:-

> "1875. August. It is impossible to get the children to bring sewing work. Parents have nothing to give them."

This comment was repeated four years later:-

> "1879. August. Children are very slow bringing needlework. The parents are very poor."

Music appeared in 1866, Political Economy in 1868 and Composition and Grammar in 1871. Examinations were held as we see in May 1871:-

> "1871. May. Examination Subjects – Reading, Writing, Composition, Arithmetic. Special Subjects – Grammar and Geography."

The 1861 Ironworks' School, later known as the Senior School and now part of the Vaynor and Penderyn Comprehensive School.

Ysgol y Graig Junior and Infants' School c1976.

The Schools had received 82 books on "Political Economy" which to say the least would appear totally unsuitable, in view of the difficulties experienced with such ordinary subjects as Geography:-

> "1881. December. Geography backward, the great difficulty being to get the children to reproduce their information in English."

The curriculum was made far more varied and systematic by the introduction of the Revised Code in 1882. The changes are indicated in the following entry:-

> "1883. April. Made arrangements for teaching Class and specific subjects under the New Code. The subjects to be taught this year are – Reading, Writing, Arithmetic which are "obligatory", Grammar, Geography, Recitation, and the following specific subjects – Algebra, Euclid, Animal Physiology, Music, Military Drill and Composition."

The appearance of these subjects on the curriculum was over a period of years as the following log book entries show:-

> "1888. May 8th. Commenced teaching music by notes – Tonic sol-Fa system."
> "1889. November 1st. Drawing lessons commenced."

Although not referred to in the list of subjects to be taught according to the Revised Code mentioned above, we find Latin introduced in 1890. It would be of interest to know how long it remained on the curriculum, where until recently they had been experiencing so many problems with Welsh first language children. However we note:-

> "1890. June. Latin taught as a Specific subject."
> "1890. November. List of subjects taught at present – Reading, Writing, Arithmetic, Recitation, Geography, Grammar, Composition, Drawing, Music, Map Drawing."

In his report to the Vaynor School Board in January 1893, Mr Matthew Owen stated that it was "his opinion that the teaching of Welsh was an advantage, but it would be unwise to introduce it for another year".

> "1898. March. We have commenced elementary Science."

1898. March. The Metric System has commenced."
1902. January. More Welsh introduced into the School."

The Education Act 1902 established Local Education Authorities and gave them the right to set up Secondary Schools. The nearest to Cefn Coed within the county of Brecon then was at Brynmawr and for 1902 we find this important mile stone recorded thus:-

> "1902. September 8th. Some boys have won scholarships tenable at Brynmawr County School."

Whether the "string band" at the Hen Dŷ Cwrdd, established in 1900 and conducted by Merthyr schoolmaster, Mr J. R. Evans, influenced the decision to start the violin class at the Cefn Coed Schools is unknown but it is nevertheless possible. As we see, in "1903. A violin class has started on the 'Maidstone plan' ". About 40 boys and girls have joined.

Welsh finally became an acceptable curriculum subject in 1906 when we note:-

> "1906. February. Breconshire Education Committee have instructed "Welsh" to be introduced into the schools."

Whether this decision was prompted by an early realisation that the language was under threat in an area already becoming anglicised is unknown but another sign of the times is shown in the next extract from the log books:-

> "1907. 'Moral Instruction', Hygiene and Temperance are included in the new Time Table."

DISCIPLINE, SICKNESS AND SCHOOL ABSENCE

Remarkable changes have taken place in Education in recent years. At the present time the National Curriculum is being introduced bringing with it a completely new system of Primary and Secondary Education. In recent years corporal punishment in Schools has become illegal and other forms of punishment rather than the rod or the birch now prevail. No longer do children in Primary Schools sit silently in serried rows but rather around tables weighing and measuring and talking freely to their friends.

Children are taller, better fed and healthier than they were during the nineteenth century. The School Medical Service and the School Psychological Service, school meals and hygiene lessons all contribute to the physical and psychological well-being of the child. Those with mental or physical handicaps receive special educational treatment either in special classes or special schools depending upon the degree and type of handicap. Truanting and delinquency and juvenile crime are some of the major problems of our major towns and cities. One notes that whereas the reasons for absence in the nineteenth century were associated with sickness due mainly to poverty, malnutrition or epidemics, strikes or social occasions the reasons given today appear to be associated with school failure, lack of interest in school, unsuitable school provision or family problems.

The atrocious conditions in this area recorded by Dr Dyke,[15] the Merthyr Medical Officer of Health during the nineteenth century, involving insanitary living conditions, no sewage system or water supply, frequent epidemics of cholera, measles, chicken-pox, diphtheria, whooping cough, mumps, small pox and scarlet fever or typhoid resulted in a child mortality regarded as one of the worst in Britain. The development of a Public Health Service, the School Medical Service and of course more recently the medical services that form part of the Welfare State have greatly reduced the mortality of both children and adults in the country generally. Reference is made in other chapters to mortality rates in this area but the seriousness of the situation may be gleaned from the fact that in 1870 the death rate of children between 5-9 years was 7.9 per thousand which was reduced to 0.5 per thousand by 1953. The almost continuous outbreaks of one epidemic or another resulted in a high level of absenteeism as the following entries show:-

> "1866. September 21st. The cholera has reduced the attendance.

1877. August. No school this week on account of measles.
1877. October. Schools closed because of fever epidemic.
1884. April. Whooping cough spreading – 25 cases.
1888. October. Diminished attendance. Typhoid Fever spreading.
1889. Two fatal cases of typhoid fever in Cefn.
1890. September. No school for a fortnight on account of scarlet fever and typhoid.
1898. February. School closed 3 weeks – Scarletina epidemic."

During virtually every year of the first decade of the present century and even up to 1920 there were outbreaks of fever, as the following entries recorded:-

"1900. November. School closed 3 weeks – epidemic of measles.
1906. Epidemic of Whooping Cough and Chicken Pox – schools closed for one month.
1908. January. This has been an exceptionally gloomy time owing to the large number of deaths and serious illness.
1920. Epidemic of measels. School closed 2 weeks."

Malnourishment was a crucial factor in the spread of diseases such as Tuberculosis and genuine efforts were apparently made to assuage the pangs of hunger during periods of industrial recession or during strikes as the following entries indicate:-

"1898. May. Because of "strike" the Drill Hall was used today as a place for soup distribution to the children, 200 were supplied."

The pattern of social unrest and strikes continued in South Wales as we note in the following:-

"1912. April 4th. Holidays are to include only Good Friday and Easter Monday. This change is advisable owing to the feeding of hungry children during the Coal Strike."

The national miners strike of 1921 was a kind of dress rehearsal for the 1926 strike and at Cefn Coed and Merthyr was found the same solidarity and courage in the face of hopeless odds. In the end the miners had to return to work, crushed and humiliated, on the owners' terms. At Cefn Coed we see families being starved into submission:-

> "1921. April 10th. The Provision of Meals' Act was put in operation in these Schools owing to the Coal Strike. On an average 250 children are fed daily."

Wage cuts and massive unemployment was soon to follow with men digging for coal in the "patches", and fish sales on the Twyn at Cefn. Sheep stealing and poaching the rivers and reservoirs for fish became part of everyday living up to 1939 and the Second Great War. These terrible days between the wars are reflected in the following harrowing entries:-

> "1921. July 21st. School canteen will close in its present method of feeding children, but the children whose fathers are unemployed will get cards to get groceries – 3s 0d week.
> 1924. February. About 120 children whose fathers are unemployed are provided with soup on alternative days by Col J. J. Jones JP, at the Church Hall.
> 1925. November. Col J. J. Jones intends continuing the soup kitchen throughout the winter.
> 1926. May 18th During the present Industrial Crisis the District Committee on Thursday last decided to feed the necessitous children in the village. Soup and two meals will be served daily until further notice."

The last entry refers to the General Strike which took place on 3rd May 1926 and the cruel effect upon the children is evidenced in the entry for late 1926, which states:-

> "1926. October 11th. Many boys are absent from school because of poor footwear, consequent upon the Industrial Crisis.
> 1926. November 11th. I have circularised all the Head Teachers of the rural areas for assistance in the form of cast off clothing and shoes.
> 1929. January 25th. Consignment of boots (120) from Lord Mayor's Fund for distressed areas."[16]

The author vividly recalls children trying on new boots in the Cefn Coed Boys' School in the early 1930s. Local distress was relieved by the Quaker Society, "the Lord Mayor's Fund" and by the "adoption" of Cefn Coed and Pontsticill by Chippenham in Wiltshire. The local Distress Committee opened a "shop" at the now demolished St Tudor's Church, on the present site of the Vaynor and Penderyn Comprehensive School gymnasium and also a cobbler's shop at 83 High Street, Cefn Coed, now also demolished and for years the author's father's workshop.

Reference has already been made to the fact that a harsh environment engendered severe discipline in schools. Corporal punishment in the form of caning, the use of the birch rod, transfer to the "Truant School" at Quakers Yard, "flogging", "keeping in" or "dismissal" appeared to be the more common forms of punishment as we see in the following excerpts from the school log books:-

> "1866. 5th June. ---- ----, and ---- were found this morning writing bawdy language upon slates and showing it to the others. Each was punished and otherwise corrected.
> 1877. I caned several girls in 2nd class for making blots on their exercise books.
> 1881. April. I try "keeping in" system to 1 p.m. and 5 p.m. as a remedy for coming late, also for laziness and insubordination.
> 1884. I am striving to reduce corporal punishment to a minimum, but it is absolutely impossible to do without it altogether.
> 1888. January. Children unpunctual in the morning. Remedy – corporal punishment judiciously administered."

Running a school a century ago was obviously not without its difficulties as the following notes record:-

> "1892. May. Difficulty of establishing discipline in the school. Obscene language freely indulged in – Lying and thieving are also two very common vices.
> 1892. September. Punished ---- for truant playing. His sister and mother came here mid-day and used most insulting language and threats. Also four lads (just left school for work) were here kicking the school door and causing other damages.

> 1893. December. The lads ---- and ---- were whipped with a birch rod in the lavatory for truant playing on Monday.
>
> 1902. A lad named ---- came to school this afternoon after an absence of over a week. He was flogged."

Many of the incidental holidays awarded to Cefn Coed pupils mark historical milestones in the life of the locality while other events recorded old customs no longer part of the folk lore of the area. We have for example the first recorded closure of the schools for a political reason:-

> "1875. May 20th. Whit Monday was a holiday and Thursday also a Parliamentary Polling Day. The School being used as Booth.
>
> 1879. May 17th. No School on Thursday – Funeral of Mr Crawshay.
>
> 1881. September. School open 7 times only by reason of the Eisteddfodau."

The name "Mabon" (Rt Hon William Abraham 1842-1922) frequently occurs between 1892 and 1898 when South Wales miners did not work on the first Monday in every month, a scheme to limit output in order to maintain wages. This was known as "Mabon's Day". Mabon, a miners agent, was elected MP for the Rhondda division in 1885, was also Chairman of the Joint Sliding Scale Association and later made a Privy Councillor in 1911. As we see:-

> "1891. May 4th. Mabon's Day. 50 boys away. Broke up for afternoon – there are so many counter attractions e.g. Penydarren Park races, Eisteddfod, Tea Parties, Studts' concern.
>
> 1891. June. Mabon's Day. 60 boys absent. Procession of Freemason Clubs and Societies.
>
> 1894. August 30th. Half holiday. Library tea at Pontsarn.
>
> 1898. April 21st. Half holiday granted because the "Foundation Stone" of the "Cefn New Library" was laid.
>
> 1899. March 1st. This afternoon a half holiday was granted in celebration of the Relief of Ladysmith.
>
> 1904. November 25th. School closed. The laying of the Foundation Stone of the New Church Hall and a Great Mission Service in Merthyr where the Revivalist Mr Evan Roberts is expected.

> 1905. July 11th. School closed owing to great attraction created by Charter Celebration in Merthyr".[17]

The Vaynor National School was opened in 1875 and was closed in 1948 when the children were transferred to Ysgol y Graig Infants' and Junior Schools. The following entries refer to important events at Pontsticill:-

> "1915. June 9th. Children show great interest in the development of the new water works now in course of construction.
> 1939. September 5th. Owing to the outbreak of War the children were sent home for the rest of the week.
> 1939. September 11th. Four children (unofficial evacuees) admitted.
> 1945. May 14th. Organised celebration of VE (Victory in Europe) day in the village. The children went in the School at 2 o'clock and took part in games until 4.30 p.m. when they marched to the Memorial Hall for tea. Games were resumed after tea followed by a Concert and dancing in the Hall.
> 1948. December 23rd. After the Christmas Holiday the children are being transferred to Cefn Coed, the authority having decided to close this school."

At the time of writing (1980) the old National School at Pontsticill still stands and is used as Sunday School. Recent efforts to demolish or sell the old School have been frustrated by the concerted efforts of old Parishioners and natives of Pontsticill. The log books of the Nantddu School, Cwm Tâf which was closed in 1927 have recently been examined but unfortunately provide very limited information regarding either the school or the locality. One would have expected to find references to the reservoir developments which completely reshaped the valley. Invariably the only comment, made every Friday for many years was "Vicar called today"!

I have purposely omitted the names of so many dedicated and fine teachers who have taught in the Vaynor Schools over the years. Many were my teachers while others became my colleagues later and the omission of their names is because some one could undoubtedly be inadvertently omitted. For this reason therefore, they must live on in the memory of the children they were privileged to teach.

REFERENCES

1. T. J. HARRIS. Education in the Parish of Vaynor Prior to 1870. Cefn Coed and Vaynor Local History Society (1955).
2. J. O. EVANS. The Cefn Coed Schools 1861-1956. Cefn Coed and Vaynor Local History Society.
3. THOMAS RICHARDS. The Puritan Movement in Wales. National Eisteddfod. (1920) p.234.
4. MARY CLEMENT. The SPCK and Wales 1699-1740.
5. M. C. JONES. The Charity School Movement. Cambridge (1932).
6. The Story of Merthyr Tydfil. NUT (1932).
7. Reports of the Commissioners of Inquiry into the State of Education in Wales. Abridged Edition 1848.
8. THEOPHILUS JONES. A History of the County of Brecknock (1809).
9. The Cefn Coed Schools' Log Books. 1862.1875 at Ysgol-y-Graig Junior School, Cefn Coed.
10. The Log Books. Ibid. June 19th 1866.
11. Reports of Commissioners op. cit.
12. Reports. op. cit.
13. ELWYN BOWEN. Some Aspects of the History of Vaynor from 1600. Unpublished MA Thesis, Swansea (1980).
14. J. O. EVANS op. cit.
15. Merthyr Public Library. DR DYKE'S Diaries.
16. The Log Books op.cit., January 1929.
17. Ibid July 1903.
18. Pontsticill School Log Book Dec 1948 at Ysgol-y-Graig Junior School, Cefn Coed.

CHAPTER X

Folk Customs And Medicines

INTRODUCTION

Of the traditional customs, some are associated with various festivities and days of the calendar, while others commemorate the chief turning-points in the life of human beings. Others cannot be classified. Many colourful customs have ceased to exist and often only the material objects linked with them remain to remind us of their former significance. One difficulty which besets us as we look at discontinued folk customs and their paraphernalia, is that we often have to make a conscious effort to re-discover what place they had in the life of our ancestors. A comprehensive study of folk customs would, in fact, take account of both the historical and the sociological approach, in an attempt to understand why they existed, and why some still persist. We may ask the question what do we mean by a folk custom?

Almost all our social life is based on habitual behaviour which is mostly drawn form the past, obviously however this does not constitute a body of folk custom. In practice, we distinguish between various kinds of customary behaviour and we reserve the term 'customs' for a different category of behaviours. We usually say that it is the picturesque, irrational or festive quality which sets them distinctly apart from the common place. Antiquity and repetition are not distinguishing marks of folk custom. It is rather an awareness on the part of the participants or observers that the behaviour involved in a folk custom is somewhat out of the ordinary and is called for by the singularity of the occasion. In other words, certain occasions call for special kinds of behaviour which will depend upon tradition and the extent to which tradition is countered and modified by current influences. Looked at from this standpoint, folk customs appear as what may be called "superfluous behaviour" distinctly patterned on traditional lines, in which a society indulges on particular occasions.[1]

Over a century has elapsed since the term 'folklore' was suggested by W. J. Thoms in 1846. Folklorists are unable to agree on the precise area of their field of study. There is no difficulty in including tales, myths, superstitions, songs, riddles, proverbs and similar traditions which have been handed down by word of mouth and which live in an unwritten form in the minds of ordinary people. The contention arises when one considers whether crafts, dances, ceremonies and games should also be included as folklore? It is necessary at this point to discuss briefly the relationship of folklore and folk customs.

The essential feature of folklore is that it is not only transmitted by word of mouth but also that it exists in people's minds or on their lips until it is finally written down by collectors. The subject excludes traditional activities of all kinds which are not expressed solely by word of mouth, and folk customs are among these traditional activities which are excluded. They are essentially actions of a particular kind carried out by people, together or as individuals and can be seen by an observer. They contain folklore in the form of set verses and music but the custom consists of the singing of them rather than of what is sung. Often folklore is the intangible background of folk customs and may help to explain the custom in terms of, for example, superstition. The custom may exist for some time after the folklore which originally gave it meaning has disappeared.

To fully understand customs it is necessary to refer to material, economic and social conditions as well as folklore. The social setting in which folk customs and folklore flourish is of a particular kind, and certain distinctive features are present which help us to understand how old customs are able to survive as living traditions, for example, local communities were largely self-sufficient and did not need to open themselves up to outside influences. People were born, lived and died in this intimate social setting where the land and its way of life was a unifying force upon the peasant life of the locality. This peasant society in Wales was made up of numerous little communities, and as the American sociologists, G. C. Homans[2] has stated that, any group of men tends to complicate the conditions of its life and to make them more interesting. They will tend to build up their original purpose, for example, the meals at a farm shearing are often festive and the day itself is an important festive occasion when bantering, joking, discussion, story-telling and formerly ballad singing took place. What actually began with an economic purpose turned out to have ramifications involving leisure activities also.

One may ask why have folk customs which have had such a long life almost finally vanished? One explanation is that Welsh country life has become less and less peasant-like in those characteristics which enabled old customs to linger on. No longer are the countryside communities the intimate little worlds they were in the last century. Apart from this process of change Welsh rural society from the eighteenth century onward was being steadily influenced by the Methodist movement and these religious reformers in their zeal attacked both harmful and harmless customs indiscriminately.

A large body of folk customs has succumbed to the forces of change both sociological and religious. We now turn to local customs and practices in the Parish of Vaynor which were many and varied. To establish the date of their origin is obviously impossible. All we know is that as Tom Lewis has stated "some are centuries old and precede many of our constitutional laws. Many have changed over the years, others have disappeared completely and possibly in our conventional and sophisticated age have little meaning and are not worthy of record. They enable us, nevertheless to understand the way of life of our forefathers and in a way to understand our own".

SEASONAL CUSTOMS

NOS CALAN GAEAF

Trefor Owen states "All-Hallows Eve, was the weirdest of the three nights during the year; on it spirits walked abroad. It was believed that on this eve, the ghost of a dead person was to be seen at midnight on every stile ... one of the oldest Calan Gaeaf customs, was that of lighting bonfires after dark ... there would be dancing, shouting and leaping around the fire as it burned".[3] A local correspondent writing in 1854 stated "it was the day of thanksgiving for the preceding harvest, all work was suspended, fires were lit upon the prominent heights. These were called "coelcerthi" or Sacred fires and carry in their names the remembrance of their original religious character. The time was devoted to music, dancing, manly games and every diversion that the imagination of youth could conceive. The custom survived in the kitchen and in the farmhouse, among the peasantry and young people and on Tuesday night many a goose was roasted and eaten with small hills of 'potch pytatos', many old stockings were emptied of their nuts and many were the apples fished up from tubs of water".[4] The old custom of "tucking apples" has now virtually discontinued.

CHRISTMAS

During the Victorian period, Christmas changed gradually from an intensely social occasion in which all the community took part to one of family celebration in the seclusion of private homes. In the wake of this change came many of the Christmas customs as we know them – the Christmas card and the Christmas tree, while the earlier observances slowly disappeared. The folk custom in the end gave way to the commercialised holiday. The Christmas card beginning in 1843 has become a convenient substitute for the older custom of the Christmas letter or personal visit to convey the compliments of the season. The custom of decorating homes with holy and mistletoe of course continues.

THE PLYGAIN SERVICE

In many parts of Wales, Christmas meant rising early (or staying up overnight) to attend the plygain service at the parish Church. Plygain, and its earlier forms 'pylgain' and 'pylgaint', are derived from the Latin pulli cantio, "cock's crow'.[5] The hours for the plygain appears to have varied between 3 a.m. and 6 a.m., the latter becoming more common as time went on. In country districts the plygain at the parish Church was attended by people from even the remotest farms. Often each person brought his or candle to help to light the Church since, until the nineteenth century, regular services were rarely held at night time and no provision for lighting was usually made.

The plygain itself was an abbreviated form of morning service interspersed with and followed by carols sung by soloists and parties. Seen against its historical background the plygain is a survival of a pre-reformation Christian service modified to suit the new Protestant conditions. Richards suggests that the plygain took the place of the midnight Christmas mass of the Catholic period and was originally associated with a communion service held later on Christmas morning.[6] Far from disappearing under the impact of nonconformity in the nineteenth century, the plygain was one of the few traditional church festivals not discarded by the chapels. The plygain service continued locally at Penderyn and Defynnog until this century and the midnight Christmas mass, known locally as the "Watch Night Service" continues up to the present day at St John's Church, Cefn Coed.

BOXING DAY OR ST STEPHEN'S DAY

A one time popular and barbarous custom in this area was 'hunting the squirrel'. Red squirrels were plentiful in those days but about 1825 a devastating blight attacked the hazel trees, the yield of nuts was poor and as a result most of the squirrels of the locality died of starvation. After that date red squirrels in the parish were few and the sport and custom died out. Another custom associated with the period between Boxing Day and the Twelfth Night was that of hunting the wren. A wren was caught and then placed in a bedecked box or wren house. A four-some carrying the little house would enter homes groaning under the weight of the burden. After singing and reciting the party would be invited into the house for refreshments and a possible money gift. Boxing Day was also known as "holming day" when animals and sometimes human beings were bled. It was thought to strengthen them. In a recently television programme the author showed the bleeding instruments which were borrowed from Cyfarthfa Museum.

NEW YEAR'S EVE AND NEW YEAR'S DAY

The custom of 'letting in' the New Year has been recorded in one form or other in many parts of the British Isles.[7] In this locality, and in Wales in general, it was marked merely by the belief that good or bad luck was brought to the house by the first visitor of the new year according to his or her sex or certain personal characteristics. The giving of gifts on New Year's Day is an ancient custom and widely observed, but more recently displaced by the growing importance of Christmas and Christmas presents. The collecting of *calennig* (New Year's gift) is a Welsh form of this custom. Though still extant it is somewhat subdued compared with even thirty years ago. The collecting of *calennig* began early in the day and continued until noon. The children of this neighbourhood formed themselves into little groups and went from house to house conveying their congratulations and good wishes for the year.

MARI LWYD

In this part of Wales the Mari Lwyd is undoubtedly one of the most popular of medieval customs. It was once part of a religious ceremony held in honour of the Virgin Mary but has become an occasion for feasting and merry making. These celebrations were held at Christmas tide and in the New Year, when a man garbed in a white sheet and wearing a horse's skull and jaws suitably draped and decorated with coloured ribbons and ornaments, walked at the head of a procession round the village. At each house a request was made for admittance and permission to sing was proffered in extempore verse. The occupants of the house replied in verse and a rhymed dialogue of a set type took place, ending with the admission of the party who were offered food and drink. Quite often a highly decorated wassail bowl was passed around the company, the wassail bowls being of wood or of pottery. Ten men were seriously burned at 'monythusloyne' (Mynyddislwyn) while making a Mari Lwyd in 1835.[8] The custom of Mari Lwyd was very popular in this district and survived far into the nineteenth century. It was also known as 'Ladi Wen' that is the White, or Holy Lady.[9]

THE GWYLMABSANT

Generally, the Gwylmabsant was observed in every parish and was the occasion for games and contests of all kinds and attended by large numbers of people. The festival was usually held on a Sunday or started on a Saturday and continued until Tuesday. The proceedings included contests in leaping, running, hurling, wrestling, cock-fighting and football. There is no known record or description of the Gwylmabsant in Vaynor, undoubtedly there was, because it is unlikely that Vaynor would have behaved differently from the adjacent parishes. Writing of the Gwylmabsant at Penderyn, David Davies states that the Gwylmabsant was held at the Inns of Penderyn starting in the first week of November and lasted for a fortnight with the dancers contributing towards the harpist. David Davies, also refers to Gwyl Cynog being held on the 7th October annually. On the eve of the festival it was the custom to keep, watch over the local churchyard while the Saint's Day was spent in hunting and feasting. One of the favourite dietary items on these occasions was a pudding made of bread, raisins, currants and sugar called 'Y Whippod'.[10] Canon Silas Harris, has pointed out that the festival of St Gwynno at Vaynor was on October 22nd,[11] and this was possibly the occasion of the *Gwylmabsant* in Vaynor.

EASTER

Easter, which commemorates the resurrection of Christ, is one of the three great religious festivals of the Christian year; the other two being Christmas and Whitsuntide. Easter day is always the first Sunday after the full moon which happens upon or next after the twenty first day of March, and if the full moon happens to be upon a Sunday, Easter day is the Sunday after. In turn, Easter decides the dates of other moveable feasts and fasts, including the nine preceding and eight following Sundays, Shrove tide, Lent, Ascension Day and Whitsun. The ancient customs observed on these days naturally changed their date from year to year in sympathy with Easter. With Easter, the Feast of the Resurrection, the period of abstinence and self-denial was brought to an end. This was celebrated by the buying and giving of Easter Eggs and on Easter Monday visiting Cefn Fair which will be referred to later.

SHROVE TUESDAY

It was as the day preceding the beginning of Lent that Shrove Tuesday was important to our ancestors. The fasting had not yet begun and this was the last day on which any feasting could take place. The old couplet

> "Dydd Mawrth Ynyd
> Crempog bob munud".

("Shrove Tuesday, pancakes every minute") aptly described the special activity of the day in this locality until recent times.

PALM SUNDAY (SUL Y BLODAU)

The Welsh name for Palm Sunday is *Sul Y Blodau* (the Sunday of the flowers), a term which refers to the widespread custom of decorating graves with flowers on this day. This practice was essentially a preparation for Easter and when new clothes were worn after the drabness of the winter. By the nineteenth century the dressing of graves had become an exceedingly popular custom at Easter and thousands of visitors came to the Cefn Coed cemetery up until recent times. The custom continues of attending to the graves before Easter. During the 1930s and 1940s the traffic at Cefn Cemetery on Palm Sunday was directed by the well known Merthyr character "Old Harry". Harry was born on the island of St Helena, the exiled Napoleon Bonaparte was sent here.

"Old Harry" a well known Merthyr character.

GOOD FRIDAY

Good Friday was celebrated in a solemn manner with a religious service in the parish church. This practice continues at St John's Church, Cefn Coed as does the buying and eating of hot cross buns on this day. The symbolical significance of the cross marked on the buns eaten on Good Friday calls for no explanation.

HARVEST

Harvest has been celebrated locally in harvest festivals from time immemorial. Churches and Chapels are decorated with the fruits of the harvest and special preachers are engaged for the services. The Churches have always celebrated with a week night and Sunday services. Thanksgiving services used to be held in the chapels for "gifts" other than the harvest. On Easter Monday 1843 for example, the congregation of Ebenezer Chapel, Cefn Coed, held a thanksgiving service in graditude to God for helping them to liquidate the debt incurred in building the Chapel. A local bard at Cefn Coed wrote an appropriate hymn for the occasion.[12] Tom Lewis mentions that during harvest, mowers in Vaynor hung their scythes at night on the boughs of apple trees. They claimed that the acid in trees, having rusted the gleaming blades, produced, after honing, a keener edge.

GENERAL CUSTOMS – COURTING

An old custom connected with courtship in Wales was the presenting of a carved wooden spoon by the lover to his sweetheart. The degree of elaboration of the love spoon not only exemplified the skill of its maker but symbolised the fervour of his passion. As well as love spoons, stay busks, knitting needles sheathes, love bobbins and even valentine cards were all associated with courtship in rural Wales. Tom Lewis has mentioned that when farmers settled in the parish hundreds of years ago they almost invariably planted a few sycamore saplings around their homesteads. He adds that the large sycamore leaves were used to wrap around butter instead of paper because paper was then scarce and expensive. One should also note that the sycamore was also used for making love spoons, bowls and plates because it is one of the few timbers that does not "taint" the food contents of a bowl for example. For the same reason it was used for making domestic spoons and also because it was a soft wood, easily carved with a penknife and a few rudimentary tools. Sycamore was used also locally for making wooden clocks. The author had a clock which had been fashioned and made locally which was entirely of wood and there were no metal parts whatsoever.

COURTING IN BED

Courting in Wales was usually secretive and surreptitious. In the past "bundling" or "courting in bed" was widely practised in country districts and this custom was celebrated in song and poem. The man after throwing pebbles at the girl's window, would use a ladder from the rick yard to gain admission through an upstairs window to the bedroom. He would leave by the same means before dawn, unseen and unheard by the sleeping household. An unwanted suitor could find himself drenched with a bucket of swill as he attempted to gain access to the house. The promiscuity permitted by traditional methods of courtship did bring in its wake a high degree of premarital pregnancy and illegitimacy. This is a surprising feature in a rural community that regarded alcohol, gambling and "breaking the Sabbath" as the gravest form of sins. This high illegitimacy rate has continued in this century in some of the rural areas of Wales. Alwyn Rees reported that in the Census year of 1931, the illegitimacy rate per thousand unmarried women aged 15-45 was as follows: England and Wales, 5.7; Montgomeryshire 10.6, Mongomeryshire Rural Districts, 13.4; Llanfyllin Rural District, 15.9.[13]

A discussion of illegitimacy in the Parish of Vaynor will be undertaken in the section on the Parish Records, the records do not show a high proportion of illegitimacy but in fact it is very difficult to obtain an accurate picture since, for example, so many illegitimate births were unreported. What often happened locally was that the newly born child was taken by night and left in the porch of the father's farmhouse. An interesting fact uncovered from the pages of the Parish Register of Marriages is the high proportion of brides and bridegrooms listed as "from within the parish".

While one recognises that there were Church regulations with regard to residence etc., does this not also suggest considerations such as, how far could a male walk after work to do his courting? Was it not also an advantage to seek a wife from within the Parish whose character and industry was unblemished? Was it not also an advantage to know the pedigree of the family? It would seem then from the evidence that there was a tendency to marry partners from within the Parish. Could one justifiably call this tendency which has persisted, possibly for centuries, a custom?

MARRIAGE CUSTOMS

Following a blessing from parents, and after a decision had been taken by the young people to marry, the parents on each side usually met to make arrangements for the wedding and the economic future of the young people. We are told that prosperous farmers in Vaynor gave their eldest daughter a dowry of seven hundred guineas, and to their second daughter five hundred guineas. The bride's family usually provided the young bride with some furniture, bedding, domestic utensils and sometimes some farm animals, items that in farming were traditionally the wife's responsibility. The bridegroom's father generally helped by, perhaps, paying the first half year's rent, by providing essential stock, lending money to cover the early critical period and generally helping as far as he could afford.

When the wedding day had been fixed it was customary to send out invitations to family and friends to attend the wedding either on a printed sheet or, more often, by word of mouth. The local bidder *(Y Gwahoddwr)* was asked to visit all the houses in the neighbourhood and invite the people to the wedding feast *(Y neithior)*. The bidding was a general invitation to the whole neighbourhood to meet at the house of the bride and groom bringing with them presents, however small, to the newly married couple. The bidder was attired in clothing suitable for the occasion, and carried in his hands a white stick of office decorated with ribbons of all colours. On entering a house, he would strike the ground thrice, ask for silence and deliver his speech in prose and in verse.

Some families present at a bidding would be paying a debt incurred years before *("talu'r pwyth")* at their biddings while others were creating a debt, which the newly wedded couple would be obliged to repay when the occasion arose. A printed handbill issued locally for a bidding read as follows:

> "As we intend to enter the matrimonial state, we are encouraged by our friends to make a bidding on the occasion of Friday 26th and 27th October 1832, at our house situate in Bridge Place, when and where the favour of your agreeable company is humbly solicited and whatever donation you may be pleased to bestow on us, then this will be thankfully received, warmly acknowledged and cheerfully and readily repaid whenever called for on a similar occasion by your most obedient servants.[14]
>
> William Williams and Catherine Garner".

In referring to marriage customs Tom Lewis states, "Engagement rings were not in fashion in Vaynor. When a young man engaged his sweetheart, he gave her an ash leaf plucked from a neighbouring tree, which he dried, pressed and placed between the leaves of the family Bible. Believing that evil spirits would be kept at bay at weddings by loud detonations, farmers fired their shot guns into the air when the wedding service was in progress. A much older custom in local weddings was to light a bonfire in the churchyard, which was fed by each well-wisher throwing a branch of a tree on top of the fire. Another popular custom was that known as "halting the wedding". As soon as the contracting partners emerged from the church, a rope or halter was drawn across to bar the way. The "halt" was regarded as the first obstacle in the life of the bride and bridegroom and one that was removed by the simple expedient of being kind".

"In the early days, the fiddle and the harp were much in evidence at weddings at Vaynor. Wedding parties used to march in procession from Cefn Coed to Vaynor Church, a fiddler leading the way. The young couple marched in mortal fear of old boots, laced with ribbons of varied colours, being hurled after them by their friends. If a nervous bridegroom dropped the wedding ring at the altar it was an ill omen. The omen was counteracted by the officiating clergyman making the Sign of the Cross over it. In order to keep the money in the blood" it had long been a practice in Vaynor among the wealthy farming families until about a century ago to inter-marry, a practice which very often resulted in mentally and constitutionally weak off-spring." As Tom Lewis has pointed out, "honeymoons were the prerogative of the rich. The wedding service over, the "poor" spent the rest of the day in a local inn singing and dancing to the rhythm of the harp or returning to the bride's house for the wedding feast where family and friends brought presents and partook of the feast. The young couple usually stayed at the bride's home on the wedding night moving to their new home the following day".

BIRTHS AND CHRISTENINGS

A birth is a joyful occasion and the joy that has come the way of a particular family was a signal for neighbourhood rejoicing. Sometimes a christening was an occasion for feasting and drinking and in some parts of Wales special christening glasses were used. Each glass held nearly a pint of ale and those at such a christening ceremony were supposed to drink a whole glassful at one gulp, the object of the toasts being the mother rather than the child. The custom of god-parents is supposed to be derived from the fact that the mother might be unwell and unable for this reason to take the child to the christening. She then would have asked a "god-mother" to do so for her. It is said that the seats usually found in the porch of a church were for god-mothers who were not church communicants, to wait while the ceremony of christening was in progress.

Frequent references are made in the old Vaynor records to the "man midwife". Here is a typical entry bearing on the subject, "For Ann Bowen and child and man midwife to her, 21s 0d (£1.05)". As Tom Lewis has shown, the "man midwife", of course, was a sort of medical man; in short, an apothecary, that is a prescriber or dispenser of remedies. Sometimes he was "trained" but more often than not he simply learned his job through practical experience. Very often, non-conformist ministers were "medical practitioners" of this sort. The Rev Thomas Morgan (1737-1813), who was raised to the Ministry of the Hen Dŷ Cwrdd, was a lay physician in this category and, during the smallpox epidemic of 1784 he assisted qualified doctors by inoculating a hundred children. As Tom Lewis has also stated, the Medical Directory of 1795, states that there were only three medical men in Merthyr in that year. Two of them were described as "Apothecary and Man-Midwife", and the third was "Surgeon and Man-Midwife". Two hundred years ago the nearest qualified doctors were at Cardiff twenty four miles away. Research conducted by the author locally and with the Keeper of Folk Medicines at the Welsh Folk Museum at St Fagans suggests that in the main, midwives of the nineteenth century were untrained and learned, their skills through experience only. In the rural parts of the Parish, neighbouring wives would assist with the birth without the midwife being present. This was probably the general custom in the remote upland farms of Vaynor during the centuries, prior to the training of nurses and midwives.

A custom that has now completely died out in this Parish is that of a different form of baptism, i.e. baptism of adolescents or even adults by immersion. "The ceremony was held at Pwll-dan-y-bont, namely the pool under the Pontycapel Viaduct at Cefn Coed. This was the venue for the Baptists of Carmel Chapel, Cefn Coed while the Cwm Tâf Baptists at Bethel Chapel, were baptised in Pwll-dan-bontyglec. While the immersions were taking place, the congregation stood on the bank singing hymns suitable to the occasion". It is worthy of note that these services were attended by the members of the Baptist Church in Pontsticill who at the beginning of this century covered the distance on foot. Reference has already been made to the custom of christening a new born child on the coffin of the dead mother at the Hen Dŷ Cwrdd in the early nineteenth century.

DEATH

Death brought manifestations of sympathy and in the interval between death and burial the bereaved family left much of the housework and farmwork to neighbours. Food was prepared for sympathising callers and for the funeral feast by neighbours. Experienced women in the locality prepared the corpse for burial while arrangements for the burial in the local churchyard or chapel graveyard was made by the men. An old religious custom, once faithfully kept to in the Parish of Vaynor was the 'Gwylnos', now never observed. It would best be described, perhaps as a kind of prayer meeting. It was held at the house of a dead parishioner the evening prior to the funeral. The service was brief and totally devoid of ceremonial. A short prayer by the minister or clergyman, a brief address recalling the virtues of the departed followed, then eventually brought the service to an end. If the coffin had not been closed, the miniature congregation walked past it in single file and to ward off frightening dreams that night, touched the cheek of the departed. Tea was served at each service. The last known "Gwylnos" in this locality was in March 1892.

Another religious custom was the 'Gwylio', the vigil. Two neighbours of the deceased kept watch over the body through the long hours of the night. Usually the "Watchers" were women. Four lighted candles, a foot long, were placed by the coffin, two at the head and two at the feet. The lighted candles were thought to keep evil spirits away, possibly this was a survival of the custom observed when Wales was Roman Catholic and similar to the Irish wake. As Tom Lewis has recorded, "The symbol of mourning today is black. In our Parish up to a century ago, it was white. At the funeral of an adult, men wore white ties and white gloves and white was the colour of their hat bands. At the funeral of a child the symbol was blue. Blue also was the colour of the cloth that draped the little coffin. Men mourners wore an inch of blue ribbon in their button-holes. Women mourners wore blue ribbons on their bonnets and tied their sandals with it, for sandals were then the fashionable wear for the women of Vaynor to wear in funerals. Ribbons, at that time were expensive and beyond the means of the poor and for this reason those who could not afford them borrowed them from their more fortunate neighbours. A coffin covered with a black cloth indicated that the deceased was an old person. The coffin bore no flowers".

Shrouds in those days were unheard of. The dead were buried in their best woollen underwear and it was considered a mark of disrespect to the departed to bury them in any other attire. Even as late as seventy years ago some Vaynor families followed this custom. Tom Lewis has suggested that "It probably originated in the time of King Charles II who, in order to encourage the woollen industry, introduced an Act of Parliament making it compulsory upon undertakers to wrap corpses in woollens and flannels before committing them to the earth".[15] "Washing the Body" was another custom rigidly observed in the parish of Vaynor. This duty fell upon a duly appointed "body washer", who was responsible to the Church vestry. According to the parish records for every corpse washed he was paid a shilling. It would seem that only the good and the respectable were favoured with these last rites, for when a hundred and seventy years ago a "begar was found ded on the road in Coad y Cymmar", his body was not washed. The bodies were washed in a tub, possibly a Jewish custom by origin.

On the day of the funeral of a communicant of Vaynor church, and also on the following Sunday, the pulpit was draped with black crape. The crape was never used twice. Every departed communicant was thought worthy of a fresh draping, although the crape, then, was seven shillings a yard. When funeral bells were used in the early nineteenth century, people could easily decide what sort of person had died. Twelve strokes on each bell indicated the death of the head of the family, eleven strokes a mother, ten strokes an unmarried man, nine a young unmarried woman, six strokes a boy and five strokes a girl

Suicides and women of immoral character were buried facing West and the eternal night while the believers were buried facing East and the everlasting light of day. In the early days, the local gentry were buried in the floor of the church. Coffins of the poor were ordered and paid for by the Vestry, six shillings was an average price and shoddy workmanship was hidden by inexpensive cloth. A black cloth wound round the family bible was a sign that there was a death in the house. When the photograph of the deceased hung on the wall, black ribbons were tied to the frame. Funerals were large of necessity, because the dead were carried from Cwm Tâf to Vaynor (five miles) and from Cefn Coed to Vaynor (three miles). Funerals of men killed in the mines were frequent and very large. Information regarding potentially large funerals would have been found out by Innkeepers at Cefn, Cwm Tâf and Vaynor prior to the funeral. Large fires were lit in the rooms downstairs in preparation for the usual large concourse of men who came for the "funeral drink" which went on for hours after the funeral. Non attendance at a funeral was considered an implied insult to the living and the dead.

AGRICULTURAL CUSTOMS

It was a custom locally among the farming fraternity that by mutual agreement probably at the Leet Court, they were apportioned mountain rights whereby they were permitted to graze a certain area by the number of sheep and ponies which they could maintain during the winter on their respective lowland meadows. This agreement was made traditionally at the Leet Court which was made up of the local Lord of the Manor where there was one, brinkers, farmers and freeholders.

The Rev J. E. Jenkins has indicated that ploughing by oxen was the custom until the beginning of the nineteenth century with well known teams in both the Tâf Fawr and Tâf Fechan valleys. He mentions that Cae-yr-eglwys above the Church and Llysiogisaf Farm, Cwm Tâf were the last places where oxen were used in ploughing. For ploughing Cae-yr-eglwys the four oxen and one horse were harnessed. Jenkins further informs us that the oxen were joined by a yoke(iau) made in four different sizes according to the number of oxen employed. The wooden yoke was placed on the neck of the ox and held in position by a wooden ring called 'eurrwy' and in some places 'gwyddrwy'. Different names were given for the yoke sizes, the 'beriau' was for two oxen to plough the 'talar' or cross ridges; the 'meiiau' was for four oxen which represented the ordinary farmer's team; the 'ceseiliau' was for six oxen employed by the better off yeomen farmers while the 'hiriau' was for eight oxen abreast kept by the lord of the manor.

Mr Morgan Rhys Jones of Garth Madryn, Penderyn informed me in 1970 that his great grandfather, Sion Jones of Bodwigiad Farm, Penderyn was the last person in this area to work oxen. He gave the names of the last team as "Captain, Sailor, Gold, Silver, Pearl and Laddie" – it is strange that they should have been given English names in an area where the first language was Welsh.

The yoke was usually made of oak or hornbeam, carved into shape, well polished and oiled. The bows by which the yoke was attached to the necks of the oxen were made of ash and were steamed before bending into shape. The ox was yoked to the plough team at about three years of age and was worked for six or seven years. Although its working life was short, when it was killed its meat provided food for the farming family for many months after it had been salted. The skin was passed on and sold to the local tanner who converted it into leather while the horns were used for various purposes – sometimes for holding the sand and mutton fat or bacon fat used in conjunction with the 'rip' for sharpening sickles or scythes in the harvesting fields. Ox dung was used as a fuel when firewood was scarce and was also mixed with clay, straw and other materials for making daub for walls of buildings. According to Jenkins, unmarried women usually led the oxen on the field and encouraged them to do their work by singing Welsh triplets and triads to them, sometimes introducing the names of the oxen in the rhymes. Legend has it that the farmyard at Llwynbrain Farm, Pontsticill was the favourite place for shoeing oxen in the parish of Vaynor. The ox was felled, its feet tied and was comforted by one of the maids while being shod with the shoe "called a 'kawan' ", which was in two elliptical parts because the ox is a cloven hoofed animal.

One part was fixed with two nails while the other part was with three.

Dr Geraint Jenkins, Curator of the Welsh Folk Museum has pointed out that the ploughman and oxherd were very important personalities in Welsh life and they were responsible for the animals, both night and day.Usually they had their beds in the ox-shed and one of their songs of exhortation is quoted in the section on ox-carts in Chapter Five. One of the closing rhymes referred to by Jenkins states:-

Duke a Gro, blaenion bro;
Mae y cwysau heb un tro-,
Dyma'r talar-tally ho.[16]

(Duke and Gro, chiefs of the vale; your furrows are straight. Behold the end-tally ho.)

There were numerous other customs associated with agricultural life such as the hiring of labour, the precedence given to senior men at the shearing benches, and the preparation and serving of food at the shearing feast. The customs of 'mutual aid' within the extended family and neighbourhood; then there were the customary sanctions imposed in farming communities, the oftentimes separate eating arrangements for family and farm servants and the wide range of folk medicinal customs employed on Welsh farms until fairly recent times. It has already been shown that most local farmers had their own lime-kilns and Tom Lewis has referred to the custom of local shepherds stroking new born lambs claiming that the scent of human hands deterred attacks from foxes.

SOME CHURCH CUSTOMS

Tom Lewis has reported that when Vaynor formed a part of the great Garth Madryn Forest, and only a dark tangled path led to the Vaynor Church, worshippers were guided to the services by the distant tinkle of the little Church bells. In later days, too, when clocks and watches were luxuries enjoyed only by a few, the bells, so tradition states, performed another useful function as they struck the passing hours on festival days and called people to church on Sundays. Seats were not provided in the old Church until about two centuries ago. It was the custom for the congregation to worship on their feet while the old were permitted "to go to the wall" to support their aching limbs. In later years the old and weak were provided with backless benches by the Parish Vestry. The gentry at Vaynor followed suit and brought chairs for themselves from their homes. As time passed, the peasantry did likewise. Many of the chairs were made of straw, as straw chairs were believed "to keep away the cymalwst" (rheumatism).

There are innumerable instances to show that the old custom of giving alms to the poor and destitute was given a prominent place in the religious life of the parish. In 1760, the Rev Anthony Martin who was curate of Vaynor from 1757 to 1776 presented Nantddu Church (St Mary's), Cwm Tâf, with a pewter alms' dish. The alms' dish was placed by the church door, and those who could afford an alm dropped it into the dish as they passed out of the service. Similarly boxes were placed in some of the Non-conformist Chapels at Cefn Coed, which invited donations "i'r tlodion' (for the poor). As Tom Lewis has observed, "The old Vaynorians do not seem to have divorced sport from religion. On Sabbath afternoons in the nineteenth century, in the Summer, the young men and women of the parish used to gather on Twyn Wryrfa (Maiden's Hill) in Cwm Tâf Fechan to dance and sing. That evening, however, they would usually be found on bended knee at Vaynor Church, uniting solemnly in the responses".[17]

The old time rectors used to make their ecclesiastical requirements known in the Vaynor Parish Almanac. The items required in 1892 were "Funds to cement the church spire, and to recast the bells. Alms receptacles, a new communion table, shrubs and trees for the graveyards and a bell for the National School". The school was at Pontsticill. As Tom Lewis has pointed out, Vaynor in the early nineteenth century seems to have been a strange mixture of coarseness and piety. When Rev William Jones became rector in 1816, he found that the members of the choir were in the habit of taking jugs of ale to the church with them. Told by the rector that the practice must stop, a wag in the choir is alleged to have retorted that the ale was drunk as an antidote for the dryness of his sermons!

Members of the Church Vestry, presided over always by the Rector, were supplied with drinks from the parish funds. An entry made in 1817 states "For ale in the vestries 19s 0d". The duty of making census returns in the nineteenth century was imposed upon someone who could count in English. This office was occupied by Rhys Hywel Rhys who wrote in the Parish Register, "To my trouble by gather the number of the population, 10s 0d"[18] (£0.50p).

FOLK MEDICINAL CUSTOMS

For many reasons folk medicines played a very important part in the lives of the people and as we have seen, many were made from herbs, some growing wild in the hedgerows, woods and fields while others were grown in the gardens. Flowers such as agrimony, wood sage, yellow flag, common centaury or herb Robert, sometimes boiled or mixed with other ingredients such as butter were used for both human and animal complaints such as lice, blood in the urine or plague. The bark of the mountain ash boiled was considered useful in the case of nerves while nearly every part of the elder tree, including flowers and berries were considered invaluable for colds, for making ointments and wines. The flowers were sometimes dried and kept for use in the Winter. Similarly the fruit juice of raspberries was taken by pregnant women to facilitate an easy birth while the blackberry leaves were thought to be efficacious for diarrhoea and medicine made from the flowers relieved piles.

Human urine was occasionally used in various localities in Wales for earache, dry skin or in the case of animals for bathing sprains or cuts or given as an additive to animal foods. Cows were given their own milk to drink after calving to restore the level of calcium in the animal. Cream made from cows' milk was used in the case of animal prolapse, sun burn, scalds or burns while butter was used for rubbing in the nose for a cold, for cracked lips, for removing freckles, as a base for ointments and for curing animal fluke. Animal excreta was used for dressing septic wounds with humans or for cows having udder problems. Colds and whooping cough was treated by drinking boiled milk to which grated horn had been added.

Perhaps it was from the pig that most materials or ingredients were obtained for medicinal purposes. A warmed slice of bacon wrapped in flannel was applied for a sore throat. Bacon fat from the frying pan was used to treat animal cuts. The thin layer called in Welsh, "y bloneg" surrounding the layers of internal fat of the pig was used to treat septic conditions. This was applied with an ointment made of 'bloneg' mixed with groundsel or leek. Ointment made from this fat was used for removing thorns and whitlows. Primarily of course the pig's fat was used for making lard for domestic use. The bladder was used by the boys as a football or for storing lard or for holding warm water placed on the head for headache. Poultices made from pig excreta mixed with potatoes were used in some parts of Wales for the treatment of 'thrush' in horses. Warm milk mixed with pig manure was given to cows with discoloured urine or applied to sheep with 'black leg'.

Ducks, chickens and geese also provided medicinal ingredients for example, goose grease was applied to the chest for bronchitis or to the throat for throat infections. A live small chick pushed down the throat of a horse suffering from tape worm was considered beneficial in north Wales while milk and eggs were given to cows locally to improve their condition. Eggs in their shells were placed in the mouths of cows suffering from a blistered tongue in some places.

Insects, fish and reptiles were also used in the preparation of medicines in parts of Wales. Rubbing a slug in a wart was one treatment while rubbing a slug in the legs of a new born child with bent legs was thought to help in straightening them. In Merionethshire one cure for whooping cough was to take two spoonful, three times a day of a liquid derived from leaving half a dozen skinned slugs covered in brown sugar overnight. Honey was used in various ways for treating coughs and sore throats. Colliers used honey on cuts to remove the blue scar incurred through injury in the mines while bee sting was felt to improve athritic ailments. Live eels were given to cows suffering from constipation in Eifionydd while the skin of an eel was tied to the painful area due to rheumatism. Boiled herrings were considered an antidote for the aftermath of too much alcohol and they were also fed to pigs to improve their appetites or to cows with red urine. Leeches were used generally throughout the country during the last century and in the early decades of this century to reduce temperature or to remove blood or for frost bite. The bleeding of farm animals using special instruments to cut the veins was a common practise throughout Wales for the treatment of 'inflammation' or for the treatment of pneumonia in human beings.[24]

Poultices and ointments were extensively used to relieve pain or septic conditions. Poultices were made from various substances such as bread, potatoes or from herbs such as groundsel, or leeks were popular. So were the juices of a large number of plants such as the greater celandine, ribwort plantain or the leaves of the sycamore. Drinks made from the dandelion and burdock were considered to be good medicines. 'Teas' made from agrimony, common centaury, milk thistle, wood betony, bog beans and other plants were taken while garlic was considered good for tape worms and paraffin rubbed in the head was thought to kill head lice. There were a number of methods employed to stop nose bleeds or bleeding from a wound. Lying on one's back or placing a penny or a large cold key on the nape of the neck was a common means of stopping the bleeding from the nose while a spider's web was used locally to stop haemorrhage from an injury. The leaves of geranium, willow or oak leaves placed over the wound were considered effective. Irritants such as ground sugar, glass or slate were blown into the eyes of animals thought to have a membrane growing over their eyes. A fright was the treatment in some cases for hiccups while children suffering from whooping cough could be relieved by taking them near to a gas works, to a road where hot tar was being used, near to where gorse was being burnt or as Tom Lewis has stated to take them to Pwll Tâf caves where a powder fuse had been ignited.

It might be argued that many folk medicines have a reasonable foundation for their use but others would seem to be reflections of belief held by former generations for example, in Eifionydd when it was thought that sheep were in pain, it was the custom to rub turpentine on its loins every new moon. This custom was derived probably from a belief in the Middle Ages that it was necessary to have an understanding of astrology to understand human anatomy. They also attributed magical qualities to certain plants and trees which are grown near their homes to afford protection against evil spirits, and in prayers and the blessings of God and His saints. Many of the folk medicines referred to are from the memory of old people, undoubtedly these are only some of these practised here and in other parts of Wales over the centuries. Mr Tom Jones for example in the section on 'Agriculture and Rural Industry' has referred to ancient remedies for curing blood in the urine of sheep, for sore tongues of sheep, for stopping the 'grub', for 'blockage', for foot rot and for scouring in sheep.

Illness brought many local callers, for it was considered obligatory for at least one member of each family in the locality to visit the sick person. They often brought gifts of food, folk medicines or money, and should the person be so ill as to require constant attention they offered their services to watch at night. Should this offer not be made, the family of the person considered it unfriendly and unneighbourly, even though the offer may not have been accepted. When a person lay ill, neighbours spread bracken or peat on the road outside to deaden the sound of carts. This practice of 'mutal aid' was extended to loaning animals or providing essential labour.

The diseases and ailments "cured" were mostly warts, eye weakness, lameness, rheumatism, earache, toothache, scrofula, skin diseases, whooping cough and ague. Many of the treatments seem strange , harsh and in some cases repulsive to our generation. One of the more simple treatments was the custom of drinking water from efficacious wells such as

Llysieuog Well noted for healing scrofula, wounds, sores and ulcers or bathing fractured limbs in the ice-cold water of mountain streams. In order to 'cure' hydrophobia it was the custom to grate enough stone to cover a three penny piece which was taken in fresh milk. Tom Lewis claims that the treatment in Vaynor, in comparison, was extremely cruel, where people who were infected with hydrophobia as the result of being bitten by a mad dog were put to death by suffocation between two feather beds. A farmer's wife, living at Tŷnewydd Farm, was thus put to death as recently as less than a century and a half ago.[19]

The dreadful scourge, smallpox, was almost a regular visitor to the parish until the middle of the nineteenth century. As soon as the epidemic was expected, women dressed in red gowns, convinced that red garments were a protection against their faces being scarred by the disease. It was claimed that chilblains were cured by thrashing the feet with boughs of holly until the blood ran. Another supposed cure was walking in the snow in one's bare feet. A sprained wrist was tied with strands of black wool and to cure toothache the point of a hot wire was inserted into the aching tooth to sear the nerve. Relief was also obtained by pouring a drop of vinegar into a cup to which a pinch of common soda had been added. The vinegar, after a redhot poker had been dipped into it, was rubbed into the gums. Corns were removed by dipping the feet in the dew ponds on Cilsanws mountain and to help heal a cut cobbler's wax was placed on the wound. Other 'cures' for corns included applying spittle mixed with chalk, applying pitch or Venice turpentine or the juice of house leek, and to prevent corns the feet were bathed regularly in cold water.

The 'cure' for all throat infections was red flannel smeared with goose grease while the grease rubbed into the chest was the certain remedy for "tighteness of breath". The cures for consumption or tuberculosis were as varied as they were numerous, they included drinking freely of malt, yolk of egg with wine, black currant jelly with good white bread, syrup of marshmallows and syrup of squills. Other remedies included, to suckle daily at the breast of a healthy female, the scent of a sod of new earth, honey mixed with vinegar, fish, fowl, lamb, veal, oysters, new milk or cider, fresh air, physical exercise, poppy heads mixed into a syrup, the dried leaves of the garden rosemary and cheerful companions.

Habitual sufferers from cold feet sprinkled cayenne pepper into their boots and the remedies for spitting blood included the juice of sage or honey, juice of nettles, a strong concoction of shepherd's purse, a teaspoonful of prunes after they had been boiled for three nights, the powder of betony with a little honey in vinegar, the juice of woundwort, decoction of St John's Wort with the juice of knot grass, and the juice of the plantain clarified. Bronchitis was said to be relieved by inhaling steam from the spout of a boiling kettle; and to strengthen weak eyes, gold rings were worn in the pierced lobes of the ears.

Wax, congealing in the ears, due to a cold, was dissolved by drinking hedgehog broth. Other applications for ailments of the ears included the juice of an onion to rid noise, juice of agrimony for foul ears, the juice of the berries of cuckoo-pint boiled in oil of roses for earache (the juice of "erings" or sea holly has the same effect"), the juice of wild marjoram for deafness, the juice of berries of ivy for running sores, the juice of nightshade for pain, or the juice of the flowers of cow parsnip for running ears.

The following words written at the turn of this century would seem particularly apt today. "In these days of worry and hurry, in the everlasting race to reach a goal of wealth and position, asthma is one of the symptoms". The following remedies were suggested:- "drink half a pint of tar water twice a day, add a tablespoonful of honey, sugar candy, bruised or good brown sugar; take a tablespoonful of brimstone in a quarter pint of madeira wine about eleven o'clock; a new laid egg in a glass of wine every morning; ten to sixty drops of elixir of vitriol in water; three or four times a day; syrup of squills mixed with marshmallows. For coughing a pill of camphor the size of a pea. For a beverage take a tea of coltsfoot or hore hound sweetened with brown sugar; relief can be obtained by smoking leaves of coltsfoot mixed with tobacco. When breathing with difficulty take fresh milk morning and evening and there is no better cure than a "conserve" made of the flowers of woodbine or honeysuckle".

Some of the most bizarre cures of the eighteenth and nineteenth centuries were those used to cure piles, others were "to prevent piles". Some of the suggested cures were "bathe with cold water; a plaster of treacle; for "blind" piles lay on a plaster of onions; a plaster of turpentine varnish; for internal piles swallow the yolk of an egg in brandy, a large leek boiled every morning and evening. A 'cure' seldom requiring repetition for bleeding piles is to boil lightly the juice of nettles with sugar. Another 'cure' was the juice of blackberries drunk or applied externally, or the leaves and roots of cuckoo pint boiled in wine. Then again the mucilage of seed of flea-wort made with plantain water into which the yolk of an egg or two and a little populeon are put is a safe and sure remedy. Alternatively the roots of hound's tongue, baked under the embers, wrapped in paste or wet paper and a suppository made of it and put up into or applied to the fundament, effectively alleviates the pains or piles. Lastly the oil of flowers of the common white mullein, or the oil of plums or oil of almonds are good against the inflamed piles".

The remedies which the old folks of former times had for the common cold were as brief and simple as they were efficacious no doubt in most cases. They were as follows:- "A teaspoonful of syrup of violets; abstain from intoxicating drinks and take a pint of cold water with a teaspoonful of treacle in it; rind of an orange, roll up inside out and a bit in each nostril; plunge your hands and feet into cold water and remain there until they get warm, this remedy also prevents chilblains; a tablespoonful of honey, butter, oatmeal mixed with three pence worth of best rum, and one egg mixed together in half pint of boiling water; the flowers of camomile boiled in posset drink provokes sweat (posset variation of the old Cymric term "posel" signifying a drink constituted of milk curdled with wine or other liquor)".[20]

For septic wounds local herbalists recommended a poultice of warm excreta straight from the entrails of a cow, claiming that the droppings were, after all only a mixture of herbs that had undergone a natural process of digestion. The antidote for the after-effects of excessive drinking of alcohol was believed to be repeated helpings of fried or boiled mackerel; and hardened drinkers thought that a meal of boiled cockles had a sobering effect on them. For healing stomach ulcers copious draughts of butter milk were drunk and for shingles farm house cream was rubbed into the effected parts. A remedy for shingles which was claimed to be infallible, was to drop a hot ember into a bowl of water. The shingles were then douched with the water. People suffering from constant drowsiness *(gwaith llech)* had the gristle just below the top of the ear, nicked with a razor until a trickle of blood flowed.[21] Tom Lewis claimed that during the cholera epidemic of 1849, "Rees Evan, the local herbalist, prescribed, as a preventative against the "horror", thoroughly chewed brassicas resulting in every garden and field in the parish being denuded of cabbages!"[22] He also prescribed peppermint drops. As already stated by Tom Lewis, "children suffering from whooping cough were carried down to Pwll Tâf cave (Ogof Pwll Tâf), where a power fuse was ignited, the fumes of which the gasping little patients were constrained to inhale. They emerged from the cave with wet, smarting eyes and often screaming with fright. Another remedy for this complaint was to drown a trout in milk. The trout, when expiring, vomited and both milk and vomit were swallowed. Yet another remedy was to drink the milk of a suckling mare. The constipated sought relief in the mineral spring of Ffynnon Llysieuog in Cwm Tâf. The water was carried away in jugs and urns and so efficacious was it considered by the medical profession that the possibility of commercially exploiting it was seriously contemplated a century ago".

Sore eyes and optic infections were reputed to be cured by daubing them with water from Ffynnon-Galon-Ddu (the well of the black heart). Young ladies daubed their eyes with its water in order to bring to them a lustre and sparkle. The well was situated a few hundred yards below the Pontycapel viaduct. Warts were said to disappear after swabbing them with water into which a red hot poker had been plunged. Another remedy was to apply to them the juice of a dandelion stalk. But the most popular remedy was to "charm" them. Betsi Tomos Powel of Cefn Coed was apparently well known for her "charming" of warts, her incantation ran like this:

Un, dau, tri,
A ffwrdd a Hi,
Ni ddaw y ddafaden
Yn ol atat ti.

(One, two, three,
Removed it shall be,
And never will the wart
Return to thee.)

Tom Lewis has referred to a large number of other local customs, as he states "It was further claimed that warts could be eradicated by burying a piece of meat in the ground; when putrefaction was complete the warts vanished. But perhaps the strangest cure was brought about by placing a few pebbles in a sweet bag and dropping it on the cross roads. Regarded as good for "stone in the kidneys" was mead. It was made of different kinds of herbs, flavoured with sweet briar, thyme, rosemary and bay leaves. These were boiled, and honey was added. It was claimed that this concoction disintegrated the "stone". A popular pick-me-up for the "run down" was the "tonic cup". The "cup" was carved out of a special kind of wood. Water was poured into it at bed time, and the contents drunk before breakfast the following morning. It was believed that the water gave piquancy to the stomach and sharpened the appetite. A cold fomentation of spent tea leaves was regarded as good for inflammation of the eyes and a wisp was said to disappear if gently rubbed with a gold ring. To purify the blood, small pellets of pitch were swallowed and to clear skin rash, a tea made of ground ivy was made. To stem excessive bleeding of a cut a cobweb was placed on the wound while bed wetting was remedied by taking the grated powder of a thoroughly roasted carcase of a mouse".[33] Pneumonia was 'cured' by wrapping the feet of the patient in the spleen of a newly killed lamb.[24]

REFERENCES

1. TREFOR OWEN. Welsh Folk Customs (1978). p.14.
2. G. C. HOMANS. The Human Group (1951). p.109.
3. TREFOR OWEN. op. cit., p.123.
4. Merthyr Guardian. January 3rd 1854. Merthyr Tydfil Library.
5. GWYNFRYN RICHARDS. 'Y Plygain'. Journal Historical Society. Church in Wales. I. (19), p.53.
6. GWYNFRYN RICHARDS, Bye Gones, 21st March 1917.
7. Wright and Lones. British Calendar Customs. England, II p.2. 1936-40.
8. Merthyr Guardian. January 10th 1835. Merthyr Tydfil Library.
9. The Story of Merthyr Tydfil by the Merthyr Tydfil N.U.T. (1932) p.156.
10. DAVID DAVIES (Dewi Cynon). Hanes Plwyf Penderyn (1905) p.86.
11. Brecon and Radnor Express. September 1st 1966. Article by CANON SILAS HARRIS.
12. TOM LEWIS. Customs and Practices. Pamphlet of The Cefn Coed and Vaynor Historical Society. (1957) p.7.
13. ALWYN D. REES. Life in a Welsh Countryside. (1950). p.180.
14. Merthyr Guardian. October 12th 1832. Merthyr Tydfil Library.
15. TOM LEWIS op. cit., p.5.
16. REV J. E. JENKINS, Vaynor: Its History and Guide (1897). p.114.
17. TOM LEWIS op. cit., p.6.
18. REV J. E. JENKINS op. cit., p.154.
19. TOM LEWIS op. cit. p.8.
20. Merthyr Guardian. May, June, July 1912. Merthyr Tydfil Library.
21. TOM LEWIS op. cit. p.13.
22. Ibid. p.14.
23. TOM LEWIS op. cit.
24. Brycheinion. Volume VII. Article on 'Llangattock Parish Scrap Book'. p.138.

CHAPTER XI

Some Recreations

INTRODUCTION

The hearth was the traditional scene of recreation and entertainment in rural Wales.[1] Local Communities did not have to open themselves up to outside influences on a large scale; their way of life was one which turned inwards upon itself, it relied almost entirely on its own resources which built up a highly integrated community, oftentimes isolated socially as well as geographically. For the countryman the most important social grouping was the family, then his neighbours, all dwelling within a few square miles of land. Within this small world, possibly a moorland tract or a secluded valley where the farms, hills, customs and traditions were intimately known, each person had an identity and 'belonged'.

During periods of intense seasonal labour or during the sheep shearing or harvest or whenever normal family life was upset by death, confinement or illness, relations and neighbours were always at hand and ready to help.

A well known local character living a hundred years ago at Cefn Coed was "Macws". Her correct name was Margaret Morgan, "Macws" being a corruption of Margaret. She was born in 1815 in "Tynygarn". The present residence of Mr Croad is built on the site of the old house. She vividly recalled oxen working at Penyrheol farm Cwm Tâf where she was employed and she also remembered carrying water for brewing purposes from the Tâf Fawr to the "Fox and Hounds" in Grawen Lane (then known as "Rhywle') with her friend Betsy Tomos Powel.

The splendid picture of "Macws" hanging in the picture gallery at Cyfarthfa Museum, Merthyr was painted by the artist, Henry Dyke Pearce, who was born in 1848 and whose father Thomas James Pearce kept a grocer's shop at 101 High Street. The Cefn people of the 1850s called his shop "Siop y Glasses Mawr" because the windows, compared with other shops were exceedingly large. He eventually sold the shop and bought Cefn brewery which his son, the artist, Henry Dyke Pearce inherited after his death in 1884. Her portrait painting was executed about 1880, when for an hour or so every day she wended her way to "Tan-y-Bryn" to sit for the artist to paint her picture. "Macws" died in April 1896 at the age of 81 years and is buried at Vaynor Church. Mr Henry Dyke Pearce died suddenly in 1895 at the early age of 47 years and was buried in Cefn cemetery.

"Macws" (Margaret Morgan) 1815-1896. An old Cefn Coed character painted by Henry Dyke Pearce (1848-1895) at Tan-y-Bryn, Cefn Coed c.1880.

By courtesy of the Cyfarthfa Museum, Merthyr Tydfil

The social life of country folk was restricted naturally to the small community within which they were involved in a wide range of roles – economic, religious, recreational, administrative, ritual, etc. This highly localised social life was given an intense quality by the repetitive and highly personal nature of their social relationships. Such was the communal life of

Vaynor. No longer are the old countryside communities of Vaynor the intimate little worlds they were. The railway and the motor car have broken down their isolation and residents now look further afield for recreation in Cardiff or even London. Within the tapestry of Welsh life in times past, recreation was an important and indeed essential element; this we now examine in Vaynor.

THE INNS OF VAYNOR

Inns have a fascinating history even as far back as 300 BC. when Pytheas, the Greek explorer reported that the inhabitants of this island made a drink called 'mead' by mixing honey with wheat. The Celts called it 'curmi' from which the modern word 'cwrw' is derived. Literature abounds in references to them. What vivid pictures are conjured up on reading Chaucer's 'Canterbury Tales' or Boswell's 'Life of Doctor Johnson'! Who fails to enjoy Longfellow's 'Tales of a Wayside Inn', and who does not appreciate the accounts of the old Welsh ballad singers, the itinerant harpists and the drovers of bygone days on their way to and from the English fairs and markets? Undoubtedly, old inns and taverns are inextricably interwoven with the life of the community.[2]

Before the fourteenth century, inns were only found in the towns, sometimes, the church built them as guest houses, especially in places visited by pilgrims. Of course, there were many ale-houses along the road but these did not provide sleeping accommodation. It was during Queen Elizabeth's reign that inns grew in importance when wheeled vehicles were introduced. When the stage coach appeared during the late seventeenth and eighteenth centuries, the inns and taverns came into their own with the improvement of roads. In Brecknock this was especially true of the Brecon to Merthyr road, resulting from the offer of the Brecknockshire Agricultural Society to pay half the cost of repairs for certain roads. One finds soon after the formation of toll gates and turnpike houses, that stage coach routes commenced and the wayside inn in the County became an important institution. Between the Morning Sun Inn Cefn Coed and Brecon during the nineteenth century there were fourteen wayside inns and ale-houses namely, the Morning Sun Inn, Crown Inn, Cefn Hotel, Red Lion (Cwm Tâf), Farmers' Arms, Millers' Arms, Tredegar Arms, the

Crown Inn, Horse and Jockey, Half Way Inn (mentioned by G. W. Manby in 1802), Storey Arms and the Old Glanrhyd Inn, the (New) Glanrhyd and the Tair Bull at Libanus.

Storey Arms Inn (demolished 1924).

When the Industrial Revolution made its impact on the country, a decline in the use of many rural inns on the highway occurred while dozens of new taverns were opened in the growing industrial areas. The following were the inns of the Parish of Vaynor in 1873.[3]

INNS AND INNKEEPERS – CEFN COED

"Green Dragon – Elizabeth Bishop; Castle Inn – **Ben Jenkins;** Greyhound – Mary Davies; Morning Sun Inn – Thomas Lewis (great grandfather of the author); Drovers' Arms – William Davies; Cross Keys – Mary Morgan; Rising Sun – John Evans; Royal Oak – Morgan Morgan; Pontycapel – William Evans; Rock and Castle – Thomas Morgan; Brecon and Merthyr Railway Inn – Thomas Hughes; Cefn Hotel – Thomas Jones; Bridgend – Jane Pearce; Station Hotel – James Jones; Railway Inn – Ann Swan; Pontycapel Brewery – Pearce and Shaplin; Globe – Thomas Thomas; White Horse Inn – Thomas Thomas (the other great grandfather of the author); Greyhound's Head – Watkin Vaughan; Corner House – William Williams; Farmers' Arms – William Williams; Crawshays Arms – William Williams; George Inn – Thomas Williams; Gwynne's Arms – John Williams."

The Rising Sun Inn at the Stocks, Cefn Coed demolished 1964.

CWM TÂF AND PONTSTICILL INNS

"Fisherman's Arms – Rees Atkins; Refreshment Rooms – Andrew Baxter; Red Lion – Daniel Harvard; Millers' Arms – Thomas Hughes; Halfway House – Meredith Jenkins; Pentwyn Inn – John Jenkins; Aberglais – William Jones; Church Tavern – John Jones; Butchers' Arms – William Meredith; Crown Inn – Jenkin Meredith; Pontsticill Inn – Thomas Powell; Red Cow – Jennet Thomas; Farmers' Arms – Micah Williams. In addition there were public houses and "cwrw bachs"."

In 1873 there were about thirty six Inns, public houses and "cwrw bachs" in the Parish of Vaynor and two breweries, the Pontycapel brewery and the Cefn Hill brewery situated near to the entrance of Ysgol y Graig School. A noticeable characteristic is that among the names of the taverns and inns were a large number of English ones, probably due to the strong anglicising influences of the Industrial Revolution. A harsh working environment produced equally harsh leisure activities and heavy drinking was, as a result, one of the scourges of this locality in the nineteenth century. "Going on the booze" meant more or less non-stop drinking for a week or even a fortnight. Wife beating was, it is said a popular pastime for some men (two men sold their wives at Merthyr) and one can understand the saying "Mae uffern yn y tafarn" (Hell is in the Tavern). In fairness, one could argue that men escaped to the taverns from squalor and the perpetual crying of children many of whom found no cure even for a minor ailment like toothache. They drank, heavily to the accompaniment of ballad singers, penillion singers and harpists. Competition in singing love-songs committed to memory was a popular pastime in the Crown Inn, Cefn Coed – Morgan Emmanuel and 'Dai Coch' were the local champions and it was said they they sang

The Farmers' Arms, Cwm Tâf, demolished in the making of Llwyn-On reservoir.

against each other for half a day.[4]

Tom Lewis has pointed out at some length that the Inns of long ago formed an integral part of local social life. The Long Room was the venue for secular activities of the local chapels and the venue also for the Church Vestry.[5] The Long Rooms were used for many purposes, at Penderyn, the Petty Sessions were held at the Lamb Inn while at Cefn Coed the inns were used for inquests, public meetings and as a base for the many Friendly Societies. Some of the inns of Vaynor acted as venues for the local intelligentsia where the members ranged from amateur versifiers to bards of some repute.

In Cwm Tâf in the summer, the favourite rendezvous on summer evenings, was Pontyglec (The Bridge of Gossip), for here was purveyed the latest news of the valley, news of courtings and jiltings, of weddings and illnesses, of deaths and removals. The winter venue for discussion and argument was the local Inn, the "Red Lion", where the stranger was cheerfully welcomed and made to feel at home. Tom Lewis informs us that it was here, one evening in the middle of the last century that the Squire of Pontardâf, when in his cups was alleged to have lit his pipe with a five pound note in mistake for a scrap of paper.[6]

The Red Lion Inn, Ynysyfelin, Cwm Tâf (c1912).

The Morning Sun Inn, Cefn Coed, was a typical old fashioned Welsh hostelry. Thomas Lewis, great grandfather of the author had built it in 1861 and from the smithy at the back one heard daily the sound of the hammer on his anvil. His customers included carters, drovers from Cardiganshire, navvies from the reservoirs at Cwm Tâf, miners and ironworkers from Merthyr. The travellers having been attended to, the tables were cleared and the rest of the evening was spent telling tales of "cannwyll y corff", and highwaymen and the like. Jokes were told until tired eyelids drove the convivial gathering to their beds. The inn was the favourite haunt of the local intelligentsia who wished to discuss, in a congenial atmosphere, not only national and international questions, but even high doctrinal points over their gleaming tankards of ale. It was at the Crown

Morning Sun Inn (c1965).

Inn, Merthyr Tydfil on 4th October 1833 that a meeting was held to consider the possibility of obtaining a Borough Charter for Merthyr and "to adopt" measures for erecting a Town Hall, a 'Lock-up' House and such other buildings as were thought necessary".[7] The meetings of the Friendly Societies referred to above were forerunners of our 'Welfare State'. They were necessarily meetings of voluntary groups having common normative values, common interests and loyalties under an appointed leader, who was usually the club secretary.

After paying their weekly dues, or collecting their allowance for sickness or a family death, the rest of the evening was usually spent in conviviality. The Friendly Societies persisted in the same inns for decades as local newspaper reports indicate, for example in August 1834, the Old Star Friendly Society held at the Crown Inn, Merthyr claimed to be the oldest friendly society in Merthyr and offered "a comfortable allowance in sickness or old age – every member at the age of 70 receives a weekly pension of 5s 0d for life".[8] When the May Rose Hill Lodge at the Morning Sun Inn, Cefn Coed closed in 1912, the local newspaper reported that "it has been held for close on fifty years".[9] Another friendly society, the United Briton Friendly Society met at the Bell Inn, Cefn Coed. Letters to this Society were recently found in the attic of the Bell Inn while it was being demolished.

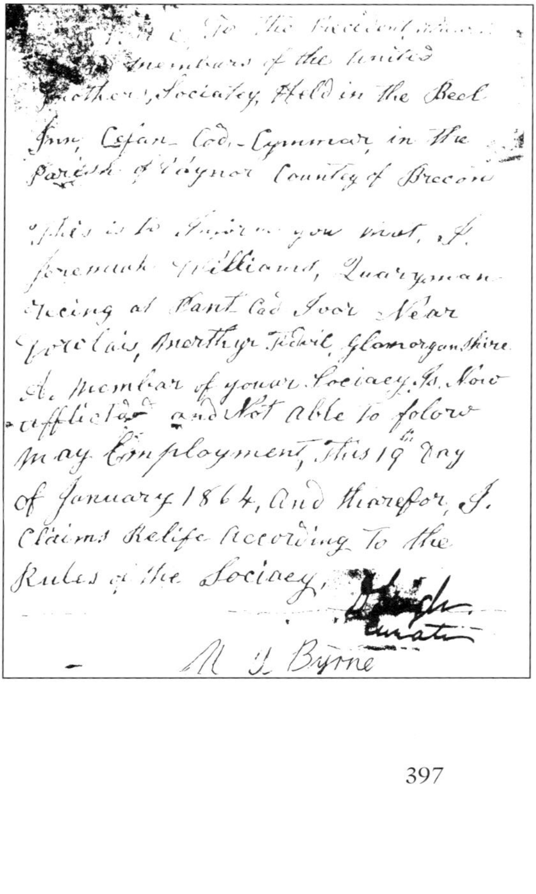
To the President, and members of the United brothers Sociaty, Held in the Bell Inn, Cefan Cod,-Cymmar in the Parish of Vaynor County of Brecon

This is to inform you that, I, Jeremiah Williams, Quaryman recing at Pant Cad Ivor Near Dowlais, merthyr Tydfil Glamorganshire A member of youar Sociacy. Is Now afflicd and Not able to folow may Employment, This 19th Day of January 1864, And tharefor, I, claims Relife According To the Rules of the Sociaey,

D Hughes
M A Byrne

When the Bell Inn Cefn Coed was demolished in the late 1970s the following letters referring to the United Brition Friendly Society were found in the attic:- "To the Precident, and members of the United brothers Sociaty, Held in the Bell In,, Cefan Cod,-Cymmar in the Parish of Vaynor count of Brecon This is to inform you that, I, Jeremiah Williams, Quaryman recing at Pant Cad Ivor Near Dowlais, merthyr Tydfil Glamorganshire. A Member of youar Sociacy. Is Now afflicd and Not able to folow may Employment, This 19th Day of January 1864, And tharefor, I, claims Relife According to the Rules of the Sociaey". This had been signed by D. Hughes and M. A. Byrne.

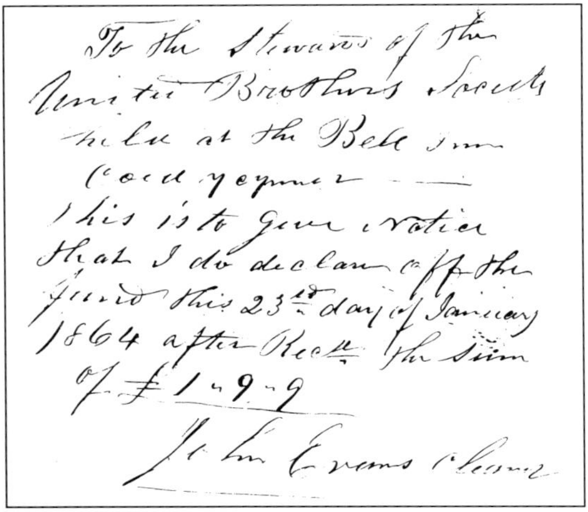
To the Stewards of the
United Brothers Society
held at the Bell Inn
Coed y cymer
This is to give Notice
that I do declam off the
fund this 23rd day of January
1864 after Recd the sum
of £1..9..9
John Evans cleaner

"To the Stewards of the United Brothers Society held ast the Bell Inn Coed y cymer.
This is to give Notice that I do declaim off this fund this 23rd day of January 1864 after Recd the sum of £1..9..9.
John Evans
cleaner".

The Bell Inn, High Street, Cefn Coed, demolished late 1970s.

The inns of Vaynor were the venues for the *Gwylmabsant* festivities and for the Saint's Day activities. These occasions lasted, according to David Davies the Penderyn parish historian, for up to a fortnight of drinking, dancing and feasting "Yn Nhafarndai Penderyn"[10] (In the Penderyn Inns).

He recounts penillion sung to the harp on these occasions and concludes with the verse:

> "O gwmmwd Ystradfellta
> O lanau afon Hepste,
> O Randir Rhigos a Chwmtaf
> Daeth bechgyn braf i fwyta".[11]

Honeymoons were the prerogative of the well-to-do, the poor usually spent the day in a local inn singing and dancing to the melody of the harp. An old toast sung after matrimony was:

> "Dyma iechyd i'r dyn sy'n cusanu ei wraig,
> Ac yn unig ei wraig yn mhobman
> Drwy garu gwraig arall pan ddylai dyn fod
> Yn cusanu ei wraig ei hunan;
> Dyma iechyd i'r dyn sydd yn siglo cryd
> Ei blentyn ei hunan bob amser;
> Pan dybiant y sigland eu plantos eu hun
> Yn siglo plant ereill mae llawer".[12]

Translated it reads as follows:-

> "Here's health to the man who kisses his wife
> And only his wife in every place
> Through loving some other woman,
> When he should be kissing his own wife,
> Here's health to the man who rocks the cradle,
> Of his own child all the time,
> When they think that they rock their own children,
> Many are rocking other children".

Funeral services over the rest of the day was invariably spent at the nearest inn celebrating the 'funeral feast' and it was a good excuse to be away from the mines and ironworks for one day at least. "Years ago, when the hunting horn resounded much oftener in the neighbouring hills", states a newspaper report of March 1913, "A favourite hostelry with the huntsmen after 'the hill' was Tafarn Ynysfelin, Cwm Tâf. Here also the "Hunter's Club" was held of which nearly all the gentry around were members. At the annual supper, there was much talking, eating and drinking. Farm labourers and other workmen were not privileged to enter the room, plenty of ale and rations were supplied to them downstairs. This liberal treatment focussed the attention of Cefnites".[13] From what has been written, it would seem that much of the vivid and rich cultural life of Vaynor in the nineteenth century was centred on the pubs.

Iolo Morgannwg had been one of the pioneers of the eisteddfod and dominated the one held at the Hen Dŷ Cwrdd in 1816. It was later in 1820 that an eisteddfod was first recorded at Merthyr but it really became important from St David's Day 1821 when the Cymreigyddion society was formed at the Patriot Inn, Merthyr. Branches were soon flourishing in other pubs and they were followed by the Cymmrodorion in 1827, Gomerians in 1828 and Brythoniaid in 1834. Essentially literary in both languages, these active societies tended to hold three eisteddfodau a year and created a lively coterie of local poets and essayists in Merthyr and district.

The Patriot Inn, Ynysgau, Merthyr c1830 where the Cymreigyddion Society was formed in 1821 and where three eisteddfodau were held annually at this time.

THE CHAPELS AND CHURCHES

For more than a century the chapels and churches have been the major centres for all kinds of pre-arranged recreation. In its early enthusiasm, Nonconformity stamped out the gwylmabsant, in this locality as David Davies states, "Tynwyd dyddiau 'Y Mabsantau' i ben tua'r flwyddyn 1866"[14] (The days of the Gwylmabsant came to an end around 1866), and Nonconformity also discouraged all kinds of secular entertainment, substituting the prayer meeting for the noson lawen (merry evening) in the home and the preaching festival for the pleasure-fair as an occasion to draw the crowds. From the beginning the chapel was not only 'the House of God', it was what the Unitarians called their chapel in the early days, the 'Tŷ Cwrdd', the meeting house of a society. As this society grew out of its extreme puritanism, it took over many of the less reprehensible elements in the old amusements as well as education, and rendered them compatible with its own standards.

Many of the activities of the chapels, which will be referred to later, were considered too secular for the Church at Vaynor and at Cefn, but by being brought in they were, as it were, sanctified. A regenerated version of the spirit of gwylmabsant survived in the Sunday School tea parties held at Vaynor, when the tea party at the pavilion was followed by open-air sports

Pontsarn station with the pavilion shown in the background (c1910).

and competitions. Drama, originally condemned locally by the chapels, eventually became accepted by all the chapels as part of their recreational and religious life. The very many activities of the Vaynor Chapels in the nineteenth century are referred to in the chapter on the History of Religion in Vaynor.

The records of the Hen Dŷ Cwrdd refer to an eisteddfod as early as 1816 attended by Iolo Morgannwg, and a "string band" in 1810 trained by one, "Billy Berthlwyd". The chapel bought "Howel Powel, a weaver a fife for 7s 6d" and in 1851 a "Viloin (Violin)" for William Jones. While "Tomos o'r Sychpant" Cwm Tâf played the "clarionet". They had a Sunday School in 1838 but the records refer to Catherine Rees attending a Sunday School in 1775, a choir in 1843, "Y Teparti Mawr" reputed to have been attended by over a thousand people in 1861, and followed by a concert. Then we read of a Sunday School picnic in 1870; buying a harmonium in 1867 and learning tonic sol-ffa in 1872; the first drama production in 1883; and Pegi Sion Rees' "cottage teas" to help the poor in the 1880s.[15] Then a great attraction came in the 1890s, when the Chapel used the truly "Magic Lantern" for the first time. By the 1890s the Eisteddfod at Christmas was a thriving and very popular event. At the turn of the century came a 'Mutual Improvement Society' and a new "String Band" which played every Sunday night under the conductorship of Mr J. R. Evans, a Merthyr Schoolmaster. This was no small orchestra.

In Tom Lewis' family, eight children played musical instruments and his brother John Lewis who was later killed underground in a local drift mine, was accepted to sing in the Carl Rosa Opera Company. A memorial poem by 'Merthyrfab' to the late John Lewis was distributed to his family and friends.

Excerpts from the records of Carmel Baptist Chapel, Cefn Coed afford fascinating accounts of some of the recreational activities of the Chapel over the last century:-[16]

> "1882. Mr Salathiel (the minister), oddiwrth y tea party £18.13s.5½d (£18.67) (From Mr Salathiel £18.13s.5½d from the tea party).
> 1888. Am ystol at yr Harmonium 2s 6d (£0.12) (For stool for the harmonium 2s 6d).
> Am yr harmonium £9.0s.0d (£9.00) (For a bread knife 12s 6d) (£0.63).

1889. Am gylleth fara 12s 6d (£0.63) (For a bread knife 12s 6d).
1889. I Mr a Mrs Jones, Y Pandy. Llogar £100 - £4.0s.0d (Interest on £100 to Mr and Mrs Jones, Pandy £4.0s.0d)
Elw oddiwrth y Tea Party £12.6s.7d (£12.33) (Profit from the tea party, £12.6s.7d).
1906. Elw y magic lantern, 16s 6d (£0.83) (Profit from the magic lantern 16s 6d).
Derbynwyd yr Eisteddfod Nadolig £1.0s.0d (Received from the Christmas Eisteddfod Church Tafarn £1.0s.0d).
1907. July Tea party y plant, Church Tafarn 7s 6d (Children's Tea Party at the Church Tafarn 7s 6d) (£0.37)".

By 1908 the Sunday School Trip was to Aberavon and by 1920 it was to Barry which we see from the following entry:-

"1920. Tea yn Barry Island. Talwyd i Newton Bros am fwyd. £31.17s.6d (£31.88) (Tea in Barry Island. Paid Newton Bros for food £31.17s.6d).
Talwyd Taff Vale Railway am train £42.2s.5d (Paid Taff Vale Railway £42.2s.5d for the train) (£42.12)".

In 1922 the Sunday School went to the Tredegar Arms, Cwm Tâf and the charges were as follows:-

"Tea yn Tredegar Arms

Car 62 adults @ 1s 4d per head	£4	6s	8d	(£4.33)
Car 92 children @ 9d per head	3	9s	0d	(£3.45)
Milk and room	1	16s	0d	(£1.80)
Nwyfa extra (Extras gas)		1s	0d	(£0.05)
Ffwrnio (Baking)		4s	0d	(£0.20)
B. D. Owen, Grocer	4	16s	4d	(£4.82)
	£15	2s	2d	(£15.11)

In 1929 Carmel was off by charabanc to the seaside but by 1943, during the War years they had returned to Vaynor as the following entries show:-

"Talwyd am pavilion Pontsarn £1.15s.0d (££1.75) (Paid for Pontsarn pavilion £1.15s.0d).

> Am train i'r plant 7s 3d (£0.37) (Train for the children 7s 3d).
> Am fwyd i Mr James £2.19s.4½d (£2.95) (For food from Mr James £2.19.4½)".

The membership of Carmel Baptist Chapel fell dramatically after World War II and there are no further references in the Chapel records to any annual outings. There are however numerous references in the Cefn Coed Schools' log books referring to low attendance or school closures due to Chapel or Church functions in the locality,[17] for example:-

> "1863. November. School thin owing to tea drinking at the Baptist Chapel.
> 1864. March. School thin owing to a concert at Ebenezer Chapel.
> 1888. August. Members away owing to tea parties at Carmel and Field Street Chapels.
> 1899. Attendance low. Rehearsal of operetta by the children of Ebenezer Church to be given at Drill Hall.
> 1900. May. Attendance low. Wesleyan tea party at Pontsarn.
> 1903. May 14th. Attendance too low to open. Singing Festival of Welsh Calvinistic Methodists and anniversary services at Carmel chapel".

The observation made by the Headmaster in 1881 regarding "weekly" tea parties seems to be borne out by the evidence available. Another quite amazing fact is that "the Welsh Calvinistic Methodists' Singing Festival and the Anniversary Services at Carmel" should have proved so popular as to close the school. I wondered whether tea drinking was perhaps a luxury in the mid-nineteenth century Vaynor but this is not so. Research has shown that Ann Thomas of Dreinos, Vaynor who died in October 1782, has a memorial stone in the Hen Dŷ Cwrdd churchyard with two upturned cups without handles and a sugar basin carved thereon, was the first person to drink tea in the parish. One sees therefore that tea drinking had been practised in Vaynor for a century or more and possibly it became much more common lower down the social scale in the nineteenth century.

The local press has weekly accounts of various Chapel and Church activities back to the last century. It is commonplace to, find entries referring to harvest Festivals, Christmas Concerts, Lectures and Eisteddfodau. One sees for example, "November 15th 1913 Vaynor Church Guild". The first concert in connection with the above guild took place at the School recently" and for the same month. "November 29th 1913 Hen Dŷ Cwrdd. The Winter's work of the Mutual Improvement Society in connection with this church was commenced on Tuesday evening when a good number of the members sat down in the school room to an enjoyable tea".[18]

Some Recreational activities in Vaynor associated with the places of worship

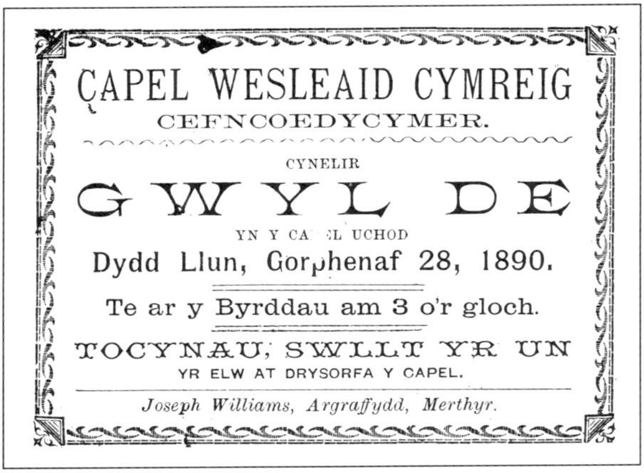

CAPEL WESLEAID CYMREIG

CEFNCOEDYCYMER.

CYNELIR

GWYL DE

YN Y CAPEL UCHOD

Dydd Llun, Gorphenaf 28, 1890.

Te ar y Byrddau am 3 o'r gloch.

TOCYNAU, SWLLT YR UN

YR ELW AT DRYSORFA Y CAPEL.

Joseph Williams, Argraffydd, Merthyr.

A tea party at the Welsh Wesleyan Chapel, Cefn Coed 1890.

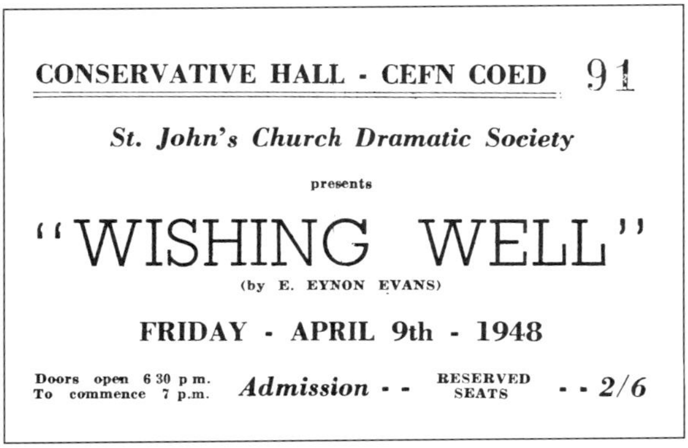

CONSERVATIVE HALL - CEFN COED 91

St. John's Church Dramatic Society

presents

"WISHING WELL"

(by E. EYNON EVANS)

FRIDAY - APRIL 9th - 1948

Doors open 6 30 p m.
To commence 7 p.m.

Admission **- - RESERVED SEATS - -** ***2/6***

The "Wishing Well" performed by St John's Dramatic Society April 9th 1948.

HEN DY CWRDD

CEFN COED.

PROGRAMME

OF THE

Mutual Improvement Society

FOR THE SESSION 1909-10.

President - - Mr. CLEDWYN DAVIES.
Vice-President - - - Mr. DAVID JONES.
Treasurer - - - Miss LIZZIE JENKINS.
Secretary - - Miss BESSIE WILLIAMS.

The Meetings of the Society will be held in the Schoolroom, on Tuesday Evenings, at 8 *o'clock.*

7594 109 *Joseph Williams & Sons, "Tyst," Merthyr.*

A programme for the Hen Dy Cwrdd Mutual Improvement Society 1909-10

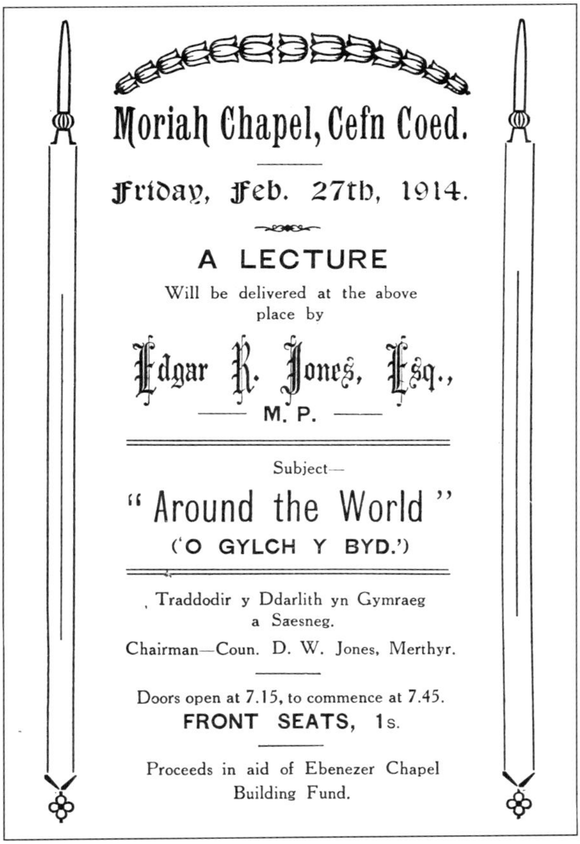

Moriah Chapel, Cefn Coed.

Friday, Feb. 27th, 1914.

A LECTURE

Will be delivered at the above place by

Edgar R. Jones, Esq., M. P.

Subject—

"Around the World"

('O GYLCH Y BYD.')

Traddodir y Ddarlith yn Gymraeg a Saesneg.

Chairman—Coun. D. W. Jones, Merthyr.

Doors open at 7.15, to commence at 7.45.

FRONT SEATS, 1s.

Proceeds in aid of Ebenezer Chapel Building Fund.

A lecture given by Mr Edgar R. Jones MP for Merthyr Tydfil, February 27th 1914.

Each denomination also had an annual Cymanfa Ganu (singing Festival) which united groups of Chapels in Cefn, Merthyr and Dowlais. Every little congregation practised the hymns and anthems contained in the Cymanfa programmes for some months before the event. The festival lasted for one day, food was available and it provided the opportunity for social intercourse between friends and relatives. The Unitarian congregation has for many years travelled to Aberdare, Trebanos, Lampeter, Llandysul, Cardiff, and Swansea to attend Singing Festivals. The extraordinary democratic energy of the chapels with their lively strong Sunday schools, their stringbands, choirs, concerts, outings, tea parties and

MR RICHARD WATKINS' MIXED CHOIR c1940

Back row: *Mr Tom Oates, Mr Trefor Jones, Mr J. Rees, Mr J. Morris, Mr David E. Jones, Mr Bill Wathan.*

Front row men: *Mr Bill Richards, Mr Tal Morgan, Mr L. Hamer, Mr I. Peters, A. N. Other, A. N. Other, Mr J. Williams, Mr Ivor Davies.*

Back row ladies: *Mrs K. J. Evans, Mrs Lewis, Mrs Fron Davies, Mrs May Morgan, Winnie Lewis, Mrs Price, Mrs E. Watkins, Mrs L. A. Thomas, Mrs S. Richards, Mrs Williams, Mrs N. Davies, Mrs E. Neale, Mrs E. James, Mrs T. Arthur, Mrs Oats.*

Middle row ladies (seated): *A. N. Other, Mrs Francis, Miss England, Mr Richard Watkins (Conductor), Mrs Watkins, Mrs Richards, Miss C. Chambers.*

Front row ladies: *Miss Doris Simons, Minnie Stroud, A. N. Other, Mrs J. Morris, Mrs J. Williams, Mrs I. Peters, Mrs Annie Nongrove, Mrs Borthwick.*

CEFN COED MALE VOICE CHOIR (1946)
Back row from the left: *J. Williams, J. Thomas, Emrys Jones, Jenkyn Rees, D. H. Jones, M. Glover, Tom Oats, A. N. Other, W. Wathan, Morgan Thomas, I. Clements, Trefor Jones, Ben Davies, Bill Richards.*
Second row: *J. Powell, A. Loring. A. N. Other, Tom Jones, Bill Mason, Bill Rees, J. Powel, D. Hopkins, C. Dunley, V. Chappell, J. Morley, D. W. Beynon, Emlyn James.*
Front row: *Morgan Williams, Tal Morgan, Tom evans, Cromwell Evans, L. Hamer, George Batten, Ivor Davies, W. Ellis (Conductor), Gwyn Williams (Accompanist), G. Williams, John Beynon, George Jones, R. Watkins, Mr Wathan.*

eisteddfodau have waned and the intense religious passions of former years has cooled into dull indifferences. Local choirs have been of great importance in the musical life of the parish of Vaynor and some singers have become nationally acclaimed.

Among the most popular and gifted singers of Wales until her untimely death in 1987 was Miss Beti Jones, a local business woman and resident of South Terrace, Cefn Coed. She overcame a severe attack of polio in her childhood to train eventually under the nationally known opera teacher, Joan Cross in London. Her beautiful soprano voice enabled her to sing very frequently in public, on the Radio and Television with some of the greatest names in opera such as Sir Geraint Evans and Mr Stuart Burrows and with the Dowlais, Pendyrus, Treharris, Penydarren and Cefn Coed Choirs. Beti was endowed not only with a superb voice, she had a compassionate personality which found expression in singing and supporting all charitable and worthwhile causes. Her last public appearance was at such a concert organised by the author at St John's Church, Cefn Coed on December 20th 1987.

The late Miss Beti Jones of Cefn Coed.

Donor Miss Anita Jones

Mr W. S. Parry, Fellow of Trinity College of Music served as an officer in the First Great War, was wounded and after the war married Margaret Lloyd daughter of James Lloyd, grocer at High Street, Cefn Coed, and for over thirty years was the Cefn Coed Postmaster. During this time he became a celebrated composer, conductor, organist, Eisteddfodwr and producer.

COR MEIBION CEFN COED 1976
(CEFN COED MALE VOICE CHOIR 1976)

Back row: *Bryn Williams, Alex Herron, Bill Williams, Selwyn Morgan, Ray Chappel.*
Fourth row: *John Thomas, Ted Murphy, J. Gighee, Gilbert Parry, John Dunne, Tom Morgan, Tom Evans.*
Third row: *David Owen, Norman Evans, John Evans, Harry Davies, Islwyn Williams, Jack Davies, Emrys Jones, Russell Phillips.*
Second row: *Charles Roynan, Dennis Williams, Bert Lewis, Graham Jones, Bertie Evans, Stan Evans, Trevor Jenkins, A. Davies, Bernard Harris, Bill Issitt, David Evans.*
Front row: *Bill Owen, Morgan Williams, Derek Marshall, Tudor Price, Dan Connors, N. Williams, Emlyn James, Vince Harris, Bill Jones, Ivor Davies, Bill Evans.*
Seated: *Bryn Willimas (Secretary), Don Aldridge (Treasurer), Mrs Joan Watkeys (Accompanist), Morgan Williams JP (Conductor), John Morris (Assistant Conductor).*

THE JEDBURGH PIPE AND DRUM BAND MARCHING THROUGH CEFN COED 1988

the villagers of Cefn Coed celebrated the Scotland versus Wales rugby International 1976 in style, by importing their own pipe and drum band from north of the border. The 46 bandsmen and supporters from Jedburgh, Roxburghshire in Scotland were invited down as guests of the Cefn Coed Male Voice Choir. The trip was organised by Mr Brynmor Williams, the choir's Secretary who liaised with Mr George Millar, Secretary of the British Legion Jedburgh Branch and also a Scottish Rugby Selector. Upon their arrival the band took up residence at the Plas-newydd Hotel Cefn Coed and their first official engagement was with the Cefn Coed Male Voice Choir in a concert at the Cefn Coed Community Centre on the 5th February 1976. This visit initiated a tradition of coming to Cefn Coed every two years on the occasion of the Scotland versus Wales International Rugby match. The Cefn Coed reciprocate by visiting Jedburgh when Wales are playing in Scotland.

THE FAIRS, FETE AND GALAS AND CARNIVALS

A number of Breconshire fairs were established by the Normans[19]. Usually, the right to hold a fair and a market was conferred by the King or the lord of the manor by grant of a special charter. Some of the fairs were given special names and at Brecon the November Fair, once held on St. Leonard's Day, 6th November was called the "Grand Mart of South Wales".[20] Although most of the fairs were established for a special purpose, such as the sale of sheep, cattle or ponies, other commodities were also sold such as boots, clogs, clothes, china, food, tea, fruit and confectionery. Some of the visitors however were too poor to buy and could only sigh and say:

> "Diflas dowlod heb ddim gwair,
> A diflas ffair heb arian."
>
> (Cheerless the loft without hay
> And cheerless the fair without money).[21]

It was the custom at some fairs to hire servants for the farms, and Old Saints' Day marked the end of one period for which farm workers, men and women, agreed to serve. Those seeking employment stood in a row on the pavement while prospective employers and their wives scanned the row and spoke to the workers prior to choosing a suitable maid or man servant. The fairs also provided the opportunity for a day of recreation, when farmers met and talked and when young men looked for brides, drank, fought and wrestled. A popular figure at the fairs was the ballad singer, much of whose time was spent wandering from fair to fair, singing ballads, relating to the latest events, or recording amusing doggerel rhymes on various themes. In some cases there was a close connection between the fairs and the Saints' days. Such was the May Fair at Brecon, attended by decades of Vaynor farm servants and farmers and held during the Festival of the Church of St John the Evangelist without the Lateran Gate on 6th May. These fairs were often in early days held on Church ground, and it was not uncommon for a tombstone to be used as a stall.

Fair night was usually an unruly affair and many people, therefore, came to be opposed to the revelry of the fair, especially during the period of the Methodist Revival. The early agricultural revolution and especially the industrial revolution brought the Welsh fairs of the southern parts of the county such as Cefn Coed Fair into some prominence, but gradually the mart and the market came to take the place of the informal bargaining of

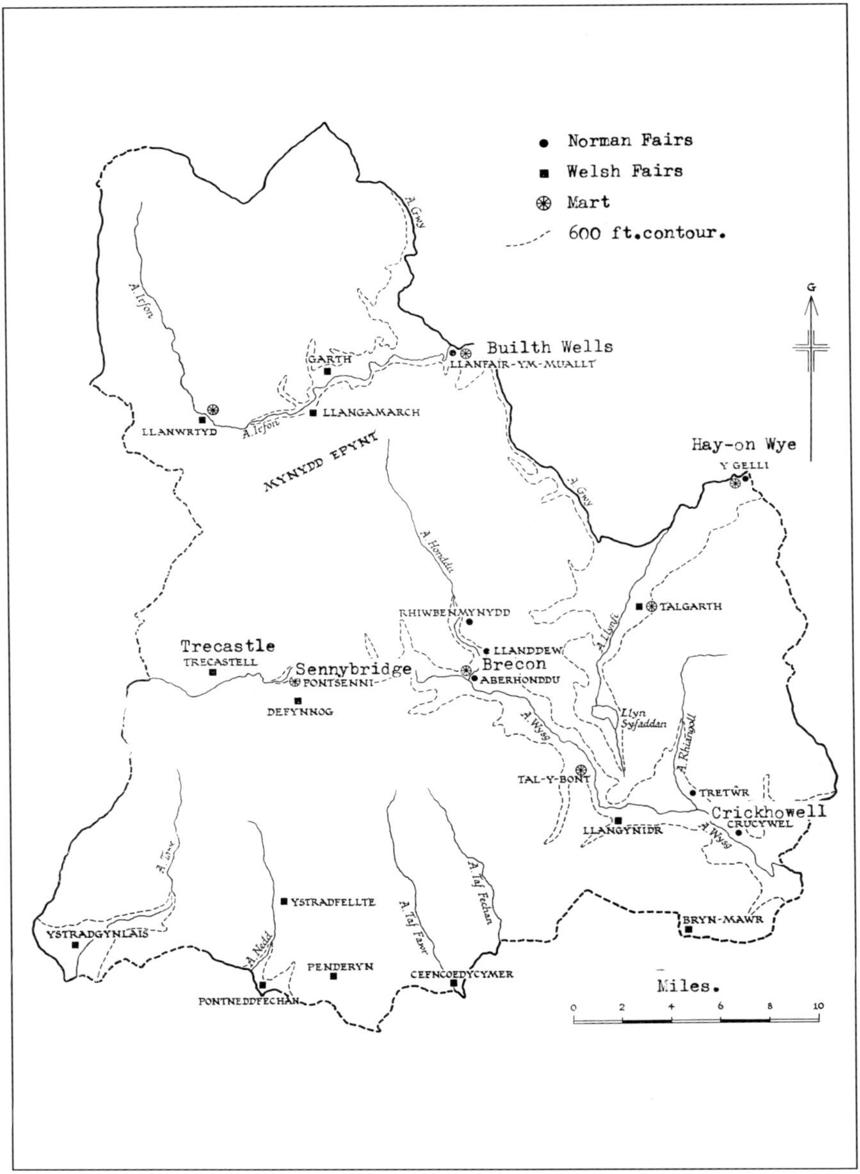

Breconshire fairs.

the old fairs, and today people travel by bus or car to the nearest town where they can have all their needs supplied. T. E. Clarke writing about 1848 stated "The fairs in Merthyr are held on March 18th, July 18th, November 18th and on September 2nd and 24th, second Monday after October 10th, and November 17th, upon a mountain called "the Waun", between two and three miles above the town, where is a large public house and some cottages".[22] During the nineteenth century, there were fairs locally at Merthyr, Dowlais, Nelson, Troedyrhiw, Cefn Coed and Aberdare.

A report in the local press for September 22th 1847 states, "The Waun was poorly attended. There were few buyers. Among the sellers were several Irishmen who had brought stock across the sea to sell among the mountains".[23] This would seem to be a report on the September 2nd Fair referred to above. There are reports too, of a "Merthyr Fair", which was apparently a quite separate fair as one sees from the following newspaper report. "Merthyr Fair: November 22nd 1834. The business of this fair on Tuesday last, though rather more extensive than for many recent years, was on a small scale ... It is an unaccountable thing, that the farmers and dealers, unless perchance they feel a peculiar attraction to the third heaven, should ascend many times in the year into the clouds at Waun to do their dealings, when there is so much better accommodation for man and horse, as well as demand and market on the surface of the valley".[24] The author also claimed that the cattle lost weight by climbing the hill to the Waun Fair!

Quite apart from the fun and enjoyment of the hiring fairs at Brecon it would appear from the following account of an October fair in 1847, that the ordinary weekly fairs were occasions for pleasure, especially for the younger generation of country folk. The newspaper report reads as follows: "October 2nd 1847. The Fair on Friday was rather gay, and spirited. Quadrupeds exchanged hands with greater alacrity than at the previous fair, and not a few became acquainted with new owners. The day was fine and the attendance of rustics, particularly of the younger generation numerous. Such gatherings, the free treating with cakes, and all gurgling and gingerbread nuts – the hearty dance and the rapid song, with the furious drive through the town and the pleasant parties made upon the way home, form striking contrasts with the busy and steady plodding of a populous commercial community".[25]

There were railway excursions too, for the fairs at Brecon; about 800 passengers travelled from the Merthyr District on 6th July 1863. Also

The Pen-Twyn Inn, Dôlygaer c1936.

deserving of notice are the excursions arranged at reduced prices from this area for the Brecknockshire Agricultural Show and the Brecon Races in September 1863. Thousands from Merthyr and Cefn Coed attended the regattas at Dôlygaer and enjoyed the teas provided at the Pentwyn Inn.

Cefn, at the turn of the century was regarded as a "rough place". It bore this unenviable reputation not because it was the haunt of criminals but rather because of the addiction of some of its inhabitants to excessive drinking. The "low characters", as the religious minded called them were not congenitally evil; when sober, they were docile enough; but on Cefn Coed Fair night they were seen at their wildest and heard at their rowdiest. The Cefn Fair was established around 1800 and in its heyday stretched from Cefn Bridge to the Station Square. It was held originally every Easter Monday and it was noted throughout the Merthyr District for its frequent fights and drunken brawls. The deeply religious only peeped at it from a safe distance while the nervous gave it a wide berth.

Tom Lewis gives a vivid account of the fair as he recalled it in his youth. He states: "To the children it was a place of enchantment and pure delight. Small boys, clutching a red and white pop gun ... little girls nursing rosy-cheeked dolls ... To the farm labourers of the parish the fair was a

Cefn Fair c1890. This fair began in the early 19th century and discontinued around 1916. The dancing bear was a feature of the fairs in Southern England and Wales.

sort of Mecca, their faces coloured like parchment, and their hair stiff and wiry from exposure to wind and rain, they sauntered from stall to stall, their hands deep in their pockets except at close of the day, when they reluctantly parted with a few coppers to purchase a few brandy snaps as a fairing for "mishtras". Courting couples, whose trysting places were usually in a remote lane, walked about unabashed ... even the sedate and fastidious threw off their reserve at the fair and were not ashamed to be seen gobbling up chip potatoes from vinegar soaked pieces of newspaper ... The cheap rings, bangles, the pins and other tawdry trinkets found ready sale ... the women were drawn to the crockery stalls where, among dust-covered ornaments, china dogs, chiffoniers and multi-coloured dishes were displayed in bewildering array ... close on midnight the fair sprung to life. It was then the beer houses disgorged their motley customers ..." The sequel to the fair was a long list of locals who had to appear before the chairmen of the Bench, Mr North. Apparently, the usual defence was invariably couched in the same terms – the collier was suffering from a blow on the head, the brain of the puddler was affected by the intense heat of Cyfarthfa, while the quarryman had never been the same since he had had sunstroke while working at Vaynor Quarry![26]

An account of Cefn Fair in the local press for April 14th 1855 provides illuminating insights into the recreational life of this district at that time. The preparations, the expectations, the "spring cleaning" of houses, the stock-laden taverns, the sheer joy of one day set apart from toil for "unrestrained festivity" bursts forth in this lovely description of Cefn Fair which reads as follows:

> "The little village of Cefn Coed Y Cymmer is classic ground and the hill of Cilsanws, named after one of the daughters of Brychan Brycheiniog was the mount Olympus of the locality in former times. The place was famous for gambling, racing and cockfighting ... neither the satire of Gwilym Morgan nor the preaching of the gospel nor the "spirit of the times" have succeeded altogether in banishing such sports from the locality ... the lustre of the past is reflected in the annual recurrences of Cefn Fair. A country fair is one of the brightest annual events in rustic life, it is anticipated as some great jubilee, a day set apart for unrestrained festivity; a day of total cessation from labour when humble men, at least for a brief period, be their own masters – gay in spirit, light in heart and happy as kings. Such an era is Cefn Fair to the younger portion of the men and women of this locality; it illumines the future and irradiates the past; it forms the theme of conversation before it comes, and of many an allusion after.
>
> Young men bestow especial care upon their dress ... and the gayer portion of Eve's four daughters evidently meditate conquest of no ordinary character, as many showed in the studied neatness of their attire, the jauntiness of their walk and the radiant expectation in every

> word and act ... the houses, particularly at Cefn, put off the sombre garb of Winter, renovate themselves – exterior and interior and assume a clean, prim and fresh appearance, becoming so important an occasion. The taverns lay in a stock of Barclay and Perkins and their external symbols receive fresh coats of varnish. On the fair day the streets are lined with stalls laden with all kinds of articles, from penny whistles to German flutes, from brandy snaps to bottled porter. "Cheap Jack" also claims purchases from the contents of his caravan, and a show or two furnish a novelty to gaping crowds. Between the stalls flows a tide of population, hundreds if not thousands share in the gaiety of the scene. Music, dancing and the Sir John Barleycorn attracts others to the public houses and the early part of the day gives place to one of a grosser and less defensible character."[27]

Such are the usual features of "Ffair Y Cefn".

Following the Methodist Revival, and also in genuine protest against the drunkenness of the local fair, Cefn Christians apparently launched a strong counter-offensive against the Fair on April 22nd 1843 by organising other activities both inside and outside the Parish as the local press reported: "Friends of Christianity in the village exerted themselves to preserve those under their care from the baneful influences of the Fair. The Church people had a school in the morning, a service at Vaynor Church in the afternoon, and a meeting at the Chapel of Ease at Cefn in the evening. The Baptists in a body went to a tea-party at Dowlais. The Wesleyans, Independents and Calvinistic Methodists assembled in the latter denominational Chapel at Coed-y-Cymmer in the morning, at Cae Pantywyll in the afternoon and at the Independent Chapel at the Cefn in the evening where addresses on the utility of Sunday School, temperance principles and deformity of drunkenness were given ... Notwithstanding the fair was attended by thousands from Merthyr and the surrounding districts".[28]

The Cefn Coed Chapel and Church goers fought a losing battle against the attractions of the fair. Throughout the nineteenth century it continued to flourish until April 13th 1912 when one reads the following report: "No fair for probably the first time since its inception about a century ago, the annual fair was not held on Easter Monday. Its discontinuance was a source of much disappointment to children and to those adults from the neighbouring valleys who had made it a practice of visiting every Easter Monday their native village".[29] This last statement is of singular interest, one sees the fair not only as a place of recreation and pleasure but also as an opportunity of meeting one's family and friends and of renewing old emotional ties with one's homeland. There are no further references to this fair except two entries in the Log Books of the Cefn Schools where one reads, "1914 March 9th. Today a new Stock Fair was held for the first time in Cefn. This interfered with our attendance" and later, "August 31st 1914. Low attendance – Cefn Fair".[30] The Cefn Fair might well have struggled on to 1916, for the following statement may be seen among the notable dates in the history of the Parish of Vaynor: "Annual Cefn Pleasure Fair, originated in 1800, discontinued 1916".[31]

A special feature of the Merthyr General Hospital was the Annual Fete and Gala held every Whitsun at Cyfarthfa Park from the 1920s and organised by the Hospital Committee. In 1950 it was taken over by the Merthyr Borough Council. The picture on the next page shows the late Mr Bert Minard of Abercanaid who won first prize at the Merthyr Tydfil Carnival in 1925.

The Little Collier (Mr Bert Minard), First Prize Merthyr Tydfil Carnival 1925.

LIBRARIES

A traveller passing through Cefn Coed on a Sunday morning about the year 1840 at about eleven o'clock in the morning might have observed a group of working men, mostly miners and iron workers, congregated around David Edwards (Dafydd Nedws) who was reading aloud the *News Of The World* word by word, line by line. Edwards translated the news into Welsh, much to the great delight and interest of his untutored listeners. One wonders what facilities existed then for scholars such as the Merthyr historian Thomas Stephens or David Edwards to obtain books locally? The claim has been made that "when the City of Birmingham opened the first Free Library in the British Isles in the forties of the last century, the innovation drew attention in educational circles. The fact is, however, that Rose Mary Crawshay had established Free Libraries in Merthyr and in seven villages round about, eight years previously. She ran them at her own expense".

In addition to books, she provided fires, lamps, draught boards, and many other games. She also paid the salaries of the part-time librarians. One of the libraries was established at 142a High Street, Cefn Coed. One of the first librarians was "Henry Tomos, Llwyn Drain, Pont-Y-Capel Road, an exceptionally intelligent collier who was prominent in the famous Chartist Movement of 1839.[32] Mrs Crawshay was obviously anxious for the physical fitness of the members, for among the books which she provided were *Dr Inman's Treatise on the Preservation of Health; The Restoration of Health* and a volume on *Neuralgia*".[33]

If the claim above regarding local libraries is correct, then one might expect to find libraries in this area about 1833 to 1835. The earliest reference found in the local press is on November 2nd 1833 where one reads: "Those Ladies and Gentlemen who still hold several volumes of work belonging to the Circulating Library lately carried on by John Howell (Printer) are earnestly requested to leave the same with his successors as early as possible".[34] In the same month one reads of a "Reading Room ", which could have been one of Rose Mary Crawshay's, Libraries; it states, "November 9th 1833, Inflammatory Newspapers. At the Reading Room in Merthyr Tydfil, one of the subscribers on entering the room on last Saturday night found several papers and the cloth which covers the table beautifully blazing towards the ceiling in humble imitation of the iron forges. The gentlemen promptly exerted himself and extinguished the flames. – No doubt it was a Whig newspaper that nearly set the house on fire".[35] In September 1834 the Commissioners of the Public Records presented Merthyr Town with fifty two books of law.

Margaret Taylor, writing of Thomas Stephens, formerly of Pontneathvaughan and then a chemist at Merthyr, author of the *Literature of the Kymry,* states that "One of his earliest and dearest projects was the formation of a library".[36] She adds that Stephens and a few others started a discussion class or conversational club "in the winter of 1846". Wilkins describes the beginning, thus "The first selection of books was Knight's Shilling Library, which I, the first librarian, carried in a box once devoted to Warren's blacking. Our next step was to the Temperance Hotel in the Glebeland, where by dint of subscriptions, about fifty volumes were put on the shelves".[37] Cefn and Vaynor residents could have availed themselves of these books or they could have attended the lectures given there as a regular feature of the institution. Stephens was a regular speaker and in 1850 spoke on "migration of the Kymry form the eastern cradle of the human race to their final settlement in the British Isles". Thomas Stephens was honorary secretary from 1846 until the end of his life. By 1861, when the library moved to Thomastown, they had nearly three thousand books and "the attendance at readings on Thursday was so numerous that the members and friends were compelled to adjourn from the Library to St David's Infants' Schoolroom. The exertions of Mr Stephens with selections of music and literature were applauded".[38]

While there was a library at Dowlais from 1845 and at Treharris from about 1860 there is no further information regarding a library in Cefn Coed until one reads in February 1872, "School removed to Heol Cae Library in consequence of the enlargement of the present school" and later in May 1872 "Heol Cae Library was vacated and the enlarged school rooms re-entered".[39] At this time, the Boys' School had about 150 pupils and the Girls' School a similar number and this suggests that the Heol Cae Library was quite a sizeable building to accommodate this number of pupils. It would appear then that Cefn residents would have had access to libraries at Cefn Coed or Merthyr from about 1833 to 1835.

There is no further information regarding library facilities in Vaynor until 1884, when the first Minute Book of the Cefn Reading Room and Library states "At a meeting convened by circular and held in the Board Room of the School, Cefn on Thursday October 2nd 1884, it was resolved that a Reading Room and Library be established at Cefn".[40] Later in October one reads: "It was decided that Mr Lloyd's house be taken for the purpose of a Reading Room and Library at an annual rent of £12 exclusive of rates. That a parish Meeting be called to enable the Committee to obtain the sum of £8 now lying with Brecon Old Bank and having been placed there for the purpose of being utilised in the event of a Library being established. That the Reading Room and Library be supported by donations and Subscriptions. That the minimum subscription be 5s 0d per annum to be paid in advance. Subscribers to be entitled to the use of the library. That a working Secretary be appointed. That a Housekeeper be engaged on the most advantageous terms to reside on the premises to look after the institution generally. To supply refreshments if necessary upon terms to be agreed".

Things were evidently moving very quickly because on November 21st 1884 it was decided to hold a public meeting to promote the interests of the institution. It was decided that ladies be allowed to become members and various people announced their intention to send the following newspapers and periodicals to the Reading Room: *The Iron Trade Review, The Ironmonger, Merthyr Express, South Wales Daily News, Chambers Journal, Western Mail, Punch, Truth, Illustrated London News, Y LLan, Engineer, Standard, Amseroedd, South Wales Daily News, Christian Herald, Seren, Baner Fach* and the *Christian Herald*. On November 28th 1884 the Committee recommended that a Mr Lewis Jones, 210 High Street, Cefn Coed be appointed caretaker of the premises and that the house be subdivided into a general reading room, a smokeroom, a library, a committee room and living accommodation for the use of the caretaker.

The Library was duly opened on December 12th 1884 and by April 14th 1885 the Secretary reported a membership of 81, i.e. 17 paying annually and 5 half yearly while 59 paid quarterly. At the same meeting, it was agreed that the playing of chess and draughts be allowed in the Reading Room provided that there was no gambling. The local gentry supported the Library and one notes for January 1885, donations from Mr Gwynne Holford (Lord of the Manor) £10, Mr R. T. Crawshay (Ironmaster) £2 and Lord Tredegar (Cwm Tâf) £2. One reads in the Cefn School Log Books the entries "1894 August 30th Half Holiday Library tea party Pontsarn" and later "Half Holiday. Foundation Stone of Cefn New Library" was laid. This probably refers to the library which still stands and is currently unoccupied (1980).

William Morgan (Pant) writing in 1893 of the Cefn Library stated, "An institution, in which the people can firstly take a special pride, ... for the intellectual elevation of the place, is the Reading Room and Library. This has been a beneficient operation for many years. The Reading Room is

High Street, Cefn Coed with a group of men standing outside the Cefn Coed library c1930.

supplied with the chief local and London dailies, together with many weekly and monthly periodicals, while the Library is stocked with about 600 volumes of English and Welsh books. A survey conducted in 1927 by one David Evans reported that "only ten (members) belong to the professional classes. Of the remainder, 50 per cent are unemployed and the other 50 per cent have such irregular employment that the wages are very small. In order to survive the institution has to appeal to the public, run Whist Drives, etc. The building is in a most deplorable condition. The Library consists in the main, of a large number of old novels, there being not a single volume of an educational standard, and the readable volumes are only for light reading. The whole library of some 1,000 volumes is useless and should be scrapped as waste paper, 90 per cent of the books being old useless fiction".[41] This report was savage in the extreme.

A new branch library was built at Cefn Coed by the Breconshire County Council in the early 1950s and the old Reading Room and Library was closed. With the closure of the Reading Room an important landmark disappeared and with it all the warmth of good companionship. It was always a great pleasure to hear good stories told by witty and intelligent colliers; where the lilting cadences of the Welsh language was the only mode of communication. It was here that the scholar had his leg pulled and the Vicar, the Rev John Emlyn Jones was teased about the strength of his cigarettes made from Franklyn's tobacco – this was their recreation. Some were so poor during the recession between the two Great Wars that they could ill afford to buy spectacles to read the books upstairs at the Library. Those who could afford to buy books might have a Bible, Biblical commentaries, the Life of Livingstone, the novels of Daniel Owen, the poetical works of Ceiriog and of Islwyn, the hymns of Williams Pantycelyn, the rudiments of Tonic Sol-ffa, a collection of oratorios, or books of songs or anthems and books on gardening.

SOME OTHER RECREATIONAL ACTIVITIES

Writers have drawn a dark picture of Cefn Coed in the nineteenth century and have laid particular stress upon its recreational pastimes. Morgan (Pant) made his point by stating, "It is a common saying that Cefn Coed was, in its early life a notoriously wicked place, for here lived the chief pugilists, racers and gamblers, of the whole district".[42] Matthew Owen, writing in 1912 and referring to sixty years previously declared, "It was then notorious for brutal pastimes, which sometimes ended in drunken riots, and even in loss of life".[43] Both writers evidently spoke with conviction, one wonders however why Cefn should have been so bad? The reason was perhaps because while Vaynor was only a mile from Merthyr it was eminently suitable for holding cock fights and for poaching. The dingles of sylvan beauty screened by a profusion of dense copses and tall overhanging trees were a poacher's paradise. On poaching nights in the rivers the only light needed by country folk to guide their faltering steps in the inky darkness was that afforded by the moon and the stars. We now briefly look at some of the other recreational activities.

RUNNING

"Not far from the old Chancel wall will be found the grave of Thomas Edmund, the 'Famous Racer' ",[44] wrote J. E. Jenkins Rector of Vaynor in 1897. Thomas Edmund was born in 1751 and died at the age of 34. He was born in Pont Sticill, the son of "Ann o'r Lan" who lived in a small cottage on the hillside overlooking the main road from Pontsticill to Dôlygaer. During the latter part of his life, he lived in a small dwelling house near the old "Cross Keys Inn", Cefn Coed where he died." It is of interest that he should have died here because the flat road lying above and below the "Stocks" Cefn Coed was one of the venues for foot racing years ago. It was called 'Heol Tafarnau', so called because there were seven public houses there. This was a popular sport locally, so much so that Thomas Lewis of the Crown Inn, Cefn boarded and trained runners at his Inn for local races around 1855. Gambling on these occasions was apparently very heavy and it is likely that this is part of the gambling referred to by Morgan (Pant) and Matthew Owen. J. E. Jenkins provides a vivid account of Edmund's most noted race, run on a New Year's Day over three miles on "the mountain from near Ystrad by Torypantau (Torpantau) to the boundary line between Brecknockshire and Glamorganshire above Tyle-y-bont Farm. The particulars of this race are preserved in an old manuscript Ballad, called "the Song of the Race".[45]

The Rev J. E. Jenkins goes on to say that "The men of Brecknockshire increased their stakes on Edmund – their "bets" were two to one. Rich and poor seemed to have plenty of money. Edmund won the race and a good sum of money. The afternoon was spent at Garn-Y-Vaynor, a place noted for good ale". Although he was a young man of unquestionable integrity it appears that he ended his days in disgrace. The story has it that having drunk too much prior to a race in London, he lost the race. When he arrived home in Vaynor, where heavy bets had been laid on him, he met with jeers and insults and steps had to be taken to protect him from acts of physical violence. Boycotted and ostracised, even by his warmest friends, he despaired of living down the dishonour and died at the age of 34 years. So ended the career of Thomas Edmund, a contemporary of Griffith Morgan, ("Guto Nyth Bran"). Thomas Edmund was the "wonder" of the Parish of Vaynor, he won every race except his last!

WRESTLING

"A favourite form of sport in the locality was wrestling (moelyd cwmp) and the best exponents of the art were to be found among shepherds. The reason is obvious" states Tom Lewis , "Roaming over the steep flanks of the Beacon ranges gave them stout limbs and powerful muscles and although their strength was ungainly rather than elegant, it provided them with all the necessary qualities of successful wrestlers." He then refers to the custom of the Shepherds of Cwm Tâf Fawr and Tâf Fechan meeting on the plateau of Pen-y-Fan on Sunday mornings, and of an occasion in 1752 when, during a wrestling match, "two of the shepherds, with legs and arms firmly interlocked, rolled over the edge of the cliff to their death hundreds of feet below".[46] One wonders whether this incident has any relationship with the following newspaper report. "August 10th 1833. Rees Davies aged twenty son of Evan Davies, Bailey Glaes, Brecon and John Davies aged nineteen, son of the Butchers Arms, Brecon fell while wrestling over 300 feet on to a ledge and were killed".[47]

FIGHTING AND BOXING

The late Alderman Tom Lewis JP has written in his history of the Hen Dy Cwrdd about the Rev Thomas Davies who was the minister there from 1790 to 1832 and as he states, "The Rev Thomas Davies was a modest, silent man who abhorred all strife and contention. His tongue, it was said, was the tongue of the gentle, his ways were the ways of peace, yet for the 43 years he spent as a local minister at Cefn Coed from 1790 on a stipend of £3.9s.6d, a quarter, could hardly be described as a "reign of peace". He was fated to make his abode near the scene of weekly rowdy encounters. The square in front of his home, Brewery House, which still stands only fifty metres from the "Stocks" at Cefn, was then known as the "Pitch" and it was here, stripped to the waist that combatants settled their differences. The clamour and shouting of drunken voices raised in anger grated on his sensitive ears and it is said that regardless of the consequences he frequently exercised his restraining influence on the contestants".

The following newspaper account refers to such an incident which occurred in this locality during the Rev Thomas Davies' time, "July 20th 1833. John Evans examined before I. B. Bruce Esq and William Thomas Esq, touching the death of William Traharne, who had died on Monday night following a blow received in fighting with the prisoner".[48] Morgan (Pant) in referring to 'Garn, Pontsticill' states, "It is well known that Garn was once, on account of its secluded situation, the rendezvous of pugilists and sporting characters. The scene of these squabbles was on the site whereon the present Baptist Chapel now stands".[49]

Synonymous with professional boxing in this area is the name of Mr Eddie Thomas MBE whose ancestors came from the parish of Vaynor. In the late 1940s Mr Thomas became British, European and Empire Welter Weight Champion and later became a world class boxing trainer. Two of his protegés, Mr Ken Buchanan and Mr Howard Winstone MBE became World Champions. The latter became Feather Weight Champion of the World in 1968 when he beat Mitsunori Seki of Japan at the Royal Albert Hall. At this time Mr Winstone was living at Somerset Close, Cefn Coed. Mr Thomas also trained Colin Jones who shared the decision for Welter Weight Champion of the world with Milton McGrory of America in 1984.

Eddie Thomas MBE, former British, Empire and European Welter Weight Champion.

Howard Winstone MBE, World Featherweight Champion

DANCING AND SMOKING

There are few references to be found relating to dancing in this area in the nineteenth century except the newspaper report of October 1847 describing Brecon Fair which said that there had been "the hearty dance and the rapid song",[50] on this happy occasion, and a second reference made by J. E. Jenkins which reads as follows: "Twyn Wyryfa, or the Maiden's Hill, is in the upper part of the parish about midway between the two valleys. The ground on the top is level, like a lawn. Here, centuries ago, the young maidens of the parish met together to dance and smoke on Sunday afternoons. There is a beautiful well close by. The New Woman, after all, is not so new as many people think. A Catherine Rees, of Tresimwm, in Glamorgan, died in 1768 aged 110 years. In a note on her life, it is stated that women in her time smoked freely, and that dancing on Sunday was a common pastime".[51] It would seem that smoking among women is not a modern custom. Women smoked pipes in Vaynor over two hundred years ago.

The pipes were made locally. It is said that women took to smoking in the first instance because herb smoking was considered efficacious for the chest. The pipes when they were old and smelly were kept in chests of drawers and coffers to ward off moths. Tobacco was not sold in the parish until about a hundred and fifty years ago,. Smokers, it is said, walked to Brecon to fetch it bringing back a supply that lasted six months.[52]

FISHING, SHOOTING AND HUNTING

The rivers of the Parish of Vaynor abounded with trout and the newspapers of the area make frequent references to poachers being caught in the Tâf Fawr on Tâf Fechan. We have the following report by a parish constable in 1820 which reads as follows: "Coed Y Cymmer May 20th 1820. Sir. I take the earliest opportunity to inform you that I have secured 2 long nets, 2 long poles, nearly 18 feet long and one basket under very heavy threat and peril. I will bring them to Brecon as soon as possible. I am, Sir, your humble servant. Thomas Lewis, Constable". The note was addressed to John Powel Esq, and apparently caused great concern at Brecon because on "May 24th 1820 at a meeting at the Grand Jury Room of the Shirehall, Penry Williams of Penpont in the Chair, an association was formed for the Protection of Game and Fish within this and adjacent counties".[53] Poachers protected themselves from the attack of the otter by wearing gaiters studded with cockle shells while poaching in the Tâf Fawr and Tâf Fechan. For generations the same families in the parish have been well known poachers of fish and game from the rivers and moors and from Mr Crawshay and Lord Tredegar. They used all kinds of devices, for example "on August 2nd 1913 at the Penderyn Petty Sessions, David John Morgan, Abercanaid was fined £1 and costs for using chloroform and lime at Tâf Fechan".[54] It is recorded too, that in a well known local pool, "A trout weighing eight and a quarter pounds, was caught in Pwll Dan-Y-Fainc, Cwm Capel by Daniel Prosser. May 9th 1886".[55]

The woodlands and moorland of Vaynor abounded with foxes, badgers, hares and rabbits. As Theophilus Jones has stated, "This district was with propriety called Garthmadryn (The home of the fox); and its inhabitants consisted principally of foxes".[56] It is therefore understandable that the fox over the centuries has been hunted and trapped by both individuals and by "Hunting Clubs", such as the one based at the Red Lion, Cwm Tâf, and more recently by the Tâf Fechan Hunt, Vaynor. Apart from the sport derived from hunting the fox, there was in addition so they claimed, a far more important reason, namely to remove by any means possible "a vicious killer" which might deprive a farmer of a hundred lambs in one season. Occasionally, one still sees a silver fox on the Brecon Beacons, a genetic "throw back" to the foxes imported from Belgium by W. S. Miller of Forest Lodge in the last century, in the hope that they might breed with the wild native red fox and that the offspring would not kill lambs.

From the pen of the poet Howel Rhys of Vaynor, we have a graphic account of a badger hunt in the poem "Can Y Daear Fochyn" and from the following newspaper account it would appear that shooting wild animals was a particularly popular sport in the last century. The account states, "December 26th 1833. The dangerous practice of every man and boy who can possess himself of a rickety gun taking it out on Christmas Day, though it may be amusement to the performers, it is no joke to the public ... we trust that the £20 penalty for killing game on Christmas Day will be levied on these reckless fusiliers".[59]

Game in the form of grouse, woodcock, black game, snipe, hares and rabbits have always been plentiful in Cwm Tâf Fawr. The greatest exponents of grouse shooting in the last century and in the first decades of this century was the family of Lord Tredegar. It was customary for Lord Tredegar and his retinue to arrive at Merthyr Station on August 11th. They would then proceed to the Lodge Cwm Tâf, known locally as the "Shooting Box", with Lord Tredegar doffing his hat to the farmers, their families and servants lining the route. From early morning of the "Glorious 12th", guns reverberated through the valley and scores of grouse were shot, especially around "Waun Tinker", this is the stretch of moorland between the Storey Arms and Penderyn. From the notes given by the old poet Thomas Jenkins (born 1817) to the Rev J. E. Jenkins in 1897 one notes that he believed that Lord Tredegar and the Duke of Beaufort were the greatest persons next to the Queen. He was probably employed as a "beater" for the grouse shoots because he was a native of the farming community in Cwm Tâf, as he states:

> "Brodor o'r Vaynor wyf fi-Cwm Tâf
> Yw'r lle tyfais i fyny;
> Yn Nantgwine ca'dd fy nhad ei eni
> Yn Aber car oedd fy nhadcu".[60]

Jenkins has translated this as follows:

> "I am a native of Vaynor,
> and was brought up at Cwm-tave Vawr;
> My father was born at Nantgwine,
> and my grandfather lived at Abercar".

In his notes he states that "Waun Tinker" which was renowned for its grouse, originally belonged to the Crown and that it was given to an old soldier, who was a tinker, by trade, in lieu of a pension. This grouse shoot had belonged to the ancestors of Lord Tredegar for many years, as we note from the following public notice dated August 9th 1834.

> "Grouse shooting, Manor of Brecon. Rules and Regulations for shooting upon the hills of Sir Charles Morgan Bart, in the County of Brecon 1834.
>
> 1. No person will be allowed to sport without leave of Sir Charles Morgan.
> 2. No person will be allowed to kill more than 2 brace of Grouse in one day, or to sport after 20th August.
> 3. No one will be allowed on any other days than those mentioned on the card nor will any person be allowed to sport on the hills situated in the several parishes of Llanspythid, Cantref (Cwm-Tâf), Penderyn (Cwm-Tâf) and Ystradfellte in the County of Brecon.
>
> A reward for two guineas, over and above what is allowed by Act of Parliament will be paid to any person giving information which may lead to the conviction of any Person found trespassing on the said hills.
>
> (Signed) P. Vaughan, Agent. July 21st".[61]

In order to enforce these regulations he employed gamekeepers, the last of whom was Mr David Jones (Dai Keeper) who lived at the Lodge (Shooting Box), the home of Lord Tredegar at Cwm Tâf in 1905.

COCK FIGHTING, BULL BAITING, OTTER AND HEDGEHOG HUNTS

Cock fighting was an established sport throughout the whole of Wales in the nineteenth century. The sport became popular in medieval times when bull baiting, bear baiting and cock fighting took the place of knightly tournament, among the common people.[62] During the Commonwealth the sport was suppressed and, though it was revived again at the Restoration, it was not until the reign of George III that it became really popular. "Cocking" was at its height at the beginning of the nineteenth century. Gruffyd Rhisiart[63] writing in 1852 in a Welsh periodical describes cock-fighting in Wales. He refers to 'Y Cocyn' which was followed by days and nights of drunkenness, ribald song, argument, courting and fighting and so on.

There was until the end of the last century a round thatched cottage at Cefn Coed called "Ty Cockyn". Was this the venue for local cock-fights? If this were so then according to Gruffydd Rhisiart, it would have had a circular pit six to eight yards in diameter with the surface peeled to a depth of six to eight inches, and the floor made even and pressed hard. During the week before the "cocyn", the birds were prepared – the dubbing, training etc was done when the birds were stags, i.e. fully feathered chickens. The feathers of the wings were cut as well as those of the tail and hackle. The comb and wattle were cut off. This was done by means of a specially forged scissors which was heated to sear the wound and prevent it from bleeding. A steel spur was secured to the bird's leg, called in the language of the 'cocyn', 'the weapon'.

During the training of the birds they were fed and nourished by the trainer or "feeder" on a special diet, which included "Sweet butter with white sugar candy and rosemary finely chopped ... wheatmeal and oatmeal mixed with ale and the whites of eggs.[64] Mr John Francis of Cefn Coed still has 'muffles' or 'hots' used by his ancestors for training fighting cocks. In training when the birds were put out to spar their spurs were covered with the 'muffles' which were in fact miniature boxing gloves made of soft white leather. This it was said improved their wind and eliminated the superfluous fat on their bodies.

A special type of cock fight, called the "Welch Main" developed in Wales and became popular in these islands. A public notice dated March 27th 1805[65] advertising a "Welch Main" reads as follows: "To be fought on Easter Tuesday. A Welch Main. By sixteen cocks for an eight days clock with a mahogany case. Value nine guineas. Stags allowed 1 ounce and henbirds, 2 ounces. Each cock to stake one guinea, the winners to have the prize, paying two guineas the second best two have three guineas, the two thirds one guinea and a half each, and the four fourths fifteen shillings and nine pence each. The cocks to be taken to the Pens on Saturday 6th April. To weigh precisely at 11 o'c lock on the day of the fighting. Fed Gratis by Henry Osman. N.B. Any person choosing to feed his own cock must be at the scale at the time appointed".

This pastime gave rise to several industries. Those who could afford them, armed their birds with silver spurs which were held to reduce the risk of infection. The spurs varied in length from one inch to three inches, according to the style of fighting practised by individual cocks. (How many spurs were fashioned in the local iron works at Merthyr?) In addition 'muffles' or 'hots' were manufactured, saws for shortening and cutting the natural spur, scissors for dubbing and removing the comb and wattles, markers for the identification of the birds and bags bearing the owners' colours for conveying the birds to the pit. Tom Lewis has referred to the "Twyn" at Cefn as the centre of fighting, but the name "Ty Cockyn" would seem to have a stronger historical connotation. Legislation to suppress cock fighting was passed in 1835 and 1849 but the sport persisted long after these dates.

It is stated that when Thomas Edwards, a youth from Aberdare, was killed while watching bull-baiting near Morlais Castle that the sport soon afterwards discontinued. The last bull-fight in the Parish of Vaynor was fought on a field formerly known as Tai Trotman, now occupied by Holford Street. Thomas Edwards was buried in the Hen Dŷ Cwrdd, Cefn Coed, in the early nineteenth century.

While the sensitive spirit recoils from the nauseating cruelty of these blood sports, one should be aware of the fact that the following newspaper report of 1833: "Brecon, otter hunting. The Brecon pack had an excellent sport on Monday". In the following verse the poet Shon Goch describes a favourite medicinal dish which he calls 'hedgehog broth'. This suggests that hedgehogs were hunted for this purpose. The poem reads as follows:

"Cawl cig eidion a chawl cig moch
Yw cawl Shon Goch o'r Caerau;
A chawl Draenog fore a hwyr
I dynu'r cwyr o'm clustiau".[66]

Jenkins has translated this as follows:

> "Broth (or soup) of bacon and beef;
> John Goch of Caerau loves most dear;
> And hedgehog broth he also takes
> When cold has settled in his ears".

THE VOLUNTEERS

THE Cefn Drill Hall was opened on January 21st 1866 and from that date this was the place of training for the local battalion of the Volunteers. Drills and band practices were held weekly and by virtue of these practices the inhabitants became familiar with the compositions of Suppe, Sousa, Godfrey and Winter. W. J. Williams,[67] writing of the Cefn Volunteers states "The training given to the youth who became volunteers was undoubtedly good for them, for the corps unified members of the different grades of society ... their evenings at the Drill Hall were enjoyable and instructive". Fire practice took place at the "Targets" on Cilsanws mountain.

Between the two Great Wars the Drill Hall was used regularly by the Territorial Army. When World War commenced in 1939 the Territorials were soon replaced by the Home Guard made up of local men under the command of Captain W. S. Parry, local Postmaster, Church organist and composer. In addition to the Home Guard other men were appointed Special Policemen under the command of Mr E. Berryman and Sgt Stubbs the local Police Sergeant stationed at Cefn Police Station. For their services during the war many of the Special Police received medals while one, David Bowen, father of the author, was awarded the Parchment of the Royal Humane Society for bravery in saving the life of a school boy David Williams from the treacherous Pwll-dan-graig pool, Godre'r Coed, Cefn in June 1944.

CEFN COED BATTALION HOME GUARD 1940

Back row: *Privates John Reid, J. Watkins, H. Gough, Vic Chambers, John Lewis, Islwyn Francis, Reg Evans, Mark Jones, M. Thomas, Henry Morgan, Frank Trott.*

Second row: *Private Tom Morgan, Private Gwilym James, Sgt Bryn Davies, Private Tom Edwards, Private A. N. Other, Private Jones, Private Alan Rotheroe, Private Howard Turner, Private D. Kirby.*

Front row: *Sgt D. T. Prosser, Corporal Vic Evans, Sgt Tudor Rogers, Sgt Arthur Miles, Lieutenant Bryn thomas, Captain W. S. Parry, Lieutenant D. Tawlfryn Jones, Sgt Major Barney McCue, Lance Corporal Frank Lewis, Corporal Ronnie Batten.*

A public Concert held at the Conservative Hall, Cefn Coed for the Presentation of Mr David Bowen (Special Constable) of the Parchment of the Royal Humane Certificate for saving the life of David Williams from Pwll-dan-graig, Godre'r Coed 2nd June 1944.
Also in the photograph are Mr E. Rees, Police Constable Flook, Mr Tal Morgan, Mr Vernon Rose (Clerk to the Vaynor and Penderyn RDC), Mr and Mrs S. Williams (parents of David Williams), Councillor Isaac Morris (Chairman of the Vaynor and Penderyn RDC), Mr David Bowen, Mr Emrys Evans BA, BSc (Director of Education for Breconshire), Mrs Davies (Headmistress of Ysgol y Graig Infants' School , Cefn Coed.

WALKING

J. E. Jenkins states that "From time immemorial, the people of the district have made it a custom to climb the Beacons annually on the first day of August:

> "Awst y Cyntaf af ar ofwy – i Ben
> Ei binacl clodadwy;
> Ow! fynediad ofnadwy!
> Fy mhen a ddaw e'n sobr mwy!"[68]

Jenkins has translated it thus:-

> "On the first of August I will go
> to the top of the Beacons
> How terrible the ascent!
> My head! will it ever come sober again?"

Walking to market, to the fair, to church or chapel was of necessity done by most people without thought because there was no other means of conveyance. T. E. Clarke has referred to a custom of around the mid-nineteenth century which has been practised locally up until the second World War, namely that of young men and women parading up and down Merthyr High Street on weekends, he states "The streets of Merthyr are thronged on Saturday and Monday nights, from eight till ten o'clock; these hours being devoted to a sort of public promenade by the working classes. Moonlight is most favourable, for although there are gasworks in the town, it is not publicly lighted, and the paving is of a bad description".[69]

THE TEA PARTIES, RAFFLES AND PENNY READINGS

In the last century, when a family was visited by some misfortune and the spectre of want hovered over their homes the system adopted to relieve them of their distress was to hold a concert, a lecture, a "raffle" or a Penny Reading. Immediately it became known that a bread winner had fallen victim to some illness or an accident at work which rendered him incapable of following his employment for a considerable length of time, a group of housewives gathered together to devise ways and means of proffering a helping-held. Their method of rendering the desired aid was to hold a series of "Cottage Teas". As Tom Lewis has written, "Every housewife on the committee was expected to hold a Tea in turn, in her own dwelling, providing too her own food and crockery".

Naturally, the carefully preserved cups and saucers from the age old corner cupboard were requisitioned with the best possible culinary skill of the hostess to provide an assortment of delicious pasties. A running commentary on the most recent village events, to the accompaniment of the clicking of knitting needles was a prominent feature of the gathering. It was the duty of Pegi Sion Rees to make the teas publicly known. To execute her duties thoroughly she carried about with her a piece of chalk with which she put a cross on the door post near the latch. When the housewife on her return observed the chalk mark she knew that Pegi had been there in her absence. Publicising the teas, however, was not the only duty imposed upon Pegi. Welsh villagers generally speaking were loathe to admit that they were in straitened circumstances. It was an essential part of Pegi's duties to investigate covertly these cases, and report the circumstances to the organisers of the the "Cottage Teas".[70]

THE GORCHEST STONE

J. E. Jenkins has referred to the fact that "on the hill above Pentwyn there is a stone called 'careg Orchest' (a feat stone). These were to be found in every parish in the olden times, before the ancient twenty four Mabawl and Grawl Gampau gave place to the present doubtful games and before football became a "profession". It is a round smooth stone and the gorchest or feat is to raise it up which an ordinary strong man can do provide he has a strong grip and large sinewy hands".[71]

OTHER GROUPS AND SOCIETIES ETC

During the present century there have been innumerable societies, clubs associations and groups involved in a great variety of social, religious, educational and generally recreational activities in the parish of Vaynor. Many of these were associated with the Chapels and Churches in the form of societies for young people such as dramatic pursuits etc while others were specially for boys such as the Cubs and Scouts or for girls such as Brownies or Guides. Other groups of young people have met since the 1940s under the aegis of the Cefn Coed Youth Club.

Many of the adult groups were associated with the different chapels and churches where dramas, cantatas and choral groups were at one time very popular. Practically every chapel had a Sisterhood or Women's League or sewing class meeting weekly in addition to meetings for Men's fellowship or Bible Study. Other groups were activated by particular interests in religion, social activities, or sporting activities such as golf or rugby. One of the oldest groups still meeting regularly is the C. W. Pearce Lodge of the Royal Antedeluvian Order of Buffaloes. Many of the popular associations such as the TocH, the Ambulance Association, the Cefn Coed Operatic Society under its celebrated composer and conductor Mr W. S. Parry and the Old Age Pensioners Association have sadly ceased to exist. During the 1920s and early 1930s Cefn Coed had a cricket club and the Cefn Athletic Football team during this period was very successful and produced some excellent footballers. Many moved from Cefn Coed to become professional footballers, such as Trevor Jones, Idris Hopkins and Ben Lewis of Field Street, Cefn, and his brothers Willie and Danny were semi-professionals.

CEFN COED YOUTH CLUB, WINNERS IN THE 1961 BRECONSHIRE DRAMA FESTIVAL

***Back row:** Annette Bush, Gill Phillips, Derek James, Gwyn James, Jim Mochan, gareth Gwenlan, Ken Williams, Mostyn Jones, Peter Price, David Tamberlin.*

***Second row:** Mrs Nancy Morgan, Mrs W. Chambers, Mr Tal Morgan, Mrs Nanwen Owen, Sian Williams, and Beryl Cox.*

***Front row:** Mr Cromwell Davies, Mrs L. Evans, Mr Selwyn Morgan (Producer), Mr Tom Owen (Warden), Mr W. J. Evans.*

In the sphere of Rugby Football, Tom Arthur born in Cefn Coed obtained eighteen International caps for Wales while playing as an outstanding forward for Neath. Edgar Francis of Cefn Coed obtained an amateur International cap for football. More recently Mr Stan Ashton of Holford Street, Cefn Coed was the Welsh International Team manager for the Welsh Snooker team and was himself the Merthyr Tydfil Borough Singles Champion 1977-80. In the world of refereeing, Mr Vivian Llewellyn formerly of Pentwyn Farm, Cwm Tâf became a famous International Rugby referee and was the referee on that never to be forgotten occasion when Cardiff defeated the New Zealand All Blacks at Cardiff in 1953. Andrew Reynolds of Gersanws, Cefn Coed was awarded a Schoolboy International Cap for football in the 1970s.

CEFN COED OPERATIC SOCIETY

Some of the cast of Yeomen of the Guard produced by Mr W. S. Parry, April 1959. Included are Arnold Garbett, Rosemary Gasson, Mrs Grace Gunter, Ira James, Moyra Sims, Mrs Kate Davies, Linda Evans, Mair Lloyd, Barbara, Minnie Edwards, Kitty Morris, and Nan Williams.

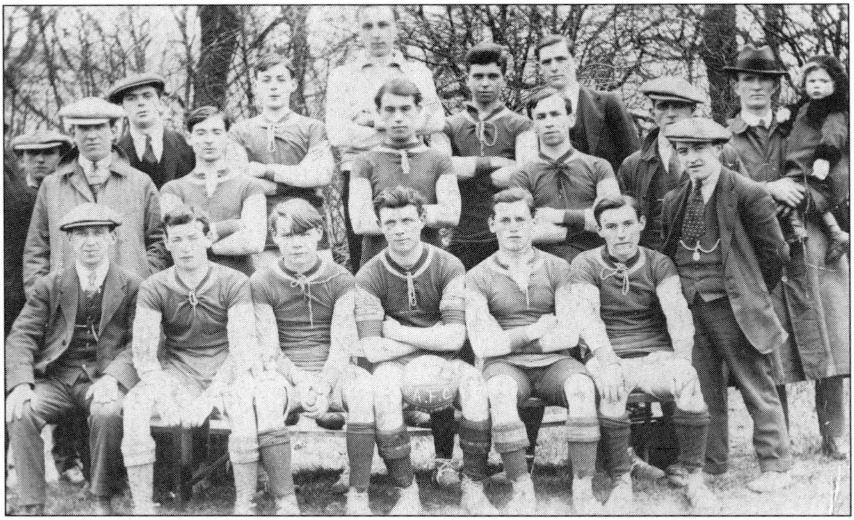

CEFN ATHLETIC FOOTBALL TEAM c1920s

Included in the photograph are:
Back row: *Mr D. R. Davies, A. N. Other, Bill Wright (Goalkeeper), Harry Law.*
Middle row: *John Davies, D. Jones, Bill Mathews, John Meredith, Tom Rees, A. N. Other, Mr Thomas (with child).*
Front row: *D. J. Rees, W. Griffiths, A. N. Other, B. Thomas (Captain), Cled Williams, Evan Davies, Tom Price.*

By courtesy of Mr Llew Williams, son of Mr Cled Williams above

CEFN COED OLD AGE PENSIONERS' ASSOCIATION

Presentation of a clock by Mr C. Lewis to the Association late 1970s. Mr Dick Morgan, Mr B. Morgan, Mr A. Williams, Mr Danny Lewis, Mr W. Jones, Mr David Thomas, Mr Will Rees and Mr Mog Thomas.
Front row: *Mr Ben Wathan, Mr Cliff Lewis, Mr Ivor Davies.*

THE ROYAL ANTEDEVULIAN ORDER OF BUFFALOES,
GRAND LODGE OF ENGLAND
C. W. PEARCE LODGE 1012 (c1960)

Back row: *D. Hourehane, I. Bowen, W. Mason, Gwilym James, Jack Williams, Ben Davies, D. W. Jones, Trefor Jones.*
Middle row: *Tom Gunter, D. T. Prosser, D. Kendry, A. Hancock, T. Mahoney, I. dyment, S. Lewis, K. Walker.*
Front row: *T. J. Lewis, John Jones, D. Lloyd, J. Evans, G. Lewis, E. Parry, D. Prosser, H. Matthews.*

Donor Mr Ieuan thomas

Laying the foundation of the TocH Hall, Cefn Coed (mid 1930s)
Back row: *Mr Tom Lewis JP, Mr Boulter.*
Front row: *Unknown, Unknown, Dr Harold Thomas, Mr S. Maggs, Mr Sam Evans, Mr Thompson, Mr Jones.*

CEFN COED AUXILIARY NURSING DIVISION c1950
Mrs Lewis (Commandant), Mrs Rugby Besley, Mrs Margery Thomas, Mrs Ruby, Mrs Dunley, Mrs Herron, Mrs Evans, Mrs Williams, Mrs betty Steele, Mrs Nancy England.

REFERENCES

1. Alwyn D. Rees, Life in a Welsh Countryside (1951), p.131.
2. D. Watkin Morgan, 'The Inns of Abercrave', Brycheiniog, Vol IV (1958) p.111.
3. Charles Wilkins, Postal Guide and Directory to Merthyr Tydfil (1873).
4. Merthyr Express article by Tom Lewis August 12th 1912. Merthyr Library.
5. Tom Lewis, Hen Dy Cwrdd, Cefn Coed y Cymmer (1947), p.90.
6. Tom Lewis, A Brief Topographical Sketch of the Parish of Vaynor. Cefn Coed and Vaynor Local History Society (1957), p.12.
7. Merthyr Guardian, September 7th, 1833. Merthyr Library.
8. Merthyr Guardian, August 9th 1834. Merthyr Library.
9. Merthyr Express, March 9th 1912. Merthyr.
10. David Davies ('Dewi Cynon'), Hanes Plwyf Penderyn (1905), p.92.
11. David Davies, op. cit., p.93.
12. Merthyr Express, January 25th 1913. Merthyr Library.
13. Merthyr Express, March 22nd 1913. Merthyr Library.
14. David Davies, op. cit., p.93.
15. Tom Lewis, op. cit., p. 199.
16 Carmel Baptist Chapel, Cefn Coed, Chapel Records.
17. Log Books of the Cefn Coed School from 1861 at Ysgol y Graig Junior School, Cefn.
18. Merthyr Express November 15th 1913. Merthyr Library.
19. Atlas Brycheiniog (1960) p.73.
20. Ibid p.72.
21. Ibid p.73.
22. T. E. Clarke, A Guide to Merthyr Tydfil, (1848), p.37.
23. Merthyr Guardian, September 11th 1847. Merthyr Library.
24. Merthyr Guardian, November 22nd, 1834. Merthyr Library.
25. Merthyr Guardian, October 2nd 1847. Merthyr Library.
26. T. Lewis. Old Characters. Cefn Coed and Vaynor Local History Society Part 2. (1956) p.1.
27. Merthyr Guardian, April 14th 1855. Merthyr Library.
28. Merthyr Guardian, April 1843. Merthyr Library.
29. Merthyr Express, April 13th 1912. Merthyr Library.
30. Log Book, Cefn Coed Schools, August 1914. Ysgol y Graig, Cefn Coed.
31. Notable Dates in the History of Parish of Vaynor Cefn Coed and Vaynor Local History Society Pamphlet. (1960). p.2.
32. Vaynor Gleanings, Cefn coed and Vaynor Historical Society, (1958), p.11.
33. T. Lewis, ibid., p.15.
34. Merthyr Guardian, November 9th 1833. Merthyr Library.
35. Merthyr Guardian, November 9th 1833. Merthyr Library.
36. Merthyr Historian, Volume 2. Article by Margaret Taylor on 'Thomas Stephens of Merthyr Tydfil' (1821-1875), p.137.
37. Merthyr Historian Volume 2, p.137.
38. Merthyr Guardian, February 19th 1864. Merthyr Library.
39. Log Books of the Cefn Coed School from 1861. Ysgol y Graig, Cefn Coed.
40. First Minute Book of the Cefn Coed Reading Room and Library in the care of the Author.
41. David Evans, The Libraries of the County Borough of Merthyr Tydfil (1927) quoted in the History of Merthyr Libraries unpublished Thesis by Ann Bowen College of Libraianship, Aberystwyth.
42. W. Morgan (Pant), The Illustrated Vaynor Handbook, p.6.
43. Matthew Owen, Breconshire (1912), p.101.
44. J. E. Jenkins, Vaynor Its History and Guide, p.32.
45. J. E. Jenkins, op. cit., p.34.
46. Tom Lewis, 'Hen Dy Cwrdd, Cefn Coed y Cymmer', p.213.
47. Merthyr Guardian, August 10th 1833. Merthyr Library.
48. Merthyr Guardian, July 21st 1833. Merthyr Library.
49. W. Morgan (Pant), op. cit. p.31.
50. Merthyr Guardian, October 1847. Merthyr Library.
51. J. E. Jenkins, op. cit., p.102.
52. Tom Lewis, 'Customs and Practises of the Parish of Vaynor'. Cefn Coed and Vaynor Local History Society (1954) p.7.
53. Historical Memoranda of Breconshire. A Collection of papers from various sources. Relating to the History of the County. Vol. II by John Lloyd (Brecon Museum).
54. Merthyr Express, August 2nd 1913. Merthyr Library.
55. Notable dates and Events in the History of the Parish of Vaynor, Cefn Coed and Vaynor Local History Society (1960), p.2.
56. Theophilus Jones, History of Breconshire, p.144.
57. W. Morgan (Pant), op. cit., p.73.
58. W. Morgan (Pant), op. cit., pp. 75.
59. Merthyr Guardian, December 28th 1833. Merthyr Library.
60. J. E. Jenkins, op. cit., p.125.
61. Merthyr Guardian, August 9th 1834. Merthyr Library.
62. I. Peate, Guide to the Collection of Welsh Bygones (1929), p.65.
63. Richard Roberts (Gruffydd Rhisiart), Chronicle y Cymdeithasau Crefyddol, X, pp. 246-52.
64. George Morgan, The New Complete Sportsman in Guide to the Collection of Welsh Bygones, by Peate, (1929), p.66.
65. A public Poster from the Welsh Folk Museum, St Fagans.
66. J. E. Jenkins, op. cit., pp.127-128.
67. W. J. Williams, 19th Century Cefn Coed (Cefn Coed and Vaynor Historical Society (1960), p.10.
68. J. E. Jenkins, op. cit., p.100.
69. T. E. Clarke, op. cit., p.45.
70. Tom Lewis, op. cit., p.199.
71. J. E. Jenkins, op. cit., p.144.